JAMES

Baker Exegetical Commentary on the New Testament

ROBERT W. YARBROUGH
AND ROBERT H. STEIN, EDITORS

Volumes now available

Matthew   *David L. Turner*

Mark   *Robert H. Stein*

Luke   *Darrell L. Bock*

John   *Andreas J. Köstenberger*

Acts   *Darrell L. Bock*

Romans   *Thomas R. Schreiner*

1 Corinthians   *David E. Garland*

Philippians   *Moisés Silva*

James   *Dan G. McCartney*

1 Peter   *Karen H. Jobes*

1–3 John   *Robert W. Yarbrough*

Jude and 2 Peter   *Gene L. Green*

Revelation   *Grant R. Osborne*

Dan G. McCartney (PhD, Westminster Theological Seminary) is professor of New Testament interpretation at Redeemer Theological Seminary in Dallas. Prior to this, he was professor of New Testament at Westminster Theological Seminary, where he taught for more than twenty-five years. He is the author of *Let the Reader Understand: A Guide to Interpreting and Applying the Bible* and *Why Does It Have to Hurt? The Meaning of Christian Suffering*. He also revised J. Gresham Machen's *New Testament Greek for Beginners*.

JAMES

DAN G. MCCARTNEY

Baker Exegetical Commentary on the New Testament

Baker Academic
a division of Baker Publishing Group
Grand Rapids, Michigan

Published by Baker Academic
a division of Baker Publishing Group
PO Box 6287, Grand Rapids, MI 49516-6287
www.bakeracademic.com

Printed in the United States of America

Library of Congress Cataloging-in-Publication Data
McCartney, Dan.
    James / Dan G. McCartney.
      p. cm. — (Baker exegetical commentary on the New Testament)
    Includes bibliographical references and index.
    ISBN 978-0-8010-2676-8 (cloth)
    1. Bible. N.T. James—Commentaries. I. Title.
BS2785.53.M36 2009
227′.9107—dc22   2009019502

09   10   11   12   13   14   15   7   6   5   4   3   2   1

To my former colleagues in the biblical studies departments
at Westminster Theological Seminary,
for their encouragement and support,

and

in memory of J. Alan Groves,
whose life so beautifully manifested the wisdom
that comes from above.

וַיִּתְהַלֵּךְ אֶת־הָאֱלֹהִים וְאֵינֶנּוּ כִּי־לָקַח אֹתוֹ אֱלֹהִים:

Contents

Series Preface

The chief concern of the Baker Exegetical Commentary on the New Testament (BECNT) is to provide, within the framework of informed evangelical thought, commentaries that blend scholarly depth with readability, exegetical detail with sensitivity to the whole, and attention to critical problems with theological awareness. We hope thereby to attract the interest of a fairly wide audience, from the scholar who is looking for a thoughtful and independent examination of the text to the motivated lay Christian who craves a solid but accessible exposition.

Nevertheless, a major purpose is to address the needs of pastors and others involved in the preaching and exposition of the Scriptures as the uniquely inspired Word of God. This consideration affects directly the parameters of the series. For example, serious biblical expositors cannot afford to depend on a superficial treatment that avoids the difficult questions, but neither are they interested in encyclopedic commentaries that seek to cover every conceivable issue that may arise. Our aim, therefore, is to focus on those problems that have a direct bearing on the meaning of the text (although selected technical details are treated in the additional notes).

Similarly, a special effort is made to avoid treating exegetical questions for their own sake, that is, in relative isolation from the thrust of the argument as a whole. This effort may involve (at the discretion of the individual contributors) abandoning the verse-by-verse approach in favor of an exposition that focuses on the paragraph as the main unit of thought. In all cases, however, the commentaries will stress the development of the argument and explicitly relate each passage to what precedes and follows it so as to identify its function in context as clearly as possible.

We believe, moreover, that a responsible exegetical commentary must take fully into account the latest scholarly research, regardless of its source. The attempt to do this in the context of a conservative theological tradition presents certain challenges, and in the past the results have not always been commendable. In some cases, evangelicals appear to make use of critical scholarship not for the purpose of genuine interaction but only to dismiss it. In other cases, the interaction glides over into assimilation, theological distinctives are ignored or suppressed, and the end product cannot be differentiated from works that arise from a fundamentally different starting point.

The contributors to this series attempt to avoid these pitfalls. On the one hand, they do not consider traditional opinions to be sacrosanct, and they are certainly committed to doing justice to the biblical text whether or not it supports such opinions. On the other hand, they will not quickly abandon a long-standing view, if there is persuasive evidence in its favor, for the sake of fashionable theories. What is more important, the contributors share a belief in the trustworthiness and essential unity of Scripture. They also consider that the historic formulations of Christian doctrine, such as the ecumenical creeds and many of the documents originating in the sixteenth-century Reformation, arose from a legitimate reading of Scripture, thus providing a proper framework for its further interpretation. No doubt, the use of such a starting point sometimes results in the imposition of a foreign construct on the text, but we deny that it must necessarily do so or that the writers who claim to approach the text without prejudices are invulnerable to the same danger.

Accordingly, we do not consider theological assumptions—from which, in any case, no commentator is free—to be obstacles to biblical interpretation. On the contrary, an exegete who hopes to understand the apostle Paul in a theological vacuum might just as easily try to interpret Aristotle without regard for the philosophical framework of his whole work or without having recourse to those subsequent philosophical categories that make possible a meaningful contextualization of his thought. It must be emphasized, however, that the contributors to the present series come from a variety of theological traditions and that they do not all have identical views with regard to the proper implementation of these general principles. In the end, all that matters is whether the series succeeds in representing the original text accurately, clearly, and meaningfully to the contemporary reader.

Shading has been used to assist the reader in locating salient sections of the treatment of each passage: introductory comments and concluding summaries. Textual variants in the Greek text are signaled in the author's translation by means of half-brackets around the relevant word or phrase (e.g., ⌜Gerasenes⌝), thereby alerting the reader to turn to the additional notes at the end of each exegetical unit for a discussion of the textual problem. The documentation uses the author-date method, in which the basic reference consists of author's surname + year + page number(s): Fitzmyer 1992: 58. The only exceptions to this system are well-known reference works (e.g., BDAG, LSJ, *TDNT*). Full publication data and a complete set of indexes can be found at the end of the volume.

Robert W. Yarbrough
Robert H. Stein

Author's Preface

The Epistle of James is perhaps best known for its declaration "Faith without works is dead" and its assertion that a nonworking "faith" cannot justify anyone. It is vital to the health of the church that we remember this. Orthodoxy is worthless unless it produces orthopraxy. Jesus declared, "By their fruits you will know them" (Matt. 7:20 KJV alt.), and he made it quite clear that not everyone who claims Jesus as Lord on the day of judgment will enter the kingdom, but only those who have done the will of the Father (Matt. 7:21–23). One cannot have Jesus as Savior without owning him as Lord, and one cannot have him as Lord without a commitment to obey him. The Epistle of James serves as a reminder that a faith claim and genuine faith are two different things.

This is not at all to set the voice of James against that of Paul. Paul, no less than James (and Jesus), insists that right belief must result in right behavior and that those who live wicked lives have no part in the kingdom of God (Gal. 5:21; Eph. 5:5). Even a mountain-moving faith, if it has not love, is nothing (1 Cor. 13:2). It is a grotesque caricature of Paul to turn his doctrine of justification by faith into a ticket to heaven by a one-time "receiving Jesus into your heart." But James's letter, perhaps even more clearly than Paul's writings, warns Christians that faith in Jesus Christ means more than saying yes to an offer of free fire insurance.

James has other concerns, of course. His letter touches on a number of issues of practical Christian life: temptation, anger, speech, care of the poor, respect for everyone regardless of social status, relationships within the church, business plans, prayer, illness, and more. But the theme that runs throughout is James's insistence that true Christian faith must make a difference in the way we deal with such life questions. In fact, James talks about faith considerably more than he talks about works as such. It is precisely because faith is so crucial that James insists that it must be genuine and active. Hypocrisy is as dangerous and insidious a problem for the church today as it was for the Christians of James's day or the Jews of Jesus's time. It is still possible, indeed easy, for religious people to deceive themselves into thinking that they are true believers and chosen by God, when all the while they belie their "faith" by living according to their own desires rather than God's. It is precisely our amazing ability to deceive ourselves that makes James's warnings so important. This commentary is offered in the hope that the epistle that it seeks to expound will be heard more clearly in the church of our day.

Several words of thanks are in order here. First, my thanks to my colleagues and the Board of Westminster Seminary for granting me a study leave to complete the manuscript. Second, I am indebted to my research assistant for one summer and now my colleague, Dr. Adrian Smith, for his help in digging up and preprocessing numerous journal articles and chapters in multiauthor works. Third, I greatly appreciate the patience that Wells Turner has shown in helping me get the details right. Fourth, I am tremendously grateful to Moisés Silva, first my teacher and advisor, then my colleague and friend, for giving me the opportunity and encouragement to delve into a book to which I had previously given little thought. Finally, how could I ever express adequate thanks to my wife, Kathy, dearest companion, most trusted advisor, faithful prayer partner, occasional research assistant, and best friend? The heart of her husband safely trusts in her.

Abbreviations

Bibliographic and General

ABD	*Anchor Bible Dictionary*, edited by D. N. Freedman, 6 vols. (New York: Doubleday, 1992)
ASV	American Standard Version
b.	Babylonian Talmud
BDAG	*Greek-English Lexicon of the New Testament and Other Early Christian Literature*, by W. Bauer, F. W. Danker, W. F. Arndt, and F. W. Gingrich, 3rd ed. (Chicago: University of Chicago Press, 2000)
BDF	*A Greek Grammar of the New Testament and Other Early Christian Literature*, by F. Blass, A. Debrunner, and R. W. Funk (Chicago: University of Chicago Press, 1961)
DNTB	*Dictionary of New Testament Background*, edited by C. A. Evans and S. E. Porter (Downers Grove, IL: InterVarsity, 2000)
EncJud	*Encyclopaedia Judaica*, edited by F. Skolnik, 2nd ed., 22 vols. (Detroit: Thomson Gale, 2007)
ESV	English Standard Version
ET	English translation
Gk.	Greek
Heb.	Hebrew
IDBSup	*Interpreter's Dictionary of the Bible: Supplementary Volume*, edited by K. Crim (Nashville: Abingdon, 1976)
JB	Jerusalem Bible
JE	*Jewish Encyclopedia*, edited by I. Singer, 12 vols. (London: Funk & Wagnalls, 1909)
KJV	King James Version
L&N	*Greek-English Lexicon of the New Testament: Based on Semantic Domains*, edited by J. P. Louw and E. A. Nida, 2nd ed. (New York: United Bible Societies, 1989)
LSJ	*A Greek-English Lexicon*, by H. G. Liddell, R. Scott, and H. S. Jones, 9th ed. with revised supplement (Oxford: Clarendon, 1996)
LW	*Luther's Works*, edited by H. T. Lehmann et al., 55 vols. (Saint Louis: Concordia; Philadelphia: Fortress, 1955–76)
LXX	Septuagint
m.	Mishnah
MHT	*A Grammar of New Testament Greek*, by J. H. Moulton, W. F. Howard, and N. Turner, 4 vols. (Edinburgh: T&T Clark, 1996–99)
MM	*The Vocabulary of the Greek Testament: Illustrated from the Papyri and Other Non-literary Sources*, by J. H. Moulton and G. Milligan (London: Hodder & Stoughton, 1930; repr. Grand Rapids: Eerdmans, 1980)
MT	Masoretic Text
NA[27]	*Novum Testamentum Graece*, edited by [E. and E. Nestle], B. Aland, K. Aland, J. Karavidopoulos, C. M. Martini, and B. M. Metzger, 27th rev. ed. (Stuttgart: Deutsche Bibelgesellschaft, 1993)

NAB	New American Bible				
NASB	New American Standard Bible				
NEB	New English Bible				
NETS	New English Translation of the Septuagint				
NIV	New International Version				
NJB	New Jerusalem Bible				
NLT	New Living Translation				
NRSV	New Revised Standard Version				
NT	New Testament				
OT	Old Testament				

OTP   *The Old Testament Pseudepigrapha*, edited by J. H. Charlesworth, 2 vols. (Garden City, NY: Doubleday, 1983–85)

PG   Patrologia graeca [= Patrologiae cursus completus: Series graeca], edited by J.-P. Migne, 161 vols. (Paris: Migne, 1857–86)

PL   Patrologia latina [= Patrologiae cursus completus: Series latina], edited by J.-P. Migne, 221 vols. (Paris: Migne, 1844–79)

PW   *Paulys Realencyclopädie der classischen Altertumswissenschaft*, edited by A. F. Pauly and G. Wissowa (Stuttgart: Metzlerscher Verlag, 1921)

RSV   Revised Standard Version

RV   Revised Version

Str-B   *Kommentar zum Neuen Testament aus Talmud und Midrasch*, by H. L. Strack and P. Billerbeck, 6 vols. (Munich: Beck, 1922–61)

SVF   *Stoicorum veterum fragmenta*, by H. von Arnim, 4 vols. (Leipzig: Teubner, 1903–24)

TDNT   *Theological Dictionary of the New Testament*, edited by G. Kittel and G. Friedrich, translated and edited by G. W. Bromiley, 10 vols. (Grand Rapids: Eerdmans, 1964–76)

TDOT   *Theological Dictionary of the Old Testament*, edited by G. J. Botterweck, H. Ringgren, and H.-J. Fabry, translated by J. T. Willis, G. W. Bromiley, D. E. Green, and D. W. Stott, 14 vols. (Grand Rapids: Eerdmans, 1974–)

Theod.   Theodotion's Greek recension/translation of the Hebrew Bible

UBS⁴   *The Greek New Testament*, edited by B. Aland, K. Aland, J. Karavidopoulos, C. M. Martini, and B. M. Metzger, 4th rev. ed. (Stuttgart: Deutsche Bibelgesellschaft, 1994)

Hebrew Bible

Gen.	Genesis	2 Chron.	2 Chronicles	Dan.	Daniel
Exod.	Exodus	Ezra	Ezra	Hos.	Hosea
Lev.	Leviticus	Neh.	Nehemiah	Joel	Joel
Num.	Numbers	Esth.	Esther	Amos	Amos
Deut.	Deuteronomy	Job	Job	Obad.	Obadiah
Josh.	Joshua	Ps.	Psalms	Jon.	Jonah
Judg.	Judges	Prov.	Proverbs	Mic.	Micah
Ruth	Ruth	Eccles.	Ecclesiastes	Nah.	Nahum
1 Sam.	1 Samuel	Song	Song of Songs	Hab.	Habakkuk
2 Sam.	2 Samuel	Isa.	Isaiah	Zeph.	Zephaniah
1 Kings	1 Kings	Jer.	Jeremiah	Hag.	Haggai
2 Kings	2 Kings	Lam.	Lamentations	Zech.	Zechariah
1 Chron.	1 Chronicles	Ezek.	Ezekiel	Mal.	Malachi

Greek Testament

Matt.	Matthew	Eph.	Ephesians	Heb.	Hebrews
Mark	Mark	Phil.	Philippians	James	James
Luke	Luke	Col.	Colossians	1 Pet.	1 Peter
John	John	1 Thess.	1 Thessalonians	2 Pet.	2 Peter
Acts	Acts	2 Thess.	2 Thessalonians	1 John	1 John
Rom.	Romans	1 Tim.	1 Timothy	2 John	2 John
1 Cor.	1 Corinthians	2 Tim.	2 Timothy	3 John	3 John
2 Cor.	2 Corinthians	Titus	Titus	Jude	Jude
Gal.	Galatians	Philem.	Philemon	Rev.	Revelation

Other Jewish and Christian Writings

Adv. Jud.	Tertullian, *Adversus Judaeos* (*Against the Jews*)
Adv. Nest.	Cyril of Alexandria, *Adversus Nestorii blasphemias* (*Five Tomes against Nestorius*)
Apoc. Ab.	Apocalypse of Abraham
Apoc. Mos.	Apocalypse of Moses
1 Apol.	Justin, *Apologia i* (*First Apology*)
2 Apol.	Justin, *Apologia ii* (*Second Apology*)
Ascen. Isa.	Martyrdom and Ascension of Isaiah 6–11
Bapt.	Tertullian, *De baptismo* (*Baptism*)
Bar.	Baruch
2 Bar.	2 Baruch (Syriac Apocalypse)
Barn.	Barnabas
1 Clem.	1 Clement
2 Clem.	2 Clement
Comm. Rom.	Origen, *Commentary on Romans*
Dial.	Justin, *Dialogus cum Tryphone* (*Dialogue with Trypho*)
Did.	Didache
Doctr. chr.	Augustine, *De doctrina christiana* (*Christian Instruction*)
1 En.	1 Enoch
2 En.	2 Enoch
Ep. fest.	Athanasius, *Epistulae festales* (*Festal Letters*)
Epist.	Jerome, *Epistulae* (*Letters*)
1 Esd.	1 Esdras
2 Esd.	2 Esdras (4 Ezra)
Gen. Rab.	Genesis Rabbah
Haer.	Irenaeus, *Adversus haereses* (*Against Heresies*)
Herm. *Mand.*	Shepherd of Hermas, *Mandate*
Herm. *Sim.*	Shepherd of Hermas, *Similitude*
Herm. *Vis.*	Shepherd of Hermas, *Vision*
Hist. eccl.	Eusebius, *Historia ecclesiastica* (*Ecclesiastical History*)
Hom. Exod.	Origen, *Homilies on Exodus*
Hom. Josh.	Origen, *Homilies on Joshua*
Hom. Lev.	Origen, *Homilies on Leviticus*
Ign. *Eph.*	Ignatius, *To the Ephesians*
Ign. *Magn.*	Ignatius, *To the Magnesians*
Ign. *Phld.*	Ignatius, *To the Philadelphians*
Ign. *Pol.*	Ignatius, *To Polycarp*
Ign. *Rom.*	Ignatius, *To the Romans*
Ign. *Smyrn.*	Ignatius, *To the Smyrnaeans*
Ign. *Trall.*	Ignatius, *To the Trallians*
Jdt.	Judith
Jos. Asen.	Joseph and Aseneth
Jub.	Jubilees
1–4 Macc.	1–4 Maccabees
Marc.	Tertullian, *Adversus Marcionem* (*Against Marcion*)
Mek. Exod.	Mekilta on Exodus
Mon.	Tertullian, *De monogamia* (*Monogamy*)
Nat. grat.	Augustine, *De natura et gratia* (*Nature and Grace*)

Paed.	Clement of Alexandria, *Paedagogus* (*Christ the Educator*)	T. Benj.	Testament of Benjamin
		T. Dan	Testament of Dan
Pan.	Epiphanius, *Panarion* (*Refutation of All Heresies*)	T. Gad	Testament of Gad
		T. Iss.	Testament of Issachar
		T. Job	Testament of Job
Pol. *Phil.*	Polycarp, *To the Philippians*	T. Jos.	Testament of Joseph
		T. Jud.	Testament of Judah
Ps. Sol.	Psalms of Solomon	T. Naph.	Testament of Naphtali
Res.	Tertullian, *De resurrectione carnis* (*The Resurrection of the Flesh*)	T. Reu.	Testament of Reuben
		Tob.	Tobit
		Tract. John	Augustine, *Tractates on the Gospel of John*
Sib. Or.	Sibylline Oracles	*Vir. ill.*	Jerome, *De viris illustribus* (*Famous Men*)
Sir.	Sirach (Ecclesiasticus)		
Strom.	Clement of Alexandria, *Stromata* (*Miscellanies*)	*Virg.*	Pseudo-Clement, *De virginitate* (*Letters on Virginity*)
Symb.	Augustine, *De symbolo ad catechumenos* (*The Creed: For Catechumens*)	Wis.	Wisdom of Solomon
T. Ab.	Testament of Abraham		

Josephus and Philo

Ag. Ap.	Josephus, *Against Apion*
Abraham	Philo, *On the Life of Abraham*
Alleg. Interp.	Philo, *Allegorical Interpretation*
Ant.	Josephus, *Jewish Antiquities*
Confusion	Philo, *On the Confusion of Tongues*
Creation	Philo, *On the Creation of the World*
Decalogue	Philo, *On the Decalogue*
Flaccus	Philo, *Against Flaccus*
Giants	Philo, *On Giants*
Good Person	Philo, *That Every Good Person Is Free*
J.W.	Josephus, *Jewish War*
Migration	Philo, *On the Migration of Abraham*
Names	Philo, *On the Change of Names*
Posterity	Philo, *On the Posterity of Cain*
Sobriety	Philo, *On Sobriety*
Spec. Laws	Philo, *On the Special Laws*
Virtues	Philo, *On the Virtues*

Rabbinic Tractates

The abbreviations below are used for the names of the tractates in the Mishnah (indicated by a prefixed *m.*), Tosefta (*t.*), Babylonian Talmud (*b.*), and Jerusalem/Palestinian Talmud (*y.*).

'Abod. Zar.	*'Abodah Zarah*	B. Qam.	*Baba Qamma*
'Abot	*'Abot*	Bek.	*Bekorot*
'Arak.	*'Arakin*	Ber.	*Berakot*
B. Bat.	*Baba Batra*	*Beṣah*	*Beṣah* (= *Yom Ṭob*)
B. Meṣi'a	*Baba Meṣi'a*	Bik.	*Bikkurim*

Demai	*Demai*	*'Or.*	*'Orlah*
'Ed.	*'Eduyyot*	*Parah*	*Parah*
'Erub.	*'Erubin*	*Pe'ah*	*Pe'ah*
Giṭ.	*Giṭṭin*	*Pesaḥ.*	*Pesaḥim*
Ḥag.	*Ḥagigah*	*Qidd.*	*Qiddušin*
Ḥal.	*Ḥallah*	*Qinnim*	*Qinnim*
Hor.	*Horayot*	*Qod.*	*Qodašim*
Ḥul.	*Ḥullin*	*Roš Haš.*	*Roš Haššanah*
Kelim	*Kelim*	*Šabb.*	*Šabbat*
Ker.	*Kerithot*	*Sanh.*	*Sanhedrin*
Ketub.	*Ketubbot*	*Šeb.*	*Šebi'it*
Kil.	*Kil'ayim*	*Šebu.*	*Sebu'ot*
Ma'aś.	*Ma'aśerot*	*Seder*	*Seder*
Ma'aś. Š.	*Ma'aśer Šeni*	*Šeqal.*	*Šeqalim*
Mak.	*Makkot*	*Soṭah*	*Soṭah*
Makš.	*Makširin*	*Sukkah*	*Sukkah*
Meg.	*Megillah*	*Ṭ. Yom*	*Ṭebul Yom*
Me'il.	*Me'ilah*	*Ta'an.*	*Ta'anit*
Menaḥ.	*Menaḥot*	*Tamid*	*Tamid*
Mid.	*Middot*	*Tem.*	*Temurah*
Miqw.	*Miqwa'ot*	*Ter.*	*Terumot*
Mo'ed	*Mo'ed*	*Ṭohar.*	*Ṭoharot*
Mo'ed Qaṭ.	*Mo'ed Qaṭan*	*'Uq.*	*'Uqṣin*
Naš.	*Našim*	*Yad.*	*Yadayim*
Naz.	*Nazir*	*Yebam.*	*Yebamot*
Ned.	*Nedarim*	*Yoma*	*Yoma (= Kippurim)*
Neg.	*Nega'im*	*Zabim*	*Zabim*
Nez.	*Neziqin*	*Zebaḥ.*	*Zebaḥim*
Nid.	*Niddah*	*Zera.*	*Zera'im*
'Ohol.	*'Oholot*		

Qumran / Dead Sea Scrolls

CD-A	Damascus Document[a]
1QH[a]	Thanksgiving Hymns/Psalms (*Hodayot*[a])
1QM	War Scroll (*Milḥamah*)
1QpHab	Pesher to Habakkuk
1QS	Rule of the Community (*Serek Hayyaḥad*)
1QSa	Rule of the Congregation (Appendix *a* to 1QS)
4QMMT	Halakhic Letter (*Miqṣat Ma'aśê ha-Torah*)
4QpPs[a]	Pesher to Psalms[a]
4Q185	Sapiential Work
4Q372	Apocryphon of Joseph[b]

Greek Papyri

BGU	*Aegyptische Urkunden aus den Königlichen/Staatlichen Museen zu Berlin: Griechische Urkunden*, 15 vols. (Berlin, 1895–1983)
CPR	Corpus papyrorum Raineri, archeducis Austriae (Vienna, 1895–)
P.Cair.Preis.	*Griechische Urkunden des Ägyptischen Museums zu Kairo*, edited by F. Preisigke, Schriften der Wissenschaftlichen Gesellschaft zu Strassburg 8 (Strassburg: Trübner, 1911)

P.Mich.	The University of Michigan Papyrus Collection, University Library, Ann Arbor, Michigan
P.Oxy.	*The Oxyrhynchus Papyri*, edited by B. P. Grenfell et al., 71 vols. (London: Egypt Exploration Society, 1898–2004)
P.Wisc.	*The Wisconsin Papyri*, translated and edited by P. J. Sijpesteijn, 2 vols., Papyrologica Lugduno-Batava 16 (Lugdunum Batavorum: Brill, 1967–77)

Classical Writers

Adol. poet. aud.	Plutarch, *Quomodo adolescens poetas audire debeat* (*How a Young Man Should Study Poetry*)
Anab.	Xenophon, *Anabasis* (*The Persian Expedition*)
Autol.	Theophilus, *Ad Autolycum* (*To Autolycus*)
Cons. Apoll.	Plutarch, *Consolatio ad Apollonium* (*Condolence to Apollonius*)
Ep.	Seneca, *Epistulae morales* (*Moral Letters*)
Epict. diss.	Arrian, *Epicteti dissertationes* (*Discourses of Epictetus*)
Hist.	Herodotus, *Historiae* (*Histories*)
Leg.	Plato, *Leges* (*Laws*)
Metaph.	Aristotle, *Metaphysica* (*Metaphysics*)
Mund.	Aristotle, *De mundo* (*On the Universe/Cosmos*)
Per.	Plutarch, *Pericles*
Rhet.	Aristotle, *Rhetorica* (*Rhetoric*)
Tranq. an.	Plutarch, *De tranquillitate animi* (*On Tranquillity of Mind*)

Transliteration

Hebrew

א	ʾ		בָ	ā	qāmeṣ
ב	b		בַ	a	pataḥ
ג	g		הַ	a	furtive pataḥ
ד	d		בֶ	e	sĕgôl
ה	h		בֵ	ē	ṣērê
ו	w		בִ	i	short ḥîreq
ז	z		בִ	ī	long ḥîreq written defectively
ח	ḥ		בָ	o	qāmeṣ ḥāṭûp
ט	ṭ		בוֹ	ô	ḥôlem written fully
י	y		בֹ	ō	ḥôlem written defectively
כ/ך	k		בוּ	û	šûreq
ל	l		בֻ	u	short qibbûṣ
מ/ם	m		בֻ	ū	long qibbûṣ written defectively
נ/ן	n		בָה	â	final qāmeṣ hēʾ (בָה = āh)
ס	s		בֶי	ê	sĕgôl yôd (בֶי = êy)
ע	ʿ		בֵי	ê	ṣērê yôd (בֵ = êy)
פ/ף	p		בִי	î	ḥîreq yôd (בִי = îy)
צ/ץ	ṣ		בֲ	ă	ḥāṭēp pataḥ
ק	q		בֱ	ĕ	ḥāṭēp sĕgôl
ר	r		בֳ	ŏ	ḥāṭēp qāmeṣ
שׂ	ś		בְ	ĕ	vocal šĕwāʾ
שׁ	š				
ת	t				

Notes on the Transliteration of Hebrew
1. Accents are not shown in transliteration.
2. Silent šĕwāʾ is not indicated in transliteration.
3. The spirant forms ב ג ד כ פ ת are usually not specially indicated in transliteration.
4. Dāgēš forte is indicated by doubling the consonant. Euphonic dāgēš and dāgēš lene are not indicated in transliteration.
5. Maqqēp is represented by a hyphen.

Greek

α	*a*	ζ	*z*	λ	*l*	π	*p*	φ	*ph*
β	*b*	η	*ē*	μ	*m*	ρ	*r*	χ	*ch*
γ	*g/n*	θ	*th*	ν	*n*	σ/ς	*s*	ψ	*ps*
δ	*d*	ι	*i*	ξ	*x*	τ	*t*	ω	*ō*
ε	*e*	κ	*k*	ο	*o*	υ	*y/u*	ʽ	*h*

Notes on the Transliteration of Greek

1. Accents, lenis (smooth breathing), and *iota* subscript are not shown in transliteration.
2. The transliteration of asper (rough breathing) precedes a vowel or diphthong (e.g., ἁ = *ha*; αἱ = *hai*) and follows ρ (i.e., ῥ = *rh*).
3. *Gamma* is transliterated *n* only when it precedes γ, κ, ξ, or χ.
4. *Upsilon* is transliterated *u* only when it is part of a diphthong (i.e., αυ, ευ, ου, υι).

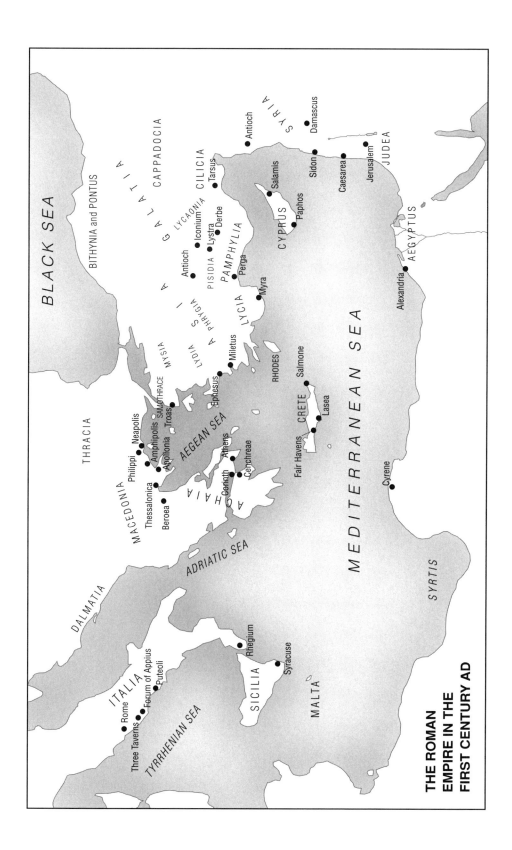

THE ROMAN
EMPIRE IN THE
FIRST CENTURY AD

BLACK SEA

BITHYNIA and PONTUS

GALATIA

CAPPADOCIA

LYCAONIA

CILICIA

Tarsus

Antioch

SYRIA

Damascus

JUDEA

Jerusalem

Caesarea

Sidon

Salamis

CYPRUS

Paphos

AEGYPTUS

Alexandria

Antioch

Iconium

Lystra

Derbe

PISIDIA

PAMPHYLIA

Perga

PHRYGIA

LYDIA

MYSIA

LYCIA

Myra

Miletus

Ephesus

Samothrace

Troas

Neapolis

Amphipolis

Apollonia

Philippi

THRACIA

Thessalonica

Beroea

MACEDONIA

AEGEAN SEA

Athens

Corinth

Cenchreae

ACHAIA

RHODES

CRETE

Salmone

Lasea

Fair Havens

MEDITERRANEAN SEA

Cyrene

SYRTIS

ADRIATIC SEA

DALMATIA

ITALIA

Rome

Three Taverns

Forum of Appius

Puteoli

TYRRHENIAN SEA

SICILIA

Rhegium

Syracuse

MALTA

Introduction to James

The document known as the Epistle of James has a unique voice in the NT. Its orientation to practical theology, its interest in true godly wisdom and consistent Christian behavior, and its large supply of memorable phrases and aphorisms that encapsulate many aspects of the practical Christian life have made it useful for purposes of moral exhortation. However, it has been a lesser influence on the development of the church's theology, and until recently it has been somewhat neglected.

Further, the second half of James 2 appears at first glance to clash with certain statements by Paul on justification by faith. This, along with the less-developed Christology of James, led Martin Luther to question its validity as an expression of the gospel of Jesus, even calling it "an epistle of straw."[1] Most of the Reformers, however, even Luther's protégé Melancthon (*Loci Communes* 9.5.12), along with most of the church throughout its history, took a more sober view and argued that James, when understood better, is not in conflict with Paul. The issue of James's relationship to Paul's theology will be examined in more detail both in the introduction and in the commentary on James 2. Indeed, a careful study of the letter leads to the conclusion that James's insistence on works is precisely because faith is important. A faith devoid of works is a faith devoid of life; a living, saving faith is one that has an effect on behavior, and therefore it is essential that a person's faith be a working faith.

---

1. The famous words appear in Luther's 1522 edition of his German Bible (an English translation is available in *LW* 35:362). Luther did not, however, exclude James from his NT. He grouped it along with Hebrews (!), Jude, and Revelation as being among the less-significant writings. Further, Luther's own theology is closer to James than he perhaps realized. In his preface to Romans he declares that real faith is "a living, busy, active, mighty thing, this faith . . . it is impossible for it not to be doing good works incessantly. It never asks whether good works are to be done; it has done them before the question can be asked, and is always doing them. Whoever does not do such works is an unbeliever. . . . Thus, it is impossible to separate works from faith, quite as impossible as to separate heat and light from fire" (*LW* 35:370–71). James surely would concur.

It is in fact the thesis of this commentary that James should be seen as a book about true faith as opposed to a false one. Far from minimizing faith, the author of James regards faith as supremely important, and it is for this very reason that it is crucial that a person's faith be genuine. People often deceive themselves, and it is quite possible for people to think that they have faith when in fact they are hypocrites. James, in the first chapter alone, uses three different words to describe this capacity for self-deceit: πλανάω (planaō, lead astray) in 1:16, παραλογίζομαι (paralogizomai, deceive) in 1:22, and ἀπατάω (apataō, deceive) in 1:26. Indeed, the issue runs all the way through James: the doubter's double-mindedness in 1:6–8, empty religiosity in 1:26, the pretense of loving neighbor while showing favoritism in 2:8–9, the empty, dead faith of 2:20, the contradiction of blessing God and cursing his image-bearers in 3:9 and of boasting while being false to the truth in 3:14, and the pretense of the merchant in 4:13 are essentially all referring to forms of self-deception. But James wants those who profess to believe in Christ to be real disciples and manifest living faith, and he wants to awaken people who complacently think that they are believers but do not act like believers—in other words, those who have deceived themselves. Further, the threats to faith that can come by way of persecution, illness, and the delay of the coming of the Lord are met with exhortations to persevere, which is the stance of faith. Truly, James as a whole is a book about genuine faith. Surely, there are few times more in need of James's insistence that faith be genuine than our own.

Controversy has continued to swirl about the book, however. Almost every aspect of interpretation, its author, its date, its original audience, its theological substructure, its organization (or lack of organization), its overall purpose (especially whether it is in any way a reaction to some form of Paulinism), its unity, and even the meaning of several of its words, phrases, and sentences have been heavily debated, and many matters remain without anything close to a scholarly consensus.

All these questions of introduction, authorship, dating, original audience, text, genre, and canonical acceptance are tangled together, and even the meaning of the text and the questions of introduction are interlinked. As a result, no obvious starting point presents itself. The question of authorship, for example, depends on when we date the letter and on the history of its use in the church, but dating is heavily dependent on identifying the original audience as well as the author, and the identity of the original audience is tied up with the author, date, and genre as well as the meaning of certain of James's statements. Change any piece, and the whole puzzle must be assembled differently.

Nevertheless, the book gives us some clues about these things, and if we listen sympathetically to its message and pay close attention to the world in which it was written, we can, with some measure of confidence, answer many of those questions. Fortunately, the book's central message is comprehensible regardless of its origins.

Character

Following the lead of Johnson (1995: 3–4), we will begin with a preliminary and brief attempt to listen to the "voice" of the letter and ascertain how it might fit in the story of the earliest church. This will give us a means of tentatively dating the letter. We can also determine how well it fits with what can be known of its putative author, whom the letter itself identifies as simply "James, servant of God and the Lord Jesus Christ." As we will note shortly, this must refer to the James who appears in Acts as the leader of the Jerusalem church, whom Paul identifies as "the brother of the Lord" (Gal. 1:19).

1. James is interested primarily in practical Christianity. He assumes the content and saving power of the Christian gospel (1:21; see "Theology" below), but his interest is on how that is worked out in life, and he denounces a kind of faith that does not act accordingly. James also packs the letter with aphorisms that encapsulate godliness and thus has contributed many pithy and memorable phrases to the Christian's wisdom vocabulary. The letter is also heavily imperatival, containing some fifty-four imperative verbs (plus a few negative aorist subjunctives that serve as prohibitions), and it displays an exhortational tone throughout.

   Our Western Christian heritage has vigorously stressed the importance of doctrine, focusing on propositional truth as crucial for Christian identity, because ideas and thoughts make a difference in actions and relationships, particularly our relationship to God. But James reminds us that the ultimate purpose of Christian instruction, the goal of doctrine, is a godly character and righteous behavior. This purpose is also found in Jesus's teaching and even in that of Paul (see, e.g., Rom. 8:29, "conformed to his image"; see also Phil. 2:12–13), but it has tended to become lost in our battles over precise doctrinal formulation. James reminds us that genuine faith is more than a matter of simply acknowledging the right concepts; it is right living in accordance with those concepts.

2. James exhibits throughout, both in vocabulary and in concept, a Jewish flavor. Many scholars have noticed the similarities between James and Jewish wisdom literature, especially Sirach (see excursus 3, "James and Wisdom"). And several scholars have pointed out that despite the distinctively literary quality of James's Greek in several passages, many of its expressions have a pronounced Semitic cast (see MHT 4:116–20; see also "Jewish Literary Background" below). Also, James exhibits in its use of the OT a common Jewish exegetical procedure of interpreting one text by reference to another (James 2 interprets Gen. 15:6 by referring to Gen. 22).[2] It uses features indicative of a Semitic rather than normal Greek style—for example, attributive genitives such as "hearer of forgetfulness" (= "forgetful hearer") in 1:25, and attributed genitives

2. Jacob (1975) notes similarities with 1 Macc. 2:52; Sir. 44:20–21.

such as "abundance of wickedness" (= "abundant malice") in 1:21 and "beauty of its face" (= "its lovely appearance") in 1:11. Even among ancient interpreters James's use of parataxis (using "and" to join two sentences where literary Greek would use a subordinate clause) was noted (Theophylact, *Commentary on James* [PG 125:1152]). Further, the law of God is termed "royal" (or better, "kingdom-related") and "liberating." James's concerns are reflective of OT ethical interests, particularly as seen in the prophets and wisdom literature. Its view of the law, like that seen in the Gospel of Matthew, is entirely positive; there is no development or even hint here of the Pauline experience of the law as an "enemy." On the other hand, James's focus is not at all on the Jewish distinctives of circumcision, food laws, or Sabbath observance, but on things such as showing no favoritism, loving neighbor, acting mercifully, caring for widows and orphans, being unselfish and honest, and persevering in prayer. Hence, the Jewishness that James exhibits is not an exclusionary kind that sees covenant in terms of ethnicity or ritual, but one that consists in godly behavior.

3. Although James only twice explicitly refers to Jesus Christ, this book is decidedly Christian. The Christian framework is implicit in several places, and the book as a whole expresses a Christian outlook (Cranfield 1965: 182–93). Particularly, James shares the Christian eschatological orientation, evident in that the motivation for ethics is chiefly the knowledge of the imminent coming of the Lord in judgment (1:9–10; 5:7–8; see "Eschatology" and "Ethics" below). Further, although perhaps some of the numerous echoes of Jesus's teaching (see "James and the Wisdom of Jesus" below) can be explained as a common Jewish heritage, the sheer number of correspondences is so great and at times so distinctive that few scholars any longer doubt a substantial link between the Synoptic tradition and James, although that link probably is an indirect one.[3] In only one instance does the similarity approach quotation of a Gospel text (the vocabulary of James 5:12 closely resembles that of Matt. 5:34–37, which also has an echo in 2 Cor. 1:17). But the content correspondence with the didactic material found mostly in Matthew and Luke is pronounced (see Hartin 1991).

4. James is multithematic in character. The letter does not evince a linear discussion of a single theme, but appears to be a collection of admonitions on faithful life, on what a life full of faith looks like. Nor is this collection linearly organized; instead, it interweaves several themes that are introduced in James 1 and then ties them together and examines the issues from various sides (see "Structure" below).

3. Several commentators have attempted to list the connections, and these lists vary considerably, but even the most conservative of them usually see in more than twenty of James's verses a correspondence with something in the Synoptic tradition of Jesus's teaching (see Deppe 1989). The correspondence with the Sermon on the Mount is particularly striking.

5. The Epistle of James, though clearly Christian, exhibits almost no christological development. James has no trace of the "union with Christ" theme seen in Paul's letters. James also exhibits little redemptive-historical reflection and, although the fact of God's mercy is central (2:13), shows hardly any interest in how the mercy of God is possible or how the death and resurrection of Jesus are related to God's mercy. Likewise, James makes no mention of the Holy Spirit.[4] Even the alleged reaction to something sounding vaguely like Paul in James 2 seems to be dealing not with the theological concerns of Paul, but with a lack of ethical consistency on the part of confessing believers, a problem often seen in Israel in the OT and one endemic to every age.

6. James exhibits a good command of Greek. Hellenistic literary imagery abounds, such as forest fires, ship rudders, horses and bits, astronomical phenomena (perhaps, but see the commentary on 1:17), mirrors, and life cycles. On the other hand, some of James's imagery is narrowly Palestinian (saltwater springs, early and late rains) and unlikely to have been well understood outside Palestine.

Several scholars have noted that the language of James is "relatively polished Greek" (Dibelius 1975: 34–38) of an almost literary character (Mayor 1897: ccxx–ccxxix; Ropes 1916: 25–27; Schlatter 1956: 77–84; Mussner 1975: 26–30; Baasland 1988: 3650–62). The author appears to be quite at home in Greek, using extensive alliteration (e.g., the alliterative π [*p*] in 1:2, 11, 17, 22) and wordplay (e.g., ἔργα [*erga*, works] versus ἀργή [*argē*, vain, ineffectual] = α-εργη [not-working] in 2:20; or the play on the double meaning of ἰός [*ios*, rust, poison] in 5:3). Further, he demonstrates a good vocabulary, using several words that are well known in classical literature but found nowhere else in either the NT or the LXX (e.g., ἐνάλιος [*enalios*, sea creature] in 3:7; κατήφεια [*katēpheia*, gloominess] in 4:9; see Mayor 1897: ccxviii), and he seems somewhat familiar with Greek popular imagery (Ropes 1916: 231). James also tends toward classical syntax in contrast to other NT writers (e.g., 5:12 preserves the classical accusative of oath with ὄμνυμι [*omnymi*, swear] as opposed to the more Semitic ἐν + dative in Matt. 5:34–35 or κατά + genitive in Heb. 6:13; see BDF §149).

It was therefore supposed by many scholars that the literary Greek style is prima facie evidence that the author is unlikely to have been a Galilean Jewish peasant. Presumably, a fairly highly educated Hellenistic Jew or perhaps even a Gentile convert with literary training could more easily write such a letter. However, some curious facts suggest a more complicated picture:

4. The πνεῦμα (*pneuma*) in 4:5 is best understood not specifically as the person of the Holy Spirit but as either the human life-spirit (i.e., that which makes a human being alive; cf. 2:26) or the divinely given spirit of wisdom and understanding, by which God equipped Israel's leaders and artisans. See the commentary on 4:5 for a more complete discussion.

1. All but thirteen of James's words are found in the LXX. Even some of James's unique words seem to have Semitic roots. The word δίψυχος (*dipsychos*, double-minded), for example, which is not found in any extant literature prior to James,[5] including the LXX, appears to be a reflection of a Semitic idiom such as that found in Ps. 119:113, where the psalmist declares his hatred for the *sē'ăpîm* [those of "divided" loyalties, i.e., the double-minded]. Similarly, Ps. 12:2 condemns the "double-hearted" (*lēb wālēb*).[6] Whatever the author's background, he was well grounded in the Jewish Scriptures.

2. James sometimes uses idioms very unlike Greek and very like Semitic style.[7] Particularly, James's use of the genitive noun as an equivalent of an adjective (e.g., in 1:17 "shadow of turning" [= shifting shadow], or in 1:25 "hearer of forgetfulness" [= forgetful hearer], or in 2:4 "judges of evil opinions" [= judges who make bad decisions], or in 3:6 "world of unrighteousness" [= unrighteous world]) is difficult to attribute to anyone other than a person whose first language was Semitic (see BDF §165). Likewise, the omission of the article in certain phrases with a possessive pronoun (e.g., "his tongue" and "his heart" in 1:26; "his way" in 5:20) echoes Semitic style (BDF §259.3). James 5:17 evinces imitation of the Septuagintal style of rendering of the Hebrew infinitive absolute via a verb with the dative of its cognate noun,[8] and in 5:18 the circumlocution "heaven gave rain" for "God sent rain" also suggests a Jewish author (like Matthew, which uses "kingdom of heaven" for "kingdom of God").

3. James uses some words of Jewish background that were either unknown outside Jewish circles (e.g., "gehenna" in 3:6)[9] or had special meanings (e.g., "synagogue" in 2:2).[10] Further, James 5:20 alludes to Prov. 10:12 in a form not evident in the LXX translation but only in the Hebrew,

5. LSJ 440 does list a reference appearing in a fragment of a manuscript of Philo, but BDAG 253 indicates that in the fragment in question (II.663 Mangey) the word appears only in a title that is not from Philo's hand.

6. In neither of these texts does the LXX render the "divided" aspect clearly. In Ps. 118:113 (119:113 MT) the equivalent is simply "lawless"; in Ps. 11:3 (12:2 MT) the Hebrew idiom is rendered literally and, probably for most Greek speakers, incomprehensibly (ἐν καρδίᾳ καὶ ἐν καρδίᾳ). But James, being of Semitic background, may have understood it, and he attempted to render the concept of divided loyalty by the novel but quite comprehensible term δίψυχος. See the additional note on 1:8 in the commentary below.

7. For more on the Semitic style of James, see MHT 4:116–20. The suggestion that the Epistle of James may originally have been written in Aramaic was both raised and put to rest by Mayor (1897: cclx–cclxviii).

8. Although James is referring to an OT event (Elijah's intercession), the LXX has no equivalent to James's προσευχῇ προσηύξατο (see BDF §198.6).

9. Of course, this word occurs in the record of Jesus's words found in the Synoptic Gospels, but though James seems to know the tradition of Jesus's teaching, he never, with the possible exception of 5:12, reflects the actual wording found in the extant Gospels.

10. Admittedly, the word "synagogue" was picked up in the second-century church to apply to Christian gatherings (Ign. *Pol.* 4.2; Justin, *Dial.* 63.14; Herm. *Mand.* 11.9–14).

suggesting familiarity with the content of the proverb apart from the common Greek translation.[11]

4. Although James frequently uses phrases that at first seem to evoke Greek rather than Jewish literature (such as "cycle of generations" in 3:6, or astronomical terms such as "parallax" and "turning shadow" in 1:17 [see the commentary on 1:17], or the illustrations of ships being steered by rudders and horses by bits), often the author either has failed to understand the original meaning of such phrases or has ignored that meaning and developed his own in a way that fits more with Semitic background than Greek. For example, much ink has been spilled over the alleged origins of "cycle of generations," which the tongue sets afire, as being in the Orphic mysteries, but the cycles of birth, death, and rebirth (reincarnation) seem totally irrelevant to James's use. It is more likely that the author is using terminology borrowed from Greek culture for his own ends rather than importing the full connotations of that terminology into his own exhortations. Likewise, the reference to God being without the "shifting shadow," such as is apparent in the movement of the sun or the phases of the moon, probably has nothing to do with the astronomical phenomena or their astrological connotations. It is instead simply an example to contrast the unchanging constancy of the God of the Bible with the constant changes of everything worldly, including the astronomical entities that the Greco-Roman world perceived as gods. Such use has more the appearance of an "outsider" to a culture borrowing the terms but ignoring their "insider" connotations. This is exactly what we would expect of a Palestinian Jewish Christian who was competent in Greek and who was familiar with the Hellenistic cultic milieu while also being critical of it.

Another feature of James's style is his frequent use of comparisons. He refers to tossed waves (1:6), plants withering (1:10–11), a corpse without breath (2:26), horse and bridle (3:3), ship's rudder and pilot (3:4), a forest fire (3:5–6), fresh and bitter springs (3:11), grapevines and fig trees (3:12), evanescent mist (4:14), moth-eaten garments (5:2), rusted metal (5:3), and that peculiarity of Palestinian climate known as the early and the late (rains) (5:7).

Sometimes James's vigorous and colorful rhetoric can be baffling, particularly if too much precision is expected. As will be argued in the commentary, this probably is not a reflection of overly subtle or secret meanings on the part of the author, but is simply the result of impassioned rhetoric, and it is a mistake to press the specific language too hard or to expect linguistic

---

11. Since the form appears also in 1 Pet. 4:8, which virtually quotes Prov. 10:12, it is difficult to argue that both James and 1 Peter, independently of each other and of Proverbs, came up with the same phrase that just happens to resemble the Hebrew of Prov. 10:12. Ropes (1916: 316) therefore feels compelled to hypothesize "that some familiar *Greek* aphorism (all the associations of which can no longer be traced) has been used by 1 Peter, while a part of the same form of words has been independently used, in a very different sense, by James" (italics mine).

precision where none was intended. I will argue that James's difficult passages often are not difficult at all in terms of the point that the author is making; it is only the imprecision of the comparisons or language that have us scratching our heads. Thus, as in the difficulty of the interlocutor's statements in 2:18, or the odd "face of his generation" in 1:23, or the question-begging reference in 3:6 to "the tongue, a fire, the wicked world, the tongue is set in our members," whatever it is that James exactly had in mind is not ultimately germane to his overall main point. It is when the oddity of an expression is pressed too hard that some of the more idiosyncratic interpretations arise, sometimes to the obfuscation of James's main point.[12] The evocativeness of the imagery serves James's interest in motivating action or behavior. It is a mistake to read him as generating excessively subtle sophistries in order to win a theological argument or philosophical debate.

Here we may draw some preliminary conclusions. The letter is Christian, but it reflects a fairly primitive stage of theological development. James evinces no concern for ecclesial authority or structure; the importance of the substitutionary death of Christ receives no mention; there is no cultic identification with Christ, no discussion of how the inclusion of Gentiles affects theology, and no reflection on how Christ fulfilled OT expectations. Although James is concerned with the problem of Christian suffering, he, unlike 1 Peter or the letters of Paul, deals with it not by reference to the Christian's identification with Christ's suffering, but by way of simple exhortations to endure because it pleases God, produces maturity, and will someday be over. On the other hand, James reflects the peculiar orientation to godly life that appears in the recorded teaching of Jesus in the Synoptic Gospels (more on this below). Yet James at no point actually cites the Gospels (at least not in the form in which we have them) or even acknowledges that the material comes from Jesus or reflects the special interests of Jesus. It is as though James is imbued with the wisdom teaching of Jesus, but not in the written form in which we now find it. All this points to a time quite early in the life of the church, prior to the theological reflections of Paul, prior to the circulation of the Gospels, and prior to the authors of Hebrews, 1 Peter, and the Johannine materials, or at least prior to the time when these other writings began to have widespread and determinative influence.[13]

Authorship and Date

Because the questions of authorship and date are interdependent, I will discuss them together. The name "James" is the equivalent of the OT name "Jacob"

---

12. This has been particularly true in the case of the interlocutor's position in 2:18, which at first read seems to be saying the opposite of what the interlocutor would be expected to say (see the commentary).

13. Of course, the lack of influence on James does not prove that he wrote chronologically prior to these documents, but at least it means that James represents a stage of Christian thinking that has not yet been determined by them, and hence it is logically prior.

(hence the adjective "Jacobean" to describe things pertaining to James). It is quite a common name in the NT as well as in Judaism generally,[14] and thus the identification of the author as simply "James, servant of God and the Lord Jesus Christ" implies someone very well known in the church. Two of the twelve disciples were named "James." The better known of these was James the son of Zebedee, brother of John, but this James was killed by Herod (Agrippa I), as we know from Acts 12:2. This happened sometime in (or possibly before) the year 44, which probably is too early for him to be the author of the letter.[15] James the son of Alphaeus also was one of the Twelve, but nothing is known of him after the earliest days of the church, and if he had authored the letter, he would have needed further identification than just "James." There was another man named "James" who might have been a disciple (not one of the Twelve) named "James the Younger" (or perhaps "Little James" or "James the Less"), but he is known only by the fact that his mother was one of the witnesses of the crucifixion, which makes him even less known than James the son of Alphaeus (unless it was the same person). The only James who seems to fit, therefore, is the James who was leader of the church in Jerusalem, indicated in Acts 12:17 and elsewhere, and whom Paul mentions in Gal. 1:19, calling him "James the Lord's brother." He is the James named among the family of Jesus in Mark 6:3. Not all students of this letter conclude that James the brother of Jesus wrote it, and shortly I will discuss the issue of whether James is pseudepigraphical, but even those scholars who do not think that James "the Lord's brother" wrote this letter acknowledge that he is the "James" intended in the salutation and in whose name it was written.

Who Was James?

The person named "James" who was leader of the church in Jerusalem, Paul knows as "the brother of the Lord" (Gal. 1:19 [cf. 1 Cor. 9:5, which mentions "brothers of the Lord" as among the church leaders who are married]). Later Christian writings (e.g., Eusebius, *Hist. eccl.* 2.23) usually refer to him as "James the Just" (Ἰάκωβος ὁ δίκαιος, *Iakōbos ho dikaios* [perhaps better translated "James the Righteous"]). This James appears three times in Acts, always in a prominent role. After the death of James the brother of John (recorded in Acts 12:2), and after Peter is miraculously delivered from prison, Peter tells the people to "inform James and the brothers" of what has happened (Acts 12:17), which surely indicates this James is already a prominent leader of the church. At the apostolic council in Acts 15:12–21 (probably occurring about

---

14. It is for this reason that, despite the media frenzy, the ossuary inscribed as that of "James brother of Jesus," even if its inscription be determined to be genuine (as appears increasingly doubtful), is unlikely to be that of the brother of Jesus of Nazareth. But whether or not that ossuary contained the bones of James, it contributes nothing toward our understanding of his letter, and its authenticity will not be evaluated here.

15. This event is neatly datable to 44 because the death of Herod Agrippa I occurred shortly thereafter (Acts 12:23), an event noted also by Josephus (*Ant.* 19.8.2 §§343–59).

five years later, in 49), James is the spokesman for the Jerusalem eldership, and it is he who sends the letter of Acts 15:23–29. Finally, in Acts 21:18–20 it is this James to whom Paul gives his report.

He probably is also included in Acts 1:14 as among those waiting in Jerusalem for the Holy Spirit, among whom are "the mother of Jesus, and his brothers." This James is also named by Paul in Gal. 2:1–10 as a leader of the church in Jerusalem, and in 1 Cor. 15:7 as one of the notable witnesses to whom Jesus appeared after his resurrection. The text of 1 Cor. 15:5–7 is also informative because of how Paul identifies those to whom Jesus appeared:

> He appeared to Cephas, then to the twelve. Then he appeared to more than five hundred brothers. . . . Then he appeared to James, then to all the apostles.

This shows that the term "apostles" is applied more broadly than just to the Twelve, and presumably it includes the person named "James" who was not one of the Twelve, which is unlikely to be anyone other than James the leader of the church in Jerusalem. Likewise, Paul in Gal. 1:19 directly refers to this James as an apostle: "I saw none of the other apostles except James the Lord's brother."

The author of Jude also mentions James by identifying himself simply as the "brother of James," which could only be a reference to this James, the brother of Jesus, the leader of the church at Jerusalem from 44–62.[16]

We also have references to James from outside Christianity in comments by Josephus (*Ant.* 20.9.1 §§197–203), who identifies him as a leader of the Christian movement and notes his death in 62 as one of the atrocities leading up to the catastrophe of the Jewish war of 66–70. Some scholars have debated whether this is one of the "Christian interpolations" added into Josephus by Christian scribes. However, Josephus's words here speak of James and the Christian movement only tangentially; his main focus is the hasty and unjust behavior of Ananus and his subsequent deposal. If this is a Christian interpolation, it is odd that the only mention of Jesus identifies him as one who is "called" the Christ. It is likely that this text serves as evidence that among non-Christian Jews of the mid- to late first century, James may have been at least as well known as Jesus of Nazareth. The closely similar but not identical account related in Eusebius (*Hist. eccl.* 2.23.21–24) generally confirms the historical plausibility of Josephus at this point. On the other hand, the story in Hegesippus's account (which Eusebius recounts a little earlier in *Hist. eccl.* 2.23.4–18) has a more fanciful character and bears the marks of forced harmonization.[17]

---

16. This also fits with the identification of "James . . . and Judas" as two of the brothers of Jesus named in Mark 6:3 ("Jude" and "Judas" are English equivalents of slightly different Greek adaptations of the one Hebrew name "Yehuda," just as both "Simeon" and "Simon" can be used to refer to the apostle Peter, whose Hebrew name was "Shim'on").

17. Eusebius seems to think that Hegesippus is of the first generation of Christians after the apostles, but internal evidence suggests that Hegesippus was more likely writing in the mid-

The Epistle of James receives little mention in extant literature until the late second and early third centuries (see "External Indications and the Church's Reception" below), by which time we begin to see traces of its wider circulation. But quite apart from this letter, James became something of a favorite "hero" for a number of diverse groups, both within and without the pale of the orthodox church. Eusebius (*Hist. eccl.* 2.1.2–5) notes that Clement of Alexandria spoke of James as the "bishop" or overseer of the Jerusalem church. Further, Clement's *Hypotyposeis* (books 6–7) describes James's martyrdom of being thrown from a parapet. (Although there are some difficulties in harmonizing this account with that of Josephus, both accounts agree on the timing.)

Other, later material on James is more dubious historically. The gnostic Gospel of Thomas found in the library at Nag Hammadi has Jesus telling his disciples to "go to James the righteous, for whose sake heaven and earth came into being" (12). More reasonable but still excessive is the report by Hegesippus that James had knees like a camel from his extended prayers, and reports that James had access to the sanctuary at the temple, which is extremely unlikely and probably impossible because James was not of a priestly lineage. Hegesippus's account of James's martyrdom, recorded by Eusebius (*Hist. eccl.* 2.23.4–18), which apparently tries to harmonize the story of James's death found in Josephus with that found in Clement of Alexandria, is equally hagiographic and historically unconvincing. The second-century document known as the Gospel of the Hebrews describes the appearance of Jesus to James in eucharistic language, clearly borrowing from a selection of NT texts and referring (like the Gospel of Thomas and Eusebius) to James as "James the Righteous."[18]

But what can we know of this James who led the church in Jerusalem, whose name appears at the head of this letter? What was his relationship to Jesus? Since he was not one of the Twelve, how did he come to have a position of prominence?

As already noted, Paul identifies James as the "brother of the Lord" (Gal. 1:19). The most natural way of understanding this, along with the mention of James as one of Jesus's brothers in Mark 6:3, is that after Jesus was born, Joseph and Mary had other children. James therefore would have been the half brother of Jesus. Once the idea of Mary's perpetual virginity arose, this became a problem, and so two other theories of James's relationship to Jesus developed. The first theory was proposed by Epiphanius of Salamis

---

second century. Likewise, the material found in the Pseudo-Clementine letters on the "Ascents of James" has no credible connection to the historical James. See Painter 2001: 36–46. Eisenman (1997) makes an exhaustive attempt to work out his earlier thesis (Eisenman 1990) that drew a connection between the "James the Righteous" of the Pseudo-Clementine material and the "Teacher of Righteousness" mentioned in the Dead Sea Scrolls. The suggestion that James was the central figure of the Qumran community caused a brief sensation in the popular media, but virtually all other scholars have rightly rejected it because it is built on too many speculative leaps and historical improbabilities. See Painter 1999: 230–34, 277–88.

18. See Martin (1988: xliv), who provides a translation of the relevant passage.

(315–403), and hence this view is called the "Epiphanian" view. Epiphanius proposed that James and the other "brothers" were children of Joseph by a previous marriage, Joseph's first wife having died prior to his betrothal to Mary. This idea is also found in the Gospel of Peter and is supported by Origen (d. 254). The second theory was proposed by Jerome (347–420), whose Latin name is "Hieronymus," and so this view is called the "Hieronymian" view. Jerome proposed that there was confusion over the name "James" because of the number of people by that name, and also because "Mary" was such a common name. Jerome thought that the "apostle" James to whom Paul referred in Gal. 1:19 was James the son of Alphaeus, and that this apostle was the same as the James son of Mary noted in Mark 15:40, leading to later confusion. On the other hand, Jerome proposed, James, the "brother of the Lord" who led the Jerusalem church and wrote the Epistle of James, was in fact a cousin of Jesus.[19] To do this, Jerome had to claim that the Greek word ἀδελφός (adelphos, brother) could mean "cousin." Augustine of Hippo (354–430) supported this view, and it came to be the dominant view up until the Reformation. Roman Catholic commentators (e.g., Hartin 2003: 16–17) have continued to support this tradition by arguing that "brother" could indicate members of a broad family network. Certainly, "brother" can be used as a social connector, as James frequently does within this letter. Unfortunately for this view, however, all those occasions in Greek literature where a cousin, or someone else within a larger family unit, is called a "brother" are instances where "brother" is being used in a general sense, as when all Israelites are called "brothers" or all the men in a military unit are called "brothers," or fellow believers are called "brothers." And in all cases where "brother" is used not as a social connector but as a means of identifying someone (brother of a named person), it always signifies someone who shares at least one parent with the named person. Since Greek has a perfectly good word for "cousin" (ἀνήψιος, anēpsios), and because never is ἀδελφός used unambiguously to mean "cousin," Jerome's view looks a great deal like special pleading.

Even in the ancient church the natural way of reading the references to James "the Lord's brother" was not unknown. Tertullian, who with his natural ascetic interests would have no reason to deny the perpetual virginity of Mary, nevertheless simply accepts that James was Jesus's younger half brother (Tertullian, Marc. 4.19; Res. 7; Mon. 8).

Likewise, the Christian writer Helvidius (wrote ca. 380) simply proposed that Mary and Joseph had other children subsequent to Jesus's birth.[20] And indeed, the reference to Mary's virginity in Matthew implies that it was not perpetual, saying that Joseph "knew her not until she had given birth

19. Jerome also appears to have depended on other, dubious sources regarding James as the cousin of Jesus, in particular the Gospel of Peter and the even more dubious Protevangelium of James. For more on this, see Mayor 1897: viii–xlvii.
20. No works of Helvidius have survived. We know of him and his theory only because Jerome specifically opposed it in putting forth his own theory.

to a son" (Matt. 1:25).[21] We may also note that since pious Jewish couples regarded it as a righteous responsibility to bear and raise children, it is exceedingly likely that Joseph and Mary would have at least tried to have more children. The occasional appearances of Jesus's siblings in the Gospel accounts (Mark 3:20–21, 30–35; 6:1–4; John 7:3–5), as well as in Acts (1:14), suggest that they were successful. Mayor (1897: x) further makes the point that since Tertullian, who wrote at the end of the second or beginning of the third century, seems to be unaware that he is contradicting any earlier tradition, it is likely that the Hieronymian and Epiphanian views arose in response to the theological need of safeguarding the idea of Mary's perpetual virginity.[22]

If James was Jesus's half brother, and probably even if he was a son of Joseph by an earlier marriage, he would have been raised in the same family. This close familiarity with Jesus since childhood makes very natural the close resemblances of the Epistle of James and the teaching of Jesus in the Synoptic Gospels.

But it appears that James earlier in his life did not share so closely his brother's expectation of the kingdom of God. Mark 3:20–21 and 6:1–4 seem to indicate at least a hesitancy on the part of Jesus's earthly family, and John 7:5 plainly says that "not even his brothers believed in him." This last text in particular is somewhat unambiguous, since "believing" in the Gospel of John is something that many people do and yet do not do.[23] But the consistent picture gleaned from these texts, plus the fact that James was not with the disciples but rather received a special appearance from Jesus (according to 1 Cor. 15:7), suggests that James was less than enthusiastic about Jesus's itinerant ministry.

But after receiving that resurrection appearance, James becomes not only active as a believer but also prominent. As already noted, it is he, not, as might have been expected, Peter, who is the de facto leader of the church whom Paul meets in Acts on three different occasions. And the early church preserved several traces of James's reputation, not just in Acts and the letters of Paul, but also in the hagiographic materials such as Hegesippus's comments recorded in Eusebius, the Pseudo-Clementine materials (both the *Recognitions* and the *Homilies* contain several references to James), the Gospel of Thomas, and Clement of Alexandria

---

21. The Greek phrase ἕως οὗ (*heōs hou*, until), as in English, does not require an end to the previous condition, but normally it does imply it.

22. See the lengthy discussion in Mayor 1897: viii–xlvii.

23. Painter (2001) in particular argues that James and the rest of Jesus's family were not "unbelievers" or opposed to Jesus's mission before his resurrection. According to Acts, Jesus's family, including James, is a part of the early church, and the appearance to James mentioned in 1 Cor. 15:7 is not said to be a "conversion" experience, any more than the appearance to Peter mentioned two verses previously. However, when Jesus responds to his townspeople's skepticism in Mark 6:4, he observes that a "prophet is not without honor, save in his own country and among his own kin, and in his own house." Coming as it does immediately after the specific mention of his brothers and sisters in 6:3, this statement would seem to be inappropriate, perhaps even odd, if in fact his own kin did honor him.

(in *Hypotyposeis*, books 6–7),[24] and even in the non-Christian Jewish source Josephus. Not all of these have much historical value, but the variety and the distribution of the tradition of James's exemplary piety suggest that he made an impact on many people entirely independently of the letter under his name.[25]

Whether this James was the half brother of Jesus or simply a close relative, virtually all scholars acknowledge that this prominent leader of the church in Jerusalem is the James referred to in James 1:1. But was this letter written by the historical James so designated?

Four Views of Author and Date

There are four commonly espoused views regarding the authorship and dating of the Epistle of James:

1. The letter was written by the historical James prior to the Galatians controversy, and even before the apostolic council in Jerusalem noted in Acts 15, thus probably in the mid- to late 40s.
2. The letter was written by James in response to Paulinism of some sort, specifically correcting the idea that righteousness can be acquired simply by acknowledging certain theological propositions.
3. The letter is pseudonymous, written at the end of the first century or early in the second century by a proponent of Jewish (non-Pauline) Christianity.
4. Much of the material of the letter goes back to James, but has been edited and assembled after his death by someone with Greek literary training.[26]

VIEW 1: THE LETTER WAS WRITTEN BY JAMES BEFORE PAUL'S LETTERS

Since the first explicit acknowledgment of the Epistle of James by Origen in the early third century, Christians have held that its author is James, known

24. Also, Eusebius (*Hist. eccl.* 2.1.2–5) informs us that Clement of Alexandria referred to James as the "bishop" (ἐπίσκοπος, *episkopos*) of Jerusalem.

25. Chilton (2001: 146–47) suggests that James was a Nazirite who saw his brother's movement as oriented toward producing more Nazirites. He supports this by reference to (1) the Amos 9:11–12 prophecy (to which James is said to refer in Acts 15:16–18), a prophecy also quoted in the Damascus Document, where it refers to the restoration of Torah, and (2) the record in Matt. 2:23 of Jesus being called a "Nazarene," which Chilton understands to be a mistaken remembrance that Jesus was a "Nazirite." The idea is brilliant, but it involves too many suppositions to be likely and is implicitly contradicted by passages such as Matt. 11:19 // Luke 7:34 (which report that Jesus was being called a "wine-drinker"). Moreover, the one passage where James is most similar to the Synoptic account is James 5:12 (Matt. 5:34), which prohibits the taking of oaths. Since Nazirites became Nazirites by taking an oath, it is difficult to see, if Jesus and James were Nazirites, how they could have prohibited oaths.

26. A fifth view, that James is an adaptation of an earlier, purely Jewish work with 1:1 and 2:1 (the only explicit references to Christ) added later, is proposed by Massebieau (1895) and Spitta (1896: 1–13). Dibelius (1975: 22–23) thoroughly debunks this view by pointing out that certain Christian distinctives permeate the book of James (e.g., the reference to the parousia of the Lord in 5:8, and the invocation in 2:7 of the "name," which can be no other than that of the Christ), and I could find no commentary of recent vintage that supports this view. See also the discussion in "Original Recipients and Occasion" below.

to Paul as "the Lord's brother." Though after the Reformation many have assumed that it was written in reaction to Paul, it may in fact have been produced prior to the letters of Paul and thus prior to the controversy that occasioned the letter to the Galatians. This is the view of Mayor (1897: cxxi–cliii), Zahn (1909: 1.91–94), and Schlatter (1956: 7), and it has more recently gained renewed support from Adamson (1989: 3–52, 195–227), Johnson (1995: 111–21), Moo (2000: 26), and to some degree Bauckham (1999: 127–31) and Brosend (2004: 5–6).

Several indications point to the Epistle of James being quite early, despite the paucity of references to it in the early church (see "Evidence: External Indications and the Church's Reception" below). One is the indication that the recipients apparently are meeting in "synagogues" (2:2), and some "rich" attendants at these synagogues are the very people who are "blaspheming the good name that has been invoked upon you" (2:7). As Dibelius (1975: 23) points out, the "name" being blasphemed can only be that of Jesus or perhaps "Christian." An implication of this is that the letter envisions a time prior to the "parting of the ways" when Judaism had expelled Christians from its assemblies.

Another indication that the Epistle of James may be quite early is that despite the heavy correspondences with the Synoptic tradition, hardly anything in James except 5:12 has any linguistic similarity to that tradition as we know it from the canonical Gospels. The one exception in 5:12 also has an echo in Paul, which suggests that it may have been circulating prior to the Synoptic Gospels (or Q, the hypothetical source for Matthew and Luke, if it existed). One possible explanation for this is that the author of James had knowledge of the teaching of Jesus prior to its "standardization" in the Gospels, independently from the (probably Petrine or at least Markan) preaching tradition that had rendered Jesus's teaching into Greek. If James were late and harking back to the Synoptic Gospels, one would expect closer verbal correspondences, such as exist between the Synoptics.

Further, the primitiveness of James's theological framework should not be overlooked. Except for the alleged interaction with Paul or Paulinism in 2:14–26 (see excursus 2, "Faith, Works, and Justification in James and Paul"), the theology of James is to a large extent a recasting of the "kingdom of God" exhortations of Jesus into a somewhat Hellenized framework, though retaining its roots in Jewish wisdom and prophetic traditions. The significant theological issues that occupied the minds of Paul, John, the authors of Hebrews and 1 Peter, and other NT writers—for example, the nature of redemption and the application of it to Jews and Gentiles, the significance of resurrection, the dynamics of sacraments, and the nature of the church—are only nascent or are simply absent in James. Yet as we have seen, James is tremendously concerned for faith in Christ (see the commentary on 2:1), for eschatological hope (5:7–8), and other concerns that are also evident in Jesus's teaching. This is exactly what we would expect of a very early Christian writing. On the other hand, Christian writings that are known to be late first or early second century demonstrate much more development, either in typological theorizing (Barnabas, Shepherd of Hermas), ecclesiology (Ignatius), philosophical development (Justin), or sacramental theology (Didache, Melito of Sardis).

Many recent interpreters have regarded the material of James 2 as directed against a "faith without works" opinion that is difficult to conceive among Jewish believers prior to Paul. This presupposes that James is addressed strictly to Jewish believers with solid ethical backgrounds, and that Paul is absolutely unique and cannot have had any precedents. We have no evidence of any Jew prior to Paul suggesting that a faith devoid of deeds can justify, but neither does Paul suggest this. I will discuss this issue of James's relationship to Paul later, but here we note that if James is reacting to Paul at all, he is reacting to a deviation from Paul that Paul himself would repudiate. In regard to James's addressees, it is not altogether manifest that the audience comprises only Jewish Christians. Indeed, the inclusion of believing Gentiles was already thematically introduced by Jesus himself, who commended the faith of people such as the centurion (Matt. 8:10) and the Syrophoenecian woman (Matt. 15:28) and mentioned nothing about circumcision or becoming a Jew. And Peter's experience with Cornelius in Acts 10 occurred prior to Paul's mission. So there very well may have been several believers of Gentile background already in the church prior to Paul's missiological activities. Yet they, because of their faith in Jesus, still could be considered as those who had been accepted by God and thus as members of the "scattered twelve tribes" (see "Original Recipients and Occasion" below, and the commentary on 1:1).

In fact, therefore, although there are some similarities of phrasing and use of OT texts (particularly Gen. 15:6) that may sound as though James is "reacting" to a perversion of Paul's notions of justification by faith, those similarities may instead be attributed to the fact that both James and Paul operated in a Hellenistic Jewish environment that was experiencing growing pains resulting from an influx of people from a Gentile background. Paul too had problems with Gentile believers who did not always apply their Christian faith to their ethical behavior (see, e.g., 1 Cor. 6). And Gen. 15:6, which both Paul and James quote, is of interest not just in the NT; Second Temple Jewish literature quite often refers to Gen. 15:6 because of its declaration of Abraham's righteousness, and understands it in relation to the offering of Isaac (e.g., 1 Macc. 2:52 RSV: "Was not Abraham found faithful when tested, and it was reckoned to him as righteousness?"). This is not to say that James would necessarily concur with 1 Maccabees, but it does indicate that Jews were connecting Gen. 15:6 with Gen. 22 prior to Paul.

Hence, it may be best to read the Epistle of James not as a tract reacting to Paul or even as a diatribe against a misunderstanding of Paul, but as entirely independent of the controversies addressed by Paul in Romans and Galatians and as dealing with an entirely different kind of problem than Paul's concern with "works of the law" (see Bauckham 1999: 127–31). If James is read on its own terms instead of as a reaction to Paulinism, the Jewish character of the book (for which, see Mayor 1897: cxxiv–cxxv), its primitive theology and lack of developed Christology, its close similarities to the Synoptic tradition (yet without actual quotations thereof), the reference to the assembly as a "synagogue," and other data point to a period not just prior to the "parting of the ways" of Christianity and Judaism, but even earlier, to a period when the church was still largely Jewish, though some Gentiles had believed.[27] To this can be added that James seems to know nothing of the controversy between Jew and Gentile that drove Galatians and Romans, and the "trials" in James seem to be more of the general type often endured by the poor at the hands of the rich, or by early believers at the hands of other Jews, than any official or imperial persecution.

Finally, if James wrote the letter after the apostolic council in Jerusalem in 49, one might have expected the letter to evince some knowledge of the controversy over the role of the law in the early church. While James consistently speaks positively of the law, as a law of freedom, a "royal" law (or better, "kingdom" law; see the commentary on 2:8), there is no indication that anyone thinks of the law negatively, but only that some professing believers are failing to live in accordance with it.

View 2: The Letter Was Written by James after Paul's Letters

Some scholars think that the Epistle of James was written by the historical James, but specifically in reaction to Paul (Hengel 1987: 253–67) and hence later, or that he was reacting to a misunderstanding of Paul's theology (Hort 1909: xxv; Tasker 1957: 31–32; Chester 1994: 48).

James 2, with its explicit denial of a "justification by faith alone," suggests that some among James's audience were propounding such a thing. But most scholars find it difficult to imagine such an idea of a Jewish audience prior to Paul. Hengel (1987) is the most vigorous proponent of the idea that James is directly challenging Paul's notions, arguing that it comes from the historical James, and that not just James 2, but indeed the whole of the letter, is in some sense a challenge to what James sees as a dangerous notion. The primitive and typically Jewish character of the theology is rooted in Jesus's teaching of the fatherhood of God and imminent eschatological expectation. Hengel thus dates the letter to the very early 60s.

Other scholars, such as Tasker (1957: 28–32), also see James as written by the historical James in reaction to Paulinism—not to Paul directly, but to a misappropriation of Paul's teaching on justification. This requires a date prior to the death of James in 62, but after Galatians and possibly Romans had started circulating (i.e., the late 50s) and had had time enough to be misunderstood. Although this may appear to compress the chronology to an undue degree, we should note that Paul himself finds it necessary to deal

---

27. Mayor (1897: xci–xciv) proposes that it is Paul who is reacting to James rather than the other way around. Zahn (1909: 1.126–28) also holds this view. However, the discovery of 4QMMT among the Dead Sea Scrolls has demonstrated that discussion of the relationship between faith, "works of the law," and righteousness or justification was in the air in Judaism generally, and it is unnecessary to suppose any direct dependency between James and Paul.

with a similar perversion of his teaching already in Romans itself (3:8). If Paul's antithesis of faith and works had already been misunderstood by the time Romans was written (probably ca. 55 or 56), then certainly James could have encountered it.[28]

VIEW 3: THE LETTER IS PSEUDONYMOUS

Several scholars (e.g., Dibelius 1975: 17–21; Kümmel 1975: 413; Popkes 2001: 69) think that the letter was written in the name of James of Jerusalem by a later Christian, probably in the late first century or beginning of the second century.

In addition to doubts expressed in the ancient church (e.g., Eusebius [*Hist. eccl.* 3.25.3] mentions that it is a "disputed" book), in the pre-Reformation period Erasmus expressed doubts about whether the Epistle of James could be attributed to the Jewish bishop of Jerusalem. Although Luther expressed his low opinion of the value of James in his introduction to his translation of the Bible, he did not couch it in terms of a challenge to its authorship, but simply criticized its content. But later scholars, particularly of Lutheran tradition, have developed arguments against its authenticity. They find it difficult to conceive of anyone advocating "faith without works" prior to Paul, and such an idea is considered especially unlikely among any Jewish audience even after Paul. Hence, the letter of James is placed much later, at the end of the first century or even into the second century, and is written not to Jews at all, but to the Gentile church at a time when in its own conception it has become the replacement for Israel, and when Paul is being understood in antinomian ways. This would mean, of course, that the letter of James is pseudonymous.

Several arguments are used to support this view. (1) There has to have been time for Paul's theology to have been disseminated so as to generate a reaction from the author. Since James died in 62, according to Josephus, there is insufficient time prior to the death of James for a misconstrued Pauline theology to have developed and become a problem in the church. Further, the idea that faith and obedience were separable is unlikely to have taken root while Christianity was still predominantly Jewish; it reflects a time when the church had lost its Jewish mooring, and the law of God is coming into question (as with second-century Gnosticism). (2) The Epistle of James is not included in the Muratorian Fragment, nor is it acknowledged or cited by name until Origen (third century). Although several sources speak of the person of James, no church father prior to Origen refers to this letter as being by him, nor does anyone explicitly indicate any knowledge of the existence of this letter. (3) The similarities with 1 Clement and Shepherd of Hermas, which sometimes have been put forward as evidence that Clement and Hermas knew the Epistle of

---

28. An additional factor possibly indicating some relationship between James and the letters of Paul is the vocative "O man" in James 2:20 as an address to a perceived opponent, a phrase that elsewhere appears only in Rom. 2:1–3 (2x); 9:20; 1 Tim. 6:11. The problem here, of course, is that Paul's material in these passages is not what appears to be in contrast with James 2—quite the contrary.

James, simply indicate that Clement, the author of Shepherd of Hermas, and the author of James operated around the same time and had similar concerns, or even that it is the author of James who is influenced by 1 Clement and Shepherd of Hermas rather than the other way around. (4) The Hellenistic imagery (such as references to controlling horses with bits, and ships with rudders) and the accomplished literary Greek style of James are unlikely to be the product of a Galilean Jewish peasant.[29] The reference in 5:7 to "early and late (rains)" (πρόϊμος καὶ ὄψιμος, *proïmos kai opsimos*) is a problem for this view; however, it is seen not necessarily as evidence of direct knowledge of the phenomenon, but possibly as coming from the use of the phrase in the Greek OT as an expression of eschatological expectation (especially Joel 2:23; Zech. 10:1).[30] The apparent "Jewishness" of the letter is not because the author is Jewish; rather, it reflects that he is writing at a time when the Greek OT and the Jewish wisdom tradition have become familiar to Gentile Christianity.

VIEW 4: THE LETTER COMPRISES MATERIAL ORIGINALLY FROM JAMES BUT REWORKED BY A LATER EDITOR

Concerned by the difficulties in assigning James to a pseudonymous Christian writer in the second century, but also giving weight to the unlikelihood of James being able to write such literary Greek, and accepting the common view that the letter of James is reacting to some kind of misuse of the Pauline tradition, several scholars (e.g., Kittel 1942: 79; Knox 1945; Mussner 1975: 8; Davids 1982: 22; Martin 1988: lxx, lxxvii; Niebuhr 1998: 431; Byrskog 2000: 170; Hartin 2003: 25, 27) advocate a two-stage view of authorship.[31] On this view, the historical James of Jerusalem is the originator of most or all of the content of the letter, but its assembly and literary Greek polishing are the work of a later redactor.

The primary reason for this view is to hold together the clear Jewishness and primitiveness of the material with the fact that it appears to respond to a perversion of Paul's theology that must have taken time to develop. A secondary reason is the matter of Greek style noted by Dibelius, Popkes, and others. These, it is argued, make it unlikely that the letter's final form is the product

29. Many scholars (e.g., Kümmel 1975: 406; Ropes 1916: 50; Dibelius 1975: 17) regard the excellent Hellenistic Greek of James as decisive proof that James of Jerusalem could not have written it.

30. Curiously, however, James's omission in 5:7 of the word "rain" led to confusion among later interpreters. Scribes who were unfamiliar with Palestinian climate (e.g., the original hand of Codex Sinaiticus) sometimes supplied the word "fruit," suggesting that early Christians did not immediately recognize the OT references. Ropes (1916: 296) acknowledges that it is "unlikely" to be "a purely literary allusion . . . made without any personal knowledge of these rains."

31. Something akin to this view may be as early as Jerome (*Vir. ill.* 2; see Martin 1988: lxxii), though Jerome is not entirely clear at this point. In the modern period, Harnack (1897: 1.485–91) proposed a two-stage authorship of James whereby some original early first-century source material (some of which perhaps even goes back orally to James of Jerusalem) was gathered and edited in the second century. Harnack saw this as the solution to the tension between an apparent lack of coherence of the whole alongside an inner unity of character and thematic interests.

of a Galilean Jewish peasant, whereas if a later redactor was using Jacobean (James's) material, that could explain how the letter could be both Jewish and Greek, both Semitically influenced and literarily polished. This view of the origin of James may also give explanation for the occasionally baffling arrangement of the letter. Although some segments of James, most notably 2:1–26; 3:1–18; 4:13–5:6, seem to be rhetorically coherent, the structure of James 1 and the interconnectedness of all the parts of James are difficult to see clearly. If in fact the arrangement of the various parts was the result not of a single writing effort but of a later editing (and possibly translating) by a redactor who wished simply to assemble and disseminate the Jacobean tradition, then the apparent disorganization is simply a real disorganization, and it is unnecessary for us to assemble some unity of the whole. Davids (2001: 66–67), for example, says that "the work is an edited collection of sayings and sermons attributed to James (and his brother Jesus) and . . . that process gives it a certain unevenness." It may be worth noting, however, that Davids goes on to acknowledge that "even then the work is not without its logic," as he demonstrated in his 1982 commentary (see "Structure" below).

In order to resolve the question of authorship, we should examine both the history of the reception of this letter and the characteristics of the letter itself within the environs of the early church to see where the letter best fits.

Evidence

External Indications and the Church's Reception

The Epistle of James is not mentioned in the Muratorian Fragment (the original of which usually is dated ca. 180), nor is it found in the early Syriac canon (Souter 1913: 225–26), though it was included in the Peshitta (the "official" Syriac translation dating from the fifth century).

The earliest explicit indications of the existence of this letter occur in Origen (early third century [see near the end of this section]). The earliest extant manuscripts of James ($\mathfrak{P}^{20}$ and $\mathfrak{P}^{23}$) are usually dated mid- to late third century.[32]

There are, however, several indications that the content of the letter was in circulation. The earliest implicit evidence of a knowledge of the Epistle of James is in Clement of Rome's Epistle to the Corinthians (also known as 1 Clement).[33] Clement, writing at the very end of the first century or the beginning of the second century,[34] does not specifically refer to James, but a

---

32. The recently published fragment known as $\mathfrak{P}^{100}$ (P.Oxy. 4449) is datable to late third or early fourth century (J. K. Elliott 1999).

33. Interestingly, Dibelius (1975: 33) regards the Epistle of Jude as the earliest implicit evidence. Since Dibelius regards Jude as also pseudonymous, he thinks it unlikely that the author of Jude would have chosen such a pseudonym ("Jude, brother of James") unless there was already known to be a letter under the name of James.

34. Like James, 1 Clement provides few clues for its date, but the letter is known fairly early on in the second century. Recently, Jefford (2006: 18–19) dates 1 Clement to the 60s based on its references to the temple that suggest it still stands. If his dating is correct, it either supports the very early (pre-Pauline) dating of James or else points to James being influenced by 1 Clement.

number of phrases in 1 Clement are so similar to the Epistle of James that if Clement is not quoting or influenced by James, then the author of James and Clement must have had some common influence. Mayor (1897: lii–liii) lays out the similarities, noting especially 1 Clem. 5; 21; 23; 30; 35; 38; 46 as having remarkable parallels (see also Hagner 1973: 248–56). Three striking examples will suffice here:

First Clement 23.3 refers to the wretchedness of the "double-minded" (δίψυ-χοι, *dipsychoi*) and the "doubting," which stands in contrast with God's approval of "singleness of mind" in 23.1 (cf. James 1:5–8).

First Clement 30.2 quotes Prov. 3:34 in the form found in James 4:6 (which differs from the LXX). Admittedly, this form is found also in 1 Pet. 5:5, but the connection to James becomes clearer when Clement immediately goes on to speak of "being justified by works and not by words."

First Clement 38.2 adjures the readers, "Let the wise man show his wisdom not in words but in good deeds" (cf. James 3:13).

Even more striking than 1 Clement's parallels with James are those found in Shepherd of Hermas, written in the late first century or the early second century.[35] Like 1 Clement, Shepherd of Hermas uses James's unique word δίψυχος/διψυχία several times, in all three of its sections (*Visions, Mandates, Similitudes*).[36] But there are even more striking parallels, particularly in the *Mandates*. Some of the more noteworthy similarities are the following:

Shepherd of Hermas	James
Herm. *Mand.* 3.1: "the spirit that God has caused to dwell in this flesh" (cf. Herm. *Simil.* 5.6.5).	4:5: "the Spirit that he caused to dwell in us."
Herm. *Mand.* 2.2–3: "Do not slander anyone. . . . Slander is an evil thing; it is an unstable demon [ἀκατάστατον δαιμόνιον, *akatastaton daimonion*]."	4:11: "Do not slander one another, brothers." 3:8: "The tongue . . . is an unstable, evil thing."
Herm. *Mand.* 5.2.3: "Now this patience dwells with those who have complete faith."	1:4: "Let that endurance finish its work, so that you will be complete."
Herm. *Mand.* 5.2.4: "Anger is first of all foolish, and also fickle and senseless. Then, from senselessness comes bitterness, from bitterness wrath, and from wrath anger, and from anger spite. Then spite, consisting of such evil things, becomes great and incurable sin."	3:17 is structured similarly: "The wisdom from above is, first of all, pure, then peaceable, considerate, compliant, full of mercy and good fruits, constant, sincere" (cf. 1:14–15).

35. Shepherd of Hermas certainly was written well before 175, since Irenaeus, writing about that time, refers to it, as does the Muratorian Fragment. If we allow time for Shepherd of Hermas to have circulated, that pushes its date to no later than the first half of the second century, possibly earlier.

36. The word δίψυχος is found only in James in the NT and indeed is unattested elsewhere until 1 Clement and Shepherd of Hermas. Seitz (1944) rejects this as evidence of Hermas's dependence on James, but as noted here, the connections between James and Hermas are much more than just this term.

Shepherd of Hermas	James
Herm. *Mand.* 8.2: "If you hold back from doing good, you do a great sin."	4:17: "For the one who knows a good thing to do and does not do it, there is sin."
Herm. *Mand.* 8.10: "Then, hear the things that follow [from faith, love, truth, etc.]: to serve widows, orphans, and to visit those in need" (similarly, Herm. *Sim.* 1.8 instructs people of means to "visit widows and orphans").	1:27: "Religion that is pure . . . is this: to look after [visit] orphans and widows in their tribulation."
Herm. *Mand.* 9.1–6: "Take out from yourself double-mindedness [διψυχία, *dipsychia*] and make your requests from God without any double-mindedness [μηδὲν ὅλως διψυχήσης, *mēden holōs dipsychēsēs*]. . . . For God is not as men. . . . You therefore must purify your heart from all the vain things of this world. . . . If you are doubtful in your heart, you will certainly receive none of your requests, for those who are doubtful toward God are double-minded [δίψυχοι, *dipsychoi*], and they never get any of their requests. But the perfect in faith make all their requests trusting in the Lord, and they receive them."	1:6–8: "Let him ask in faith, not doubting in any way, because he who doubts is like a wave of the sea that is blown and tossed about. Let not such a person think he will receive anything from the Lord; he is a double-minded [δίψυχος, *dipsychos*] man, unstable in all his paths" (cf. 1:13; 4:8).
Herm. *Mand.* 9.11: "Faith is from above [ἄνωθεν, *anōthen*], from the Lord, and has great power."	5:16: "The prayer of a righteous person is very powerful and effective."
Herm. *Mand.* 11.8: "The one who has the divine spirit from above [ἄνωθεν, *anōthen*] is meek and quiet and humble and abstains from all evil and vain desires of this world."	3:17: "The wisdom from above [ἄνωθεν, *anōthen*] is . . . pure, then peaceable, considerate, compliant, full of mercy and good fruits, constant, sincere."
Herm. *Mand.* 12.5.2: "If therefore you resist him [the devil], he will, being conquered, flee from you."	4:7: "Resist the devil, and he will flee from you."
Herm. *Mand.* 12.6.3: "Fear the one who is able to save and destroy all things."	4:12: "There is one lawgiver who is able to save and to destroy."
Herm. *Sim.* 2.5: "The rich man has much wealth but is poor in the things of the Lord. . . . The poor man is rich in intercession and confession, and his intercession has great power."	2:5: "Has not God chosen the poor in worldly things to be rich in faith?" (cf. 1:10–12; 5:16b).
Herm. *Sim.* 8.6.4: "who have blasphemed the Lord in their sins, and have, moreover, been ashamed of the name of the Lord by which they were called [τὸ ὄνομα τοῦ κυρίου τὸ ἐπικληθὲν ἐπ᾽ αὐτούς, *to onoma tou kyriou to epiklēthen ep᾽ autous*]."	2:7: "Are they not the ones who blaspheme the good name that has been invoked upon you [τὸ καλὸν ὄνομα τὸ ἐπικληθὲν εφ᾽ ὑμᾶς, *to kalon onoma to epiklēthen eph᾽ hymas*]."

Although occasional resemblances might be expected, and some similarities might be due to a common Jewish wisdom tradition,[37] it is difficult to

---

37. For example, the advice "Resist the devil and he will flee from you" in Herm. *Mand.* 12.5.2 and James 4:7 has close parallels in T. Iss. 7.7; T. Dan 5.1; T. Naph. 8.4.

attribute all these to happenstance,[38] and it seems hard to deny that Hermas must have had some knowledge of the material of James. This knowledge could have been of the material in a form not yet collected into the Epistle of James as we know it, which would allow for the two-stage view, but it makes the late-date pseudonymous view quite unlikely.

Other similarities to James are found in the Pseudo-Clementine literature, Didache, Epistle of Barnabas, and the second-century apologists Justin, Irenaeus, and Clement of Alexandria, but most of these can be attributed to the common Christian milieu rather than to any direct influence from James (see Johnson 1995: 66–68). Indeed, even the similarities to 1 Clement and Shepherd of Hermas sometimes have been understood in terms of a common influence,[39] though if one does not reject out of hand the possibility that James might be early, it is easier to assume that James influenced Hermas and Clement than to suppose without further evidence some common source.[40]

The earliest undeniable reference to James occurs in Pseudo-Clement, *Virg.* 1.11.4: "Nor did they heed what the scripture says: Let not many among you be teachers, brethren, nor let all be prophets. He who does not transgress in his speech is a perfect man, able to tame and to subjugate his whole body." Most of this is an almost exact quotation of James 3:1–2 and is identified as "Scripture." Although no indication of the author is given, it is clear evidence that James not only was known (Ropes 1916: 51–52) but also was regarded as canonical in the early third century.[41] As the Pseudo-Clementine literature also contains several (rather hagiographic) references to James, the author of *De virginitate* certainly would have esteemed as canonical a letter that he thought had been written by James.

38. Mayor (1897: lviii–lxii) adduces these and several other parallels in detail. Although Ropes (1916: 248) is cognizant of the parallels, he is still able to claim that "there is no evidence of literary dependence," presumably because in no case is there exact verbal correspondence. Similarly, Dibelius (1975: 31), even though he acknowledges that Herm. *Mand.* 9.1–6 is "the best interpretation of James 1:5–8 imaginable," rejects Hermas's dependence on or knowledge of James. One suspects that this is an application of the dictum "If the data do not fit the theory, they must be disposed of."

39. Seitz (1944: 131–40) proposes a now lost apocryphal work as a background for both James and Shepherd of Hermas.

40. Young (1948) suggests that it was James that used Shepherd of Hermas rather than the other way around. This is unlikely, however. Shepherd of Hermas has echoes of the Gospels, Paul's letters, and Revelation, as well as James. No one suggests that Hermas is a source for those NT books. Further, as Dibelius (1975: 235) points out, where James warns against certain potential developments, Hermas seems to know of real and specific problems (e.g., Herm. *Vis.* 2.3.1; Herm. *Mand.* 3.3; Herm. *Sim.* 6.3.5, all of which envision Christians enmeshed in shady dealings, untruthfulness, and scheming). Shepherd of Hermas represents a later, more developed social situation than that of James.

41. For the dating of *De virginitate*, see *ABD* 1:1060–61. Westcott (1881: 186–87) dates it into the late second century, which would put recognition of James even earlier, but a citation within the Pseudo-Clementine *Recognitions* is datable to 220 at the earliest, which means that unless the citation was added later (which is quite unlikely), the original work cannot have been written prior to mid-third century (Schneemelcher 1992: 493).

The earliest extant witness to both cite the letter and identify James as its author is Origen (d. 254), who refers to James some thirty-six times (Johnson 1995: 130). When referring to James 4:7 in his *Hom. Exod.* 3.3, Origen attributes the letter to "James the apostle." When referring to James 4:4 in his *Comm. Rom.* 4.8, he refers to it as written by James "the brother of the Lord" (see also Origen, *Comm. Rom.* 4.1; *Hom. Lev.* 2.4; *Hom. Josh.* 7.1).[42]

The evidence from Eusebius (writing ca. 324) is somewhat problematic. Although he accepts the letter as genuine (*Hist. eccl.* 2.23; 3.25), he acknowledges that it is one of the disputed books ("antilegomena") and that some regard it as spurious (*Hist. eccl.* 3.25.3). It appears, though, that some of the doubt about the provenance of James and the identity of its author is a by-product of the difficulty generated by the suggestion that Jesus had a brother. As noted above, Jerome (*Vir. ill.* 2), for example, had to hypothesize a complicated and unlikely explanation for "James the Lord's brother" in order to protect the notion of Mary's perpetual virginity (see Tasker 1957: 19). The letter may have had slow acceptance also because it contributed little to the christological controversies (although James 1:17 sometimes was seen in connection with John 3 as evidence for Christ's deity [e.g., Cyril of Alexandria, *Adv. Nest.* 5.4]). Further, the fact that James of Jerusalem was being claimed as a source for the "secret teaching" traditions in the Gospel of Thomas and the Apocryphon of James (both found at Nag Hammadi), along with James's lack of stature compared with Paul or one of the Twelve, may have contributed to the early church's hesitancy regarding James's letter.

However, the letter's cache of practical wisdom continued to influence other Christian writers from time to time, and it was almost universally accepted as authentic in the Eastern churches by mid-fourth century, as is evident from its inclusion in the Catechism of Cyril of Jerusalem (348) and Athanasius's well-known Easter Letter (367 [*Ep. fest.* 39]). Likewise in the West, both Jerome (*Epist.* 53.8) and Augustine (*Doctr. chr.* 2.2) accepted it without question, and the book was included in the canon agreed on at the third Council of Carthage in 397 (Westcott 1881: 440). With rare exceptions,[43] the Epistle of James was no longer disputed until the Reformation period.[44]

Internal Evidence: Palestinian Indications

There are several indications within the Epistle of James of its author's Palestinian Jewish origin:

---

42. Hort (1909: xxvii) thinks that Origen's predecessor Clement of Alexandria also knew of the Epistle of James. Although Clement does not specifically cite James, in *Strom.* 5.1 he describes a faith that is not vain and alone (τὴν πίστιν τοίνυν οὐκ ἀργὴν καὶ μόνην), a possible echo of James 2:20. But if Clement was alluding to James, he used the phrase quite differently, since what makes a faith not vain and alone for Clement is not deeds (as in James), but "investigation" of the "deeper things" of Christianity, something quite foreign to James.

43. According to Westcott (1881: 442–43), Leontius says that Theodore of Mopsuestia (d. 429) rejected it.

44. For more on James's use in the early and medieval church, see Johnson 1995: 130–40.

1. The reference to the "early and late rains" in James 5:7 is to a peculiarly Palestinian phenomenon. This may be an allusion to Joel 2 rather than an appeal to something in the hearers' experience, though even Ropes (1916: 296), who does not think that James wrote the letter, acknowledges that the author seems to think of it as natural, which hints at a Palestinian author who knew the phenomenon from personal experience. Further, James in fact omits the word "rain" in 5:7, which has led to some manuscripts (e.g., Codex Sinaiticus) supplying the word καρπός (*karpos*, fruit, harvest), precisely because of unfamiliarity with the phenomenon.
2. The reference to the sirocco (scorching east wind) in 1:11 also suggests direct experience of Palestinian climate.
3. A reference to the chaotic character of the sea in 1:6 reflects Jewish aversion to the sea.
4. The sweet and bitter springs of 3:11 are an interesting feature of Palestinian geography, especially in the Rift Valley.
5. Although olives, grapes, and figs are common enough throughout the Mediterranean, they are a prominent feature in Palestine horticulture.
6. The reference to "day laborers" in 5:4 suggests an agrarian social environment like that in Palestine (although, of course, other places in the Mediterranean world were similar).
7. The reference in 3:6 to the tongue set afire by "gehenna," without further explanation, either requires a date after the Gospel tradition had circulated enough that Christians would be familiar with the term or comes from the author's Palestinian Jewish parlance. The word does not occur in the LXX, Josephus, or Philo.

One can also note similarities (as well as some differences) to the material attributed to James in Acts 15. Admittedly, the historical value of Acts has often been questioned, and Haenchen (1971: 590), for example, has little doubt that the speeches of Acts, including that of James, are simply the invention of the author of Acts,[45] who is writing long after the alleged events. But Hemer (1990) and Lüdemann (1989) have ably demonstrated the historical character of Acts (see also Barrett 1999). The markedly Jewish flavor of James's letter recorded there in particular, and the absence of any hint of the destruction of Jerusalem, far from giving the letter of Acts 15 a veneer of Lukan invention,

45. Haenchen is, like many others, following the path laid down by Dibelius in several works, one as early as 1926, where Dibelius claims, "These speeches, without doubt, are as they stand inventions of the author. For they are too short to have been actually given in this form; they are too similar to one another to have come from different persons; and in their content they occasionally reproduce a later standpoint (e.g., what Peter and James say about the Law in chap. xv)" (Dibelius 1936: xv; the German work was originally published in 1926). For a thorough reexamination of the whole subject of the historical roots of the speeches in Acts, and the way in which Dibelius and other scholars have tended to treat them, see Bruce 1974: 53–68. See also Gempf (1993), whose analysis of ancient historical recording of speeches demonstrates decisively that although recorded speeches were not intended as transcriptions, they were conceived to be faithful representations of historical events.

give it a certain aura of authenticity.[46] In any case, both the actions of James recorded in Acts and the speech and letter recorded in Acts 15 comport well with what we have in the letter before us. Mayor (1897: iv) notes several similarities of vocabulary that are uncommon elsewhere in the NT and especially the following rather unusual phrasing features:

1. The use of χαίρειν (*chairein*, greeting) in the salutation in both letters (Acts 15:23; James 1:1). This is a standard greeting in Hellenistic letters, but it is rare in the NT. In fact, the only other use of χαίρειν as a letter greeting in the NT is the letter of Claudius Lysias to Felix recorded in Acts 23:26.
2. The reference to the name being called "upon" the people (Acts 15:17; James 2:7), using the passive of ἐπικαλέω (*epikaleō*, call) with the preposition ἐπί + accusative, to mean "God's name invoked upon people," that is, for those people to be designated as belonging to God. This is not typical idiomatic Greek, and it is found only in these two places in the NT. It is, however, an idiom found in the LXX (e.g., Bar. 2:15).
3. The imperative ἀκούσατε (*akousate*, listen) with the vocative ἀδελφοί [μου] (*adelphoi* [*mou*], [my] brothers; cf. Acts 15:13; James 2:5). However, a similar address is used in speeches by Stephen (Acts 7:2) and Paul (Acts 22:1), suggesting that it may be a standard Jewish speech opening (cf. 1 Chron. 28:2; Jdt. 14:1).

In addition to the linguistic similarities, the character of James in both Acts and the Epistle of James is that of a mediator, one who is seeking to bring reconciliation and avoid strife. Finally, Paul notes that James in Jerusalem, along with Cephas (Peter) and John, did place one obligation on Paul, "to remember the poor" (Gal. 2:9–10), exactly as one might expect from the writer of the letter of James (see James 1:9–10, 27; 2:1–7, 15–16; 5:1–6).

There is one apparent difference, however: James's letter in Acts 15, as well as his recorded speech, express concern for what appear to be cultic issues—"abstain from what has been sacrificed to idols, and from blood, and from what has been strangled, and from sexual immorality" (Acts 15:29)—whereas the Epistle of James has no concern whatsoever for these matters. But what is James's actual concern in Acts 15:29? The first (idolatry) and the last (sexual immorality) might be understood as moral concerns that Gentiles perhaps do not realize are important, but abstention from eating blood and things strangled appears to be a concern with Jewish food laws, matters that Jesus implicitly declared obsolete (according to Mark 7:19) and that the vision

46. Indeed, the rationale for supposing that the speeches in Acts are inauthentic seems largely to be based on the dubious notion that Acts is an attempt to obscure the deep divide between Gentile (Pauline) and Jewish (Petrine) Christianity, a divide postulated on the basis of the clash reported in Gal. 2. But it has often been demonstrated that Gal. 2 supposes Peter's acknowledgment of his error and gives no indication whatever of an ongoing rift. See Bockmuehl 2006: 121–36. On the character and historical nature of James's speech in particular, see Bauckham 1996.

of Peter in Acts 10, as well as the explicit teaching of Paul, indicates are superseded.

One commonly held answer is that James was restating the Noahic prohibition of Gen. 9:4, which would apply to all Noah's descendants (i.e., all humankind). Although Gen. 9 says nothing about things strangled, the purpose of killing food by strangulation was specifically to retain the blood, so presumably that prohibition could be a simple extension of the prohibition against eating blood. The prohibition against blood is further reiterated in Lev. 17:10, where the alien in Israel is included: "If any one of the house of Israel *or of the strangers who sojourn among them* eats any blood, I will set my face against that person who eats blood and will cut him off from among his people."

Another view is that James was supporting a practical, perhaps temporary, compromise to facilitate fellowship between Gentile and Jewish Christians. Especially given the severity of the prohibition in Lev. 17:10, it would have been difficult for a Jewish Christian to eat with a Gentile who was eating blood. Thus, the Acts letter was a mandate of concession rather than moral principle, and James's entire admonition would serve more or less the same way Paul advised in 1 Cor. 8.

The best way of approaching the problem, however, probably is along lines proposed by Witherington (1998: 539–44), who observes that all four of James's concerns, not just the middle two, have to do with pagan worship: eating sacrificed food, eating blood, eating strangled animals (so as to retain the blood), and cultic sex. All four of these matters were means of cultic identification with pagan deities, symbols of absorbing the power and life of a god. Since such activities were a common part of Gentile social life, recent converts from pagan backgrounds might not immediately have grasped that their new allegiance to the true God implied total abandonment of such public cultic activities. It certainly appears that the converts in Corinth had difficulties of this sort, given Paul's concern in 1 Corinthians with both cultic fornication and cultic meals. Even Paul recognizes that if someone declares to the believer that a food has been offered to an idol, one should not eat it, not because eating is anything in itself, but because of the religious connotations of eating under those circumstances.

It is still true, of course, that the Epistle of James makes no mention of that, but no author can mention everything in every letter, and there is no incompatibility between James's letter in Acts 15 and the Epistle of James.

Language Issues

As we have already observed, James appears to be stylistically sophisticated. The letter displays a large vocabulary as well as a fund of illustrations and rhetorical polish that are somewhat surprising if a Palestinian Jewish peasant is the author.

Mayor (1897: xlii) recognizes that Galilean Palestine was Hellenistic, and its residents would have known the lingua franca. Some towns within Galilee (e.g., Sepphoris, less than five miles from Jesus's hometown, Nazareth) were so dominantly Gentile that it is difficult to suppose anything being spoken there other than Greek. It is likely that tradesmen would have had some familiarity with the common language.

The most thorough study of the use of Greek in northern Palestine is by Sevenster (1968), who specifically examines the case of the Epistle of James (1968: 3–21) and concludes that the bilingual character of northern Palestine, and the fact that several cities in Galilee were almost entirely Greek-speaking, make it likely that James and the other disciples were fluent in Greek and possibly even capable of a degree of literary facility.

Further, Greek was known and used beyond northern Palestine. The discovery of the Greek Minor Prophets scroll fragments in a cave near Nahal Hever (Wadi Hebron)[47] gives indication that biblical texts in Greek were circulating in southern Palestine, another indication that Palestinian Jews knew Greek. Indeed, their knowledge of their Bible was to some degree influenced by that translation, since a literate Jew could readily refer to a Greek translation or even own a personal copy, but the Hebrew texts could be read only under prescribed circumstances. This, rather than a late Gentile origin, is most likely the explanation for the dominant presence of Septuagintal readings throughout the NT, including James. However, like the Nahal Hever fragments, the Greek OT readings in the NT, including those in James, not infrequently give evidence either of editing back toward a Masoretic type of reading or of an independent Greek translational tradition.

Amanuensis or Collator?

The definitive work on amanuenses in the Greco-Roman world by Richards (1991) shows, particularly in the case of Paul's letters, that the degree of compositional contribution by secretaries could vary widely, from simply taking dictation, to slight editing, to heavy editing, to coauthorship, to virtual composition in the case of stylized standard letters. Richards identifies certain explicit and implicit marks of the use of an amanuensis, but James has no explicit marks, and given that we have only one letter from James to consider, it is difficult to do more than hypothesize regarding implicit indications. The one consideration that might apply is that the language of James is stylistically more like what one would expect from an educated Hellenist than from a Palestinian Jew whose knowledge of Greek would have been only secondary. As already noted, since Greek was the lingua franca of the entire Mediterranean region, and since James would have grown up in a racially mixed area, it is likely that he learned Greek from childhood, and there is no reason he could not have written in Greek. Further, once he assumed a leadership role in a church that was rapidly spreading in the Greco-Roman world, it would have been appropriate for him to educate himself more broadly in Greek literary

47. For a description, transcription, and translation of these fragments, see Tov, Kraft, and Parsons 1990.

conventions. The use of certain phrases and illustrations in ways somewhat different from their classical use (such as the astronomical terms in 1:17 and the echo of Orphic language in "cycle of generation" in 3:6 [see the commentary for details]) might be an indication of a self-educated writer. However, it is also possible that James used a secretary and may have given his secretary a fair degree of autonomy in word choice, phrasing, and even organization. This could explain the "relatively polished" Greek compositional style of James without recourse to pseudonymous authorship.

This is at some remove, however, from the hypothesis of a collator, someone who apart from James's direction assembled and edited a variety of his material (see view 4 under "Four Views of Author and Date" above). In this last case, both the content and the organization are essentially that of the redactor, and it is more difficult to see how it can legitimately be called a letter from James, since the collator would be not an amanuensis but the author. If James is the product of a collator, then even if the material is in some sense Jacobean, the ascription in 1:1 appears to make the letter pseudonymous. However, the typical marks of pseudonymous literature are absent from James (see "Historical Context Issues" below).

Historical Context Issues

Bauckham (1999: 21) points out that "when Jerusalem was no longer in practice but only in symbol and hope the centre of the Jewish world, the frequent communication with the Diaspora which gave the mother church its role in relation to the churches of the Diaspora can hardly have continued." Hence, the form of James, as a "letter to the Dispersion" would have been anachronistic after the year 70, when the Romans captured and destroyed Jerusalem.

Further, as noted above, the primitive character of the theological material in James suggests an early stage of the church's development, if not prior to Paul's mission and theological reflections, then certainly prior to the wide distribution of his letters to the Romans and the Galatians.

But James's practical application of the basic Christian theology, namely the Jewish ethical religion and Jesus being both Christ and Lord (2:1), is very much along the lines apparent in the Jesus tradition. Indeed, as will be noted below, the influence from the content of the Synoptic tradition of Jesus's wisdom is patent, which is exactly what one might expect from a time when Jesus's teaching is being handed on but the church's theological development is in its infancy.

Surprisingly, the primitiveness of the theological framework of James does not strike Dibelius, who dates James very late, as odd, perhaps because he identifies the genre of James as "paraenesis" (exhortation), which is by nature nontheological. It is noteworthy, however, that no other unambiguously late Christian document has such a primitive Christian theological framework. Even documents of a primarily moral or practical nature such as the Didache display a more explicit Christology than is evident in James.

That James is concerned primarily with praxis, not doctrine, ought also induce caution with respect to identifying the specific historical context. Problems of conformity of behavior to asseverations of belief are perennial and not specific to any occasion. James nowhere addresses doctrine as a point of contention. The assumption is always one of agreement on doctrine. This is why the attempt by Popkes (1986: 16–21) to identify the situation of the addressees as false teaching in the late first century fails to convince. As Burchard (1980a: 318–19) had already demonstrated, the problem in James is one not of false teaching but of disputes and controversies within the community. No judgment of date or situation can be made on the basis of the general exhortations of James.

We should also note that if James is late and pseudonymous, it is unusual in that it lacks certain characteristics typical of pseudonymous literature:

1. elaboration of the author's identity or authority
2. warning against heretical teaching
3. emphasis on tradition
4. insistence on proper lines of authority and submission, or an interest in ecclesial structure
5. concern with a supposed delay of the parousia[48]

All these point to James's context as more characteristic of the church of the first half of the first century than that of the second century.

Conclusion

In the attempt to determine the authorship of a document, it seems reasonable to begin with that document's own claims and then evaluate whether such claims fit the internal and external evidence. If the author of this letter is James, brother of Jesus, then several lines of evidence converge:

1. The letter shows marked similarity to James's letter in Acts 15, in both vocabulary and in character.
2. The letter's interests reflect to a large degree the interests of Second Temple Judaism in wisdom, particularly in the tradition that had followed the lead of Sirach, who saw God's law as the ultimate expression of wisdom (see "Jewish Literary Background" below). This bespeaks a Jewish writer of the Second Temple period. But the letter also has a distinctly Christian cast to it, and its interests are not only those of wisdom but also of eschatology and of Christian community and discipleship.
3. The letter appears to have been written before the christological developments found in Paul's letters, 1 Peter, and the Johannine literature, or at least it does not explicitly take up those developments.
4. The letter appears to have been written before the parting of ways between Judaism and Christianity (e.g., James's reference in 2:2 to "your synagogue").

---

48. Indeed, in James the imminence of the parousia seems to be a vital assumption shared by author and audience.

5. Thus, the letter is likely to have been written before the notions of supersessionism or displacement of Judaism had taken hold in the church (as happened in the second century).

6. The letter exhibits a close connection of content with Jesus's ethical instruction yet without conformity to the language of the Synoptic tradition, just as might be expected if James was written prior to the congealing of that tradition in the written Gospels and/or their (Greek) sources.

7. The letter shows no trace of the concerns of the so-called early catholicism of the second century: church order, the maintenance of uniform doctrinal tradition through ecclesial authority, the gnostic heresies, and so on.

8. The primary use of "early and late (rains)" in 5:7 is not as a reference to Scripture (although an allusion certainly may have been in the author's mind) but as a direct illustration of the farmer's patience, which suggests that the author had firsthand knowledge of the phenomenon.

There are only two difficulties with assigning the letter to a time prior to the Jewish war: (1) James's supposed reaction to Paulinism; (2) the relatively polished Greek style. First, as I have already argued, the letter has only the appearance of a reaction to Paulinism because it is supposed that "easy believism" is inconceivable before Paul. In fact, however, Hellenistic pagan religion divorced ethics from religion, and at a stage when Gentiles were being included in the messianic Jewish community (as a grafting in rather than a displacement of Israel), James needed to warn these new believers against this unethical religion, declaring it useless. As I will argue below, the situation in the earliest church involved Gentiles coming into the messianic community, and some of these Gentiles may very well have had trouble connecting the requirements of covenant obedience with their newfound belief in God's provision of salvation. Also, James's concern with self-deception and hypocrisy, if the Gospels are any indication, is just as relevant to Jews as it is to Gentiles. As I point out in excursus 2 ("Faith, Works, and Justification in James and Paul"), James's concern is with a "workless faith," which is effectively a nonfunctioning faith, and Paul is miles from advocating anything like this. It still could be that James is reacting to a perversion of Paul's theology that developed much later (as with Marcion), but this scenario does not fit with the other issues noted above.

The second alleged difficulty, the polished Greek style, is less of an issue once it is observed that since James was from the mixed Gentile territory of Galilee, it is no wonder that he knew Greek quite well. On the other hand, the form of his letter is quite non-Greek; it is cyclical with regard to several thematic concerns rather than a linear development of an argument (see "Structure" below). In this it is similar to other letters that aver authorship by Galilean Jews: especially 1 John and 1 Peter, which, curiously, also evince good Greek writing (1 Peter more than 1 John) and thus also are regarded as spurious by many critical scholars. Since I have read works in what appears to me to be excellent literary English written by people whose first language is not English, I am unconvinced by any argument that a "Galilean peasant" could not have learned to write good literary Greek. Even if it be conceded as unlikely that James of Jerusalem had the ability to write literary Greek well enough to produce this letter, it would still be well within the realm of possibility that in addressing a letter to the Diaspora (which would have to be in the lingua franca), James acquired the services of an accomplished amanuensis. As Bauckham (1999: 24) observes, if Josephus, who knew Greek very well, employed assistants to help give his works a literary polish (*Ag. Ap.* 1.9 §50), there is no reason why James could not have done so. This in no way would vitiate James's authorship.[49]

Original Recipients and Occasion

When Dibelius (1975: 1–3) doubts that the letter of James is a "real" letter, he not only doubts that the author truly is James; he also thinks that the audience is fictional. Thus, although some of the pieces that were collected into the final "epistle" as we have it may originally have addressed some specific circumstance, the "paraenesis" nature of the assembled document has no particular "life situation" that determines its meaning or significance. This, of course, assumes that the letter has no overall coherency, an assumption that will be challenged more directly when we look at the structure of the Epistle of James.

If James does have coherency of intentionality, however, then there are several indications that he is addressing a real audience. This real audience may have been relatively nonspecific (Bauckham 1999: 25–28), which is what one would expect of a letter addressed to "diaspora" congregations of various types scattered through the Mediterranean world, but nonetheless "real" in that there are real circumstances being addressed and real people whom the author wishes to influence. The clearest indication of this reality is found in the constant use of second-person plural pronouns when James is describing a problematic situation. So, for example, in attacking favoritism, James says, "If someone comes into *your* synagogue" (2:2); and in the illustration of a workless profession of faith he says, "If a brother or sister is without clothing and lacks daily food, and one *of you* tells them, 'Go in peace, stay warm, and eat well'" (2:15–16); and warning against strife, he asks, "Where do the battles *among you* come from?" (4:1). This linkage of "you" with specific problems runs throughout James. The way he raises the issues, even if they are not evident in all the churches of the Diaspora that he had in mind as potential recipients, and even if he draws those issues hyperbolically, gives the impression that the problems are quite real and that he has heard about some specific things that ought not to be taking place.

---

49. The possible use of an amanuensis by James should be distinguished from the suggestion of Davids (1982) and others of a two-stage authorship, whereby the actual letter does not involve the intentionality of James himself.

A further indication is that James consistently addresses his readers as "brothers." "Brothers" was a term Jews used to refer to fellow Jews. So, for example, 2 Macc. 1:1 RSV: "The Jewish brethren in Jerusalem and those in the land of Judea, To their Jewish brethren in Egypt, Greeting and good peace." This appears as well in Acts, where "brothers" can mean either "fellow Jews" (2:29; 3:17; 7:2; 13:15, 26, 38; 22:1; 23:1, 5, 6; 28:17) or "fellow Christians" (1:16; 6:3; 15:7, 13). Paul frequently uses the word to address fellow believers whether Jew or Gentile, and it also means "fellow believers" in 2 Pet. 1:10 and 1 John 3:13.

Thus, I conclude that James's letter was addressed to real believers, not a fictional audience.

The Audience as Diaspora

James addresses his letter to "brothers" whom he designates as "the twelve tribes of the dispersion (diaspora)" who meet in "synagogues." What is the makeup of this "diaspora" brotherhood? Do the terms imply a Jewish audience, either Jewish believers in Jesus or both Christian and non-Christian Jews?

James's opening is similar to 1 Pet. 1:1–2. The term "diaspora" was used in Judaism to refer to Jews who had been "scattered" away from Palestine (e.g., Ps. Sol. 9.2). It is used in Acts 8:1 of Christians, where the ἐκκλησία (ekklēsia, church) of Jerusalem has been scattered (διεσπάρησαν, diesparēsan) in Judea and Samaria, and then in 8:4, where they are called the "scattered ones" (διασπαρέντες, diasparentes). Hence, one might quickly conclude that this letter was written to Jewish Christians. The reference to the readers as "the twelve tribes" also points in this direction. And certainly there are indications that James regarded his readers as members of the one family of God commonly called "Israel." But we know from Acts that some Gentiles were being converted even before the Pauline mission and certainly before the controversy over circumcision arose. Since James is addressing churches outside Palestine, it is likely that some of them had Gentile converts, but these converts would have been as much a part of the Christian "synagogue" (2:2) as Jews, indeed more than Jews who had not believed in Jesus as the Christ. It is only as we remain locked into an ethnic definition of "Israel" that the question even becomes relevant. I submit that, given his insistent rejection of favoritism, ethnicity was irrelevant for the author of this letter.

Was the Audience Christian or Jewish Non-Christian?

Although the theory is seldom proposed anymore, at the end of the nineteenth century two scholars (Spitta 1896: 1–13; Massebieau 1895) independently suggested that the Epistle of James was originally purely Jewish, not Christian, material to which 1:1 and 2:1 had been added. The theory is based on the Jewish character and allusions in the letter and the fact that apart from two passing references, no mention is made of Jesus, and no theological observations or exhortations are based on anything distinctively Christian (not found in Judaism).

This view is definitively countered by Dibelius (1975: 22–23), who notes that not only is there no indication, either internally or externally, that 1:1 and 2:1 were added, but also several features of James evince a Christian environment:

1. In 1:16–18 God is Father, and believers are "brothers" and the "firstfruits" of creation who have been "planted by the word of truth" and are "destined for the crown of life." These are Jewish images indeed, but the peculiar combination of them is distinctively characteristic of Jesus. Further, while rare in Judaism, they are all commonplace in the early church.
2. In 2:7 believers are suffering for "the name." As Dibelius (1975: 140–41) notes, this can only be the name of Christ, because if the "name" refers to Judaism or Israel (or Abraham?), it would not set the name-bearers over against the "rich" (2:6) who come into the synagogue.[50]
3. In 5:7–8 James gives as the motive for patience the imminence of the parousia of the Lord. Not only is the term "parousia" the distinctive word for early Christian expectation of the return of Christ in judgment, but also the event is said to be "at hand," using the same exact word (ἤγγικεν, ēngiken, the perfect tense of ἐγγίζω, engizō) that the Gospels use to describe Jesus's announcement of the nearness of the kingdom of God.

The several parallels with Jesus's teaching as reported in the Gospels, especially James 5:12 (cf. Matt. 5:34), make it quite likely that James is in some way related to the Jesus tradition.[51]

Was the Audience Ethnically Jewish or Gentile (or Mixed)?

Scholars generally have been divided into two camps. Those who think that James is early and written by James tend to see the audience as ethnically Jewish, either a mixture of non-Christian and Christian Jews (Adamson 1989: 11–12; Allison 2001)[52] or simply Jewish Christians outside Palestine (Zahn 1909: 1.89–91; Moo 2000: 23). Those who regard James as pseudepigraphal and late usually (Allison [2001] being a noteworthy exception) adduce arguments for a primarily or entirely Gentile audience, for whom "twelve tribes" has become a cipher for Christianity[53] that has "replaced" Israel as the people of God

---

50. Dibelius ignores another implication of this: Christians and non-Christian Jews are still meeting together in the same synagogue when James is writing. This can hardly fit the second-century setting that Dibelius envisions.

51. Dibelius (1975: 23), who regards James as written late, also thinks that James 2:14–26 must reflect a reaction against Paulinism, which would support the Christian character of James.

52. Bauckham (1999: 16) suggests that since "early Jewish Christians thought of themselves, not as a specific sect distinguished from other Jews, but as the nucleus of a Messianic renewal of the people of Israel . . . what James addresses in practice to those Jews who already confess the Messiah Jesus, he addresses in principle to all Israel."

53. As in 1 Pet. 1:1, which most recent scholars think is addressed to Gentile believers, partly because of the paucity of evidence of Jews living in the areas designated in 1 Pet. 1:1, and partly

(Popkes 2001a: 63, 70; Vouga 1984: 24–26; Baasland 1988: 3676–77). Popkes (2001b: 90), who holds the letter to be pseudepigraphal and fairly late (end of the first century or early second century), notes the conspicuous absence of key Jewish terms and elements such as Israel, Israelites, Jews, Moses, Jerusalem, temple, priesthood, Sabbath, circumcision, food laws, fasting, Jewish feasts (not even Passover), and any references to particular Jewish groups, and he concludes that this is because "these items were not of interest in his [the author's] present mission in relation to his addressees." The conclusion is true as far as it goes, but this does not mean that the audience was Gentile or that those items were of no interest to writer or audience. It means no more than that they were not the point at issue. With the exception of 1:1, the book of Proverbs mentions none of these things either. Does this mean that Proverbs was not written by or for Israelites, or that neither author nor intended audience of Proverbs cared about these things?

On the other hand, if James of Jerusalem wrote the letter, is it necessary to suppose that his audience was exclusively or even dominantly ethnically Jewish? Chilton (2001: 143–44) thinks that Acts 15 presents James as trying to preserve the distinction of Jew and Gentile within the church and argues that James is implicitly rejecting the allegedly Pauline "redefinition" of Israel. If so, we could expect a letter from him to be consciously addressed more or less exclusively to Jewish disciples of Jesus Christ. But what appears to be operative in Acts 15 is that James is accepting the inclusion of ethnic Gentiles into the people of God, and his injunction regarding eating blood and fornication is meant not to maintain a distinction, but to preserve the unity of the believing community. Thus, the ethnic distinction ultimately is unimportant. Gentile converts do, says James in Acts 15, need to observe certain features, such as abstaining from idols and from consuming blood or strangled animals, all of which had religiously symbolic value, and avoiding fornication, which, given the context, may be particularly focused on the ritual fornication that was also an aspect of Hellenistic cultic life.

Further, the James of Acts 15 refers to Amos 9:11 (God's promise of rebuilding the fallen tent of David) as a reflection of how Gentiles are included. If Gentiles are indeed included in the "tent" of David, it means that they are included in the restored messianic community. It would be strange to think of them as "non-Israelites" or pagans outside God's people. As Davids (2001: 67) puts it, "In James's view, as far as he reveals it, all followers of Jesus were in some sense Israel." In James's view, in other words, the determinative factor is not ethnicity, but faith.[54]

If in fact the James of Acts 15 is also the author of the Epistle of James, then it may be that its "Jewish" flavor, and its address of the intended recipients in

---

due to texts such as 1 Pet. 1:18; 4:3, which seem more appropriate to an audience of Gentile background.

54. Moo (2000: 23) thinks that the recipients "were almost certainly Jews," but he notes that some scholars see the "twelve tribes" not as a literal reference, but as a metaphor for the totality of God's people.

language that implies that they are Jews, are not so much an ethnic indication as a reflection of James's acceptance of Gentiles who trust in the Christ as ingrafted into "Israel." Indeed, in 2:25 the author presents just such an individual from the OT, Rahab the Gentile harlot, as a star example of someone whose deeds manifest faith and who consequently is justified and included among God's people. The inclusion of Gentile converts, then, does not at all call into question the "Jewish" flavor of James any more than it does the book of Joshua.

Other evidence also supports the Jewish character of James. Zahn (1909: 1.89–90) notes that James makes no mention of such typically "Gentile" sins as idolatry and fornication. If James is, as I have argued, early and not a reaction to Paul, the church probably is still largely Jewish, and the Gentiles who are now included probably were mostly "God-fearers" who already had some prior exposure to Jewish ethics and religion. But the presence of Gentile converts may also have opened the door for the pagan disconnection between religion and ethics to have crept into the church even before Paul's mission, and thus there is no need to suppose a form of "Paulinism" as the background for James 2.

It is often supposed that, especially if James's audience was Jewish, he could only be reacting to a form of Paulinism, because prior to Paul no Jew would ever suppose that faith without works could avail anything. However, the Gospels give plenty of indication that Jesus constantly encountered Jews who, though they paid lip service to the law, failed to perceive and practice its priorities (see especially Matt. 23). The kinds of works of faith that both James and Jesus propound are things such as showing no favoritism, caring for the destitute, showing mercy, avoiding judgmentalism, and the like. Both Jews and Gentiles have often had difficulty in fulfilling these responsibilities.

Arguably, James in 2:1–13 was showing readers that neglect of the poor and showing favoritism to the rich is functionally equivalent to ignoring Torah. James 2:8 assumes that the readers agree with Lev. 19:18, but the author avers that showing favoritism runs counter to it, and indeed Lev. 19:15, just three verses earlier than the love command, specifically forbids favoritism. James's true target is neither the Pauline notion of justification by faith nor even a perversion of it; rather, it is the endemic and widespread problem of hypocrisy.

In any event, certainly some Gentiles had become Christians prior to Paul's letters (and indeed the tensions generated by such Gentile converts joining the [Jewish] Christian community is the provocation for the Galatians controversy). Further, the problem in James is not a soteriological issue; it is the practical issue of hypocrisy and a disconnection between faith assertions and behavior. I think it not unlikely, therefore, that James's audience is mixed Jew and Gentile, but that James thinks of his audience as "Israel" regardless of ethnic background, and he is not addressing any form of Paulinism.

Location of the Addressees

James specifies no location of his intended audience in any way other than by the term "diaspora," which one would normally take to mean Jews outside Palestine. However, as already noted, if addressed to Jewish Christians, it could even include Jews within Palestine. Although Judea had had a period of political independence following the Maccabean revolt, the resulting state was hardly anything that could be seen as a fulfillment of the prophetic expectations, and according to Wright (1992: 268–69, 299), even Jews geographically in Palestine may still have regarded their condition as one of exile. Further, 1 Peter, if it is addressed to Gentiles (as seems likely),[55] gives evidence that the early church soon adopted the language of "exile" and "diaspora" in spiritual rather than literal terms. It is more likely, though, if the author is James in Jerusalem, that he is addressing a circular letter not to the Christians in his own city but to Christians "scattered" outside Palestine, many of whom were of Jewish ancestry, but also some of Gentile origin who may have become "people of God" by virtue of their acceptance of Jesus as Christ and Lord (as James terms Jesus in 2:1).

If the letter is pseudepigraphal, the location of the intended audience is guesswork, and it may in fact have no specific readers in mind at all (Popkes 1986: 9–52). Even if written by James of Jerusalem, as a "diaspora letter" it may have simply been intended for general circulation, but as I argue below (see "Social Situation"), the vividness of James's illustrative material suggests that he at least had in mind some real problems that he had heard about. Given that the letter's earliest echoes are from 1 Clement and Shepherd of Hermas, it may be that the letter had its first readers in the western parts of the Mediterranean, but on the other hand, its first acknowledgment as being from James occurs in Eastern Christendom. Beyond conjecture we cannot go.

Social Situation

Are the situations described in James 2 (showing favoritism, neglecting those in need), James 4 (traveling merchants, bickering among brethren), and James 5 (withholding wages) purely hypothetical examples, or do they reflect real situations? Since James is a "circular" letter without specific addressees, there is a "generalized" quality to the whole of it that may suggest that the situations implied in the letter are simply hypothetical or constructed. However, the vividness with which some of the situations are described, such as the man dressed in fine clothes with gold rings (2:2), or the brother or sister without adequate food or clothing (2:15),[56] or the merchants taking mercantile journeys without reference to the Lord's will (4:13) suggest something more than general hypothetical situations. James appears to have heard some disturbing news, and he is addressing real problems.

55. As most modern commentaries on 1 Peter point out (e.g., Achtemeier 1996: 50; Michaels 1988: xlv), 1 Pet. 1:14, 18; 2:9b–10; 4:3–4 imply that the intended readers of 1 Peter had Gentile backgrounds. Jobes (2005: 23–24) suggests that ultimately the racial background of the recipients of 1 Peter does not matter because the author regards his hearers as covenant people of God through faith in Christ and thus as truly "Israel" whatever their background. This is, in my view, likewise true of James.

56. As noted already, the partitive genitive "of you" in 2:16 is more naturally read as assuming specific real people than general hypothetical ones. See also the commentary on 2:16.

The letter seems to address Christians as those whom the rich "drag into court" (2:6), which would imply that the intended recipients are not among the wealthy. The rejoicing of the lowly in 1:9 and the denunciation of the rich in 5:1–6 also imply this, and "the poor" are the "rich in faith and heirs of the kingdom" (2:5). Some interpreters (e.g., Dibelius 1975: 39–40) understood "the poor" as a Second Temple Jewish metaphor, a reference to the pious, the faithful, the religious, the 'ănāwîm of, for example, Ps. 86:1; cf. 132:15. Recent interpreters (e.g., Tamez 1990) have been more inclined to regard literal material poverty as in view, reflecting the social dynamics of benefactor and patron, meaning that most or virtually all of James's intended audience was lower class, servants and dependents who were tempted to seek patronage by showing favor to those who could grant it.

However, the target of James's exhortations does not appear to be the destitute; rather, it is those who have at least some means of sharing but are reluctant to do so, or those who wish to dissociate from the "man in shabby clothes" and curry favor with the "gold-fingered." Although there was no social stratum equivalent to our modern middle class, the target audience is, generally speaking, neither the rich nor the truly destitute (such as orphans and widows; Bauckham 1999: 188).

It is nevertheless probably too restrictive to ask questions such as whether there were rich Christians in James's church. James exhorts all believers both to identify with the poor and to exhibit God's character in caring for the poor, not as a "benefactor" or patron but as one who knows that he or she is also poor. This is the intention behind 1:9–10, which calls upon the rich man to rejoice in his humble position (or perhaps humiliation). The point is not just irony; it is a call to recognition that God's values are not those of the world.

Communal Orientation

Hartin (2003: 4–5) represents the viewpoint of many that James exhibits primarily a communal interest and ethic as opposed to an individual one (see "Ethics" below). Thus, Hartin (2003: 13) sees the purpose of James as "socialization," that is, the process of social formation whereby the people addressed are drawn into and instructed in the ethos and values of a social group, in this case the community addressed as the "twelve tribes in the dispersion." The purpose of the letter, then, is not merely to demarcate and identify the characteristics of a community, but to exhort those who wish to be associated with that community to conform to those characteristics. But whereas community responsibility and "socialization" certainly are a concern of James, they are by no means the only concern. Patience in suffering (5:7), keeping oneself "unspotted" by the world (1:27), resisting the devil (4:7) and drawing near to God (4:8), and being a friend not of the world (4:4) but of God (2:23) also are concerns, and these at the very least involve some degree of individual intentionality. Of course, to some extent almost all practical life concerns are bound up with social environment, but James's interest in holiness is certainly as much the individual's relation to God as it is the community's social consciousness and responsibility.

Text

Johnson (1995: 4–6) discusses the state of the text in some detail and indicates that it is "relatively stable and homogenous," though it is not as well represented as the Gospels and Paul's letters in manuscripts prior to the major texts (Sinaiticus, Vaticanus) of the fourth century and later. Further, there appear to be no examples of a "Western" form of the text of James, probably, as Davids (1982: 59) suggests, because of the letter's obscurity in the first few centuries, particularly in the West.

The early papyri from the third century are quite fragmentary: $\mathfrak{P}^{20}$ (James 2:19–3:9), $\mathfrak{P}^{23}$ (James 1:10–12, 15–18), and $\mathfrak{P}^{100}$ (James 3:13–4:4; 4:9–5:1).[57] $\mathfrak{P}^{54}$ is later (fifth or early sixth century) and also is fragmentary (James 2:16–18, 22–26; 3:2–4). $\mathfrak{P}^{74}$ is late (seventh century) but probably is rooted in an earlier text tradition (it most often resembles Alexandrinus and, to a lesser extent, Vaticanus), and it contains sections of every chapter of James. On the other hand, $\mathfrak{P}^{74}$ also offers a number of unique readings, as will be noted in several of the additional notes in the commentary. The only early witnesses to the whole of James are the great uncials Sinaiticus, Alexandrinus, and Vaticanus (ℵ, A, B). Uncial C (fifth century) contains most of James, up to 4:2. There are also several ancient translations, including one valuable Old Latin manuscript designated "ff" (the Corbey manuscript), which is almost identical with B except for twenty-one interesting and unique variants.[58]

Most of the significant textual variants in James are traceable to attempts to deal with some of the idiosyncracies and difficulties of James's phrasing. Specific text-critical issues are addressed in the additional notes to each section of the commentary.

Genre and Purpose

James falls into the class of Jewish literature known as a "diaspora letter," which presents itself as a circulating epistle sent by a person of recognized authority in Judea to Jews located outside the land. Diaspora letters typically give advice on how to maintain integrity as the people of God in the midst of a non-Jewish world, and they articulate some expectations regarding the future (Niebuhr 1998). The Aramaic letters of Gamaliel are of this sort, and similar epistles are seen in 2 Macc. 1–2; Bar. 6:1–73 (the so-called Letter of Jeremiah); 2 Bar. 78.1–87.1. The short letter of James found in Acts 15:23–29 is also of this type. As noted earlier, there are some interesting similarities between the letter reported in Acts and the Epistle of James.

James's presentation of itself as generally within this genre of epistle still leaves several questions unanswered. Is James a real letter? What is its purpose?

---

57. For a description of $\mathfrak{P}^{100}$, see J. K. Elliott 1999.

58. For example, Corbey drops "of faith" from 1:3, yielding the reading "knowing that your probation produces endurance." The text of the Corbey manuscript is most easily accessible in Mayor 1897: 2–27.

What is the rhetorical character or function of the letter? Should it be classed as genuinely Jewish literature, or is it primarily a Greek document with a Jewish veneer?

Is James a Real Letter?

Curiously, James is the only letter of the NT to begin with a classic Greek salutation: χαίρειν (*chairein*, greeting). We do see this greeting in two reported letters in Acts 15:23 and Acts 23:26, but not in any of the letters of Paul (who has replaced the standard greeting with χάρις καὶ εἰρήνη, *charis kai eirēne*, grace and peace) or in any other NT letter. If James is pseudonymous and written late, it probably is not a letter from an individual to a specific audience, but is a literary epistle that simply has been put in the form of a letter for artistic purposes or to give it some kind of authority. The distinction between "literary epistle" and "real letter" goes back at least to Deissmann (1927: 233–45) and probably is implied by the judgment of Ropes (1916: 1) that it is a letter in form only. Dibelius (1975: 1–11) in particular argues that James is a "literary" epistle that is public and artistic, not a real communication between specific people. But the distinction between "real" and "literary" letters is unclear. How "specific" does an audience have to be for a letter to qualify as "real"? A study of ancient Greek letters by J. L. White (1988) demonstrates that the Greek "letter" was a very elastic genre and was used for a variety of purposes in a variety of forms. The specificity of the audience could vary from a single intended recipient to only the vaguest of general audiences. Especially the "diaspora letter" type has an intended breadth of audience. Further, as discussed above, James does appear to have at least some specificity of audience and is responding at least to some potential if not actual situations, particularly the preferential treatment of rich visitors condemned in James 2 and the intraecclesial bickering that called forth James's reprimand in James 4.

Rhetorical Purpose and Origins

James has a large number of commands and prohibitions, but these are not "bare" imperatives, as with apodictic law codes such as the Ten Commandments. Rather, James admonishes and exhorts his readers to manifest the life of faith by obedience—in other words, to behave according to the precepts that they already have acknowledged. James tries to convert his readers not to a new opinion but to an appropriate life. He assumes that the audience already accepts the precepts and truth of the Christian message, and he presumes that they already know and accept the ethical teaching of Jesus (see below under "Old Testament Connections") as well as the truth of his lordship (2:1). However, there is some disconnection between profession and behavior, which is calling into question the genuineness of the profession. To convey how serious this matter is, he uses a wide repertoire of both Greek and Jewish rhetorical devices.

SIMILARITY TO GREEK RHETORICAL FORMS

Aristotle (*Rhet.* 1.3.3) identified three general types of rhetoric: legal (forensic), deliberative (mostly political), and epideictic (ceremonial).[59] Where legal rhetoric tries to prove a case, and deliberative tries to persuade toward a course of action, epideictic is less specific, though generally it praises or blames an individual or group. Aspects of all three types can be seen in James (such as making a case in 2:20–26, or casting blame in 4:13–5:6), but in general, James exhibits the characteristics of deliberative literature, which attempts not just to persuade people that something is true, but to move them to a course of action (Kennedy 1984: 147). Certainly, the heavy use of admonitory language in James indicates a concern not so much to inform as to influence behavior.

Diatribe (to attack an argument). Undeniably, James shows a familiarity with certain Hellenistic rhetorical devices. Ropes (1916: 10–18) demonstrates that James has many features of the Greek diatribe form, and he argues that the whole of James may be seen as a diatribe. Diatribe is used mostly to attack a position, argument, or course of action as wrong and uses a number of forceful rhetorical devices to achieve its end. Recently, Watson (1993a: 119) notes several specific features often found in Greek diatribes that appear also in James 2:

Introduced "dialogue" with an imaginary interlocutor (2:18–23)

Iteration of the objections and false conclusions of the interlocutor (2:18–19)

A series of questions and answers (2:20–23)

Questions designed to lead the reader to reject the conclusion (2:20)

Outright censure (2:2–7, 8–13, 14–17, 18–20)

Illustrative vices (2:2–4, 15–16)

Harsh vocatives ("you idiot" in 2:20)

Maxims and quotations (2:8, 10, 11, 23)

Irony and sarcasm (2:18–20)

Personification ("judgment" in 2:13, "faith" in 2:17, 26)

But although the latter part of James 2 exhibits diatribal features, as also do parts of James 4–5, it seems to be pressing things too far to say that the genre of James as a whole is a diatribe. It is difficult, for example, to see the exhortation to prayer in James 5 as attacking a position.

Paraenesis (to provide exhortation). Dibelius, whose commentary was originally published in 1921, acknowledges the diatribal aspects that Ropes had pointed out, but he argues that the diatribe was simply one device among many used for a variety of exhortations. Dibelius (1975: 3) designates James

59. For a good survey of how James fits in the scheme of Hellenistic moral literature, see Johnson 1995: 16–24.

as being an example of "paraenesis," which he defines as "a text which strings together admonitions of general ethical content." Such texts have no overall controlling theme or purpose and no discernible formal structure; they simply assemble some exhortations, precepts, and pithy sayings. They do address a particular (though possibly fictional) audience, but the material is connected, when there is any connection at all, only by catchwords.

Such a classification has the advantage of connecting the Epistle of James to both its Greek origins and its Jewish background, since Jewish ethical teaching in Hellenistic context also lay behind other "paraeneses" (Dibelius [1975: 4] points to the two paraenetic chapters in the book of Tobit [4:5–19; 12:6–10] as examples). It further has the advantage of explaining why there seems to be a lack of continuity even in the meanings of certain words in close proximity in James. Thus, the apparent shift from a positive meaning of πειρασμός (*peirasmos*, testing, temptation) in 1:12 to a different, negative meaning of the cognate participle πειραζόμενος (*peirazomenos*, being tempted, tested) in 1:13 is not an interpretive conundrum; it is simply the result of connecting two originally unconnected sayings by means of a similar word being used in each.[60] Dibelius further points to two other characteristics of paraenetic literature: the repetition of identical motifs in different places, and the impossibility of fitting all the admonitions into a single set of audience and circumstances. Thus, there is no identifiable "life situation" for interpreting James. It is simply a repository of ethical and sapiential injunctions.

Paraenesis versus protreptic discourse. Ever since Dibelius's definitive study, the paraenetic or hortatory character of James has been widely recognized.[61] But to say that James has features in common with Greek paraenetic literature is quite different from identifying the entire letter of James as a paraenesis. One of the principal marks of paraenesis as a genre is its lack of focus or organizing theme. But although James is difficult to outline linearly, a close study of the letter indicates that it is far from lacking in theme or focus. Most recent scholars have perceived various themes that give coherence to James,[62] and few scholars now support Dibelius's pronouncement that James has no formal structure. Further, work on paraenetic literature by J. Gammie (1990) suggests that a distinction should be made between "paraenesis" as a genre and what Gammie calls "protreptic" discourse. Whereas paraenesis is marked by "the enumeration of precepts or maxims which pertain to moral aspiration and the

60. Dibelius (1975: 7) notes similar catchword (mis)connections in 1:4 and 1:5; 1:26 and 1:27; 2:12 and 2:13; 3:17 and 3:18; 5:9 and 5:12; 5:13–18 and 5:19–20; along with a couple other possibilities. He then devotes three whole pages to noting similar catchword connections in Pseudo-Isocrates' *Ad Demonicum*, Tobit, and other NT admonitory passages, most strikingly in Rom. 12:13–18 and Gal. 6:2–10. But few regard Rom. 12 and Gal. 6 as incoherent, so these comparisons appear to undermine Dibelius's theory.

61. Of course, the recognition that James is an exhortation is nothing new, but Dibelius's classification of James as a type of Greek paraenetic genre has been a starting point for discussion.

62. For example, several scholars have pointed to holiness or perfection as a principal theme running through James (see J. H. Elliott 1993).

regulation of human conduct" (Gammie 1990: 51) and a lack of thematic unity, protreptic discourse is marked by sustained arguments (in James, especially evident in the diatribe of chapter 2, but see also 3:1–12; 4:13–17; 5:1–6, 13–18) and a clear focus on a limited number of issues. Protrepsis aims not merely to present a convincing case for the truth or error of a position, but to persuade the audience to make a change in behavior or make a new commitment (see Baasland 1988: 3652; Hartin 1999: 47–49; Wachob 2000: 48). This fits James, in particular his concern for believers' responsibility toward the poor, his discussion of the difficulty with godly speech, his exhortations toward peace, his interest in prayer, and, tying it all together, his mandate that an asseveration of faith must be matched with correlative behavior (explicit in 2:1, but implicit throughout; see "Controlling Theme: Genuine Faith" below; and excursus 1, "Faith as the Central Concern of James"). Thus, Johnson (1995: 24) no doubt is correct to classify James as "protreptic discourse in the form of a letter."

Protreptic literature (from the Gk. verb προτρέπω, *protrepō*, turn) is a kind of conversion literature, but it is not so much a call to adopt new religious concepts as a call to adopt a different lifestyle or behavior pattern, that is, to repent. James is addressed to those who already name the name of Jesus as Christ and Lord (2:1). But in a sense Christians too, just as Israel did so often in the OT, need a constant call to behavioral "turning back." It is neither difficult nor uncommon for those who name the name of Christ to slide back into "friendship with the world" (4:4), a divided loyalty that James calls "double-mindedness" (literally "two-souledness") in 1:7, and if they do so, they must repent (4:8–10).

Jewish Literary Background

Several scholars (Ropes 1916: 24; Dibelius 1975: 17–18; Popkes 1986), while recognizing that James comes from a Christian environment that was cognizant of its Jewish ethical roots, notice the letter's marked similarities to Greek forms and its use of certain Hellenistic phrases, plus the letter's inscription in good literary style, and conclude that it was written by someone with a background in Hellenism and written for an audience of Hellenistic, mostly Gentile, Christians. Thus, it was not by James of Jerusalem, who was an Aramaic-speaking Galilean Jewish peasant. But several other scholars (Mayor 1897: cxxiv–cxxv; Schlatter 1956: 21–36; Gertner 1962; Baasland 1982; Mussner 1998; Bauckham 1999) notice that the strikingly Jewish features of James are not just superficial or artificial, nor are they simply the remnants of the Jewish origins of Christianity; they reflect an inherently Jewish character. Cladder (1904) examines James's style and vocabulary and demonstrates James's resemblance to certain psalms as well as to Jewish wisdom literature. Although we may reject the thesis of Spitta (1896) that James is a strictly Jewish (not originally a Christian) document, Spitta was right in seeing James as firmly situated within Jewish wisdom tradition.[63]

63. Spitta (1896), in his footnotes throughout his exposition section, draws an extensive list of parallels to James from Sirach, Wisdom of Solomon, Judith, 4 Maccabees, Psalms of Solomon,

Meyer (1930) even goes so far as to propose that the book of James is a Jewish book structured on the Testaments of the Twelve Patriarchs, and the "James" in whose name it is written is a reference not to James of Jerusalem but to the patriarch Jacob ("James" and "Jacob" are identical in Greek). Meyer's volume then works out how the segments of the Epistle of James correspond to the patriarchal names. The whole approach is inventive and involves a number of unlikely stretches and unsupportable hypotheses, and few other scholars have been persuaded, but Meyer does point out a number of resemblances of James to Jewish literature of the period.

More recently, Beck (1973) observes similarities between James and the Qumran documents 1QS (Rule of the Community) and 1QSa (Rule of the Congregation).[64] Even a century ago, Hort (1909: x–xi) noted that James in certain ways bridges Judaism and Christianity[65] and pointed out that "the Epistle of St. James marks in the most decisive way the continuity of the two testaments."[66]

Old Testament Connections

Although James is widely regarded as closely allied with the wisdom literature of the OT, one of the letter's strongest OT connections is to Lev. 19, particularly Lev. 19:10–18. Note the following echoes of Lev. 19 found in James:

19:10   Show concern for the poor and the sojourner (cf. James 2:1–6, 15–16, 25)

19:12   Do not swear falsely (cf. James 5:12)

19:13   Do not oppress neighbor (cf. James 5:1–6)

19:15   Do not show partiality (cf. James 2:1–11)

19:16   Do not slander or falsely accuse (cf. James 4:11)

19:17–18   Do not hate brother in heart or take vengeance, but love neighbor as self (cf. James 2:8; 4:1)

Johnson (1982: 399) observes that only one verse of this passage in Leviticus (19:14, which forbids cursing the deaf and putting a stumbling block before the

Jubilees, 1 Enoch, 4 Ezra, Apocalypse of Moses, Testament of Abraham, and *m. 'Abot* as well as from OT texts. Although none of these, with the exception of the half dozen OT citations, represents anything close to actual quotations, the interest and style of addressing practical ethical concerns, and the recurring connections between wisdom and God's law, so much like Sirach, show very well the deeply Jewish character of the Epistle of James.

64. Beck (1973) goes so far as to find the structure of James based on 1QS, but the controlling concerns of the documents are radically dissimilar, and Beck's argument is burdened by much special pleading. See Cheung 2003: 53–54.

65. Mussner (1975: 136) suggests that James may also in our own time provide a bridge between Catholic and Protestant Christianity.

66. The view that James is addressed to non-Christian Jews as well as Christians is propounded by Allison (2001), who argues that James was written to reassure Jews that Christians were faithful to Torah.

blind) has no parallel in James[67] and concludes that "James made conscious and sustained use of Lev. 19:12–18 in his letter."[68] Since James quotes Lev. 19:18, it is hard to argue that James was unaware of the significance of Lev. 19 for his own ethical admonitions. On the other hand, it might be nearer the mark to say, with Bauckham (1999: 74–83), that James as a disciple of Jesus is adapting the ethical teaching of Jesus, for whom Lev. 19 seems to play a determinative role. Much of this is also found in the Sermon on the Mount (Matt. 5–7) and/or the parallel Sermon on the Plain in Luke 6. Further, the reflections of Lev. 19 found in James sometimes have the character of their form and content in Jesus's sermon more than in Lev. 19 itself. Note especially how the warning in Lev. 19:12 against swearing falsely is reflected in James 5:12, not directly, as it is in Lev. 19, but in the intensified and generalized form found in Jesus's teaching recorded in Matt. 5:34–37. In fact, none of the allusions to Lev. 19 in James is without some parallel in Jesus's teaching recorded in the Gospels.

James shares much with Proverbs, as well. James, like Proverbs, wants readers to acquire wisdom and regards wisdom's source as God and its character as ethical. Twice James quotes from Proverbs (James 4:6; 5:20). There are also several allusions: Prov. 2:3–6 (get wisdom) has an echo in James 1:5; Prov. 27:21 (on being tested) can be seen behind James 1:3; James 2:6 reflects the concern for respecting the poor also seen in Prov. 14:21; Prov. 16:27 has the same concern for the tongue seen in James 3:6; and James 4:14 has an echo of Prov. 27:1; other parallels may be seen. But these parallels also may be found in other Jewish literature. If James was alluding to these passages from Proverbs, he was likely doing so only unconsciously.

Rather unlike Proverbs, on the other hand, James speaks with a voice resembling that of the OT prophets at points. In particular, his excoriating indictment of rich landowners in 5:1–6 is quite unlike wisdom literature. It rather sounds like Amos pronouncing woe to those at ease in Zion (Amos 6), or like Jeremiah warning against the coming "day of slaughter" (verbally echoed in James 5:5). Again, though, this is a further point of similarity with the nature of Jesus's wisdom teaching. Jesus also spoke as both sage and prophet, and James appears to be following Jesus's example.

Relation to Extrabiblical Jewish Wisdom Literature

Sirach

Of all Jewish wisdom books, James's closest resemblance is to the Jewish Wisdom of Jesus the Son of Sirach, generally known simply as Sirach (or by its

---

67. Actually, even Lev. 19:14 has a remote echo in James's admonition against cursing a fellow human being made in God's image (3:9–10).

68. Johnson might also have mentioned Lev. 19:10, which forbids stripping a vineyard bare so that the poor and the sojourner might have something. James too is concerned for the poor and requires a response to their neediness (1:26–27; 2:15–16) as well as honoring them (1:10–12; 2:6).

Latin title, "Ecclesiasticus"). Mayor (1897: lxxiv–lxxvi) lists some thirty-two points of similarity, several of which occur more than once in either Sirach or James or both. The warning in James 3 about the dangers of the tongue and the difficulty of controlling it also is of great concern in Sir. 19:6–12, 16; 20:5–7, 18–19; 28:13–26. At several points Sirach not only has similar interests, but even uses phrasing quite similar to James. For example, Sir. 15:11–17 addresses the same concern as James 1:12–15 in much the same way:

> Do not say, "Because of the Lord I left the right way"; for he will not do what he hates. Do not say, "It was he who led me astray"; for he had no need of a sinful man. The Lord hates all abominations, and they are not loved by those who fear him. It was he who created man in the beginning, and he left him in the power of his own inclination. . . . Before a man are life and death, and whichever he chooses will be given to him. (RSV)

Or compare Sir. 5:11, "Be quick to hear, and be deliberate in answering," with James 1:19; and also Sir. 5:13, "Glory and dishonor come from speaking, and a man's tongue is his downfall," and Sir. 19:16, "Who has never sinned with his tongue?" with James 3:2. James also shares with Sirach the odd imagery of hoarded gold and silver "rusting" (Sir. 29:10; James 5:3).

Much of Sirach itself is in fact a recasting of material in Proverbs, though with two differences: true wisdom is located in God's revealed law (something only implicit in Proverbs itself), and the motive for true wisdom or obedience to Torah is the eschatological hope.

Bauckham (1999: 74–83) makes a convincing case that given the deep connections between the content (though not the wording) of Jesus's teaching as found particularly in Matthew and Luke and the sayings of James (see "James and the Wisdom of Jesus" below), the Epistle of James is a recasting of the wisdom tradition of Jesus in much the same way as the wisdom of Sirach uses Proverbs as a lens for understanding Torah. As Sirach understands true wisdom as rooted in Torah, and true Torah as giving expression to wisdom, so James has adopted and adapted the tradition of Jesus's teaching to undergird his concept of true wisdom "from above," as James 3:17 terms it. At several points in the commentary, other similarities to Sirach will be noted.

Wisdom of Solomon

Although there are fewer cases of verbal similarity between James and Wisdom of Solomon than are seen in Sirach, many characteristics of the outlook and interests of James are also seen in Wisdom of Solomon.

Like James, Wisdom of Solomon operates with both the wisdom tradition and the apocalyptic mentality of Second Temple Judaism (see Burkes 2002). The motivation for wisdom is the judgment of God (Wis. 1–6), as it is in James. Wisdom in Wisdom of Solomon functions much like the Holy Spirit, just as in James (see Kirk 1969), and indeed wisdom *is* God's Spirit (see, e.g., Wis. 1:6–7; 9:17). As such, wisdom is a divine gift (Wis. 1:2–5; 7:7; cf. James 1:5). Wisdom does not come to those who put God to the test (Wis. 1:2; cf. James 1:13), but it does come to those who ask in faith (Wis. 7:7). The rich are condemned for the oppression of the righteous poor (Wis. 2:10; cf. James 5:1–6). Earthly cycles, heavenly phenomena, and the nature of animals provide illustrative material in Wisdom of Solomon (7:18–20) just as in James (1:17; 3:6–7).

However, other aspects of Wisdom of Solomon seem foreign to James. James knows nothing of the personification of wisdom as in Wis. 8 and displays no interest in how wisdom functioned in the creation of the world or the history of Israel. The similarities between James and Wisdom of Solomon testify that both operate within the broad interests and ideas of wisdom in Second Temple Judaism, but they give little indication of a direct use of Wisdom of Solomon by the author of James. Although it is possible and even likely that James knew of the Wisdom of Solomon, that book does not function as an immediate source for James.

Sentences of Pseudo-Phocylides

Unlike Sirach, Pseudo-Phocylides,[69] like James, focuses on the universals of Jewish ethics, not the distinctives of Judaism: circumcision, Sabbath observance, and food laws. Similarities of Pseudo-Phocylides with James may be seen in the following Sentences:[70]

10: "Do not cast down the poor unjustly, do not judge partially" (see also 137; cf. James 2:1–4).

11: "If you judge evilly, subsequently God will judge you" (cf. James 2:4, 13; 4:11–12).

19: "Give the laborer his pay, do not afflict the poor" (cf. James 5:1–6).

20: "Take heed of your tongue, keep your word hidden in (your) heart" (cf. James 1:21, 26; 3:2–12).

22: "Give to the poor man at once, and do not tell him to come tomorrow" (cf. James 2:15–16).

27: "Life is a wheel" (cf. James 3:6).

46: "For [gold's] sake there are battles and plunderings and murders" (cf. James 4:1–3).

50: "Be sincere to all, speak what is from your soul" (cf. James 3:17).

63: "Anger that steals over one causes destructive madness" (cf. James 1:20).

69. The Sentences of Pseudo-Phocylides is a didactic morality poem written in the name of an ancient (sixth century BC) philosopher. As it exhibits a vigorous monotheism and opposition to paganism, but without any discernible evidence of Christian influence, it was written probably by a Hellenistic Jew early in the Christian era. See *OTP* 2:565–72; Harnack 1897: 2.589.

70. Citations of Pseudo-Phocylides are from *OTP* 2:574–82.

124–26: "Speech is to man a weapon sharper than iron. God allotted a weapon to every creature; the capacity to fly to birds, speed to horses, and strength to the lions" (cf. James 3:3–8).

144: "By a tiny spark a vast forest is set on fire"[71] (cf. James 3:5b).

None of these several similarities exhibit the close verbal parallels with James that are seen in Shepherd of Hermas. These are of a general sort, and they find echoes elsewhere in moral literature. Therefore, resemblances probably do not indicate that James knew or was using the Sentences of Pseudo-Phocylides, or that the author of the Sentences knew James; however, they do suggest that the authors of both James and Pseudo-Phocylides moved in a similar environment (Hellenistic Judaism), and that both were concerned about living as the people of God in an unsympathetic world. This might suggest that the author of James was not Palestinian, but as already noted, even Palestinian Judaism was Hellenized, and James's roots in Judaism are even more fundamental than those of Pseudo-Phocylides.

James has similarities to other Second Temple Jewish wisdom literature as well, but these are even less likely to indicate any dependence. It should be clear, however, that James is "at home" in this tradition, which has melded OT wisdom, law, and eschatology (effectively the three parts of the OT canon) into a general practical theology informed and motivated by the commitment to Jesus as the Christ, the Lord of glory.

Eschatological Motivation for Exhortations

The book of Sirach was written probably in the early part of the second century BC (Coggins 1998: 18–19). Sirach was concerned with wisdom and understood the ultimate source of wisdom to be God's law, Torah. Although we see inklings of this notion already in Proverbs, which states that the fear of the Lord is the beginning of wisdom (Prov. 9:10; cf. Job 28:28; Ps. 111:10),[72] Sirach, along with Wisdom of Solomon, also introduced to the Jewish wisdom tradition a strongly eschatological note that had been only marginally present earlier. Since wisdom as Torah obedience in this life sometimes results not in earthly bliss but in earthly suffering, the motivation for wisdom/obedience is not simply that things will go better in this life, but that one will be rewarded in the coming age. Most Jewish wisdom writings subsequent to Sirach, and indeed virtually all Jewish literature in the century prior to Jesus, adopt this eschatological motivation. Essentially, the prophetic (eschatological) tradition and the wisdom tradition have merged. The eschatological element is thus also seen in James. For example,

71. P. W. van der Horst, in *OTP* 2:579, places this verse in brackets because it is found in only one manuscript. It possibly was imported into that manuscript from James, though it is also found in Philo, *Migration* 21 §123.

72. In Ps. 19:9 (possibly also in Ps. 34:11) the "fear of the Lord" appears to have become metonymous for God's law.

James 5:7–8 gives as an example the farmer waiting patiently for the harvest, which is a model of the Christian waiting patiently for the parousia of the Lord.

James 1:9–12 reminds readers of the coming eschatological reversal, when the humble will be exalted and the exalted will be made low.

James 1:21 and 5:20 remind readers of their expectation of the salvation of souls.

James 5:1–3 warns of the fiery judgment coming upon the wicked who oppress the poor.

As Bauckham (2001: 111) points out, "Recognizing that James is wisdom instruction does not require us to play down the eschatological element in James." Nor does the eschatological element mean that James has departed from the genre of Jewish wisdom. It rather is thereby distinguished from Greek wisdom, which, since it has no temporal eschatology and no single divine judge, is not oriented toward a future manifestation of divine righteousness.

Further, note that James's eschatology lies closest to that of Jesus, who spoke of the eschatological judgment as a harvest (Matt. 13:39; cf. James 3:18), referred to the Son of Man's coming in judgment as his parousia (Matt. 24:27, 37, 39), understood the judgment to be a lifting up of the lowly and a casting down of the high (Matt. 23:12), and warned of the fiery judgment that is coming upon those who care nothing for the poor (Matt. 25:41). And that brings us to the literature that in general bears the closest relationship to the content of James: the teaching of Jesus.

James and the Wisdom of Jesus

At several points in the preceding survey we have noted that James closely resembles the recorded teaching of Jesus. James does not cite the words of Jesus in the form that we have them in the Gospels (although 5:12 comes fairly close to Matt. 5:34–37), nor does he explicitly refer to Jesus's teaching, except in a general sense in 2:1. Nevertheless, as many scholars have noted, a great deal of James's instruction has a marked similarity to what we find in Jesus's ethical instruction in the Synoptic tradition.[73] The most thorough study of this matter was undertaken by Deppe (1989), who examines some sixty writers on James from 1833 to 1985 on the question of James's parallels to Synoptic tradition. Deppe finds a wide variety in the specific texts that scholars have seen as parallels, possibly because many of the apparent parallels also occur elsewhere in Second Temple Jewish literature, but he concludes that regardless of whether any one particular alleged dependency is real, the sheer number of correspondences makes it difficult to argue that there is no

---

73. Kittel (1942: 84) refers to the "echoes" (*Anklänge*) of the Lord's word that are interspersed through James.

relationship whatever.[74] This is especially true of the marked correspondences to the Sermon on the Mount (Matt. 5–7) and Luke's corresponding Sermon on the Plain (Luke 6).[75]

James and the Sermon on the Mount/Plain

The Jewish character of the Gospel of Matthew has often been observed, and James's relationship to Matthew is also close (see Schlatter 1956: 19–29). Thus, it is not surprising that James exhibits a high degree of correspondence with Matthew's presentation of Jesus's ethical teaching found in the Sermon on the Mount (Lohse 1957). We may point to the following correspondences:

James		Matthew 5–7
1:2	Joy in suffering	5:11–12 (Luke 6:22)
1:4	Be perfect	5:48 (Luke 6:36)
1:5–6	Ask in faith	7:7 (Luke 11:9)
1:10	Riches are like grass	6:30 (Luke 12:28)
1:17	The Father gives good things	7:11 (Luke 11:13)
1:19–20	Do not be angry	5:22
1:22–23	Hearing and doing	7:24–26 (Luke 6:47–49)
2:5	God chooses the poor	5:3, 5 (Luke 6:20)
2:10	Doing the whole law	5:18–19
2:11	Murder and adultery	5:21–30
2:13	Mercy triumphs	5:7 (Luke 6:36)
3:12	Fruit indicates the tree	7:16–18 (Luke 6:43–44)
3:18	Peacemakers	5:9
4:4	Serving two masters	6:24 (Luke 16:13)
4:8	Pure in heart	5:8
4:10	God exalts the humble	5:5
4:11 (5:9)	Do not judge	7:1–2
4:13–15	Not worrying about future	6:34
5:2–3	Moth-eaten treasures	6:19–21
5:10	Prophets as examples	5:11–12
5:12	Do not swear	5:34–37

74. Deppe (1989) himself conservatively maintains that there are eight "conscious allusions" in James: 1:5; 2:5; 4:2, 9, 10; 5:1, 2, 12, plus another ten ethical themes that are paralleled: joy in trial (1:2; 5:10–11), faith and doubt (1:6), warning against anger (1:19–20), hearing and doing (1:22–25), faith and action (2:14), the love commandment (2:8), mercy (2:13), serving God versus loving the world (4:4), refraining from judgment (2:12; 4:11–12; 5:9), and perseverance leading to blessing (1:5; 5:10–11). To this list I would add the theme of eschatological reversal evident in 1:9–11, as well as in the "conscious allusions" noted above (2:5; 4:9; 5:2–3). James 1:9–10 particularly, in contrasting the rich with the humble rather than the poor, appears to echo Luke 1:52–53. Deppe thinks that all told, there are about twenty-five verses that evince enough correspondence to indicate dependency of some sort. See also Mussner 1975: 48–50.

75. Whether or not the Sermon on the Mount in Matthew and the Sermon on the Plain in Luke are redactional adaptations of the same event or record two different sermons with similar material, they present a coherent image of one dimension of Jesus's teaching.

The clearest example is the last one. The similarity here is quite evident:

James 5:12 NIV	Matthew 5:34–35, 37 NIV
Above all, my brothers, do not swear	But I tell you, Do not swear at all:
—not by heaven	either by heaven, for it is God's throne;
or by earth	or by the earth, for it is his footstool;
or by anything else.	or by Jerusalem, for it is the city of the Great King.
Let your "Yes" be yes, and your "No," no, or you will be condemned.	Simply let your "Yes" be "Yes," and your "No," "No"; anything beyond this comes from the evil one.

The Jewish tradition, and the wisdom literature of the OT itself, advised caution in the use of oaths, but the outright prohibition of them seems to be a unique characteristic of Jesus's teaching, which we also find in James, even to the mention of "neither by heaven nor by earth" and the admonition to let yes be yes and no be no (this last being evident also in 2 Cor. 1:17). In addition to this very close correspondence, the sheer number of correspondences seems to rule out pure coincidence.

Other Correspondences to the Jesus Tradition

The correspondences are not entirely restricted to the Matthean Sermon on the Mount. A few correspondences are found only with the Lukan Sermon on the Plain and not in Matthew, especially the reference in James 4:9 to eschatological reversal in terms of laughing and weeping (cf. Luke 6:25). In addition to the above, other similarities to Jesus's teaching outside the Sermon on the Mount may be noted, such as James 1:6 (believing and not doubting), which resembles Matt. 21:21 (= Mark 11:23).

Further, it is not only the content of James's teaching that bears such close affinity to the teaching of Jesus; even the wisdom forms used in James are patterned after those found in the Gospels. Bauckham (1999: 56) observes that James's wisdom sayings (2:10; 4:4), comparisons or parables (1:23), beatitudes (1:12), woes (5:1–6), and models (5:10–11) have antecedents in the forms that Jesus uses.

Conclusion

What is to be made of this? Certainly, one would expect some correspondence of James with Jesus's teaching, simply because they come from the same milieu of early Christianity, which had evolved from within Judaism (Penner 1996: 254). However, the extent of correspondence, and the unique character and similar phrasing of the prohibition of oaths, make it more likely that James knew Matthew (or vice versa), or that both James and Matthew had access to variants of a particular text (such as a pre-Synoptic form of Q, as Hartin 1991: 141–72 proposes), or that both James and Matthew were disciples of a particular tradition, namely the teaching of Jesus. Given the lack of verbal correspondence, this last possibility seems the likeliest explanation.[76] James and Matthew (and at points Luke and Mark) are similar because their authors were disciples of Jesus. But the similarities fall far short of anything like the verbal correspondences seen among the Synoptic Gospels. James is probably therefore either writing prior to the formal solidification of the Greek tradition of Jesus's words, and thus "quoting" in a different form than we have it in the Synoptics, or (more likely) he is paraphrasing and reapplying the ethical teaching of Jesus.[77]

Bauckham (1999: 97–107) notes that not only are particular texts similar, but also the overall tenor of James's wisdom is similar to Jesus's teaching in its (1) radical reinterpretation of Torah, (2) rejection of social stratification, (3) appeal to eschatological motivation, (4) emphasis on God's mercy over judgment, and (5) concern for the reconstituted people of God. The author of this letter has absorbed not just several of Jesus's sayings, but indeed the very ethos of Jesus's ethical vision.

James and 1 Peter

James bears a certain curious relationship to 1 Peter. Although they are stylistically quite different, both are deeply concerned with the problem of Christians suffering (James 1:2–4; 1 Pet. 1:6–7). Admittedly, whereas 1 Peter has an intensely biblical-theological approach to the issue, understanding suffering as meaningful because of participation in the sufferings of Christ, James takes an entirely pragmatic approach, understanding it as building maturity or wholeness. But despite this difference, there are some intriguing linguistic and other similarities.[78] Both address their audiences as "diaspora." Both letters cite or allude to Prov. 3:34; 10:12 (James 4:6; 5:20; 1 Pet. 5:5; 4:8). Curiously, the forms of the citations of Prov. 3:34 in James 4:6 and 1 Pet. 5:5 are not just alike, but together they are unlike the LXX or any other text form. Both letters also allude to Isa. 40:6–8 (James 1:10–11; 1 Pet. 1:24–25). For both James and 1 Peter the word of God is a generative seed (James 1:18; 1 Pet. 1:23; see Bauckham 1999: 155–56). Mayor (1897: cxiv–cxv), who sees these and a number of other correspondences, therefore supposes that the author of 1 Peter knew James and modeled his letter after it, arguing that

76. Wachob (2000: 17–18) says that the Epistle of James, by not specifying that the material comes from Jesus, effectively "attributes the wise sayings of Jesus to James." In addition to presupposing that James is pseudepigraphical, this reflects a Western way of thinking about texts, which requires proper acknowledgment of sources and avoidance of "plagiarism." It is like saying that the book of Sirach, in "adapting" Proverbs, is "attributing" the wisdom of Proverbs to Jesus the Son of Sirach. In most cultures, especially ancient ones, words and ideas were not "owned" by their first utterer, and wisdom in particular, even when its source is known, is a shared, communal thing (as Wachob himself appears to acknowledge).

77. This would apply also if any of the sayings in James suspected of being *agrapha* (words of Jesus not found in the canonical Gospels) are in fact such. The sayings in James 3:18; 4:17; 5:20 sound like they could be references to traditional teaching stemming from Jesus, but there is simply no way of knowing.

78. For a thorough discussion, see Schlatter 1956: 67–73. Bauckham (1999: 155–57) has a more succinct and accessible discussion.

the much more extensive christological development of 1 Peter puts it later. Certainly, 1 Peter exhibits more theological development, but the similarities between James and 1 Peter are, like James's similarities with the Sermon on the Mount, more indicative of a common milieu than of direct dependence. The relationship between James and 1 Peter is much better understood as the result of both stemming from a Jewish Christian Hellenistic environment in which Christian profession is becoming dangerous. The use of Prov. 10:12 (love covers many sins, which James only half quotes in 5:20) and Prov. 3:34 suggests not direct dependence, but only that both these texts had become important parlance broadly in early Christianity and were being adduced on occasions of persecution or suffering. The common text form of Proverbs and the dependency on a similar collection of OT texts suggest a currency of certain OT texts in the Christian community, which in the first century was by no means very large.[79] But the uses of the texts, the underlying theological development, and the style and vocabulary of the two letters are so different that direct dependence in either direction is unlikely.

Was James a Reaction to Paul (or Later Paulinism)?

As discussed above (see "Authorship and Date"), Hengel (1987) sees James as over against Paulinism not just in terms of the "faith versus works" question, but in the way James and Paul see Christianity. Where Paul takes a practical and cosmopolitan approach to wealth, seeing the wealthy as those who have responsibility to contribute to the support of the poor and to facilitate Christian mission, James simply exhibits an unremitting negativity toward monetary wealth generally, so much so that the rich are seen as necessarily excluded from the kingdom of God. Where Paul is concerned with Jewish-Gentile relations, James is simply focused on social responsibility. Where Paul tells people that they should desire to be teachers, James exhorts people to be reluctant to be teachers.

But Hengel overstates the matter. No doubt there are differences of emphases, but it is not evident that the differences reflect a deliberate purpose on James's part to polemicize against Paulinism. While it is arguable that the latter part of James 2 may be confronting a misreading of Paul, most of the other differences can more easily be explained with reference to their different audiences.

Most scholars who view James as a reaction see it more as a reaction to a later development of Paul's thinking than to Paul himself. Dibelius (1975: 179) acknowledges that if the author of James is reacting to Paul, then he understood Paul poorly, but Dibelius also bluntly declares that *"his remarks in 2.14ff are still inconceivable unless Paul had previously set forth the slogan 'faith, not works.'"* Likewise, Dunn (1977: 251–52) regards it as "obvious . . .

---

79. And, of course, if James and 1 Peter indeed were written by their namesakes, the two authors were colaborers who may have shared a particular Greek translation/recension of Proverbs.

that what is reflected here is a *controversy within Judaism*—between that stream of Jewish Christianity which was represented by James at Jerusalem on the one hand, and the Gentile churches or Hellenistic Jewish Christians who had been decisively influenced by Paul on the other." Similarly, Painter (2001: 58) thinks that James is "clearly an attack on what is understood to be Pauline teaching" (see also Painter 1999: 83–85).[80]

However, many older scholars (Beyschlag 1897: 7; Zahn 1909: 1.124–25; Mayor 1897: cxxi–cliii; Schlatter 1956: 7), as well as some more recent ones (Johnson 1995: 111–21; Bauckham 1999: 127–31; Brosend 2004: 5–6), argue that James should be read on its own terms rather than as a reaction to Paul or Paulinism or at least prior to making a judgment whether it is a reaction to Paul (Schlatter 1927: 419). The fact that Dibelius, along with others who regard James as "inconceivable" apart from Paulinism, concedes that James is opposing "an abuse of Pauline tradition that is quite at odds with what Paul himself advocated" (cf. Popkes 2001b: 90–92) ought to alert us to the possibility that James is reacting to neither Paul nor Paulinism but to something else.

In fact, James's similarities with Paul's language in Galatians and Romans in the last twelve verses of James 2 (which is the only place where there are similarities more specific than the general context of early Christianity) are best seen as the result of a common Jewish heritage (Bauckham 1999: 131–33). They are not in direct dialogue, and they are addressing entirely different problems (Childs 1984: 438–43; Chester 1994: 28). When James speaks about the limitations of faith, he indicates that the problem is one of a truncated notion of faith, a false and empty faith that does not do what genuine faith does. This has nothing to do with Paul's problem, which related to certain expressions of distinctively Jewish commitment to Torah (circumcision [Gal. 5:3]) and confidence in one's Torah observance or ethnicity rather than in God's mercy (Rom. 3:27; Gal. 6:13–14), nor is the faith that James attacks anything like what Paul calls "faith," which "works through love" (Gal. 5:6; see excursus 2, "Faith, Works, and Justification in James and Paul").

But, one may argue, surely it is inherently quite unlikely that any Jew prior to Paul ever supposed that faith without works did count with God, and so James could not have faced this problem prior to Paul. This line of argument presupposes two things: (1) there was, for Jews, no problem of empty profession of faith prior to Paul; (2) James was addressed to Jewish Christians exclusively.

I argued above, regarding the second presupposition, that it could very well be that James is addressing an audience that he regards as "Jewish" in the

---

80. Moo (2000: 26) suggests that James 2 is a reaction to a misunderstood form of Paulinism, but is prior to the meeting of Paul and James in Jerusalem recorded in Acts 15 (AD 49), since there they are said to have achieved mutual understanding. This view is difficult to maintain because it assumes not only that Paul did clearly delineate faith in opposition to works of the law before Galatians, and that this was propounded prior even to Paul's confirmation of his message that he indicated in Gal. 2:2, but also that the position had time to be misunderstood and presented as an "easy-believism" by Jewish believers all prior to the apostolic council at Jerusalem. This is as unlikely as Mayor's view that Paul was reacting against James.

sense that they are among God's elect people, even though not all of them are genetically the offspring of Abraham, Isaac, and Jacob, and among pagans the connection between religion and ethics could be very loose indeed (see "Original Recipients and Occasion" above).

Regarding the first presupposition, as to whether Jews were likely to think that an empty profession of faith without obedience would have been salvific, it is worthwhile to observe carefully exactly what it is that James is attacking. The "works" that James is concerned with, the "works" that people who profess faith must have, are things such as showing no favoritism, showing mercy, and caring for the poor. James makes no mention at all of circumcision, Sabbath observance, and purity laws. Now, if one reads the Gospels, one can find plenty of cases where Jesus berates his fellow Jews precisely for failing to do the kinds of works that are most important to God, focusing instead on Sabbath observance or food laws (e.g., Matt. 12:1–7; 23:25–26). The scribes and the Pharisees that Jesus so readily calls "hypocrites" were devoid precisely of those "works" that James insists are a necessary correlate of real faith, even though those same scribes and Pharisees undoubtedly would have vigorously proclaimed their "faith" in one God. And indeed, that is precisely how James characterizes such pseudo-faith: as a declaration of belief in one God (the primary article of faith attested in the Shema [Deut. 6:4], a touchstone of the Jewish faith), a faith that James derides as one that the demons can profess, though they shudder at it. Put simply, James's concern is not with how one is put into right relationship to God, but with hypocrisy, and that was as much a problem in Judaism as anywhere else. Thus too, James does not oppose works to faith, but rather points to the absurdity of their separation (Blondel 1979: 148).

So, even if James is addressing a purely Jewish audience, there is no reason why James's diatribe against "faith without works" has to be a reaction to Paul or a misunderstanding of Paul. It could very well be simply another echo of the teaching of Jesus. But in fact I think it also likely that at least some of James's audience were of Gentile background.

It thus appears that James has features that can be linked to Greco-Roman moral exhortations, and to OT wisdom and poetry, and to OT prophetic material, and to Jewish Second Temple literature, and to certain other NT writings, both Gospels (especially Matthew) and other NT writings (especially 1 Peter).[81] On the other hand, James bears little resemblance to the letters of Paul, beyond what may be expected of their common Christian milieu. Even if the alleged "response" of James to Paul in James 2 is in fact a response to Paul's letters or teaching, it seems to move in a different sphere, deal with different problems, using similar vocabulary differently.

81. Resemblances can, of course, also be shown to later Christian literature such as Shepherd of Hermas, as well as later Jewish material such as the Sentences of Pseudo-Phocylides. I have already argued that the strong verbal resemblance to Shepherd of Hermas is an indication that James was already circulating in the early second century.

All this is best explained if James was written prior to the later heavily christological development of the church as seen in Paul and 1 Peter, prior to the parting of the ways between Christianity and Judaism, by a person of Palestinian Jewish background who was a disciple of Jesus of Nazareth, but written to a Hellenistic Christian audience, perhaps many of whom were of Gentile origin, but had, by virtue of belief in Jesus as Lord, become reckoned among God's people (see further Johnson 1995: 26–88). James, coming as it does from a Jewish source with Jewish theological background and assumptions, and Jewish identification of ethics and wisdom (wisdom from above is pure, peaceable, etc.), is fundamentally Jewish in outlook and grounding, but is addressed to Hellenized believers, either Gentiles, or Jews who had been acculturated into a Hellenic world. Thus, as a good preacher who "stands between two worlds," applying Scripture (the OT and Jesus's teaching) to a world different from that in which Scripture (both the OT and Jesus's teaching) was originally given, James speaks the wisdom of God using the forms, imagery, and rhetorical devices of Hellenism.

The Epistle of James is therefore very much a "real" letter from one person to others, even if we cannot identify the circumstances of specific people, because this is neither an isolated theological tome nor a response to a specific church's problems; it is a practical admonition intended for circulation. It seeks to evoke from those who claim to have faith the kind of behavior that manifests faith. It applies the righteous wisdom of the sage Jesus of Nazareth to the Hellenized "diaspora" who have professed belief in this Jesus as the Messiah (Christ) and Lord (2:1), using the language and style that communicated well in their broad Mediterranean environment.

Controlling Theme: Genuine Faith

Several concerns seem to recur in the Epistle of James. Davids (1982: 23–25) lists several of these in his attempt to outline the structure of James. Simply reading James for content yields the following issues:

Hearing and doing the word (1:18, 21–27; 2:1–26; 3:2; 4:11)
Speech control (1:19–21; 3:1–12; 4:11–12, 13–17; 5:9, 12)
Suffering, endurance, perfection (1:2–4, 12–15; 5:7–12)
Wealth and the desire for it (1:9–11; 2:6–7; 4:1–4, 13–17; 5:1–6)
Love, mercy, humility (1:27; 2:8, 13, 14–17; 3:13–16)
Wisdom (1:5; 3:13–17)
Prayer (1:5; 5:13–18)

Davids (1980: 97) thinks that the problem of suffering is the controlling matter, but although that is a concern at the beginning and the end of the letter, most of the central portions do not directly touch upon that problem. Suffering is explicit only in 1:2, 12. And the concern with suffering is indirect:

it is the response to suffering in faith and endurance that is James's interest. Unlike 1 Peter, he does not develop a theology of suffering per se.

I propose that the overall theme of James, the matter that occurs not just at the beginning and the end but throughout, and that drives the deep concerns of the whole letter, is that genuine faith in God must be evident in life (see Cranfield 1965: 338–45), and that if one wishes to avoid false faith (i.e., hypocrisy), the "faith said" must correspond to the "life led."

Genuine faith "saves" (5:15)[82] and is indispensable (1:6–8), but a faith devoid of works is a contradiction, an absurdity (Blondel 1979: 148). Indeed, the entire book of James is, in one sense, about the importance of true faith and the danger of a false, self-deluded, hypocritical faith. James's diatribes against hypocrisy are one of the many features of the letter that bear uncanny resemblance to the teaching of Jesus.

James's interest in genuine faith is introduced at the beginning of his letter in his exhortation to stand firm in the face of the difficulties that his readers may encounter, described as a testing of faith (1:3). It is also the request made in faith that is the key to wisdom (1:6). Lack of faith, on the other hand, or "doubting," is the cause of instability and failure (1:8). Faith is also presented as the crucial factor at the end of the letter. It is specifically the prayer of faith that rescues the sick person and eventuates as well in the forgiveness of sins (5:15). But more broadly, although the word "faith" is not used throughout, it lies at the root of the whole of James's exhortation. The patient waiting in 5:7–11 is nothing if not a presentation of the character of faith. Hence, the great diatribe in James 2 against a "fake" faith, a faith without deeds, is all the more trenchant because a "false faith," something that looks like faith but is not, is perhaps the most dangerous idea in circulation for someone who names the name of Christ (2:1). The tongue is dangerous because it can give the appearance of "faith" by praising God, but if it is simultaneously cursing those made in God's image, its employer is engaging in self-deception.

In fact, the matter of self-deception, which is what false faith is, is raised throughout the letter. The illustration of the person looking in the mirror in 1:22–24 is basically about the capacity for self-deception. This self-deception is also an explicit concern in 1:16 and 1:26 and is implicit in 2:4.[83] Self-deception is deeply troubling precisely because one can deceive oneself into thinking that one has faith when there is none.[84]

---

82. Although the sense of physical salvation certainly is present in the beginning of 5:15, there is probably an overlay of spiritual deliverance (forgiveness of sin) as well, as is implied by the remainder of the verse. This is also the case with the similar language in Luke 7:50.

83. In 2:4 "judges with evil thoughts" (RSV, ESV, NIV), which I render in the translation in the commentary section as "judges rendering perverse verdicts," is in Greek κριταὶ διαλογισμῶν πονηρῶν (kritai dialogismōn ponērōn), literally "judges with bad reasoning processes," possibly another indicator of the self-delusion of those who are gathered in the name of Christ but are showing favoritism to the wealthy.

84. For more on the centrality of genuine faith in the letter of James, see excursus 1, "Faith as the Central Concern of James."

Structure

James presents itself as a "letter to the dispersion," which, as noted above, was a type of circular letter addressed from some central figure, usually in Jerusalem or elsewhere in Palestine, to the Jews of the Diaspora, those "scattered" throughout the Hellenistic world. Such letters generally address how to preserve one's Jewishness in the midst of a world antagonistic to Jewish culture, faith, and values. The content of James certainly fits this character, though James is interested particularly in the form of Jewish faith and values advocated by Jesus. But the Epistle of James does not fit the pattern of most other NT letters. Its ending seems quite abrupt (though Francis [1970: 125] shows that abrupt endings without personal greetings are not unknown among both public and private correspondence). More significantly, James 1 appears to raise a number of items in sequence without an immediately discernible pattern, and often it is difficult to see the connection between the various components of the letter.

The difficulty of finding a convincing linear structure in James has resulted in a plethora of unconvincing or only partly convincing suggestions as to its organization or overall structure. Dibelius (1975: 1–11) seems to cut the Gordian knot when he identifies the genre of James as "paraenesis," which by definition has no overall controlling structure. According to Dibelius, as the genre admits of no overall coherent structure, it is fruitless to try to identify one in James. Dibelius could support this analysis by pointing to the "disorganized" character of Q, to which James has many connections. But just as later scholarship on Q has questioned Dibelius's judgment that Q is simply a "stratum" of tradition without a theological message, so it is now questioning his judgment that James is simply a collection of ethical exhortations with no connection to the Christian message. Increasingly, scholars who study the Gospels are finding the ethical teaching of Jesus at the core of James's message (e.g., Betz 1985: 35).

Dibelius is in some ways reiterating a judgment made by Luther, who also saw no order or method in James (*LW* 35:397; 54:425). But Dibelius acknowledges that pieces of James do have coherent structure. In particular, 2:1–13 is a unit, bearing the marks of a treatise (Dibelius 1975: 124–25), a thematically coherent collection of ideas that has the characteristics of both diatribe and sermon. But this coherency is only within the pericope; it does not apply to the book as a whole.

Further, some scholars have even seen parts of James to be contradictory. For example, Amphoux (1981) observes that not only is the style of the two interjected "Come now" sections (4:13–17; 5:1–16) different from the rest of the letter, but also they seem directly contradictory to the denunciation of judgmentalism in 4:11–12 (cf. 2:12–13). Amphoux thus argues that at least these two sections represent a divergent voice from that found earlier in James 4 and in James 2. The alleged contradictory character of these two interjections will be discussed in the commentary, but James is, after all, an exemplar of the genre of wisdom, and in wisdom literature it is not infrequent that seemingly contradictory theses are deliberately juxtaposed to demonstrate the complex character of wisdom.

P. H. Davids and the Double-Opening Theory

Operating with a two-stage authorship theory, Davids (1982: 23–25) accepts Dibelius's judgment that the various pieces of the Epistle of James were gathered by a later editor, but he attributes to the later editor more skill and intentionality than Dibelius was able to see. In particular, Davids builds on the observations of Francis (1970) that Greek epistles sometimes evinced a "double-opening" structure whereby the concerns of a letter first are sketched out and then slightly more unpacked before the body of the letter. Following this lead, Davids finds not a simple linear structure to James, but two series of thematic introductions followed by a development of the main themes in reverse order, with some closing exhortations piled up at the end:

I. Double-Opening Statement (1:2–27)				
	1. First segment:	Testing produces joy (1:2–4)	Wisdom through prayer (1:5–8)	Poverty exceeds wealth (1:9–11)
	2. Second segment:	Testing produces blessedness (1:12–18)	Pure speech contains no anger (1:19–21)	Obedience requires generosity (1:22–25)
	[Summary and Transition] (1:26–27)			
II. Body (2:1–5:6)				Excellence of poverty and generosity (2:1–26)
			Demand for pure speech (3:1–4:12)	
		Testing through wealth (4:13–5:6)		
III. Closing Statement (5:7–20)	Endurance in the test (summary of the three major themes; 5:7–11)			
	Rejection of oaths (5:12)			
	Helping one another through prayer and forgiveness (5:13–18)			
	Closing encouragements (5:19–20)			

This line of approach is promising. First, James does seem to exhibit a double opening somewhat along the lines articulated by Francis. Second, Davids rightly recognizes that certain themes recur in several combinations in James.

Unfortunately, close examination of Davids's outline tends to raise certain questions. For example, "excellence of poverty and generosity" seems a strange and narrow way to describe James 2, and "testing through wealth" poorly represents the stern character of the two warning sections that rebuke merchants and landholders. These seem, rather, to be carefully worded titles designed to make the facts fit the theory. Further, even the groupings seem somewhat incoherent. For example, the middle grouping—"wisdom through prayer," "pure speech contains no anger," and "demand for pure speech"—mixes together elements only loosely related (wisdom, prayer, anger, control of the tongue). And there is much material in 3:1–4:12, for example, that could fit under the poverty/wealth paradigm (e.g., 4:3). And verses such as 4:10 ("Be humble before the Lord, and he will exalt you"), which seems closely related to 1:9 ("Let the humble brother boast in his exaltation"), is yet in an entirely different division. Finally, the fact that the latter part of James 5 is treated as something of a bag of leftovers might suggest that James's structure is not quite so neat.

On the other hand, Davids's proposal is helpful in showing that the various parts of James are not, as some maintain, unrelated to each other. There is indeed, as I will argue below, a cyclic thematic recurrence, and Davids has shown that James is not simply an incoherent assemblage of miscellaneous exhortations.

Rhetorical Approaches

Recently, several attempts have been made to understand James in terms of its rhetorical effect. Rhetorical analysis focuses on how a text functions as an effort to affect people or cause something to happen. An example of an attempt to use rhetorical analysis to resolve the problem of James's structure is seen in Baasland 1982. Baasland recognizes that James is at heart a kind of wisdom instruction, but he also argues that the presentation of that instruction is framed as a *horatio*, a language event that urges people to do something or behave in a certain way. In particular, Baasland (1982: 122) notes that the opening of James (1:1–18) introduces all the main themes of the book, which then are set forth, argued, and drawn from. Baasland outlines James as follows:

1. *Exordium* (1:2–18): introduction to the matter to be dealt with
2. *Propositio* (1:19–27): setting forth the thesis to be argued
3. *Argumentatio*
   a. *Confirmatio* (2:1–3:12): proving the case
   b. *Confutatio* (3:13–5:6): disproving possible objections to the case
4. *Peroratio* (5:7–20): applicational conclusion

Wachob (2000: 59–113), more carefully restricting himself to the clearly identifiable unit of 2:1–13, finds the "complete argument" described in *Rhetorica ad Herennium* 2.18, 28 as the operating framework for this segment. He regards 2:1 as the theme (*exordium*), 2:2–4 as the reason (*ratio*), 2:5–11 as the proof (*probatio*), divided into an argument from example (2:5–7) and an argument from judgment based on law (2:8–11), and 2:12–13 as the *conclusio* or *peroratio*.

Hartin (2003: 128) refines and expands this to include the second half of James 2 and 3:1–12 as well (similarly, Watson 1993b), so that 2:14 is the theme, 2:15–17 the *ratio*, 2:18–19 the proof or *confirmatio*, 2:20–25 a development (in this case embellishment by example), and 2:26 the *conclusio*. In James 3, 3:1 is the theme, 3:2 the reason, 3:3–5a the proof, 3:5b–10 the development, and 3:11–12 the conclusion.[85]

The problem with these kinds of rhetorical analyses is manifold. First, rhetorical scholarship has been no more successful than any other type in producing a clearly identifiable and agreed-upon structure for James. Second, close examination of the material itself, away from the proposed outline, shows that the rhetorical model accomplishes its analysis by pushing the material of James into the framework and minimizing the fact that, at points, this is forced. For example, does James's discussion on "wisdom from above" versus the "earthly wisdom" really function to disprove possible objections to James's concern? Is 2:2–4 a reason or rationale for not showing favoritism, or is it rather an example of favoritism happening in the church? Is 2:20–25 simply an embellishment and different in rhetorical design from 2:18–19? Third, even when the analysis is restricted to a clearly identified segment (such as in Wachob 2000), one can, given the wide range of types of rhetorical argument in the classical literature, to some degree choose the model that seems to match one's theory about James's concerns at any particular point and then, after some massaging, find that it "fits." Does this truly help us better understand James?

Rhetorical analysis of James does, to its credit, recognize that the letter's overall purpose is not simply to "prove a point" or "make a case." Instead, James assumes that his readers share a number of basic theses and truths that he puts forward (Wachob 2000: 194–95) and then seeks to move his hearers to action. In other words, the problem is not that his audience has different assumptions and ought to change their minds; instead, it is that the audience, who are assumed to agree with James's theology, may be living in ways inconsistent with that theology. (Whether that inconsistency is real or hypothetical is not crucial, for such inconsistency is always a potential problem.) However, simply trying out classical rhetorical structures and making James, or some part of James, fit one of them offers us no help in recognizing the structure of the letter.

Further, such rhetorical analysis, although it does bring to light aspects of James's concern for Christian behavior, assumes that the author was

---

85. Later on in his commentary Hartin (2003: 203) treats 3:13–4:10 as another rhetorical unit, based on the topos of "envy" (following Johnson 1983).

consciously following a Greek pattern or else (unconsciously) developing a classically based rhetorical pattern in accordance with a Greek education. The fact that James has to be massaged into one pattern or another ought to warn us that although it is possible that James was indirectly influenced by such patterns of presentation in the broad Mediterranean culture, such influence is only a function of his linguistic environment and does not represent a conscious rhetorical effort.

Toward Resolving the Structure of James

Although Davids's outline seems forced, and his application of the "double-opening" (addressed in the body in reverse order) appears somewhat manipulated to fit his theory, I think that he has hit upon the general path to a solution to understanding James's structure. The difficulty in outlining arose because, as Western thinkers, we are used to the linear organization and thinking patterns of the Greek tradition, such as we frequently find in Paul. As Bauckham (1999: 112) points out, however, "It is a mistake to think that coherence in James must be sought in the form of a logical sequence of thought running through the whole text." Too much demand for logically linear coherence will simply result in Dibelius's conclusion that James has no coherence. But if James comes from a Palestinian Jewish environment, and in particular a Galilean Jewish background, we might expect something unlike typical Greek (or Western) linear letter structures, rhetorical or otherwise (cf. Schlatter 1927: 418).

Much more progress is made, therefore, when attention is given to central thematic elements rather than to searching for similarities to pre-existing Hellenistic forms. One of the most promising studies in this direction is that of Cheung (2003: 181–94), who highlights James's thoroughly Jewish character by identifying the Shema as a unifying thematic principle in the epistle. The Shema is theologically foundational for James, but beyond being a simple statement of fact (to which even demons can agree, 2:19), the unity of God implies his integrity, which should also be manifest in the unity and integrity of God's people. Thus James's concern that his faithful hearers be "perfect" (i.e., whole and complete, 1:4; 3:2) as well as mutually respectful and supportive, and his attacks against the non-integrity of double-mindedness, strife, self-deception, falsehood, favoritism, and hypocrisy, run all the way through the letter and are integral to a genuine commitment to the God who is one.

My own method in approaching James is as follows:

1. Identify the chief concerns of the letter by observing how much time the author spends on each of the issues and how vigorously they are presented.
2. Observe the structure within the smaller units that are clearly recognizable as such (2:1–13; 2:14–26; 3:1–12; 3:13–18; 4:1–10 [or 4:1–12]; 4:13–17; 5:1–6; 5:7–11; 5:13–18). By this we may discover within each unit a controlling thematic interest, with various related issues and perspectives, around which central theme other issues orbit.

3. Determine how these concerns are presented and interrelated.
4. Once we have a general picture, return to the first task of reidentifying the chief concerns and begin the process again.

We already noted the observation by Johnson (1982) that many aspects of James have a connection to Lev. 19:10–18, and that probably this reflects Jesus's own interest in the ethics summarized in Lev. 19. But these reflections are not systematic, or at least the organization is far from obvious. It rather appears that James, writing to the "diaspora" gatherings of Christians, has a number of mostly ethical concerns: suffering, constancy, care for the poor, showing no favoritism, speech ethics, unselfishness, conduct in recognition of God's sovereignty, forgiveness, and intercessory prayer.

Further, the studies noted above have made it clear that James 1 is a kind of précis or "epitome" (see Johnson 1995: 15; Bauckham 2001: 112) that summarily presents the themes of the letter, though not in a straight line but cyclically and from a variety of angles. Also, the "double opening," though perhaps not quite as neat as Davids drew it, does appear in principle to be operating: the several themes of the body of the letter are introduced and reintroduced. Then James 2:1–5:6 presents a series of admonitions that tend to focus on one of these issues while relating some of the other issues to that central one. The end of the letter, 5:7–20, in echo of chapter 1, draws a few remaining things together and to a close, focusing primarily on patience and intercessory prayer. As I will show below, the fundamental motif that runs straight through James is his concern with genuine faith.[86]

Structural Indicators

In the process of observing James's structure, certain features became manifest that seem to be functioning as structural markers, in particular the use of the vocative "brothers" and the use of proverbs as "closers."

"Brothers" as Discourse Marker

The vocative "my brothers" often serves to introduce a new segment, but some segments lack it (e.g., 4:1), and sometimes "my brothers" occurs in the middle of a discussion (3:10), so it cannot be used by itself to identify topic shifts (contra Moo 2000: 122). However, as noted below, "brothers" does often introduce segments and might serve as a secondary marker.

Proverbs as "Closers"

One reason James has been regarded as an example of Jewish wisdom literature is the density of apophthegms (short, pithy aphorisms), catchy turns of

86. Johnson (1995: 14) argues that the organizing principle in James is the polar opposition of "friendship with the world" and "friendship with God," an approach earlier developed in Johnson 1985. However, I think that at points it is a stretch to see this as the controlling rubric throughout James, and the opposition of friendships fits much better as one aspect of James's concern with genuine faith.

phrase, and summary proverbs in the book. Bauckham (1999: 63–69) suggests that these summary proverbs also serve as a structuring device.

Clear, short, apophthegmatic "sayings," often embedded in exhortation and sometimes concluding the several segments, can be seen at these locations:

1:20:   Human wrath does not work God's justice.

2:13a: Judgment is merciless to those who show no mercy.

2:13b: Mercy triumphs over judgment (cf. 4:6).

2:26:   Faith without works is dead (cf. 2:17).

3:5:   The tongue is little but makes big boasts.

3:18:   The fruit of righteousness is sown in peace for those who make peace (cf. Matt. 5:9).

4:4:   Friendship with the world is enmity with God (cf. 1 John 2:15).

5:16:   The prayer of a righteous person has effectual power.

In addition, if it is correct that in 4:5a the "scripture" that James has in mind is not 4:5b but rather the quotation of Prov. 3:34 in 4:6, then possibly the saying of 4:5b is another of these proverbial sayings rather than an intended Scripture reference (see the commentary):

4:5:   The spirit he has caused to dwell in us yearns toward envy.

Several other verses have some of the character of a proverbial saying, but are more expansive and less pithy:

1:12:   Blessed are those who endure temptation, for being proven, they will receive the crown of life.

1:27:   Religion that is pure and undefiled with God and the Father is this: to watch over orphans and widows in their distress and to keep oneself unstained from the world.

2:5:   God has chosen the poor with respect to this world to be rich in faith and heirs of the kingdom (cf. Luke 6:20).

2:10:   Whoever keeps the whole law but stumbles in one thing is guilty of all things (cf. Matt. 5:19).

3:2:   Whoever does not stumble in word is a perfect person, able to control the whole body.

3:8:   No one can tame the tongue; it is an unstable evil, full of deadly poison.

3:12:   A fig tree does not make olives, or a vine produce figs. Nor does a salty spring make sweet water.

4:12:   There is one lawgiver and judge, who is able to save and destroy (cf. Matt. 10:28).

4:17: To the one who knows a good thing to do and does not do it, there is sin.

5:20: The one who turns a sinner from the wandering way will save that sinner's soul from death.

All of these are in the form of observations and applications of wisdom and are expressed as third-person indicatives. But several of James's direct imperatives, while in the form of commands rather than proverbs, also have similar memorable and trenchant style:

1:19: Everyone should be quick to hear, slow to speak, slow to anger.

3:1: Not many of you should be teachers, knowing that teachers will receive greater judgment.

4:7–8: Resist the devil, and he will flee from you; draw near to God, and he will draw near to you.

4:10: Humble yourselves before the Lord, and he will exalt you (cf. Luke 14:11).

This pithy style not only has given rise to a large number of widely memorized verses in James, but also may be a key to the letter's structure.

THE PARALLEL STRUCTURE OF JAMES 2 AND JAMES 3

One of the clearest clues to the structuring of James lies in the parallel structure of James 2 and James 3. Even Dibelius acknowledges that James 2 seems to consist of two distinct parts, 2:1–13 and 2:14–26. The same bipartite structure may also be seen in James 3. The very close parallel structure is even more observable if we lay it out as follows:

Favoritism, and Works Generally (2:1–26)	Speech, and Wisdom Generally (3:1–18)
"My brothers, do not have" (2nd plur. pres. impv. verb; v. 1)	"My brothers, do not be" (2nd plur. pres. impv. verb; v. 1)
"for"	"for"
conditional sentence to demonstrate preceding (vv. 2–4)	conditional sentence to demonstrate preceding (vv. 2–3)
"Listen" (v. 5)	"Look" (v. 4)
first concluding (double) proverb (v. 13)	first concluding (double) proverb (vv. 11–12)
Secondary Development: Faith That Works versus Empty Faith (vv. 14–26)	Secondary Development: Wisdom from Above versus Earthly Wisdom (vv. 13–18)
"What good is it?" (v. 14)	"Who is wise?" (v. 13)
if clause with negative example (vv. 15–16)	*if* clause with negative example (v. 14)
development (vv. 17–25)	development (vv. 15–17)
concluding proverb (v. 26)	concluding proverb (v. 18)

This structure may also be observed beyond just these two chapters. Starting with James 2, James may be seen as comprising a series of discourses, circulating around the themes introduced in James 1: persecution and suffering, faith and perseverance, speech ethics and wisdom, poverty and wealth. Each of these discourses is marked off by an opening rhetorical question or a command (2:1; 2:14; 3:1; 3:13; 4:1; 4:11; 5:7; 5:12; 5:19), accompanied by the vocative "brothers," and is closed by a short summary proverb or saying (2:13; 2:26; 3:12; 3:18; 4:10; 4:12; 5:11b; 5:18; 5:20). This leaves only one interposed section, 4:13–5:6, which bears something of the character of woe oracles (see the commentary). It is not addressed directly to "brothers" as an exhortation but rather stands both as a warning to those who are oppressing the brothers and as a reminder to the oppressed that solace is at hand.[87]

Although James 4 roughly follows the same pattern as James 2 and James 3, it is not as tightly parallel as they are. Possibly, the discourse beginning at 4:1 already closes with 4:12, because 4:13 seems to be an entirely new subject. But 4:12 is not proverbial, and 4:13 is neither a rhetorical question nor a prohibition. This could call into question whether James 4 fits the pattern at all, but the difference may be because in James 4 the author is beginning to move into the final series of warnings and exhortations.

Summary and Outline

In addition to the thematic concern that runs through James (the necessity that faith be genuine), there is the structural device of summary apophthegms. James seems to close out the various segments of the body of his letter (after James 1) by using apophthegms as "summary statements" or conclusions to his several concerns, and I think that Bauckham is correct that these pithy sayings thus constitute a marker of the letter's organization.[88]

Also, James regularly addresses his hearers as "brothers," and although sometimes "brothers" can appear in the middle of a section, he seems regularly to use it at the beginning of each section. This, coupled with the use of apophthegms as summary statements, allows us to delineate the structure of James. Bearing in mind James's overall interest in genuine faith, I offer the following outline:

    I. Salutation (1:1)
    II. Overview of the life of faith (1:2–27)
       A. Faith and wisdom (1:2–8) ["brothers"]
       B. Pride and wealth (1:9–12)
       C. Faith and testing (1:13–18)
       D. Doing the word of God (1:19–25) ["brothers"]

---

87. The analysis here is similar to that of Bauckham (1999: 63–65) in that he too has taken his literary cues from the vocative "my brothers" and the concluding aphorisms.

88. Although my outline differs somewhat from Bauckham's, both are based on the same notion and thus are broadly similar.

These segments, with the exception of the interjected woe oracles, have a basic formal structure, most beginning with a vocative "brothers" or some variant thereof (marked above with ["brothers"]) and closing with a summary proverb or apophthegm (marked above with [apophthegm]).[89]

Theology

Dibelius (1975: 11) declares, "James has no theology." Presumably, he means that James, by virtue of its genre as "paraenesis," neither articulates a coherent Christology nor develops a soteriology. The theology of James is assumed more than expounded in the letter, and to some degree the reader of James must extrapolate the underlying theology by reading the letter against the background of James's Jewish framework and Christian commitment. Certainly he shares, as do all the NT writers, the common convictions of Judaism that

89. Remarkably, given James's close connections with the Synoptic Gospels, this is not dissimilar to the way apophthegms come at the end of some of the didactic stories about Jesus (e.g., picking grain on the Sabbath, which ends with the summary conclusion "the Son of Man is lord of the Sabbath"; Matt. 12:1–8; Mark 2:23–28; Luke 6:1–5).

there is only one true God, who is unconstrainable by reference to an idol or a particular place. God is the only judge and lawgiver (4:12). He will come in judgment (5:8–9), and when he does, he will exalt the humble and bring low the rich (1:9–10). He has spoken in the OT (2:11; 4:6). He grants life (1:12). He is unstinting and generous and does not revile (1:5). All of this is held in common with Jewish theology generally.

James is mainly concerned, however, with what may be called "practical theology," in that the author's interest is in the application of theology to lifestyle, and his goal is to manifest the character of God rather than articulate the nature of God.[90] This focus on the character of God, and of Jesus, rather than on the nature of God is seen in James's repeated references to God as "Father" (1:17, 27; 3:9), inasmuch as he both creates and cares for his people, and to the fact that he is a giving God (1:5, 17; 4:6). This focus is also apparent in that God's word or God's law is looked at in terms not of abstract truth but of its effect on character. And when Christ is specifically mentioned, the focus is on personal allegiance (1:1) or the character issue of not showing favoritism (2:1).

In this next section, which concludes the introduction, certain aspects at the forefront of James's theology will be noted (fatherhood of God, Christology, eschatology, and ethics). The reader should also consult the four excursuses at the end of the book, which take up some important topics in James's theology at greater length.

Fatherhood of God

Although the notion of God as Father has a presence in Judaism prior to Christianity (Wis. 14:3), it occurs rarely. It is, however, a hallmark of Jesus's teaching that God not only is Father to his people, but also may be invoked as a personal Father. This is also applied in James, who once again is seen echoing the theology of his teacher and brother, Jesus.

Three texts in James refer to God as πατήρ (patēr, father): 1:17, 27; 3:9. These are examined by Ng (2003), who notices in each case a particular allusion to the OT at work, and this allusion points to a particular characteristic of God that is being put forward by James. The predominant feature in all three is that God is creator (as of the heavenly lights in 1:17 or of humankind in 3:9). One might add to this the implied fatherhood of God in the generation of his people as a firstfruit of creation by the "seed" of the word (1:18). But the eschatologically redemptive dimension is also in view, in particular with reference to God's care for the poor and his concern for the fatherless (implied in 1:27), which so often figures in the OT. As Ng observes, God's fatherhood is far from an overbearing patriarchal notion of fatherhood as might be seen in Roman culture. Instead, it is, as is so often seen in the teaching of Jesus, the image of a protector and

---

90. These two approaches are put in terms of Jewish theology, which asks, "Who is God?" as opposed to Greek theology, which asks, "What is God?" (see Bauckham 1998a: 8). I do not think that they are all that separable, but certainly there can be a difference of emphasis.

provider and one who sets the pattern for the "family traits," which include especially caring for the poor and fatherless (1:27) and respecting fellow human beings (3:9). It is because God cares as a father that those who bear his name (2:7) are expected to exhibit this character trait as well.

The fatherhood of God may also lie behind James's frequent reference to his hearers as "brothers." Just as the OT regarded God as Father of the people of God (Israel), so James regards God as Father of the people of God to whom he writes, and this makes them all, in effect, brothers and sisters, with commensurate familial responsibilities.

Christology

James contains little explicit Christology. The exhortations are more generally theological than christological, like Jewish theology generally.[91] This is not to say that James is devoid of Christology. Baker (2002) makes an interesting case that in James, Christ is implicitly regarded as the teacher and Lord of the church. As such, Christ shares the quality and offices of God. Whether or not James can be pressed quite so far, certainly basic Christian convictions are in evidence:

1. In 1:1, James is identified as a "slave of God and Jesus Christ." Jews called themselves "slaves" only with reference to God, and this formula thus implies recognition on some level of Christ's deity.
2. In 2:1, Christ seems to be the critical factor in the expected obedience of the hearers, making Christ the embodiment of Torah. By referring to Christ as "Lord of glory" (or "glorious Lord"), the author makes at least a vigorous association of the exalted status of Christ with the exalted status of God. Paul uses the same phrase in 1 Cor. 2:8, and a good case can be made that the phrase was derived from early Christian christological interpretation of Ps. 24 (see Bauckham 1998b: 243). Further, Jews had faith in God, not in other creatures, and the expression ἔχειν πίστιν τινος (*echein pistin tinos*, literally "to have faith of someone") means "to believe in" (Mark 11:22). Admittedly, many commentators understand the phrase πίστις Ἰησοῦ Χριστοῦ (*pistis Iesou Christou*) to mean "faith of Jesus Christ," the faith that Jesus himself held. This is addressed more thoroughly in the commentary, but at this point we simply note that at the very least the text speaks of faith that is in some way defined by a commitment to Jesus as the Messiah (Christ).
3. In 5:7–9, James refers to the coming παρουσία τοῦ κυρίου (*parousia tou kyriou*, arrival of the Lord) and says that the παρουσία ἤγγικεν (*parousia*

---

91. The comment by Hartin (2003: 5) that the letter thus serves as a bridge to Islam as well as Judaism might make sense if James is seen strictly as a moral admonition. But despite James's paucity of explicit christological statements, the theological undergirding of James, like Judaism, is that of a personal, covenant-making God, which is quite different from Islam's fatalistic and static concept of Allah. And, as is argued here, James is not quite so devoid of Christology as it might first appear.

ēngiken, arrival is near); that is, the judge is at the door, reflecting Jesus's announcement of the coming kingdom and the coming Son of Man in the Olivet Discourse (Matt. 24; Mark 13; Luke 21).

So at the very least, James operates within an early Christian faith commitment to Jesus as the Christ, the glorious Lord, who will come in judgment, to whom the author is committed as a "slave." James's Christ thus differs sharply from the "christs" of other Jewish literature (contra Jackson-McCabe 2003), who are simply the actualizers of God's violent overthrow of "the wicked" and the restoration of the literal kingdom of Israel. Further, for James a commitment to Jesus as Lord (2:1) implies love, not vengeance; peace, not strife; respect for everyone, not favoritism; and humility, not triumphalism (see "Ethics" below).

Eschatology

Eschatology in James is focused on the expectation of coming judgment and is put forward principally as a motivation for faithful obedience to God. It therefore stands in the OT prophetic tradition. Further, as James is so taken up with the question of behavior being consistent with faith, it is arguable (so Baasland 1982: 122–24) that the whole of James should be seen from the perspective of eschatological judgment. Popkes (1986: 44–45), observing that the explicit eschatology of James is confined to the outer framework of James (1:1–18; 5:9–20), concludes (with Lohse 1957: 12–13) that eschatology plays little role in the central concerns of James. But Baasland argues that even the broad ethical exhortations of James 2–4 are better understood with the eschatological frame in the background (see also Burchard [1980b: 28–31], who sees James 2:14–26 as eschatologically driven). Once this is recognized, the implicit background of judgment can be seen in several respects:

> Eschatological reversal (1:9–11; 2:5; 4:6, 9–10; 5:1–3)
> Eschatological deliverance/salvation (1:21; 2:5; 5:11, 15, 19–20)
> Eschatological judgment (2:12–13; 3:1; 4:12; 5:4, 9)
> Eschatological reward (1:12)

Further, even James's use of the *telos* word group may entail an eschatological dimension. Eschatology thus pervades both the ethics and the encouragements found throughout James.

This eschatology is also distinctly Christian. The expectation is framed in terms of the parousia of the Lord in 5:7–8, using language closely aligned with that in the Olivet Discourse (see Matt. 24:27, 37, 39 and pars.) and also seen in Paul's letters (1 Cor. 15:23; 1 Thess. 3:13; 4:15; 5:23; 2 Thess. 2:1). There is also a close connection with Jesus's eschatological expectation, as James in 5:8 uses the very term (ἤγγικεν) used in the Gospels to describe Jesus's announcement of the nearness of the kingdom of God.

Ethics

As James is concerned for faith, he is concerned for ethics, which in Jewish thinking is faithful obedience. Recent scholars (e.g., Wachob 2000) rightly observe that the ethical exhortation of James, like that common to Matthew and Luke (the alleged Q source), is not, as Dibelius (1975: 48–49) supposes, secondary to the Christian faith, but is inherent to and inseparable from the Jesus tradition that lies at the core of that faith. Although some scholars have gone to the opposite extreme of finding *only* ethics at the core, and Christology and the redemptive story as secondary, even James, as noted above, roots his ethics in faith in Jesus Christ as Lord (2:1) and the reality of the rebirth through the implanted word (1:18, 21). Certainly, however, James's emphasis and dominant interest is in his ethical exhortation, because faith without ethical consequences is an implicit denial of the reality of that faith.

As with Jesus, therefore, James exhibits no interest whatsoever in the specific markers of Jewish ethnicity: circumcision, food laws, Sabbath; his interest is in knowing and doing "the good" (4:17).

Two Dimensions: Individual and Communal

James's ethical interest is exemplified by the two matters of 1:27 that are said to be true religion: keeping oneself unspotted by the world, and visiting widows and orphans in their distress—in other words, personal ethical purity (holiness) and interpersonal responsibility (love). The stress in James falls on the latter dimension: controlling the tongue, caring for the poor, not showing favoritism, not being envious or greedy, not withholding wages, praying for one another, and so on, summarized in the love command (2:8). But this is not to deny the dimension of personal purity.

Hartin (2003: 4–5) and Ward (1966) rightly observe that the community dimension of Christianity stressed in James is a badly needed corrective in our individualistic society. By no means, however, does James thereby mitigate individual responsibility, any more than the OT does. For example, an individual's own desire is the source of enticement (1:14), and anyone who is aware of "what is right to do" and yet fails to do it is guilty of sin (4:17). James does stress, though, that Christians do not live life alone; each one is part of a family, a brotherhood.[92]

The community to which James is writing appears to be determined not by ethnic derivation or cultic markers but by faith, specifically faith in Jesus as the Messiah (2:1). Nevertheless, like ethnic Israel, members of the community can be called "brothers," with responsibilities akin to those of family. This is a particular application of James's conviction (which no doubt he got from Jesus) that the summation of the law is found in the love of neighbor (2:8). The concept of "brotherhood" entails a mutual responsibility of believers.

This mutual responsibility is evident first of all in James's teaching on intercessory prayer in 5:13–20. As will be noted in the commentary, James, contrary

92. See the exegesis of 1:2, footnote 4, for clarification of this gender-specific term.

to our usual way of thinking, ties the promise not only of physical healing, but also of forgiveness, to the prayers of those praying for the sick person (5:15). While we have little difficulty with physical healing due to intercession, here James links spiritual healing and intercession, which makes mutual confession and intercession indispensable to the health of the congregation (5:16). This is possible because the spiritual health of the whole people is interlinked with that of the individual, so individuals must confess to one another and pray for one another. One can also appreciate, therefore, the importance of mutual forgiveness and mercy among the congregation (4:1–6, 11–12). As God graciously forgives, so must his people do so among themselves.

A second aspect of this mutual interdependency and responsibility comes in the identification of "you" with the poor (2:5–7). By setting "you" over against the oppressive rich in 2:6, James shows that the believing community is sociologically linked with the poor. Further, it is the poor who love God and will inherit the kingdom because they are rich in faith (2:5). It is all the more important, then, that not only compassion but also respect be shown to the poor (and thus no favoritism shown to the rich). The world attaches respect to fine clothes and gold rings, but the church is to attach respect to the image of God (3:9), which pertains to all human beings.

A third aspect of mutuality is material care. As already noted, James summarizes one aspect of true religion as concern for widows and orphans in their distress (1:27). This aspect also appears in his illustration of an empty faith, where pious words rather than provision are offered to the inadequately clothed and fed (2:16). Although the illustration serves primarily to drive home James's point ("What good is that?"), his choice of illustration, and the reference to "one of you," strongly suggest that James is responding to some actual unfaithful behavior (behavior inconsonant with faith) along those lines. In any case, James certainly would concur ardently with 1 John 3:17: "If anyone has the world's goods and sees his brother in need, yet closes his heart against him, how does God's love abide in him?"

Such mutual concern for well-being is given one further application in James's indictment of employers who withhold wages from those who depend on them (5:1–6). In tones resembling Amos 8:4–6, James decries the wickedness of such greed and threatens judgment like the dreadful "slaughter" prophecies of Isa. 34:2; Jer. 12:3; 19:6. The obvious implication is that such behavior is so radically out of step with genuine faith that only judgment and humiliation are in store for those who do such things.

Two Motivations: Past Word and Future Hope

James looks at the motivation to the ethical life from two directions: from the past, the commitment to Christ and the presence of the gospel (the implanted word) in the life of the believer, and from the future, the certainty of coming judgment.

Ethical behavior is expected of those who aver faith in Christ (2:1) because the gospel, the "word of truth" (1:18), which is also the "implanted word"

(1:21), is able to save souls. The first motive for obedience is thus seen in James's treatment of the perfect law—the law of liberty, which is the same as the "implanted word" (Laato 1997: 50–51). The faith in Jesus Christ as Lord must be a manifestation of the character of God.[93] Because God shows no favoritism, neither must those who profess faith. Because God shows mercy, so must his people (see Laws 1980: 304).

Several commentators have followed the lead of Seitz (1944) in seeing the origin of James's term δίψυχος (dipsychos, double-minded) in the two tendencies (yĕṣārîm) discussed in rabbinic Judaism (also evident in Qumran [see Seitz 1958]): an evil tendency (yēṣer hārāʿ) and a good tendency (yēṣer haṭṭôb). Certainly, one could see in James's use of "desire" in 1:14–15 (ἐπιθυμία, epithymia) and 4:2 (ἐπιθυμέω, epithymeō) some notion of an "evil tendency" in the human heart, but instead of a counterbalancing "good tendency," James points to the implanted word (1:21), which is the freedom-bringing teaching (tôrâ) of God, or to the act of repentantly drawing near to God (4:8). In Sir. 15:14–15, although God left humankind in the power of their own "inclination" (διαβούλιον, diaboulion), one can nevertheless choose "to do faith" (πίστιν ποιῆσαι, pistin poiēsai). Similarly, in James one can choose to follow desire, which leads to sin and death (1:14–15), or one can receive the implanted word (1:21), which leads to salvation, and one can look into the perfect law (1:25) and find freedom.

Does this call into question Paul's teaching that humans are powerless to do what is right (Rom. 5:6; 7:14–24)? It should be clear by now that James is not speaking about whether a person has self-contained power to do what is right; rather, he is presuming the Christian commitment of his audience and the presence of the implanted word, the law of God, written on the heart.

The other motive for ethics or faith-driven behavior is eschatology. Not just past commitment, but also future hope, is a motive for obedience, especially perseverance in obedience when obedience becomes difficult. This eschatological rootedness of ethics in James sets it apart from typical Jewish or Hellenistic wisdom (Wall 1990), though the lines between late Jewish wisdom and eschatology were already starting to blur by the first century.

In Greco-Roman culture, a strong motivation for ethics was found in the alternatives of shame and honor. A person behaved a certain way because it entailed honor; other behavior was avoided because it entailed shame. But James, like Judaism generally, found the source of shame or honor not in social approval or disapproval but in God's approval or disapproval on judgment day. God will humble those who have honor now in the world (1:10–11; 5:1–6), whereas those whom the world rejects, the "poor," will be exalted (2:5). James therefore urges people to "humble yourselves" so that God "will exalt you"

---

93. See the commentary for a defense of reading the objective genitive here: faith *in* Christ rather than faith *of* Christ. But even if 2:1 is referring to the faith *of* Christ, James still is making it clear that "you" to whom he is speaking are expected to evince behavior in accordance with some kind of assumed commitment to Jesus Christ as Lord.

(4:10). Eschatological motivation applies not just to the hope of eschatological reversal, but also more generally, so that the coming judgment is the motive for not grumbling (5:9), for showing mercy (2:13), for sowing peace (3:18), and even for all speaking and acting (2:12) and ordering day-to-day plans (4:14).

Consciousness of the eschatological dimension makes it possible to avoid two errors. The first error is to think that it is up to us to bring about justice. James makes it clear that although we seek to administer mercy and alleviate suffering, judgment is reserved for God alone (4:11–12; cf. 2:4). This is why James warns against anger, because it does not bring God's justice (1:20).[94] The other error is to suppose that since God will bring justice, no action of any sort is required. But as already noted, the believing community manifests the eschatological reality by demonstrating mercy in the present.

JAMES'S SPECIFIC AREAS OF ETHICAL INTEREST

Speech ethics. This is a common matter for discussion in wisdom literature, and James addresses the issue of faithful speech (speech in accord with faith) not only in his discussion of the untamable tongue (3:1–12), but also in 1:19–20 (the inability of human anger to work true justice), 1:26 (failure to bridle the tongue makes one's religion worthless), 4:15–16 (warning merchants not to speak without consulting God), 5:12 (which warns against oaths), and 5:13 (where suffering and cheerfulness are to result not in grumbling or boasting but in prayer and praise).

Wealth ethics. This is another common feature of wisdom, which also recurs throughout James. Obviously, it is of concern in James 2, in terms both of responsibility to use wealth for the health of others and of wealth not being linked to honor, at least not in a positive sense. But we also see wealth's transience in the reminder of eschatological reversal (1:9–12) and in the dangers of desire for wealth in its production of greed (4:1–6; 5:1–6). James even classes material greed with murder (4:2) and adultery (4:4).

Note that James has no interest in changing governments or corporations; he addresses believers, and he is concerned with the failure on the part of those who aver faith in Christ to respond to social needs or, even worse, to refrain from participating in greedy behavior. James knew only of an economic environment where very few were wealthy, and they retained and increased their wealth by their linkage to the political power structures and by exploiting those who were dependent on them. An economic environment of capitalization, a middle class, and productivity gains was inconceivable in James's world. Thus, the Epistle of James should not be treated as a manifesto for a return to "zero sum" economics. Nevertheless, we must keep in mind that James's harsh warnings still address those who shut their ears

---

94. Literally translated, the phrase is "the righteousness of God." In my view, translations such as "the righteousness that God requires" (ESV, 2001 ed.; the revision of 2007 reads "the righteousness of God") and "the righteousness that God desires" (NIV) are misleading. James's point is that human anger does not bring about God's justice. See the commentary.

to the cries of the poor, who pretend that profligacy is morally neutral, or who gain from oppression or exploitation. If someone who professes faith in Christ is participating in corporate greed or self-indulgent consumerism or is indifferent to human needs, then the genuineness of that person's faith surely is called into question.

Time ethics. This topic comes into view in 4:13–15. Since time is a resource, just like money, it too must be acknowledged as God's provision and used in accordance with his will. Christians habitually acknowledge this in attaching the letters "D.V." (*Deus volente*, God willing) to their stated plans, but what James 4:13–15 entails is not formulaic but rather involves the submission of all plans to God's purposes. As Jesus expressed it, "Not as I will, but as you will" (Matt. 26:39), which means at least seeking God's will in all of our planning.

Humility. This is another of James's recurring ethical concerns, and this too is attendant on the recognition of the eschatological reversal. Because the humble will be exalted (1:9; 2:5; 4:6; 5:15), it is wise to be humble (3:1, 13; 4:10) and to associate with the humble (1:27). Conversely, pride and boasting in worldly superiority are evil (3:14; 4:16).

A corollary of humility is mutual respect. Favoritism is a travesty of genuine faith, not only because it is contrary to the character of God (2:1 [cf. Rom. 2:11; Eph. 6:9; 1 Pet. 1:17]), but also because it denies the eschatological reality of the gospel and even violates the direct command of God (2:9). That believers must respect everyone is a consequence of the fact that people are made in the likeness of God (3:9). But such an ethic cut at the heart of the ordinary means of social advancement in the Greco-Roman world. Advancement came through benefaction, a system whereby a politically powerful and wealthy individual would be "patron" to dependents. In rejecting favoritism toward potential "benefactors," James cuts across the path of normal social advancement. People in our own culture customarily defer to the wealthy and influential, adulate the famous and beautiful, and shun the poor and unwashed. But James, like Jesus before him, sees God as choosing the poor over the rich. Believers therefore should be all the more careful to identify with the humble of the world.

Perseverance. Finally, James is interested in the quality of believers' perseverance under trial (1:2–3, 12; 5:7–11). As is noted in excursus 4 ("James and Suffering"), it is not suffering per se that is of ethical value to James, but suffering as an opportunity to exhibit endurance or steadfastness and to grow to be mature (τέλειος, *teleios*, literally "perfect").

SUMMARY

James exhibits an honor system that differs from that of the Greco-Roman world in which his hearers lived (Hartin 2003: 143–46; *DNTB* 518–22), and consequently he also holds to a wisdom that differs from that of the world. Where wealth and political power mean honor in the world, in James it is associated with dishonor. Where poverty means shame in the world, in James it means being rich in faith. Where patronage functions in the world to bring honor, in James one finds honor by respecting all. Where wisdom in the world is that which brings earthly success, in James it is the exhibition of gentleness, impartiality, and peace. May the church again hear James's call to seek honor from God and the wisdom that comes from above.

I. Salutation (1:1)

The "greeting" of James as an opening to the letter follows the standard classical form for a salutation. It identifies the sender and the addressees, concluding with the word "greetings." In spite of its commonness in secular Greek literature (cf. the letter of Claudius Lysias to Felix in Acts 23:26–30), the only other Christian letter in the NT to follow this form is the brief letter, also from James, recorded in Acts 15:23–29 (see Acts 15:23). Later Christian letters moved toward the use of "grace," "mercy," and/or "peace" in various combinations (all of Paul's letters, 1 Peter, 2 Peter, 2 John, Jude, Revelation), and thus we may have here an indication that James was written before the peculiarly Christian adaptations of the greeting had become standard.

On the other hand, James's salutation shares the address to those in the "diaspora" (or "dispersion") with 1 Pet. 1:1, and the self-identification of the author as a "servant" or "slave" of Jesus Christ resembles the opening of a couple of Paul's letters (Rom. 1:1; Titus 1:1; see also Gal. 1:10; Col. 4:12) as well as 2 Pet. 1:1 and Jude 1. As a letter to people "in the dispersion," it signals that it is intended, like 1 Peter, not for a specific church or persons, but as a general exhortation addressed to Christians in a variety of locations and circumstances.

Exegesis and Exposition

[1]James, servant of God and the Lord Jesus Christ, to the twelve tribes in the Diaspora, greetings.

"James," the same biblical name as "Jacob," is a common name in the NT. The author gives no further self-designation except the phrase "servant of God and the Lord Jesus Christ." A more complete analysis of the authorship question appears in the introduction to this commentary, but it is fairly easy to deduce that this James is the half brother of Jesus. According to Acts 12:2, James the apostle, the brother of John, was killed by Herod Agrippa in the year 44, and that is probably too early a date for this letter. The other one of the Twelve named James, son of Alphaeus, is barely known in the early church and would have needed to identify himself more fully had he been the author. But James the half brother of Jesus is widely known as a leader of the Jewish Christian community in Jerusalem. He is mentioned several times in Acts, is noted by Paul in 1 Cor. 15:7 as the recipient of a special appearance by the resurrected Jesus, and was highly respected as a man of

1:1

piety and godliness even outside Christian circles (Josephus gives him more notice than Jesus). He is sometimes given the designation "James the Just" or "James the Righteous." Even commentators who do not think that James the Just wrote the letter agree that he is the one who is being designated as the author in the first verse. Although there are a few difficulties with James being the author of this letter, most of what we know of this James fits quite well with its contents.

As noted above, this is not the only letter in the NT purporting to come from James the Just. Acts 15:23–29 records the substance of a brief encyclical letter from James to the church, indicating the agreement of the Jerusalem church with the Gentile mission of Paul. There James, like Paul, advocated acceptance of Gentile converts as full members of the new covenant community, though without the requirement of circumcision. He did, however, instruct them to abstain from certain Gentile behavior patterns: fornication and eating meat offered to idols, blood, and strangled things.[1] This concern with practical Christianity gives a picture much like the one that we get from the Epistle of James. Further, James's insistence on remembering the poor, noted by Paul in Gal. 2:10, fits well with the concerns of the Epistle of James.[2]

In this letter, however, James identifies himself simply as a "servant of God and the Lord Jesus Christ." Since James includes no definite or indefinite articles with these words, it is possible to read this phrase as "servant of Jesus Christ, God and Lord." But it is more likely that he is simply closely associating the two nouns: Lord Jesus Christ and God. In any case, we must remember that when a Jew put the words "God" and "Lord" together, the Lord in view could only be God (cf. 1:7, where "from the Lord" means "from God"). No matter how the verse is read, James is setting forth a very high Christology, identifying Jesus not just as Christ (Messiah) but also as Lord, mentioned in the same breath with God. Further, Jews saw themselves as servants of God, not of any earthly king or master, and as Dibelius points out (1975: 65), the term "servant" or "slave"[3] "expresses a definite relationship to the God to whose cult a person is committed." So again James's declaration of being a "slave" to the Lord Jesus is an implicit acknowledgment of Jesus's deity.

1. Since this is not a commentary on Acts, it is inappropriate to go into detail on why these particular prohibitions were included in James's Acts 15 letter, but it is not difficult to recognize that fornication was a particular problem among Gentiles, whose sexual ethics were similar to those of our own time, and that the proscribed eating habits were activities largely tied up with pagan worship rituals. For more on this, see near the end of the section "Internal Evidence: Palestinian Indications" in the introduction.

2. There are several interesting points of contact between the Epistle of James and the brief letter recorded in Acts 15:23–29. On this, see "Evidence" under "Authorship and Date" in the introduction.

3. The Greek word δοῦλος (doulos, servant) could also be translated "slave." The English word *servant* is sometimes used to describe even executives and rulers (who refer to themselves as "public servants"), but the social class of δοῦλοι typically had only slightly more self-determination than slaves of recent centuries.

It is interesting that although James is a brother of Jesus, he makes nothing of his physical relationship.[4] Were this letter pseudepigraphal, one would have expected the author to have made more of James's unique relationship with Jesus, as indeed was done in certain quarters of the church in centuries following. However, this James identifies himself not as Jesus's brother but as Jesus's servant, thus classifying himself along with all his readers.[5]

The Jesus whom James serves is further identified as the Christ. It is easy to forget that to a first-century Jew, "Christ" was not a name but a title, meaning "anointed one" ("messiah"), the deliverer and king expected by the Jews. The fact that James writes to "the twelve tribes in the Diaspora," whether that phrase is regarded as literal or figurative, reinforces that for him, "Christ" means the expected deliverer of Israel.

The "twelve tribes in the Diaspora" is, of course, a reference to Israel. Although many Jews had some knowledge of their tribal connections (e.g., Paul the Benjaminite, Symeon the Levite), the twelve tribes as distinct and discernible units or clans within Judaism were a thing of the past, especially the "northern" tribes (though the Samaritans probably were largely derived from northern Israelites). But the OT and later Jewish writings sometimes speak of the twelve tribes as an aspect of the restored Israel (Ezek. 47:13; T. Benj. 9.2). The notion is also evident at Qumran (1QM 2.1–3) and may lie behind the Gospel of Matthew's record of Jesus sending specifically twelve disciples to the "lost sheep of the house of Israel" (Matt. 10:5–6).[6] Since early Christians (Acts 26:7), following Jesus's lead (Matt. 19:28), regarded the community of believers in Christ as the fulfillment of the promises of restoration, James does not hesitate to apply this OT designation of restored Israel (cf. Ezra 6:17) to his hearers.

The "diaspora" is literally the "scattering" or "dispersion" or "sowing" of seed. In Hellenistic Jewish literary contexts "diaspora" was a way of referring to the fact that after the destruction of the northern kingdom of Israel and after the exile of Judah, ethnic Jews/Israelites were "scattered" throughout the Middle East and in subsequent centuries were even further "scattered" into Europe and North Africa. The Greek translation of Deut. 28:25 used the word in the prophecy that Israel would be dispersed throughout the kingdoms of the earth (the Hebrew text says that Israel would be a "horror" to all the kingdoms of the earth), and in the first century the term was well known among Jews as a reference to the Jews who lived outside Palestine (see John 7:35). Hence, if taken literally, James appears to be addressing his letter to Jews dwelling outside Palestine.

However, James appears to be addressing not Jews in general but Christians, either specifically Jewish Christians or Christians generally. Although

4. Interestingly, the only other NT writer to identify himself simply as "servant" is James's brother Jude.

5. The LXX designates Moses, David, and the prophets as "slaves" of God (Mal. 3:24 [4:4 ET]; Ezek. 34:23), connoting a unique relationship, but in a Christian context this designation applies to all believers (cf. Rom. 6:16–22).

6. For more on the "twelve tribes" as an expression of Second Temple Jewish hope for a restored Israel, see Jackson-McCabe 1996.

some scholars have tried to argue that James was originally a non-Christian Jewish letter that later was "Christianized" by the addition of 1:1 and 2:1 (see "Was the Audience Christian or Jewish Non-Christian?" in the introduction), several aspects of James clearly indicate a Christian provenance. But is James written specifically to Jewish Christians, perhaps those who are still active in their local synagogues?

Although the Jewishness of James is quite visible, James appears to regard the Christian community as the manifestation of the present people of God. Even if James is writing to Jewish Christians, therefore, his letter is not exclusive of Gentile Christians, and nothing in the letter suggests that James's audience is necessarily exclusively Jewish. Whatever the case, this letter has as much to say to Gentile Christians as it does to those of Jewish background.

There are, however, some good arguments for at least a large part of the audience being ethnically Jewish (e.g., their assembly is still called a "synagogue" [2:2]—the only time that word is used in the NT letters). In its earliest stages (as in Acts) the church comprised mostly Jewish believers and also regarded itself as being in close continuity with (ethnic) Israel,[7] but at the same time it recognized that what Jesus had accomplished entailed a change of concept of what constituted Israel. The new Israel was no longer so much a matter of ethnicity as one of religious commitment or faith (cf. Rom. 2:28–29; 1 Cor. 10:18; Gal. 6:16; Phil. 3:3). Ethnicity, therefore, if present at all, had little prominence in this designation of the recipients as "twelve tribes."

If James is intended not for literal Jews in general (as over against Gentiles) but for Christians (Jewish or otherwise), then the "twelve tribes" is metaphorical. Is, then, "diaspora" perhaps also metaphorical, that is, a referent not to geographical displacement but to the scattering of Christians in the Mediterranean world?[8] The term "diaspora" also appears in 1 Pet. 1:1, and given that that letter almost certainly is addressed to Gentile Christians,[9] it appears that the early church was using the term to refer to the fact that Christians were spread throughout the world by God for the purpose of being salt and light to the Gentiles. We see this happening in Acts 8:1, where members of the Jerusalem church are "scattered" (διεσπάρησαν, *diesparēsan*) in Judea and Samaria, and in Acts 8:4, where they are called the "scattered ones" (διασπαρέντες, *diasparentes*). The letter of 1 Peter also emphasizes that Christians are "aliens and strangers," outsiders because this world is not their true home (1 Pet. 2:11). Whether or not James has this distinct a purpose in the use of the term, his concern with Christians as sufferers (see 1:2) and God's sovereign purposes (1:18) at least means that he is thinking along lines similar to 1 Peter.

---

7. This fits with many other lines of evidence that James is an early letter, perhaps the earliest book in the NT (see view 1 under "Four Views of Author and Date" in the introduction).

8. Bede, in the earliest extant commentary on James (*Super divi Jacobi epistolam* [PL 93:10]), suggests that this refers specifically to the Christians "scattered" in the persecution that followed the death of Stephen (noted in Acts 8). But this is too restricted a reference.

9. Several texts in 1 Peter (1:14, 18; 2:9b–10; 4:3–4) indicate that probably it was originally addressed at least largely to Gentile converts from a pagan background.

II. Overview of the Life of Faith (1:2–27)

All of James 1 serves to give an overview of James's concern with the life of faith, or faithful life. All the concerns that will later be developed in James 2–5 are introduced here: the importance of genuine and unwavering faith, the nature and desirability of wisdom, not just hearing but doing God's word, the importance of self-control, the problem of self-deception, the dangers of wealth and the corresponding blessing of the poor, and the importance of prayer. The two overarching concerns of faith and wisdom[1] are presented in the opening paragraph. James is especially interested in the importance and indispensability of genuine faith and unyielding conviction, and this interest runs right through the letter. But it is also clear from this opening that James's audience is facing problems that are putting that faith to the test, problems that require wisdom. James writes his letter in response to the sufferings, trials, and temptations that threaten the integrity of the community of those who have believed in Jesus as Lord and Christ. The horrors of life can leave a believer confused, uncertain, uncomprehending, and floundering. Joy, which is the fruit of knowing God, and wisdom, which is the ability to handle life, seem remote and unattainable. James reminds the audience that trials are part of the package of faith and yield good fruit at the end of the day.

Although wisdom is a concern in James, of even greater concern to him is the faith of his hearers. Here in the opening statement it is "your faith" that is being proven, and it is by faith that one must ask of God, because without faith a person is unstable. James makes it clear time and again that it is precisely because faith is so important that actions and attitudes incompatible with faith must be attacked. Although the Epistle of James often is thought of as the NT book about the importance of works, it is genuine faith that concerns James. Works are important precisely because they are indispensable to true faith.

These verses therefore serve as an overview of the issues that confront the suffering community called to be God's people of faith in the world. In this way again James resembles 1 Peter, but whereas 1 Peter addresses the issues of faith and suffering primarily by reference to the redemptive-historical acts of Christ that are applied to believers by virtue of their identification with Christ, James addresses those issues by reference to the "wisdom" tradition of Jesus's teaching.

James has already introduced the overall concern of his letter by referring to Christians as those in the "diaspora." They are a suffering community that

1. See excursuses 1 and 3. See also Mayor 1897: 209–13; Lenski 1938: 538.

is "dispersed" in order to bring the seed of the word to the world. Being "in the diaspora" means that his readers face many problems and tasks in life, especially the likelihood of suffering, the necessity of faith and wisdom, and the danger of pride and wealth. So in his opening statement James lays out for the readers the issues that face such a community: trials (1:2–3), endurance (1:3–4), wisdom (1:5), and persevering faith (1:6–8). In the following verses he will introduce another complex of issues: pride and humility (1:9–10) and wealth (1:10–11), concluding with trials again (1:12). These are the issues that occupy the remainder of the letter, not in simple sequence but in various combinations and with various applications. They are all common issues in wisdom literature, and indeed James is often considered to be the "wisdom book" of the NT (see excursus 3, "James and Wisdom").

A. Faith and Wisdom (1:2–8)

Sometimes 1:2–8, along with 1:9–11, is regarded as a "double introduction" because there seems to be a kind of repetition of material within it (Francis 1970; Davids 1982: 22–28). Undoubtedly, these verses introduce the central concerns of the entire letter, but efforts to make the "double introduction" tidy (e.g., Davids 1982: 29) seem forced. Therefore, rather than press the opening into some kind of neat package, it is better simply to acknowledge that here in James 1 the author surveys broadly and repetitively the matters of concern to him.

Many commentators have noted that the Epistle of James often uses series of "link words" to develop a concern or a group of concerns. The link words are easy to see here in the Greek of 1:3–8 and can even be seen in translation: testing of faith produces *endurance* → let *endurance* have its *perfect* work → that you be *perfect* . . . not *lacking* in anything → but if someone *lacks*, he should *ask* from God → but he should *ask* not *doubting* → for he who *doubts* is like a wave.[1]

The first set of these provides a series of causal links (a sorites): testing (πειρασμοί, *peirasmoi*) → proof (δοκίμιον, *dokimion*) → endurance (ὑπομονή, *hypomonē*) → perfect (τέλειος, *teleios*), a series echoed in 1:12, where the end result is the "crown of life." These links in 1:2–4 bear an interesting resemblance to two other NT passages, Rom. 5:3–5 and 1 Pet. 1:6–7.[2] These passages likewise are concerned with suffering in the believer's life, the necessity of faith in endurance, and the joy that transcends suffering, and both passages comprise a sorites on suffering involving joy, trials, testing, endurance, and eschatology:

| Romans 5:3–5 | "We rejoice in our sufferings, knowing that suffering produces endurance, and endurance produces character, and character produces hope, and hope does not put us to shame. . . ." |
| 1 Peter 1:6–7 | "In this you rejoice, though . . . you have been grieved by various trials, so that the tested genuineness of your faith . . . may be found to result in praise and glory and honor at the revelation of Jesus Christ." |

1. Mussner (1975: 62) suggests that the chain may even begin with the greeting (χαίρειν, *chairein*) in 1:1 and joy (χαράν, *charan*) in 1:2, but since this involves unrelated semantic domains, it seems a bit too subtle. It would be like suggesting that a person hearing the phrase "carry that carefully" would make a connection between "carry" and "carefully" because of their phonic similarity.

2. For a comparison of the three passages, see Davids (1982: 65–66).

The similarities are strong in form and general content, but only loose in wording. Here we have not literary dependence, but a common theme in Christianity that stems from Jesus himself (Matt. 5:11). Suffering has an eschatological purpose (see excursus 4, "James and Suffering").

Exegesis and Exposition

[2]Regard it altogether joy, my brothers, when you encounter various trials, [3]and know that the ⌜proving⌝ of your faith produces endurance. [4]And let that endurance finish its work, so that you will be complete and whole, not lacking in anything. [5]But if someone among you does lack wisdom, he must ask from God, who gives to everyone unreservedly and who does not reproach, and wisdom will be given him. [6]But he must ask in faith, not doubting in any way, because the one who doubts is like a wave of the sea that is blown and tossed about. [7]Such a person should not think he will receive ⌜anything⌝ from the Lord; [8]he is a double-minded man, unstable in all his paths.

1:2 The passage begins with a command: "Regard it altogether joy." A large part of the life of faith is one's attitude toward things in life and one's response to events. We often can do little to control our environment and the things that happen to us, but we can control the way we think about them and how we react to them. Knowing how to interpret events and actions is a large part of wisdom, and the faithful attitude of the Christian is one of joy.

Still, to count testing as joy is a truly radical proposal. How can a trial be regarded as a joy? And how can it be regarded as "altogether" or "all" joy? As Ropes (1916: 129–30) says, the word "all," functioning essentially adverbially, heightens the effect of joy, and he suggests the translation that I have adopted: "altogether joy."[3] Hence, the NIV reading, "consider it pure joy," though possibly somewhat misleading (see the next paragraph), is semantically not far off. Although James later gives further reasons for joy in testing (1:12), here he indicates that testings are to be regarded as occasion for joy because they are an opportunity to endure and prove faith-keeping and because they lead to wisdom.

This is not to say that there is no component of sorrow in trials as well. James is not advocating masochism. The reason for the joy is not the suffering per se but rather its fruit, the character traits that it induces: endurance, maturity, and wisdom. The strange ability to experience joy at the same time as sorrow is a hallmark of genuine faith.

The connection between wisdom and enduring trials is found elsewhere in the NT (see especially 1 Pet. 1:6; 4:12–13) and is known also in Jewish wisdom thinking (Wis. 3:4–5; Sir. 2:1; 2 Bar. 52.5–6). The connection is especially clear

---

3. Compare Laws 1980: 50: "only joy, unmixed with other reactions." Mayor (1897: 31) takes the "all" as simply indicating a superior degree to "great" or "much." BDF §275.3, like the NIV, suggests "pure joy."

in Sir. 14:20–15:10 (esp. 15:6), which locates joy in wisdom, the path of which involves discipline and testing (Sir. 4:17; 22:6).

But there may be another reason why the enduring of trials may be counted as joy: they are an indication of the nearness of the end of the age (Davids 1982: 67–68; but cf. Laws 1980: 52). At least it is a reflection of the biblical hope already found in Ps. 126:5 NASB: "Those who sow in tears shall reap with joyful shouting."

James addresses his audience as "my brothers." In the OT "brothers" was used by Israelites to refer to fellow Israelites (e.g., Lev. 25:46; Deut. 15:3). The term is also used in Acts to mean "fellow Jew" (e.g., Acts 2:29; 3:17), and in both Acts and in the NT letters generally to mean "fellow Christians," both male and female.[4] James throughout the letter (1:2, 16, 19; 2:1, 5, 14; 3:1, 10, 12; 4:11; 5:7, 9, 10, 12, 19) addresses his audience as "brothers." The church was the people of God, who call upon God as Father (1:27), and who thereby are his children and hence are siblings.

Hartin (2003: 57) makes the observation that James, unlike the book of Proverbs or Sirach, does not address his readers as his children or sons, but employs a term that implies equal footing: "brothers."

Many commentators attempt to answer the question of whether these "trials" or testings are particular and real sufferings that the original hearers were experiencing (e.g., Martin 1988, who argues that 2:6 and 5:1–6 sound like real situations) or whether James is simply speaking in general (Ropes 1916: 134; Laws 1980: 52). But we can understand James's meaning without having to answer this question. All believers eventually experience trials of some sort, and at such times these encouragements apply.

Much more difficult is the identification of precisely what kind of "trials" or "testing" is involved here. The Greek word πειρασμός (peirasmos) can mean either "test" or "temptation." I will discuss the difficulties of translation of the term when dealing with 1:13, but the general notion of "trial" or "testing" functions well here. The context makes clear that James is thinking of the various pressures often applied against believers that threaten their well-being, which may very well cause believers to doubt the sovereignty of God in their lives. James therefore encourages his hearers to think differently than they might be inclined to think, knowing that when faith is tested, it is proven genuine by the test and becomes purer and stronger as a result.

The words "and know" translate a Greek participle that could simply be translated "knowing." Although the participle could be causal ("*because* you know that the proving of your faith produces endurance"), it more likely shares in the imperatival force of the controlling verb "regard" (Davies 1955: 329). Hence, **1:3**

4. The English term *brethren* is perhaps less connotative of male siblings than *brothers*, but is antiquated. In case it is not already obvious to the reader, we should note that in accordance with James's actual usage, terms such as ἀδελφός (adelphos, brother) and ἀνήρ (anēr, man; see note 24 below) and their corresponding pronouns are to be understood as inclusive of people without respect to gender.

James is also commanding his hearers to consciously recognize that the proving of faith produces endurance, as a way of helping them regard testings as joy.

Most commentators (e.g., Davids 1982: 68; Dibelius 1975: 72; Mayor 1897: 33; Moo 2000: 54) take the word "proving" in the sense of "test" or "means of testing," regarding δοκίμιον (*dokimion*) as an alternate spelling of δοκιμεῖον (*dokimeion*; see LSJ 442). In Prov. 27:21 LXX the δοκίμιον of silver and gold—the way objects are proven to be gold or silver and are delivered of their dross—is to put them in the fire. The "proof" of the gold is in the heating. Deissmann (1901: 259–62; followed by many grammars, e.g., BDF §263.2; MHT 3:14), however, argues that both here and in 1 Pet. 1:7 it is more likely to be simply an adjective, equivalent to δοκιμός (*dokimos*, tested, proven). In the neuter this can be an abstract substantive: "that which is proven." If "faith" is then taken as a partitive genitive, the result is "that part of your faith which is proven genuine works patience," and if it is an epexegetical genitive, the result is "that which is proven genuine, namely your faith, works patience." Both alternatives are awkward, and given the common substitution of ι for ει in NT Greek (BDF §23), it is easiest to take it as the noun "test" or "means of testing." Thus, testing is cause for joy (1:2) because the means of testing (i.e., suffering) manifests faith as being true, just as fire manifests the beauty of gold.[5]

The term "faith" is complex. In Jewish contexts it carries many of the features of the Hebrew word *'ĕmûnâ*, which implies not just belief in something but also fidelity, commitment, and truth. James sometimes is considered to be a book about "works," but in fact James's great concern with faith is what drives the entire book. His concern with works results from his concern with genuineness of faith, precisely because faith is so important.

Thus, the "proving of your faith" could mean (1) that which proves that one is truly committed and faithful, or (2) proof that one's trust is not misplaced (i.e., that God is faithful), or (3) the process of testing or proving of commitment (i.e., the purifying of faith). The first option fares poorly because "endurance" would be not the result of the proving, but its cause. The second option makes sense, but appears not to be the subject matter that James is speaking of at the moment. Therefore, the likeliest candidate is the third option: it is the process of the proving of one's faith that works out for the believer's patient endurance and maturation.[6]

Although Paul and James sometimes are set against one another, at least at this point Paul is in agreement with James that testing is good because it brings endurance (see Rom. 5:3–4). In James the sequence is testing → endurance → maturity/wholeness, whereas for Paul the sequence is testing → endurance → character → hope. The sequence is completed in James with reference to wisdom, and for Paul with reference to the Holy Spirit. It has been observed

---

5. In 1 Pet. 1:7, on the other hand, the adjectival meaning "tested" works better.

6. An epexegetical genitive ("the proof that *is* faith") is grammatically possible but semantically unlikely.

that often where other NT books speak of the Holy Spirit, James (who, with the possible but unlikely exception of 4:5, never mentions the Holy Spirit) speaks of wisdom (Kirk 1969). Paul occasionally refers to the Spirit as the "spirit of wisdom" (Eph. 1:17), and he sets God's Spirit and wisdom over against human wisdom (1 Cor. 2:4, 13; cf. 12:8).

The term for "endurance" (ὑπομονή, hypomonē) is a common one in Greek moral literature, especially among the Stoics. There it refers to patiently enduring whatever comes without allowing distress to influence one's convictions, thinking, or lifestyle (Plutarch, *Cons. Apoll.* 117). Endurance is a particularly desirable characteristic for a soldier (Plato, *Leg.* 12.942). The Greek term thus has a more active character than the English word "patience," which connotes passivity.[7] James, like Paul, has taken the term and applied it to the Christian's faithfulness in staying the course in the face of opposition. Also like Paul, and unlike the Stoics, James commends endurance not for the sake of distancing one's soul from the world of pain and dirt, but in hope of eschatological exaltation (e.g., 1:9). Endurance therefore is closely related to the biblical notion of faith.

The command to let endurance finish its task (or "have its complete [or perfect] work") reminds the hearers that testing has a purpose, a goal that is good. James does not want his hearers to defeat that purpose by impatience, by abandoning long-term obedience for the sake of comfort or inappropriate escape from testing.

1:4

It is unnecessary to ask, as some commentators do, what the "work" is.[8] James simply indicates that there is a "perfecting" or maturing purpose behind the testing and endurance, here described as threefold: maturity, completeness, and being fully equipped (not lacking in anything).

The maturing of the believer is simply becoming what God intends that a human being should be. In other words, to be mature is to be what Jesus was as a perfect human being, a goal both prescribed and made possible for believers by Jesus. When used of humans, the term τέλειος (teleios; see the first additional note on 1:4 concerning this word) typically refers to their being "full-grown," complete or mature (BDAG 995), though in certain contexts it can mean "perfect" in a moral or aesthetic sense (Rom. 12:2). Reflected here is Jesus's command that his disciples "be perfect" (Matt. 5:48), which gets echoed throughout the NT (1 Cor. 14:20; Phil. 3:15; Col. 4:12; cf. 1 Pet. 1:16). Endurance under pressure is a means of growth toward this completeness,[9] a

---

7. Note that James uses the word to describe Job in 5:11, and Job can hardly be said to be passive in his endurance.

8. Cantinat (1973: 66), for example, identifies it as love because Paul, in a passage parallel to James (Rom. 5:4–5), refers to love of God in the believer as the epitome of the chain of perfecting process, and Rom. 13:8–9 and Col. 3:14 speak of love as the culminative virtue and the summation of the law. This certainly fits and can perhaps be seen elsewhere in James (2:8), but it is not a necessary conclusion.

9. There is, of course, no thought of suggesting that anyone in this life ever reaches the goal of perfection and can then stop striving toward it (see Phil. 3:12–16).

completeness that is, to be sure, eschatologically determined (Mussner 1975: 67) but already in development in the believer.

Maturity (perfection) and completeness mean that the believer has integrity, unlike the man of divided mind in 1:6–8. The combination of "perfect" with the word for "complete" (ὁλόκληρος, holoklēros) suggests another dimension to the imagery: sacrifice. Offerings that in the OT were acceptable to God had to be perfect and whole, that is, without defect. Although James is not speaking in a cultic context here, this may very well have evoked the notion of the believer as, to use Paul's language, "a living sacrifice, holy and acceptable to God" (Rom. 12:1; cf. 1 Pet. 2:5). Thus, James joins Peter and Paul in attesting that trials are somehow a necessary part of the process of preparing believers for presentation to God.

"Not lacking in anything," or being fully equipped, perhaps also carries forward the priestly notion of proper investiture and preparation, but may be more closely associated with military imagery, being fully outfitted for battle. Since endurance was the prime virtue of a soldier, this certainly fits. Whatever the particulars of the image in James's mind, the meaning is clear: the strengthening of endurance through trials is an important aspect of Christian life, and without it the Christian is ill-equipped for service to God, whether that service be viewed in military, athletic, or priestly imagery (all of which are used in the NT at one point or another).

1:5 The most important thing not to lack is wisdom. The fact that at least some of James's readers apparently do lack wisdom suggests that patient endurance has yet to complete its work in them. Wisdom, generally speaking, is skill at life, particularly the ability to make sound judgments and speak the right words. The wisdom of James is not just skill at life, however, but the divinely given ability to live in a godly way (as will be developed in James 3) and to endure testing (Davids 1982: 71). In the later OT and in Jewish wisdom literature wisdom sometimes becomes hypostatized almost as though it were a person (a process begun in Prov. 8:22–31). In Sir. 24 it almost appears that wisdom is identified with God's Spirit, and at times James seems virtually to speak of wisdom the way Paul would speak of God's Spirit (Kirk 1969).[10] Whether or not that is in the author's mind, the wisdom that James is concerned with is tied up with the ability of the believer to live the life of faith. It therefore is not the wisdom of earthly success; it is the wisdom that bears the character of God (James 3:17).

Note, however, that this wisdom is not obtained by pursuing suffering, by hard work, or by any other such effort; it is acquired by asking.[11] The charac-

---

10. The connection becomes even closer when we remember that the passage in Matthew that speaks of God's generosity (Matt. 7:7–11) is understood in the parallel account in Luke to refer to God's giving of the Holy Spirit (Luke 11:13).

11. "He must ask" represents a third-person imperative traditionally translated as "let him ask." The point, though, is not that James is suggesting *allowing* a person to ask; rather, he is indicating that one *must* ask if one truly wishes to obtain wisdom. See also the additional note on 1:5.

ter of God himself provides the basis for such asking. God gives to all, is not devious or backhanded in his gifts, and does not upbraid people for asking. This declaration of the character of God as generous is effectively a central message of the gospel: God provides what he demands. Recognition of this character of God is faith, and nonrecognition of God's generous character is doubt. To doubt God's generosity is to cast aspersions on his character, and that makes wisdom unattainable. Once again we see the importance of faith in James.

That which is asked for and given is wisdom, the kind of wisdom that 3:17 calls "the wisdom from above."[12] However, the fact that the true wisdom from above must be received as a gift from God does not mean that human activity and thought are uninvolved. We look to God for our daily bread, but daily bread is also linked to our daily work. If we do not work, we may not be able to eat. As there is an indirect link between working and having bread, so too there is an indirect link between struggling to understand and obtaining of wisdom. At the very least, the believer needs to ask for it. But all this does not alter the fact that if wisdom comes, it comes as a gift, not as an earned wage.

The emphasis of the progressive participle διδόντος (didontos, gives) probably is not iterative—that is, God gives over and over again (though this is true)—but general. That is, it is the character of God to give; it is an inherent attribute (cf. Matt. 7:7–11). He gives to all. This may refer to the fact that God sends rain both to the just and to the unjust, but here James may have in mind "to all those who ask." That is, God gives without respect of persons; God shows no favoritism (one of the themes in James 2).

The Greek term translated "unreservedly" (ἁπλῶς, haplōs) is somewhat ambiguous. It is the adverbial form of the word for "simple, single, genuine, pure" and thus (like the dative of its cognate ἁπλότης) can mean "simply, singly, sincerely, plainly, purely" (see BDAG 104), as it does in all but one of the dozen or so occurrences of the ἁπλο- stem in the LXX. A derivative meaning "generously" or "graciously" (as in 3 Macc. 3:21) is sometimes proposed (Hort 1909: 7–8; Cantinat 1973: 69), and this certainly fits with the next attributive phrase, "without reproach." But the word is more likely intended to stand in contrast to the "doubleness" of the doubter in 1:8. The point is that unlike the giving done by many humans, God's giving is not devious; it is without complications or double-dealing; it comes "without strings attached," "without reservation" (Riesenfeld 1944; Mussner 1975: 68). Laws (1980: 55) suggests that both meanings may be in view. Whatever nuance is intended, God's giving stands in contrast to that of the pagan deities, whose gifts frequently came with twists and undesirable consequences. God's gift is sincere, openhanded, and free of hidden motives or trickery.

---

12. The verb "will be given" (δοθήσεται, dothēsetai) has no designated subject in the Greek, and thus "it will be given him" could be taken as a general comment about God's giving whatever good things are asked for in faith (cf. 1:17). One may infer from the context, however, that what James has in mind here is the "wisdom" that is lacking and thus asked for at the beginning of the verse. Hence, my translation supplies the subject: "wisdom will be given him."

God "does not reproach" or upbraid those who come begging at his door. When believers acknowledge their lack of wisdom, God does not dismiss or rebuke them. Although the Greek word ὀνειδίζω (*oneidizō*) in the NT often means "to revile" (Matt. 5:11; Mark 15:32; Rom. 15:3; 1 Pet. 4:14), here it probably carries more the classical meaning of "reproach," as it does in Matt. 11:20. Of course, this does not mean that God never upbraids, but he does not upbraid people for asking for something in faith. Again, this puts God in contrast with humans who are stingy and grudging (cf. Ps. Sol. 5.15–16).

One might ask why anyone would ever think that God would reproach someone for asking for wisdom. Jews were especially conscious that God is the source of wisdom, and asking for wisdom was the wisest thing that Solomon ever did. To my mind, this is one of several small indicators in James that he may have been addressing a wider audience than simply Jewish Christians, since people of Gentile background might very well have had the notion that a god would reproach someone for the presumption of asking for a boon.

Wisdom, suffering, and maturity (perfection) are very much linked together in the Jewish wisdom tradition and, in turn, to the NT development of Christology, which sees Jesus as the wisdom of God, the firstborn of creation, who has endured suffering as a righteous man, who was made perfect thereby, and who brought true understanding. Although James does not develop this christological aspect of wisdom, he is in line with the Jewish tradition behind it.[13]

1:6–8 A request of God must be made in faith. This could be understood to mean that it is up to believers to convince themselves that God will give them what they ask for and somehow to expunge all traces of uncertainty from their minds.[14] But this kind of self-hypnosis is not what James is getting at here. The "faith" required for asking is trust in the character and promises of God. Conversely, the "doubting" of which James speaks is not uncertainty about whether or not something is God's will, and it is not doubt about one's worthiness. It is a wavering of commitment to God (see Rom. 4:20: Abraham did not waver by unbelief) and the doubting of God's character (Mussner 1975: 70), especially casting aspersions on God's unstinting and unreproaching beneficence. This doubt results in an unwillingness to take a stand.

Thus, the doubter is depicted as a "wave" or billow in the sea that is blown by the wind and tossed back and forth. A wave is passive, susceptible to change and manipulation, because it has no shape of its own. It is always shifting, never solid, never sure where or what it is, without foundation. So too all the doubter's paths—whatever choices in life he or she makes (see p. 92)—are inherently unstable.

13. See Luck (1967), who finds the prototype to James 1:2–4 in Wis. 6:12–21.
14. Dibelius (1975: 70–80) notes that this is the sense of a similar exhortation in Herm. *Mand.* 9.1–7 and in Barn. 19.5, and he concludes that here it also means confidence that God will give what is asked. But "faith" here needs to be defined in relation to James 2:14–26, and the "doubt" in view here is best understood as the wavering of allegiance (Ropes 1916: 140) or distrust of God (Mussner 1975: 69), not the failure to expunge uncertainty.

The word here translated "doubt" is specialized in its Christian meaning.[15] The NT use of the verb διακρίνω (diakrinō) in the middle or passive voice to mean something like "to doubt" is reasonably well attested (see Matt. 21:21; Acts 10:20; Rom. 4:20), but in ordinary Greek the word means "to distinguish, separate, divide" (LSJ 399). In fact, it has this meaning in James 2:4. The special meaning of the word in the NT probably developed because "doubt" is a form of passing judgment on God's word[16] and is therefore the opposite of faith. The word doubt can be misunderstood, however, in that in common English parlance it is used to mean any uncertainty or questioning. But James does not mean that a believer may never have a measure of uncertainty regarding whether something is God's will; rather, he is condemning a lack of commitment, a divided loyalty (DeGraaf 2005: 741–42), or an indecision or hesitancy (Cantinat 1973: 21) that questions the integrity of God.

Therefore, the implicit command to "doubt nothing" does not mean that one should believe everything anyone says; it means that one should in no way hold back from commitment or divide one's loyalties. The negative μηδέν (mēden, nothing, in no way) is adverbial here, as it is in the parallel in Acts 10:20, where Peter is told to "go with [the men from Cornelius] without any hesitation [μηδὲν διακρινόμενος] because I [God] have sent them." James is telling his hearers that they should in no way fail to commit to God and must wholeheartedly and single-mindedly trust his character and promises.

As is so often the case, James's teaching can be traced back to that of Jesus, who also condemned double-mindedness by pointing out that no one can serve two masters (Matt. 6:24; Luke 16:13).[17]

The warning of 1:7, "He should not think that he will receive anything from the Lord," would be unnecessary if the doubting involved was simply doubting that the gift would be given. The problem is that this kind of doubter, a fence-sitter unwilling to commit wholeheartedly to faith in Christ and the actions that flow from it, might actually think it possible to receive something. James may have had in mind people who were toying with acknowledging Jesus as the Messiah, or those who had done so but were clinging to their non-Christian habits. They were attracted to Jesus the Christ but were vacillating.

This may explain James's use in 1:8 of "double-minded," referring to someone of a divided mind (δίψυχος, dipsychos). A person of double mind is ultimately trying to serve two masters. In some ways, such "double-mindedness" is the essence of sin and unfaithfulness (compare the "double-hearted" [lēb wālēb] of 1 Chron. 12:33; Ps. 12:2).[18] One cannot live a life of integrity and

---

15. The closest that a Greek passage outside the NT comes to the meaning "doubt" is perhaps Arrian, Epict. diss. 4.1.148, which refers to the "questioning" of some physicians.

16. At 1:6 a few late manuscripts even insert the word ἀπιστῶν (apistōn, unbelieving, faithless) before διακρινόμενος.

17. Str-B 3:751 refers to a parallel in the midrash Tanḥuma 23b, 24a on Deut. 26:16: "When you pray to God, do not have two hearts, one for God and one for something else."

18. Interestingly, Sir. 2:12–14 describes the double-hearted person as one who loses ὑπομονή (hypomonē, patient endurance), and Sir. 1:28 warns against approaching God "with a divided

faith if one is waffling on such a basic issue, and thus "doubters" are unstable. As Davids (1982: 75) points out, "For James there is no middle ground between faith and no faith." (See further the comment at 4:8, where James commands the "double-minded" to sanctify their hearts.)

The "paths" or "ways" is a favorite metaphor of wisdom literature, both Jewish and Hellenistic.[19] "Paths" refers to one's choices and lifestyles. The person who, literally speaking, is most "unstable in his paths" is, of course, a drunkard, reeling around crookedly and unsteadily, without clear direction, and so James is comparing doubtfulness to inebriation. Those who are double-minded are morally incapacitated and have difficulty discerning a wise path when they see it. They are unstable because they are unsteady, unable to stay the course (the Greek word ἀκατάστατος, akatastatos, implies unsettledness or fickleness). They are unstable in "all" their ways because their lack of a faith commitment affects every area of life.[20] All this instability is reflected in the image of a wave blown about.

James speaks so harshly of the doubter precisely because faith is so important. Faith is the grounding that prevents one from being tossed around like a sea billow (cf. Eph. 4:14, which uses similar imagery of immature people being blown around by every wind of teaching in human cunning). And without faith, one's life is chaotic, without direction or moral compass.

Additional Notes

1:2. The unusual word περιπίπτω (only twice elsewhere in the NT), which James uses to refer to "encountering" various trials, is the word used at Luke 10:30 to refer to someone "falling among thieves," and at Acts 27:41 it pertains to a ship "falling among" shoals, that is, encountering a threatening power. Already James is beginning to manifest his vivid language.

1:3. A very few late manuscripts (110, 1241, and a few others) read δόκιμον for δοκίμιον. As noted above, the meaning of the former ("that which is proved genuine") is possible, and the adjective δόκιμος is more common, so a scribe might have dropped the second *iota* deliberately. Metzger (1994: 608), however, notes that in the Greek papyri, δοκίμιον was used as an adjective meaning "proven" (cf. MM 167–68). The same textual variation occurs at 1 Pet. 1:7 (though with different witnesses), even though there δοκίμιον is used in a somewhat different sense.

1:4. The τελειο- word group is a favorite of James (1:4, 17, 25; 2:22; 3:2), as it is for Philo (e.g., *Spec. Laws* 4.26 §140; *Flaccus* 3 §15). Aristotle (*Metaph.* 4.16) defined "perfect" as "that beyond which there is no further advance in excellence or quality in its genus, which lacks nothing of its own excellence." Davids

---

heart" (ἐν καρδίᾳ δίσσῃ, *en kardia dissē*). It is, however, unnecessary and possibly misleading to parse out the two minds or hearts into the good and bad impulses discussed in early rabbinic theology, despite the evidence of its influence in Herm. *Mand.* 11–12. The real issue in James is faith versus unbelief ("un-faith") and the difference between the behaviors that accompany them.

19. See, for example, the Tabula of Cebes (for English translation, see Fitzgerald and White 1983), which speaks of "two ways" in much the same way Jesus does in Matt. 7. Later Christian moral tradition also uses "two ways" imagery (see especially the Didache and Barn. 18).

20. Later, James will point out the instability of unbelief/faithlessness especially as it affects the tongue, which is an unstable, evil thing (3:8).

(1982: 69), however, points out that James's use is unlikely to be that of the Hellenistic philosophical schools, but instead draws on the Jewish apocalyptic and wisdom tradition. It thus carries the weight of the Hebrew words for which the LXX uses τέλειος, namely *šālēm* and *tāmîm*. Although the word certainly has moral dimensions,[21] the burden of the word in James's usage is the completeness or maturity or wholeness of the person who is "perfect," not pre-eschatological sinlessness. Such wholeness also implies integrity, which stands in contrast to the divided-mindedness of the "two-souled" (δίψυχος) man of 1:8. Compare in the LXX the "undivided heart" (τελεία καρδία = *lēbāb šālēm*) in 1 Kings 8:61; 11:4; 15:3; 1 Chron. 28:9.

1:4. Mayor (1897: 35) notes that the word "lacking" (λειπόμενοι) in the passive voice meant in classical Greek "being left behind." However, its use here in James 1:4–5, as also in 2:15, probably is as a middle, for which BDAG 590 gives the glosses "fall short, be inferior, lack." "Lacking" is, of course, the opposite of being "perfect" and "whole."

1:5. The word σοφίας is a genitive of separation that functions with λείπω to indicate that which is missing (BDF §180.4).

1:5. The words "he must ask" in the translation above represent a third-person singular imperative in Greek (αἰτείτω), traditionally rendered as "let him ask." The point is that James is telling people to do something but is addressing them indirectly, using the third person. Modern English has no exact equivalent for this. Older English stated third-person commands with "let," as in, for example, "Let her speak" (= "She should/must speak"), which now, however, connotes something like "Allow her to speak" (see Wallace 1996: 485–86). However, "should" or "must" with a verb approximates the indirect third-person imperative, and so usually in my translation of James I have rendered third-person imperative constructions with "he should" or "he must" rather than "let him."[22] When the subject is impersonal (as in 1:4: "let endurance finish its work"), I have either retained the form (since the third-person imperative there is effectively a periphrasis for a command to cooperate or at least not to interfere with endurance doing its work) or shifted to some other appropriate second-person imperative (as in 4:9; 5:12).[23]

1:6. James's description of the doubter being "tossed about" may reflect the influence of Sir. 33:2, which sees the hypocrite as resembling a boat in a storm, but the imagery is closer to Isa. 57:20–21: "The wicked are like the tossing sea; for it cannot be quiet, and its waters toss up mire and dirt. 'There is no peace [*šālôm*, wholeness],' says my God, 'for the wicked.'"

1:7. Some manuscripts omit the word "anything" (τι), which keeps wisdom as the direct object, but James probably is pointing out that any prayer devoid of faith has no reason to expect an answer.

1:7. The use of the negative present imperative μὴ οἰέσθω as opposed to the aorist subjunctive might indicate a command, "he should stop thinking," rather than the simple "he should not think" (so BDF §336.3; MHT 3:76). In my judgment, however, this example fits better with the category of BDF §336.2,

---

21. Hartin (2003: 72) notes three dimensions to this "perfection": wholeness, righteousness, and obedience.

22. Compare 1:5 in the NIV ("he should ask") and 1:7 in the ESV ("that person must not suppose"). The rendering of an imperative with "should" or "must" is even occasionally done with second-person imperatives when the subject "you" is augmented with a noun or adjective, as in 3:1, where "be (ye) not many teachers" is properly rendered "not many of you should be teachers" (cf. NIV, ESV).

23. James 4:9 works as a third-person imperative in English: "Your laughter be turned to mourning," but since this use of the imperative infinitive ("be") is also outmoded, and since the context is a series of second-person commands to repentance, I have rendered it in the translation below as a second-person imperative: "Turn your laughter into mourning."

indicating the general character of "thinking" as an ongoing action. The difference from an aorist subjunctive prohibition would in any case be subtle, and probably it ought not to be pressed.

1:8. By repunctuation, ἀνήρ could be taken as the subject of λήμψεται in the previous verse (as RSV has it: "That person [the doubter] must not suppose that a double-minded man . . . will receive anything from the Lord"). But it is better to take it as appositional, as reflected in my translation. The trenchant use of apposition appears to be a stylistic feature of James (cf. 2:4; 3:2, 6, 8; 4:12).

1:8. The word ἀνήρ (like Heb. ʾîš) often is more gender specific than ἄνθρωπος, but in none of the six occurrences in James does it function in contrast with γυνή; rather, it serves in a general way (1:8, 12, 20, 23; 2:2; 3:2) and thus is equivalent to "a person."[24] Although in James ἄνθρωπος also sometimes appears as the general term for a person (as in 1:19; 2:20, 24), it frequently serves to underline humanity as opposed to individuality or personhood (e.g., 5:17: Elijah was a human like us; 3:8: no human can tame the tongue; 3:9: we curse other humans even though they are made in God's likeness).

1:8. The word δίψυχος is unattested prior to James, and it may have been coined by him or by another Christian (Porter 1990), possibly in reflection of the Hebrew idiom of being "double-hearted" (Ps. 12:2 [12:3 MT; 11:3 LXX]; cf. Sir. 1:28).[25] The word δίψυχος is quickly picked up in the early postapostolic period (e.g., 1 Clem. 11.2; 23.3; 2 Clem. 11.2; δίψυχος and its cognates occur more than fifty times in the Shepherd of Hermas; also cf. Did. 4.4; Clement of Alexandria, *Strom.* 1.29). See Marshall 1973.

24. See L&N 1:104. Although BDAG (79) classifies most occurrences of ἀνήρ (*anēr*) in James under the general heading of "adult human male," it does so under the specific heading of a focus on characteristics of being a person rather than in contrast to female humans, or specifically with reference to "maleness." James certainly is not suggesting that only male humans are capable of being double-minded or that doubt is an especially masculine trait.

25. For similarities to the "double-minded" notion in the Dead Sea Scrolls, see Wolverton 1956.

B. Pride and Wealth (1:9–12)

The second of James's opening statements raises the issue of wealth. It links both to the previous material on testing (1:2), because testing shows the evanescence of earthly riches and prepares the poor person for the crown of life. The earlier command to find joy in testing is given further development here, because testing brings down the wealthy (it shows how transitory wealth is) and will bring up the poor so that they can receive the eschatological blessing of eternal life. James also indicates something of the "already" character of the eschatological hope, because the person in humble circumstances now can "glory" in the future state.

Exegesis and Exposition

⁹The humble brother should glory in his exaltedness, ¹⁰and the rich one [glory] in his lowliness, because as a flower in the grass he will pass away. ¹¹For the sun rises with scorching heat and withers the grass, and its flower falls and its lovely appearance is lost. So also the rich man in his ventures will fade away. ¹²Blessed is the man who endures testing, because having been proven he will receive the crown of life that ⌜he⌝ has promised to those who love him.

The verses of 1:9–11 sometimes are considered an opening salvo against wealth, **1:9–11** a warm-up for the even harsher language of 5:1–6. But although the rich man is viewed as a man in danger, and although elsewhere James rails against the deceitful practices of the wealthy, the main problem here is not wealth per se but certain attitudes toward wealth, both on the part of the wealthy themselves and on the part of those who would pander to them. The intended audience, early Christian believers, almost certainly comprised mostly poor folk,[1] and the focus here is on encouraging these poor, reminding them of the eschatological reversal, when the poor will become rich.

The word "humble" (ταπεινός, *tapeinos*) ordinarily focuses not on economic poverty but on lowliness, either humble status in society or humble attitude. However, it can refer to the economically poor, since they are almost always of low status in society. Since here James contrasts the "lowly" man with the "rich," it is clear that James is addressing not those of humble attitude, but those of humble position. According to Jesus, one of the principal marks of

---

1. Though they are not, for the most part, destitute. See the comments in the introduction regarding the social situation of the original audience; see also Edgar (2001), who points out that the readers are being challenged to move away from the patronage systems of the ancient Mediterranean culture toward exclusive allegiance to God.

the arrival of God's kingdom is the preaching of good news to the poor (Matt. 11:5, echoing Isa. 61:1). It was good news for the poor who were hearing Jesus (not so good for the rich) because it was news of eschatological reversal: the exalted would be made low, and the low would be raised up. In 1:9–12 James makes reference to this expected eschatological reversal.

The word here translated "should glory in" (καυχάσθω, *kauchasthō*) is difficult to translate. It is a third-person imperative and thus perhaps could be more forcefully translated as "must glory in," though the purpose is encouragement, not compulsion.[2] The more difficult matter, though, is the word's semantic domain. Sometimes rendered "boast," it signifies either the feelings or the declarations of pride and joy that result when someone or something that is dear to one is recognized and honored by others (see BDAG 536). The term therefore can be used in either a good sense ("delight in, be proud of, rejoice over") or a bad sense ("brag about").[3] The determining factor is whether the cause of the delight is appropriate. Boasting in one's racial identity or intelligence, for example, is inappropriate because it takes delight in the wrong things and takes glory away from where it belongs. Some might say that it was wrong for Paul to "glory" in the Corinthian believers (the same Greek word is used in 2 Cor. 9:2 and other places), but being proud of someone who is dear to you does not necessarily take glory from God. (Hence, it is right for parents to be proud of their children as long as it promotes rather than detracts from God's glory.) Paul can even glory in or boast of his weakness (2 Cor. 12:9) because it signifies all the greater glory of God, and James tells Christians that they too can "boast" in their humble circumstances.

We have already noted that the "brother" signifies a believer. Unbelievers, be they ever so poor, have no such reason for delight, because they have no eschatological hope. It is the humble *believers* of low earthly station who are told to rejoice in their high position, because God has chosen the poor in the world to be wealthy in faith (2:5).

James's contrast between the rich and humble in 1:10–11 raises the question of whether James envisions rich Christians who "glory" in knowing that they will be brought low, or whether he simply is reminding readers that the flip side of exaltation of the lowly is the humiliation of the exalted. Grammatically, it appears that the verb ("he should glory") of this verse should be borrowed from the parallel previous verse,[4] thus yielding that the wealthy person should glory in humiliation. But it is difficult to make sense of this. If

2. See the additional note on 1:5 regarding the translation of third-person imperatives.

3. Paul, the only other NT writer to use the word, uses it both negatively and positively (cf. Gal. 6:13 with 6:14).

4. Mayor (1897: 43) puts it strongly: "No interpretation is admissible which does not supply the imperative καυχάσθω." Hartin (2003: 69) is also persuaded by the grammar, claiming that "if James were thinking of the rich person as outside the community he would have indicated that more clearly within this ambiguous phrase." But biblical language is simply not as precise as Mayor's generation would have liked. Cantinat (1973: 78) points to the poetically structured parallelism of 1:9 and 1:10, but this by itself does not determine the question.

the term "brother" too should be borrowed from 1:9, the meaning is that the believer who possesses wealth should "glory" in knowing that such wealth is transitory and unimportant and that one's hope is in the Lord. This reading would parallel 1 Tim. 6:17. The boasting would then be a kind of reverse boasting, as though the word "glory in" were in quotation marks, or a heroic acceptance of a future humiliation for the greater good of one's soul.[5] This construction also entails providing an understood subject (such as "his riches") for the verb "will pass away" rather than the rich believer per se.[6] The fading of wealth could then be one of the eschatological "testings" of 1:2 and 1:12 in which a wealthy believer might rejoice. But the withering of the flower in OT imagery refers to judgment and perishing, and it is difficult to see how one could rejoice over the expectation of being humiliated on judgment day, since the humiliation in question would be condemnation. Further, the verb "will pass away" most naturally has "rich man" as its subject.

Thus, several commentators propose that the verbal force of "glorying in" is either bitterly ironic or has faded out in 1:10–11, and that James is simply pointing out that the rich person will be humbled, that as a flower fades in the heat,[7] so too will the rich person fade away and be no more.[8] As is likely the case also in 5:1–6, James thus is not addressing some rich believers and telling them to be glad that they will be humbled; rather, he is simply encouraging humble poor believers by pointing out that rich people, along with their riches, are transitory and ephemeral. The OT passages (Job 14:2; Ps. 103:15; especially Isa. 40:6–8) that use this imagery say even more: *all* human beings are transitory and ephemeral. People become substantial and vital only by their relationship to God's steadfast love (Ps. 103:17) through his eternal word (Isa. 40:6–8). The person who is wealthy in earthly goods is frequently immune to recognizing that which truly would provide substance and value and hence is generally "poor in faith."

If it is correct to date the material content of James as quite early in the community's development, it means that the line between Judaism and Christianity had not yet been sharply drawn. Although James obviously is addressed

5. Historically, this has been the most common way of interpreting this verse (e.g., Calvin 1948: 286; Mayor 1897: 43; Moo 2000: 68–69; Mussner 1975: 74; Ropes 1916: 148; Hartin 2003: 69). Other commentaries, however, turn away from this view (e.g., Dibelius 1975: 85; Laws 1980: 63; Davids 1982: 76–77; Martin 1988: 23).

6. Blomberg (1999: 149) points out that the reference in the following verse (1:11) to "its lovely appearance" (literally "beauty of its face") could be understood as analogous to the rich brother's wealth that fades; that is, the wealth is the outward show of beauty. But as Blomberg goes on to recognize, it is not the wealth that fades, but rather the wealthy, and "the beauty of its face" is more likely simply idiomatic for "its lovely appearance."

7. Sometimes the "burning heat" (καύσων, *kausōn*) is understood to refer to the burning wind of the sirocco, since the text that James is echoing (Isa. 40) appears to do so. But the sirocco is not a function of the rising of the sun, so this does not appear to have been in James's mind.

8. The verb παρέρχομαι (*parerchomai*, pass away) is used by Jesus to refer to the passing away of heaven and earth (Matt. 5:18 [= Luke 16:17]; Matt. 24:34–35 and pars.) and thus is associated with judgment (cf. 2 Pet. 3:10) and the change of the ages (2 Cor. 5:17).

to people who have believed in Christ on some level (2:1), that belief was still in the process of being formed and applied. Therefore, asking whether the "rich man" of 1:10 is a "believer" may be asking a question foreign to the issues that James is addressing (Dibelius 1975: 85 argues that "the poor" is in some ways a biblical designation for "believers" and hence is not a purely economic term). Certainly, there are at least some "rich men" who have some relationship with the community, or else passages such as 2:1–4 would be unnecessary. On the other hand, James later states plainly that it is the poor in worldly things who are heirs of the kingdom (2:5), and the rich appear in the role of enemies (2:6) who even blaspheme the name of Christ (see the commentary on 2:7) and are "fat for slaughter" because they oppress the poor (5:1–6). At least we may say that James's Christian audience was mostly poor, almost by definition.[9] If, however, there are rich believers in James's purview, then if they have any hope in God's kingdom, they will necessarily be "glorying" in their imminent "loss of all things for the sake of knowing Christ," even as the poor believers glory in their imminent gain of all things in Christ.

It was a common error in the first century, as much as today, to suppose that one's prosperity is the result of "living right." It was assumed that wealth and worldly success were signs of approval by God (or the gods). Indeed, even today people sometimes are plagued by the idea that earthly success is a sign that God is pleased with them, or that earthly struggles are evidence of God's displeasure. James, like Jesus, forcefully corrects that notion. The kingdom of God involves an "eschatological reversal,"[10] an exalting of the humble and a humbling of the exalted (cf. Matt. 23:12), and it is the weak, poor, and humble whom God has chosen, not the successful, prosperous, and talented.

Therefore, even though James is unlikely to have had in mind a "heroic" eschatological boasting on the part of the wealthy believer, 1:9–10 does (probably deliberately) echo Jer. 9:23–24: "Let not the wise man boast in his wisdom, let not the mighty man boast in his might, let not the rich man boast in his riches, but let him who boasts boast in this, that he understands and knows me, that I am the LORD who practices steadfast love, justice, and righteousness in the earth."[11]

We should also remember that the Jewish wisdom genre is a literature full of contrasts, hyperbole, and generalized absolutes.[12] The material about field

9. As noted above, in Matt. 11:5 Jesus denotes the presence of the kingdom of heaven by pointing to the fact "the poor are evangelized." It is the poor who are targeted as recipients of the gospel.
10. Hauck (1926: 55) observes that 1:11 is an implicit reference to eschatological judgment.
11. Recently, Williams (2002) substantially reinforces this connection between James and Jer. 9 and argues for the "heroic" view of the rich believer rejoicing in eschatological lowliness.
12. That 1:11 probably is standard Semitic proverbial material is possibly evident in its series of "gnomic" aorists: ἀνέτειλεν (*aneteilen*, rises), ἐξήρανεν (*exēranen*, withers), ἐξέπεσεν (*exepesen*, falls), ἀπώλετο (*apōleto*, perishes). Most commonly, gnomic (general) truths are expressed in Greek with the present tense (Goodwin 1881: 54 [§157]). The use of the aorist, however, though not entirely foreign to Greek (Goodwin 1881: 53–55), is more common in the NT (MHT 3:73), possibly because it corresponds well to an axiomatic use of the Hebrew perfect,

flowers drying up under the sun's scorching heat is a standard reminder of judgment and the evanescence of human life (cf. Job 14:2; Ps. 37:2; 90:5–6; 103:15; Isa. 40:6–8; 51:12; 2 Bar. 82.7). James is closest in wording to Isa. 40, which he may be consciously echoing. But the Isaianic contrast with the word of God that abides forever is missing in James, which is making use of the imagery only to warn of the transience of wealth and therefore the transience of those who take their identity from wealth. As a flower's beauty vanishes in the face of adversity, so the wealthy will fade away in their pursuits, very much like double-minded doubters are unstable in their ways (1:8). The earthly attractiveness of wealth and the reflected attractiveness of those who have wealth are simply doomed to perish.

How do we who live in relative economic prosperity, especially as compared with the great majority of the world's peoples, apply this passage? Should we as believers quickly divest ourselves of as much material prosperity as we can manage? Or should we instead ignore James's comments as the impractical hyperbolic rantings of an overly enthusiastic ascetic?

Either reaction fails to deal with the real problem of wealth that James is concerned about, both here and in James 2 and James 5. Wealth leads the wealthy to arrogance, pride, and ruthlessness, to faith in themselves instead of in God, and it works against their citizenship in God's kingdom. Wealth also can lead the poor person to envy, sycophancy, and obsequiousness. It is not, however, wealth as such that is the problem; instead, it is the rich person's attachment to it and the poor person's lust for it, a confidence in it rather than in God, and a rich person's self-exaltation above the concerns of the poor.

Therefore, although I do not think that James had in mind a "wealthy brother" rejoicing in the knowledge that wealth is transitory, that may be the best way to apply it. Wealthy Christians who are deeply conscious of the transitoriness of wealth, who do not get attached to it, who do not place confidence in it, who do not find their identity in it, and who do not use wealth to put themselves above others may indeed "glory" or "boast" in knowing that ultimately their position is a lowly one. Wealthy Christians know that since it is the poor whom God chooses (2:5; cf. 4:6), their wealth places them in a precarious position, and their only true reason for glory is the same as that of the poor: they know, and are known by, a gracious God (Jer. 9:23–24).

We might also note that economic poverty by itself does not guarantee that the poor will in fact glory in the Lord. James here commends not the poor per se (for which the normal word is πτωχός, *ptōchos*), but the lowly or humble (ταπεινός, *tapeinos*). A poor person's lust for riches may result in committing evil, and admiration for wealth may result in pandering to the wealthy, as is made clear in James 2. No one is exempt from the temptations of wealth.

---

a tense commonly translated into Greek as aorist. See 1 Pet. 1:24, a direct quotation of Isa. 40:6 using aorists for the Hebrew perfects.

1:12   It is unusual to group 1:12 with 1:9–11. Most commentators notice the theme of "testing/temptation" in 1:12 (the word πειρασμός, *peirasmos*, can mean either "testing" or "temptation") and therefore take that verse as introducing the subject of temptation in 1:13–15.[13] Further, it is difficult to see 1:12 as somehow connected with the eschatological reversal material of 1:9–11.

Nevertheless, I agree with a few recent commentators (Moo 2000: 71–72; Johnson 1995: 174–76; cf. Penner 1996: 144–47) who think that the break should be between 1:12 and 1:13, with "testing/temptation" as simply the catchword that provides a pivot to the new subject. Note that the testing in 1:12 is a cause for blessedness and is of a different kind than the temptation in 1:13–15, which is a cause of sin. Further, the endurance of testing in 1:12 forms an *inclusio*, or verbal bracket, with 1:2–3, where endurance and testing are likewise linked positively. The sun with its scorching heat in 1:11 is an image for testing, reflecting the experience of suffering in the desert. Finally, 1:12 has the character of a saying, or proverbial form, one of several in James that evince the wisdom character of this letter. James typically uses these "proverbial sayings" to conclude or encapsulate a matter rather than introduce a new subject (see, e.g., 1:27; 2:13, 26; 3:11–12, 18; 4:17; see also "Structure" in the introduction).

This means that the lack of wealth or the imminent loss of it is, like many other things, a form of testing, a testing that has value to the believer because it helps to establish, to give "proof," that he or she is one who loves God.

Note that 1:12 is framed as a beatitude, similar to those in Matt. 5:2–12 and Luke 6:20–23 and elsewhere in Jewish wisdom literature.[14] Jesus's beatitudes are surprising: how can anyone regard the poor, those who mourn, those who are starved for justice, or those who are meek as blessed? Yet Jesus calls them so, because the kingdom of God invites a much different perspective on things. Likewise here, how can the struggling man or woman being tried in the fires of suffering be regarded as blessed? Yet, as James says in 5:11, those who have endured such things are later recognized as indeed being blessed. And like Jesus's beatitudes, these strange blessings are blessings because of the imminent eschatological reversal, which will result in the crown of life for those who endure. The blessedness in view, while applicable to the present, is possible now because of the expectation of the blessedness of the future estate.[15]

We should also note that the word *blessed* does not mean quite the same as the English word *happy*. The latter refers mostly to a present emotional state, the former to the state of relationship with God, a "wholeness," as it were, that while truly a present reality, has its primary manifestation in the future.

---

13. For example, Hauck 1926: 56; Mussner 1975: 85 (although Mussner also sees the connection with 1:2–11). Dibelius (1975: 88) regards it as entirely independent of either the preceding or the following verses.

14. Note especially Job 5:17: "Blessed is the one whom God reproves."

15. Compare 1:25, where the one who does not just hear the law but does it "will be blessed" (note the future tense ἔσται [*estai*, he will be]) by his doing. God's approval (blessing) is now, but its manifestation is future. See the commentary on 1:25.

This future manifestation of wholeness and blessedness is here called the "crown of life," the result of successfully enduring persecution. It is the eschatological victory wreath[16] bestowed upon those who are faithful in the love of God. "Crown of life" is found elsewhere in the NT only in Rev. 2:10, where it is likewise the reward for endurance in persecution.[17] The phrase could simply be equivalent to "living crown," standing in contrast with the fading garland that victors in the arena wore. But more likely this is an epexegetical genitive: the crown that is life (Laws 1980: 68; Davids 1982: 80). The OT and much other Jewish literature use the word *life* to refer to the fullness of human destiny in personal relationship to God, particularly eschatological life (see R. Bultmann, *TDNT* 2:855–61). Hence, the promise of the "crown of life" to those who love God is equivalent to the "kingdom which he promised to those who love him" in 2:5.[18] This sums up the reason why James exhorts his hearers to rejoice when they are beset with various tests: the testing, the suffering, the endurance, the wisdom, and the faith are designed to lead to eschatological life; and thus 1:12 concludes the opening exhortation (1:2–12). Suffering and eschatology are bound together throughout James.

In James 2:5, as also in Rom. 8:28 and 1 Cor. 2:9, all of which mention God's promise of eschatological reward, the phrase "those who love him" is not so much a condition for inclusion in eschatological life as a stock description of the faithful who will receive it.[19] Their love for God is manifest in their faithful endurance.

Additional Notes

1:11. ἀνέτειλεν . . . ἐξήρανεν . . . ἐξέπεσεν . . . ἀπώλετο often are identified as "gnomic" aorists (see MHT 3:73; BDF §344), probably in reflection of the aorists in the LXX of Isa. 40:6–8, which translate the Hebrew perfect tenses literally with ἐξηράνθη and ἐξέπεσεν.

1:11. The word used by James here translated as "ventures" (πορεία) is literally "journeys" or "comings and goings."[20] The metaphor might be evoking the image of a merchant being cut off "in mid-career"

---

16. Crowns could be symbols of sovereignty (2 Sam. 12:30) or of festivity (Wis. 2:8), but this crown is a reward for endurance and thus is like the crown in an athletic contest. One might think of the victory wreath as being more of a Gentile than a Jewish image, but the idea of a victor's wreath for endurance does occur in Jewish wisdom texts (Wis. 4:2; Sir. 1:18; 6:31; Bar. 5:2; cf. *m. 'Abot* 4.19) and also elsewhere in the NT (1 Cor. 9:25; 2 Tim. 2:5; 1 Pet. 5:4).

17. Although a few scholars who date James late think that he borrowed the expression from Revelation, it is more likely that both John the seer and the author of James found the phrase in early Christian or Jewish vocabulary. Both life and a crown are gifts of wisdom in Proverbs (3:18; 4:9).

18. "Crown of life" in Judaism is the gift of eschatological life to those (Jews) who faithfully endure to the end (Ascen. Isa. 9; 2 Bar. 15.8). It evokes the "victory wreath" or "crown of glory" (T. Benj. 4.1; Bar. 5:2).

19. Note also, in the commandment against idolatry, the description of the faithful as "those who love me and keep my commandments" (Exod. 20:6; Deut. 5:10).

20. Of course, the English noun *venture* also used to refer primarily to travel rather than business endeavors, a meaning still preserved in the phrase "venture forth."

(Laws 1980: 65), or James may be anticipating his reference in 4:13–15 specifically to the rich merchant's travels (so Mussner 1975: 75), but probably he is simply indicating that the rich person pursues wealth heedlessly of the fact that such ventures will someday cease and be seen to be worthless.

1:12. Some manuscripts supply either "God" (ὁ θεός) or more commonly "the Lord" (ὁ κύριος) as the subject for the verb "promised." The context makes the subject clear anyway.

C. Faith and Testing (1:13–18)

"Testing" is the catchword that occurs in 1:12 that serves to pivot to the subject of behavior under temptation, which is the same word in Greek (πειρασμός, *peirasmos*). However, 1:12 is related to 1:13–15 not just by catchword, but even more by contrast. In 1:12 the endurance of testing results in "life," while in 1:15 the progress of temptation results in "death." But the subject matter of 1:13–15 deals with a somewhat different problem: if testing is used by God for the perfecting of his people, does that mean that God is at the root of our temptations and sin? James answers this in two ways: negatively, by showing that for God to tempt someone to sin would be contrary to his very character, and positively, by showing where sin really comes from, the heart of the sinner.

Thus, although testing has a positive effect when endured faithfully, there is an unfaithful response to testing that turns it from an opportunity for endurance to an occasion for sin. When looked at like this, testing is "temptation." James therefore guards against the possibility of attributing to God the enticement to sin, because God is the source not of evil but of good.

The reproductive metaphor is carried throughout this paragraph. The metaphor of conceiving and giving birth to evil (1:15) is found elsewhere in the Bible (Ps. 7:14). But in the latter half of the paragraph it is God who is the creative agent. It is indeed God who is personally the "Father," who uses the seed of the word of truth to give birth to ("bring forth") believers, who are then a kind of firstfruits, a first harvest of creation. This paragraph is full of contrasts with previous material. Unlike the unstable person, God is unchanging and unshifting. Unlike desire and sin, which produce death, God produces living beings. Unlike the darkness and shadow that sin brings forth, God begets lights.

Further, James here holds in tension both the eternal unchangeableness of God himself and the eschatological, time-developed character of his relation to creation. His offspring, believers, are the firstfruits of the harvest at the end of this age. The generative "seed" that produces that harvest is the effectual "word of truth," which is implanted and thereby able to "save souls" (1:21).

Exegesis and Exposition

[13]No one, when being tested, should say, "I am being tempted ⌜by⌝ God," for God cannot be tempted by evil, and he himself does not tempt anyone. [14]Rather, each person, being lured forth and ensnared, is tempted by his own desire. [15]Then the desire, having conceived, gives birth to sin, and the sin, when it grows up, brings forth death.

¹⁶Do not be deceived, my dear brothers. ¹⁷Every good bestowal and every perfect gift is from above, coming down from the father of lights, with whom there is no variation or ⌜shifting shadow⌝. ¹⁸According to his purpose he brought us forth by the word of truth, so that we might be a kind of firstfruits of his created beings.

1:13   In the context of a strong belief in God's sovereign disposition of every-thing, it is easy to slip into the pattern of blaming God for one's own failure. Adam did it: "The woman whom *you* gave to be with me . . ." (Gen. 3:12). And the request "Do not lead us into temptation" (Matt. 6:13 NASB; Luke 11:4) could be misconstrued to suggest that God is the agent of temptation to evil.[1] This struggle to maintain the balance between acknowledging God's total sovereignty and maintaining his nonresponsibility for sin is as much a theme of Jewish wisdom literature as it is of modern theological controversy. Something very similar to James is found in Sir. 15:11–12 JB: "Do not say, 'The Lord was responsible for my sinning,' for he is never the cause of what he hates. Do not say, 'It was he who led me astray,' for he has no use for a sin-ner." English translations of James 1:12–13 compound the difficulty because English uses different word roots for external pressure to evil (testing) and internal pressure to evil (temptation), whereas Greek uses only one (πειράζω, *peirazō*; its noun form is πειρασμός, *peirasmos*). In 1:13 we see a shift from the external "push" to sin to the internal "pull," and this requires a shift of words in English ("when being tested . . . 'I am being tempted'"), which obscures the wordplay in Greek. Temptation is, of course, a form of testing, and sometimes commentators try to preserve the wordplay by blending the two meanings of πειράζω so that a single meaning can serve for both occurrences, but this then obscures the shift of meaning. Equally misleading is to assume that the word retains a single notion of "testing" and read the one meaning throughout the passage, as Davids (1982: 80–83) attempts to do.

Already Bede (PL 93:13–14) distinguished between exterior testing (which God permits) and interior testing (which comes from the devil or our own "fragile nature"). This shows that Latin readers, who also used one word in both senses, easily understood the shift of sense of πειράζω and cognates in 1:13. There are some modern languages in which the word for "testing" and for "temptation" is, as in Greek, the same, and native speakers of such languages have indicated to me that they have no difficulty differentiating or discerning the shift of meanings that occurs in 1:13, because the context makes it clear which sense is intended in each case. The statement that God is not tempted by evil removes the ambiguity for the reader.[2]

Hence, James is not contradicting what he clearly knows from the OT Scriptures (see Gen. 22:1, "God tested Abraham," where the LXX uses the

---

1. Jeremias (1967: 104) suggests that James may have had the Lord's Prayer specifically in mind here and was cautioning against its misuse.
2. For other ways of understanding the phrase "tempted of evil," see my further comments on 1:13 and the additional notes on 1:13.

verb πειράζω). Indeed, James's preceding paragraphs implicitly acknowledge that God does allow testing into the believer's life. However, "God himself does not tempt anyone [to do evil]." James's inclusion of the word "himself" here[3] is a way of acknowledging that although God is sovereign over the acts of his creatures, and although God may permit temptation and even use it in the believer's life, God himself is not the one who tempts to evil (which would make God the author of the sin). God tests by allowing and even ordaining external pressure, but he himself does not try to lure people into sinning. Paul adds that God will not allow believers to be tempted/tested beyond their capacity and also always provides a way of escape (1 Cor. 10:13).

God does not tempt to evil, because to do so would be contrary to his character: he cannot himself be tempted by evil, and so he cannot be tempted to tempt. But it is quite natural for sinful people to want to blame God as the ultimate cause of their failures; it is a further layer of the self-deception that James warns about in 1:16, 22, 26.

Here we should note that James's statement that God "cannot be tempted by evil" (literally "is untempted of evil") could be taken in other ways. Hort (1909: 23) thinks that it means that God is "inexperienced in evil" and therefore cannot tempt.[4] Davids (1978; also Davids 1982: 81), following Spitta (1896: 33), argues that it means that God "ought not to be tempted by evil men," on the grounds that there are no examples in Greek literature where ἀπείραστος (apeirastos) means "cannot be tempted." However, James is no stranger to using rare words with a slightly different meaning than in standard classical texts, and the natural effects of the privative *alpha* and the verbal adjectival ending (-τος) make the understanding "cannot be tempted" quite natural. Further, in an example that Davids gives for his own suggested meaning (Pseudo-Ignatius, *Philippians* 11), ἀπείραστος is, in the translation that he cites,[5] rendered "cannot be tempted," and thus he seems to undercut his own argument. Admittedly, the quotation is in reference to Matt. 4:7 (where Jesus quotes the command in Deut. 6:16 not to test the Lord), so Davids may still have an argument here.

3. Although the emphatic use of the nominative αὐτός in Attic Greek (see Smyth 1920: §1206a) was fading by NT times, it does retain some emphasis in most NT occurrences (MHT 3:40–41), not only where αὐτός is in predicate position to an explicit nominative, but also where a subject is assumed. In James the nominative of αὐτός occurs elsewhere only in 2:6–7 (twice). There, both occurrences of αὐτοί are unnecessary as simple pronouns, and in context they appear to underscore the "they" (the rich), translated below as "are *they* not the ones who drag you to court . . . are *they* not the ones who blaspheme. . . ." Here in 1:13 also the αὐτός is redundant if simply functioning as a pronoun, and most likely it is underscoring the "he" (referring to God). In other words, James stresses that God is not the one directly involved in the tempting.

4. Hort (1909: 22–23) postulates that James was thinking of the more common Greek word ἀπείρατος (apeiratos, inexperienced) rather than the rare ἀπείραστος (apeirastos, untried, un-temptable). But even apart from lack of textual evidence for the former, James clearly is playing on the πειρασ- stem. Of course, the phrase still could mean that God "has not been tempted" rather than "cannot be tempted" (see BDF §182.3), but James's concern here involves not the experience of God, but the character of God.

5. Davids uses the English translation by A. Roberts and J. Donaldson in *Writings of the Apostolic Fathers* (Ante-Nicene Christian Library; Edinburgh: T&T Clark, 1867), 1:480.

But Pseudo-Ignatius was written probably in the fourth century or even later, and even in reference to Matt. 4:7, Pseudo-Ignatius is more likely to be asking "Who can tempt the one who *cannot* be tempted" (possibly with James 1 in mind) than "Who can tempt the one who *should not* be tempted."[6] Most translators and commentators therefore rightly understand this to be a comment about God's incapacity for evil, not the inappropriateness of putting him to the test,[7] though of course the latter is also true, even if that is not what James had in mind.

1:14–15 The abilities to tempt and to be tempted are rooted in an evil capacity within the person. It is this capacity within that is of concern to James in 1:14, and he illustrates it, first using the language evocative of fishing or trapping ("lured and ensnared"), then with the imagery of sexual reproduction.

Things start with "one's own desire" (τῆς ἰδίας ἐπιθυμίας, *tēs idias epithymias*), which places responsibility firmly on the shoulders of the individual (Moo 2000: 75). "Desire" refers not to human emotions or wants generally, as though James were advocating a stoic avoidance of all normal human passions, but to the desire to do evil and the desire for self-exaltation and personal gratification or for safety at the expense of right.[8] James later (4:1–2) uses the word ἡδονή (*hēdonē*, pleasure, illicit desire for pleasure) in parallel with the verbal form ἐπιθυμέω (*epithymeō*) to refer to these desires. In Matt. 5:28 Jesus indicates that certain kinds of desire are, in themselves, already sin; however, James is interested not in developing a precise theory of evil, but in making it clear that the processes of sin do not originate with God (and, subordinately, in warning of the danger of allowing the deadly chain of events to start).

The individual being tempted through the agency of his or her desire is lured forth, that is, drawn out and baited (δελεάζω, *deleazō*, lure, entice, is a verb derivative from δέλεαρ, *delear*, bait). These terms ordinarily are used to describe the process of catching fish or animals with nets or lines and bait.[9] James does not speak directly of Satan doing the baiting, because his focus here is on the responsibility of the individual, though later (4:7; and probably

6. Similar criticism can be directed at Davids's other example from *Acts of John* 57.

7. Davids is driven to Spitta's view probably because he wants to continue the meaning "test" rather than shift to "tempt."

8. Wisdom literature often uses ἐπιθυμία in this sense (e.g., Wis. 4:12; Sir. 18:30–31; 23:5; cf. Rom. 7:7–8). The term sometimes is understood as a reference to the *yēṣer hārāʿ*, the "evil impulse" (Marcus 1982; Davids 1982: 83), and no doubt it could refer to such. However, in rabbinic theology the *yēṣer hārāʿ* was supposed to be countered with the *yēṣer haṭṭôb*, or good impulse. Further, the *yēṣer hārāʿ*, at least in some texts (Gen. Rab. 9.7; *b. Yoma* 69b), was created by God within humans to test them, an idea running opposite to James. In any case, the evil and good impulses within a person are not the focus of James's interest, and a reference to the evil impulse here, even if James concurred with the notion, would be a distraction from his main focus on the responsibility of the individual.

9. Mayor (1897) cites the poet Oppian, 3.316; 4.359. The fact that the terms seem to be out of the expected order (drawing out, then baited) supports the suggestion by Moo (2000: 75) that these fishing terms were used so often in a spiritual sense that the original, literal sense had faded.

3:6) he does indicate satanic involvement in the provoking or evoking of evil behavior.

In the environment of James's audience this focus on individual responsibility (each one enticed by one's own desires) was not universally acknowledged. People of pagan background often regarded themselves as pawns in the hands of supernatural forces. Further, the moral focus and unit of responsibility frequently was the family, the tribe, the nation, the community. In the modern West the opposite has been the case, and responsibility has until recently been overly individualized. But now, in the twenty-first century, James's focus on the individual may again be worth emphasizing. Contemporary enthusiasm for focusing on corporate responsibility should not obscure that individuals, as individuals, are responsible for the consequences of their moral choices, as also for their choices in belief.

Once the bait is taken (and the tempted person is "ensnared"), the metaphor shifts to the sometimes slow but always inexorable processes of reproduction. This is a natural shift, since in wisdom tradition illicit sexual seduction often is described in terms of luring, enticing, and snaring (e.g., Prov. 7:21–23). The desire "conceives" (cf. Ps. 7:14); it is seeded or fertilized. James leaves unspecified what the seed is. In 1:18 the seed that produces God's offspring is "the word of truth." Although it is risky to press analogies in James, it is reasonable to see that the fertilizing agent for sin is falsehood. Snares and bait are always false. When the human will yields to desire and gives credence to the lie, it gives birth to sin. And sin then grows up and "brings forth" or "births" death (using another word for "giving birth," which again manifests James's sharp irony). Just as endurance can achieve a "perfect work," fully equipping the believer for life (1:4), so sin, when it achieves its maturity or "perfection," yields its natural fruit, death.

"My dear brothers, do not be deceived" sometimes is taken as introducing a new paragraph, and sometimes as closing the preceding sentences. If the latter, it could be an appeal to prevent the wiles of temptation from taking root and bringing forth sin. And this is a warning worth hearing, because when the luring and baiting are going on, most times those to whom it is happening are unaware of it. The heart is deceitful and desperately wicked, and one never in this age becomes immune to the deceitfulness of sin. But the appeal in 1:16 to "my dear brothers" resembles that of 1:19; 2:5. In those texts the development of an exhortation follows the address. So the exhortation not to be deceived probably is more closely linked to the character of God expressed in 1:17. But 1:16 may also be understood as bridging 1:13–15 and 1:17–18 (Dibelius 1975: 99; Davids 1982: 86; Moo 2000: 76), and here the whole is presented as a single paragraph. The readers are not to be deceived with regard to God's character by thinking either that he is the source of temptation or that truly good things have a source other than he. And it is precisely the knowledge of God's character, both what he is not and what he is, and the knowledge that believers are his offspring by the word of truth, that protect one against the deceitfulness of sin.

1:16

"Not being deceived" is the antidote that prevents the reproductive processes of sin and death. The word used here for "be deceived" (πλανᾶσθε, passive voice of πλανάω, *planaō*) means "to be misled, led astray" (BDAG 821; the active voice means "to wander"), and in this context of luring and enticing, the choice of verb underscores the danger of being lured away from the truth (cf. the very similar use in James 5:19: "if someone among you is led astray from the truth"). Although this sentence often is read to mean "Do not be deceived about the nature of temptation" (i.e., do not think that it comes from God), the intent here is more likely to be "Do not be deceived (lured) by temptation." The way one is "not deceived" and thus avoids the chain of sin and death is by way of the "word of truth" (1:18) and a healthy knowledge of God's character.

In 1:22 and 1:26 it is *self*-deceit that is most insidious and dangerous. This is implicitly the deceit in view in 1:16 as well. The use of the negative progressive imperative μὴ πλανᾶσθε (*mē planasthe*, do not be deceived) implies that people are not to allow themselves to be deceived; that is, if they are deceived, it is because they deceive themselves, which is an action manifesting an absence of faith. Here in James 1 the author introduces three sources of self-deception that he will return to later in the letter: (1) questioning the goodness of God (1:16–17; cf. 4:1–8), (2) hearing the word without acting on it (1:22; cf. 2:14–26), and (3) having no control over one's speech (1:26; cf. 3:1–18).

1:17–18 Not only is God not a tempter, he is the giver of good. Whereas temptation takes, God gives. And God's gifts are always good (cf. Matt. 7:11). The good and perfect gift par excellence that God freely gives and is "from above" is, as we saw in 1:5 and will see again in 3:15, wisdom.

"Lights" in the plural is rare, but it occurs in Ps. 135:7 LXX (136:7 ET), which refers to God as the one who made the lights. The phrase "father of lights" has no close antecedent in either Jewish or Hellenistic literature, but in a Jewish environment the phrase most likely would be understood to refer first of all to God as the creator of sun, moon, and stars, as in Gen. 1:14–18 and the already noted Ps. 136:7 (Hauck 1926: 66; for other possibilities, see the additional notes). God's creational activity often is associated with wisdom in Jewish literature (e.g., Prov. 8; Sir. 43:1–12). But since in James 1:18 God is said to bring forth "us," there may also be an implication that believers are also the "lights" in view. Some may object that this is too Hellenistic or Johannine for James, but James bears a close relationship to the Gospel of Matthew, particularly the Sermon on the Mount (see, in the introduction, "James and the Sermon on the Mount/Plain"), where Jesus describes the disciples as the "light of the world" (Matt. 5:14). Daniel 12:3 and the War Scroll (1QM) found near Qumran (which refers to the faithful community as the "sons of light") should put to rest any doubts as to whether a Palestinian Jew could have conceived of believers as "lights."

It is instructive that James uses such a personal and relational image of God not just as "creator" of lights, but also as "father." This is in line with the reproductive metaphor running through this paragraph (1:18: God "brought us forth," i.e., gave us a new life as his children), but it is also a clear reminder of the Christian emphasis on God's fatherhood in relation to believers. God's general fatherhood is found elsewhere in Judaism,[10] but his designation as personal father is a distinctive emphasis of Jesus that is unique or nearly so.[11] It is rarely if ever applied personally in Second Temple Judaism outside of Christianity, but James shares Jesus's faith in God's personal fatherhood (1:27; 3:9).

With God, there is "no variation or shifting shadow." The language is evocative and difficult (see the fourth additional note on 1:17), but the main point is clear: God is unchangeable and entirely trustworthy (cf. Mal. 3:6). Ordinary heavenly lights produce shadows, but God's light is shadowless. Ordinary lights wax and wane, shift, move around, go through phases, and fade; even the sun is occasionally eclipsed. And all such lights cast shadows that are both inconstant and evanescent. Several heavenly lights are also known in Greek literature as "wanderers" (πλανῆται, planētai; Plato, Leg. 821b; Aristotle, Mund. 392ᵃ 13; cf. Jude 13), but God cannot be made to wander, nor does he entice people to wander. God's light is unchanging; it is not subject to variation. Unlike the sun and moon, God's light cannot be overshadowed, nor does it make "shifting shadows" (cf. 1 John 1:5: "God is light, and in him is no darkness at all"). The literalistic but memorable turn of phrase "no . . . shadow of turning" used in the KJV, even if not an exact representation of the semantic equivalent of the metaphor that James uses, captures the notion of God's faithfulness and steadiness. Given the instability of the world in which the nascent community of believers lived, the solidity and reliability of the wisdom of God was important, and the steadiness of the believers as lights is an important corollary in demonstrating that divine wisdom to the world.

Furthermore, just as God does not vary or generate shadows, his gifts are not subject to variation or trickery. They do not turn into something else when received, and they, unlike human gifts, never contain traps or enticements.

Standing opposite the unplanned pregnancy and birth of sin in 1:14–15 is the deliberate and intentional reproductive activity of God in 1:18: it is "according

10. Philo, for example, frequently connects God's fatherhood with his being the Creator (Creation 2 §10; 5 §21; 25 §77) and therefore sometimes refers to God as the "father of the universe" (e.g., Creation 24 §72) and "father of everything" (Creation 2 §7; 24 §74; Confusion 28 §144). He refers to God's assigning the dominion of the sun and moon as the work of the Father: "The sovereignty of the day the Father has assigned to the sun, as a mighty monarch; and that of the night he has given to the moon and to the multitude of the other stars" (Creation 18 §56). It is as creator that God is also called the father of all humans (Names 22 §127).

11. One Dead Sea Scroll text (4Q372 fragment 1, line 16) presents the patriarch Joseph as addressing God as "my father." But in 4Q372 Joseph speaks not so much as an individual but as a paradigm of the nation of Israel in subjection to the Gentiles, crying out to God for deliverance. To my knowledge, this is the only Second Temple Jewish text that has any individual addressing God as "my father," until Jesus did so, who also encouraged his disciples to do likewise.

to his purpose."[12] Just as God deliberately brought forth the heavenly lights by a word (Gen. 1), so he brings forth believers by "the word of truth." This phrase could be translated "true word," though retaining the phrase "word of truth" puts the emphasis where it should be: it is not just a word that happens to be true, it is the word of Truth. Truth in the NT carries a practical dimension as well as an intellective one. Truth often is not just something that one knows, but something that one does (Gal. 5:7; 1 John 1:6). Likewise for James, the truth is the whole of practical righteousness included in the Hebrew term *'ĕmet*, encompassing both thought (truth) and deed (fidelity). In the NT this word of truth is the gospel, which both conveys the knowledge of God and ultimate reality (2 Cor. 6:7; Eph. 1:13; Col. 1:5; 2 Tim. 2:15) and transforms its recipient (John 8:32; 17:19; 1 Pet. 1:23–25).

The "word" as a reference to the gospel of truth has its roots in Jesus's "seed" parables (see Matt. 13:18–43, where the "seed" of the parable of the sower is interpreted as the λόγος [*logos*, word] of the kingdom, the gospel). In John 17:17 Jesus's prayer makes it explicit: "Your word is truth." As we will see in the next section (1:19–25, especially in 1:25), the word that transforms and produces life is also called the "perfect and ever-abiding law of freedom," which transforms the one who gazes intently into it. Almost certainly this is a reference to Scripture (see the commentary on 1:25), though it is not the bare letters on the page; rather, it is the personal knowledge of the person of God that the text conveys that creates true disciples who can be lights in the world, reflecting the light of God and standing at the beginning of the eschatological redemption.

The imagery of seeding with the word of truth is picked up again in 1:21, where the implanted word is like seed planted in the ground, or semen in the womb, that produces new life (cf. 1 Pet. 1:23–25; 1 John 3:9). God's purpose in bringing forth his people was that they be, as it were, "firstfruits"[13] of the created entities. "Firstfruits" were the first harvest or finest produce that was set apart as an offering to God and was considered God's special possession (Exod. 23:19). The firstfruits offering sanctified the whole harvest. The use of the term for the church does not, however, imply that James thinks that since the church is the firstfruits, all humankind eventually will be saved.[14] In the LXX the Greek term (ἀπαρχή, *aparchē*) is used not just for actual fruits or crops, but also for anything that is the first of an acquisition or is a thing of value. Thus, gold and silver can be "firstfruits" (Exod. 35:5 LXX). Firstborn sons can also be called "firstfruits" (Gen. 49:3; Deut. 12:17; Ps. 105:36 [104:36 LXX]), and firstborn sons were, like the firstfruits of harvest, designated as set apart to the Lord (Num. 3:12) and consequently had to

---

12. James identifies the bringing forth of people by the word as a function of God's deliberate purpose, using the participle βουληθείς (*boulētheis*, willing; cf. Eph. 1:11). James thereby highlights that salvation is God's doing, not that of humans (Martin 1988: 39).

13. James uses the indefinite pronoun τινα to "soften the metaphorical expression" (BDF §301.1), hence the translation "a kind of firstfruits."

14. For a refutation of this notion, see Palmer 1957.

be symbolically redeemed (Num. 18:15), possibly as an echo of Gen. 22. Indeed, Israel as a whole is designated God's "firstborn" (Exod. 4:22). In the NT, firstfruits represent the beginning of God's redemption of all creation (Rom. 16:5; 2 Thess. 2:13; Rev. 14:4). Christ himself is the firstfruits of the resurrection (1 Cor. 15:20, 23). The term therefore is eschatological as well as cultic,[15] and James's designation of believers as "firstfruits" not only declares them to be holy, but also places them in the category of those who are already experiencing the full redemption that the rest of creation still awaits. A further implication of this is that the "firstfruits" are the exemplars who reflect God's character to the world. This may be one reason why James is deeply distressed by those who claim to have faith but do not evince that character.

Additional Notes

1:13. The meaning of "seek to seduce to evil" for the verb πειράζω is attested in secular Greek sources as well (e.g., Apollonius of Rhodes, *Argonautica* 3.10).

1:13. "Tempted by God" is literally "tempted from [ἀπό] God." A few manuscripts, including א, have ὑπό, but since that is the easier reading and is much less widely attested, ἀπό is preferred. The unusual choice of preposition perhaps stresses that not only is God not the agent of temptation, he is not its source (Mayor 1897: 48). But the use of ἀπό in the sense of "by" is found elsewhere in James (1:27; 5:4), and Mayor's suggestion seems overly subtle.

1:13. According to Mayor (1897: 50), Luther gave ἀπείραστος an active sense, translating "God cannot tempt to evil," but this, in addition to postulating an unlikely use of the predicate adjective, makes the following phrase redundant, and I could find no recent commentators who hold that view.

1:13. God is untemptable "of evil" (κακῶν; genitive plural). The word "evil" here could be either neuter (i.e., God cannot be tempted to do evil things) or masculine (i.e., God cannot be tempted by evil persons). As noted above, Davids (1982: 81) argues for the latter, noting the similarity with Deut. 6:16, which forbids Israelites from putting the Lord to the test. But here the word probably is meant to refer to God's character being untemptable rather than to the impropriety of evil people putting God to the test, which would be somewhat off the topic.

1:14. The quickly shifting mixture of imprecisely used hunting and fishing terms to describe sin is not unusual in Jewish literature. For similar metaphors, see 1QHᵃ 11.26; 13.8 (García Martínez and Tigchelaar 1997–98: 1.167, 171).

1:17. "Every good bestowal and every perfect gift" is an attempt to render the two different Greek words for "gift" in English (cf. RSV: "endowment" and "gift"). Based on distinctions by Philo (*Alleg. Interp.* 3.70 §§196–97), δόσις sometimes is seen as the act of giving and δώρημα as the thing given, but James may simply be using poecilonymy (a piling up of synonyms) to emphasize God's generosity, or he may be quoting an extant "saying" or expressing himself poetically.[16]

---

15. The cultic force is simply the holiness of the firstfruits, not that they are a redemptive sacrifice. They are the down payment for the rest of humanity that will be redeemed (Dibelius 1975: 106), not the cause or means of their redemption.

16. The words make a (slightly defective) hexameter line, and Paul uses "do not be deceived" as an introduction to a Greek moral quotation in 1 Cor. 15:33, so it is possible that James is quoting something, but if so, it is unprovable, and in any case it matters little for interpretation

1:17. In the clause πᾶν δώρημα τέλειον ἄνωθέν ἐστιν καταβαῖνον the verb ἐστίν could be taken either with καταβαῖνον periphrastically ("every perfect gift from above is coming down") or, as in the translation above, with ἄνωθεν (see Wallace 1996: 648). The difference has little effect on the sense, since either way, the gift is both from above and coming down.

1:17. The phrase translated "father of lights" could conceivably mean "father of men" (Amphoux 1970). The classical word φώς (man; LSJ 1968) is distinguishable from the common NT word φῶς (light) only by its accentuation, and early manuscripts generally lack accents. The former is found as late as the second century AD (Rylands Papyrus 77.34), and James demonstrates a fairly classical style of writing. But all the native Greek-speaking church fathers who discuss this passage understand it to mean "father of lights." Further, if James had meant that God was the "father of men," he chose a very confusing way of saying it.

The rare plural "lights" most often refers to the sun and moon (e.g., Ptolemaeus, *Tetrabiblos* 37, 38; Plutarch, *Per.* 6.4).[17] The phrase "father of lights" is unusual and possibly unprecedented,[18] but as noted above, the common meaning of lights as "sun, moon, stars" makes good sense and fits with the wisdom genre, which focuses on God as creator (cf. Ps. 136:7–9 [135:7–9 LXX]).

1:17. Much discussion has developed over the difficult phrase τροπῆς ἀποσκίασμα, for several reasons. First, some important witnesses (𝔓[23], ℵ [original hand], B) read τροπῆς ἀποσκιάσματος. To make sense of this, Ropes (1916: 162–64), who prefers this reading, reads the preceding η as an article rather than a conjunction ("with whom is no variation that is of a changing shadow"). There are other variant readings as well that make little sense without emendation, which indeed several scholars are willing to offer, but this is unnecessary because the commonly found text makes sense as it is.[19]

Second, assuming that the most widely distributed text is correct, the meaning of the words is complicated by their resemblance to astronomical terms. The word ἀποσκίασμα is an extremely rare term for "shadow." It is used to refer to the variations in shadows due to changes in position of heavenly bodies, such as the changing shadows on the moon (Aëtius, *De placitis philosophorum* 2.30.3) or the moving shadow of a sundial (Plutarch, *Per.* 6.4).[20] It does not mean "eclipse," as some

---

except to reinforce the probability that δόσις and δώρημα are not to be strongly differentiated. See Davids 1982: 86.

17. I therefore have no idea why Davids (1982: 87) claims that "Hellenistic thought apparently did not use φῶς to designate heavenly bodies."

18. Hauck (1926: 66) and Str-B (3:752) refer to Apoc. Mos. 36; 38 as an antecedent in Jewish literature. Laws (1980: 73) critically assesses this reading of "father of light(s)" in the Apocalypse of Moses as well as in T. Ab. 7.6 and concludes that they are of doubtful relevance as background to James. Although the original Life of Adam and Eve story upon which the Apocalypse of Moses is based may be pre-Christian, it is only in the Greek Apocalypse of Moses that the phrase is found, and the Apocalypse of Moses ordinarily is dated two or three centuries later than even a late date for James. With regard to the Testament of Abraham, the context indicates that the "father of light(s)," also called the "man of light" and "glorious man," is not God, but the angel Michael sent to take Abraham's soul (T. Ab. 7.8). Taking a different path, Verseput (1997a) suggests that James 1:17 is an echo of Jewish morning and evening benedictions recited, when the greater and lesser lights of God's creation trade places, to remind believers of the coming eschatological re-creation. It seems unlikely that James's readers would have been able to pick up on such subtle allusions.

19. Admittedly, this runs counter to the usual rule of preferring the *lectio difficilior*, but the unintelligible variations in question can be explained on other grounds.

20. Plutarch uses a masculine form, ἀποσκιασμοί. His context is referring to the fact that even though natural phenomena, such as the shadows (ἀποσκιασμοί, *aposkiasmoi*) of a sundial or the lights (φῶτα, *phōta*) of signal fires, can be explained naturalistically, this does not mean that they cannot have further significance.

older commentators suggested. The word τροπή often appears as a technical term for "solstice," when the location of sunrise changes direction, though it can also have a nontechnical sense of "change" or "variance" (LSJ 1826). In concert with James's description of God as the "father of lights," the reader naturally gravitates to some kind of astronomical explanation. But if James did use astronomical terms deliberately, he was using them loosely, not technically,[21] to evoke the common Jewish and Hellenistic fascination with the regularity and the predictable change of astronomical objects and also to contrast these with God's unchangeableness. Again, if some of James's original audience were of Gentile background, this would be an especially important contrast because it would reinforce the distinction between the true God, who does not change, and the pagan gods, such as Jupiter or Apollo, who do.

1:17. The reproductive language "brought us forth" could be understood, as Elliott-Binns (1956) does, as referring to creation rather than a redemptive "bringing forth." However, Rom. 8:18–25 uses similar language to describe the yet-to-come redemption, and as noted earlier, the contrast with the reproductive process of sin, plus the fact that the active agent in God's "bringing forth" is the word, make a decisive case for this being a reference to redemption (Moo 2000: 79).

Neither does the word "created entities" (κτίσματα) simply mean "humanity" (contra Elliott-Binns 1956: 154–55). The word is used in Wis. 9:2 to refer to creation over which humankind has been set to rule. The "firstfruits" are not simply the "first converts among a lot of other converts"; they are the "princes," as it were, who will rule over redeemed creation. The bringing forth and maturing of the "firstfruits" of the created entities is therefore also likely to be seen by James as an eschatological event, a sign of the imminence of the end.

1:18. Mussner (1975: 95–96) sees a baptismal formulary source behind 1:18, pointing to the language of "putting off" (ἀποτίθημι) in 1:21, and the language of rebirth by the word as evoking baptism. Of course, any references to God's regenerational activity could be connected to baptism, but to find such wherever possible is unnecessary (Davids 1982: 93).

---

21. Note his similar nontechnical use of words that sound like technical philosophical language in 1:21 (ἔμφυτος λόγος, *emphytos logos*) and 3:6 (τρόχος τῆς γενέσεως, *trochos tēs geneseōs*). He also may have been borrowing the entire phrase; the appearance in most manuscripts of the abbreviation ἔνι (= ἔνεστι), though ℵ, P, and a few other Greek manuscripts have the more common ἐστιν, may indicate that James is quoting or semi-quoting from some no longer extant text and investing it with his own meaning.

D. Doing the Word of God (1:19–25)

The word of truth of 1:18, when it is fruitful, has certain practical effects. In 1:19–25 James begins to point out in general terms what those effects are. The passage consists of a number of sentences that have a "proverbial" character and could function independently of context: "Be quick to hear, slow to speak and slow to anger. . . . The wrath of man does not accomplish the justice of God. . . . Lay aside all filth and abundant malice. . . . Receive the implanted word that can save you. . . . Be doers and not hearers only." But these are not just collected sayings; all of them are related to the character development of those "firstfruits" whom God has brought forth by the word. It is the *word* that ties all these things together. Hence, this hortatory material grows out of the material in 1:17–18 relating to God's fatherhood by the word. The mandate of 1:19a specifically connects to the previous material by linking the wise behavior and ethical mandates of 1:19b–25 to "being aware" of God's implanted word.

Exegesis and Exposition

[19] ⌜Be aware⌝ [of these things], my dear brothers. And everyone be quick to hear, slow to speak, and slow to anger, [20]for man's anger does not work God's justice. [21]Therefore, laying aside all filth and abundant malice, in meekness receive the implanted word which can save your souls. [22]And be doers of that ⌜word⌝, not just hearers who delude themselves. [23]⌜For⌝ if someone is a hearer of the word and not a doer of it, that person is like a man observing his natural appearance in a mirror—[24]he observes himself, but no sooner has he gone away than he has forgotten what he looked like. [25]But the one who gazes intently into the perfect law of freedom, and continues to do so, becomes not a forgetful hearer but an active doer. Such a one will be blessed in his doing.

1:19   "Be aware of these things" in 1:19 is simply one word in Greek (ἴστε, *iste*), which could be either imperative ("Know!") or indicative ("You know").[1] Those who understand an indicative here take it as referring to the previous material as the basis for the following imperatives. Those who take it as an imperative usually take it to mean "Pay attention to what I am going to say next." The latter comports better with the way similar introductory imperatives in 1:16 and 2:5 (which include the vocative "my dear brothers") usually are taken. However, the following phrase begins not with "that" but with the conjunction δέ (*de*, and, but), which seems out of place if the command "Everyone

---

1. For comment on the textual situation, see the first two additional notes on 1:19.

be quick to hear" is what the readers are supposed to "know." Also, 1:19b does not convey some new thing to know; it gives some imperatives that are a practical outworking of the content of the preceding verses. Thus, 1:19, like 1:16 above (and 2:5 below), should be understood as a bridge verse. "Know" is imperative and calls attention to what follows, but it also urges readers to understand the material of 1:13–18 as preparation for the practical injunctions that follow.[2]

Throughout this letter James addresses his audience as "my brothers." As 2:1 makes clear, he is referring to fellow believers in Christ (the term is inclusive of men and women). Here he makes his attachment to them even stronger: "my dear [literally 'beloved'] brothers."

"Everyone be quick to hear, slow to speak, slow to anger" reads like a typical proverb, and it corresponds to several proverbial wisdom passages (Prov. 15:1; Eccles. 5:1–2; 7:9; Sir. 5:11).[3] In context, though, James is not just giving good advice for living; he has something specific in mind: being quick to hear "the word of truth," which is synonymous with believing it. And it is not just hearing, but a hearing that results in slowness to speak and slowness to anger. As we will see in 1:26; 3:10; 4:11, control of the tongue is a major component of true faith, and the problem of anger is brought up again in 4:1.

Human anger does not bring about God's justice (literally the "righteousness of God"). The "righteousness of God" can be understood in three ways: (1) as a genitive of source (the righteousness that God gives), (2) as an objective genitive (the righteousness that God requires), (3) as a descriptive (or subjective) genitive (the righteousness that God does). The first of these—the righteousness attributed to the believer by virtue of being united with Christ (as Paul speaks of in, e.g., Rom. 5:17; Phil. 3:9)[4]—is outside James's purview here, since the passage is concerned with the behavior of the believer rather than God's provision for sinners. The second option, the righteousness that God requires, is found in several English translations (e.g., NIV, ESV, 2001 ed.) and is supported by the fact that the phrase "to work righteousness" (ἐργάζεσθαι δικαιοσύνην, *ergazesthai dikaiosynēn*) occurs also in Acts 10:35, where it means "to do what is right." On this view, "to work the righteousness of God" is simply to do what pleases God (Moo 2000: 84). Hence, 1:20 might simply mean that human anger does not do what pleases God. But if this is all that James is saying, it seems an awkward way to say it. The phrase "work God's righteousness" is better taken, as in the third option, as referring to bringing about God's justice, that is, the accomplishment of that which is justice in God's eyes, a "setting things to right" (cf. Matt. 6:33). James's point, then,

1:20

---

2. This would also be true if ἴστε is taken as an indicative (as at Heb. 12:17) instead of imperative. The only other NT occurrence of ἴστε is at Eph. 5:5, where its mood is also ambiguous.

3. For "must" as translating the third-person imperative, see the second additional note on 1:5.

4. The meaning of the phrase in Romans has recently come under scrutiny again, but this is not the place to engage in that discussion, since it is not what James has in mind here.

is that although the wrath of a human being may indeed work what looks like "justice" to humans, it does not bring about the divine justice; it does not reflect the righteous character of God, nor does it accomplish that which God would regard as true righteousness.

If this is correct, then here James confronts an easily made error. When someone sees injustice and roils in anger over it, it would seem as though giving vent to that anger, perhaps even to the point of violence, is just and right because it may serve to counter the perceived injustice. It may even be effective sometimes in mitigating that particular injustice, though if history is any guide, it may also end up doing little more than substituting a new set of injustices for the old. But the biblical testimony is consistent that God reserves vengeance for himself (Deut. 32:35; Rom. 12:19), and as James himself says in 3:9, cursing a fellow human being is inconsistent with the praise of God, in whose image human beings are made.

Given James's own forthright and vigorous comments on injustice within the church, however, this is by no means an endorsement of a quiescent acceptance of the status quo. But how does one "work God's righteousness" if not by wrath? The answer, in the next verse, is fairly easy to understand but somewhat difficult to swallow: the justice of God is worked by combating evil not in anger but in meekness or gentleness, by receiving the implanted word-seed of God.

1:21 "Laying aside" or "putting off" is the term used for taking off a garment (in preparation for vigorous physical activity), and the image of putting off evil is common in moral exhortation (in the NT, see Rom. 13:12; Eph. 4:22, 25; Col. 3:8; Heb. 12:1; and especially 1 Pet. 2:1, which bears close similarity to the present text), usually in apposition to a positive command. The garment to be put off is metaphorical "filth." The term for the "filth" (ῥυπαρία, *rhyparia*) that believers are to shed is a rare word that connotes sordidness (BDAG 908). It occurs in the NT only here, and the cognate adjective for "filthy" (ῥυπαρός, *rhyparos*) is also almost unique to James (2:2, where it again refers to a garment; the only other NT occurrence is Rev. 22:11). James may be using an OT image from Zech. 3:3–4, where the angel commands someone to remove the high priest Joshua's "filthy garments" (ἱμάτια τὰ ῥυπαρά, *himatia ta rhypara*), which are his iniquities, and to clothe him with clean vestments. The use of this term, together with the reference to the "abundant malice" or overflowing of evil, shows James's awareness of the extreme horridness of the human predicament, recognizing as well that even "brothers" (fellow believers) must be exhorted to put it aside.

The main clause of 1:21 is the imperative δέξασθε τὸν ἔμφυτον λόγον (*dexasthe ton emphyton logon*, receive the implanted word), which sets the controlling purpose of the sentence. By implication, therefore, the circumstantial participle "laying aside" is also something that James expects his hearers to do.[5] This may seem difficult, because thus far James has treated his audience

---

5. All English translations available to me that do not simply render ἀποθέμενοι (*apothemenoi*) with an English participle translate it as an imperative, including KJV, ESV, NIV, NJB, NLT, RSV, NRSV, NET.

as already being Christians. Believers, in addition to having laid aside filth, have already received the word. So if one can paradoxically be commanded to receive a word that has already been implanted (see the exegesis of 1:21 further below), it is not inconsistent for James to expect his hearers to lay aside that from which they have already been cleansed.

"In meekness" (ἐν πραΰτητι, *en praytēti*) could be taken either as modifying "receive" (as virtually all English translations) or "laying aside" (as the punctuation of NA[27] implies). In my judgment, the phrase seems to fit more naturally with "receive," but since "laying aside" is syntactically dependent on "receive," it is not crucial to resolve the question. Since "in meekness" stands in contrast with anger, it may not so much be describing the way in which the word is received as noting an essential circumstance of its reception. That is, the one who receives the word must be characterized by meekness in all of his or her activity.

Meekness stands in contrast with anger (cf. Titus 3:2) and registers the attitude of faith. It is the attribute commended by Jesus in the third beatitude: "Blessed are the meek, for they shall inherit the earth" (Matt. 5:5). Meekness, along with righteousness and truth, is one of the triad of virtues that the king rewards in Ps. 44:5 LXX (45:5 MT; 45:4 ET). It is also one of the fruits of the Spirit in Gal. 5:23. Many commentators and preachers have rightly challenged the notion that meekness means taking on a "doormat" personality, allowing oneself to be trampled on. They point out that Jesus refers to himself as meek and lowly in heart (Matt. 11:29), but he never permitted anyone to trample on him.[6] But the fact that meekness is not "doormatness" is no excuse for arrogance. In Matt. 5:5 (echoed in James 2:5) Jesus declared the meek to be the inheritors of the earth, precisely in opposition to the way things appear. The world neither rewards nor respects gentleness, meekness, and humility, but these are the key to proper reception of God's word and the implementation of God's righteousness. Worldly wisdom admires arrogance, self-assurance, and the captaincy of one's own soul, but the entirely different wisdom of God is meek (James 3:13), for it is the attitude of the poor.

The phrase "abundance of malice"[7] is elucidated by Jesus's comment in Luke 6:45b: "The evil person out of his evil treasure produces evil, for out of the abundance of the heart his mouth speaks." The word for "malice" (κακία, *kakia*) could indicate wickedness generally or, specifically, the inclination to harm others (as is likely in Rom. 1:29; Col. 3:8; see BDAG 500; Lightfoot 1879: 214). The assumption is that everyone has not just a few peccadillos that must be disposed of, but an abundance of malice or wickedness.

To "receive the word" means both to believe the gospel (Acts 8:14; 17:11; 1 Thess. 1:6) and to act on it (Matt. 7:24), these ultimately being the same

---

6. John 10:18 tells us that throughout his passion and execution, Jesus was always in control.

7. Here is another example of the "attributed genitive" (Wallace 1996: 89–91) so characteristic of Semitic literature.

thing. The word that is to be received is "implanted" (ἔμφυτος, *emphytos*), another word that is unique to James in the NT. In Greek literature generally it typically means "inborn, natural" (LSJ 551), but if it is inborn, it cannot be received. Therefore, the "implanted word" (*logos*) is not the "innate reason" of the Stoics,[8] but the gospel, which has taken root in the believer's life (cf. Barn. 9.9), but needs constantly to be listened to, believed, and acted upon.

As James has identified the life-giving word (1:18, 21) with the law of liberty into which one may gaze and become a doer (1:25), the reference to the word as implanted also evokes the promise of a new covenant in Jer. 31 (Moo 2000: 87). Jeremiah prophesied of a time when God would write his law upon people's hearts (Jer. 31:33).[9] Here is evidence that James implicitly shares the redemptive-historical perspective of other NT writers who saw Jeremiah's prophecy of a new covenant fulfilled in the coming of Jesus Christ (Matt. 26:28 and pars.; Rom. 11:27; 2 Cor. 3:6; Heb. 8:8–12; 10:16).

That the word may be described both as implanted and as something that must be received may appear paradoxical, but it well describes the "already/not yet" character of the saving activity of the gospel, reflecting also the biblical tension between divine sovereignty and human responsibility in the working out of the believer's deliverance from evil. It is already implanted in the believer and cannot fail (good seed that is received into the ground will always grow up and bear fruit), but the human subject also is not yet fully matured and is responsible continually to accept, believe, and act upon that word.[10]

Another way of rendering "save your souls" is "rescue your lives." "Save your souls" could be both misleading and confusing in our time. It is misleading because "soul" in modern parlance typically refers to the spiritual, nonphysical aspect of humans that is self-conscious. On the other hand, neither should "lives" here be understood in a strictly physical sense. The Greek word ψυχή (*psychē*, soul, life), the word often used in the Greek OT for Hebrew *nepeš*, carries a more general notion of life or personhood considered as a whole, that is, a human being's personal identity (cf. Mark 8:35; John 10:11). So the implanted word is able to rescue the whole person of the one in whom it is implanted.

"To save" is also confusing because the word "salvation" and the verb "save" in our age usually are connected to a vaguely defined notion of religious experience or fundamentalist fervor, which is far from the biblical meaning of the

8. For reasons why ἔμφυτος λόγος in James cannot mean "innate reason" as in the Stoics, see Dibelius 1975: 113. Although James is sometimes compared to Justin Martyr, who comments that non-Christians sometimes speak moral truth "because of the seed of the word which is implanted [ἔμφυτος] in every race of men" (*2 Apol.* 8), James clearly means something different.

9. Jeremiah 31:33 uses the verb "write," not a word meaning "plant" or "sow." Nevertheless, the notion of an interior word of God certainly is there, as it is also in Deut. 30:14 (cf. Rom. 10:6–8).

10. See Cantinat 1973: 105; Dibelius 1975: 114. Laws (1980: 83) objects to this notion, insisting that the aorist tense of δέξασθε (*dexasthe*, receive) carries "the sense of a single rather than a progressive action." However, that view reads too much into the use of the aorist tense, which says nothing at all about the progressiveness of the action or the lack thereof.

term. The Greek word σῴζω (*sōzō*) simply means "to keep alive, rescue, deliver from bondage or oppression or disease" (LSJ 1748). It is extremely common in the Greek OT, especially in Psalms, and often is juxtaposed with the giving of life (e.g., Ps. 137:7 LXX [138:7 MT]): "Though I walk in the midst of trouble, you will give me life; you stretched out your hand against the wrath of my enemies, and your right hand delivered [ἔσωσεν, *esōsen*] me." The last verse of James (5:20) shows the eschatological and spiritual nature of this "salvation of the soul" when he points out that the one who turns someone back to the Lord will save that person's "soul" from death and cover a multitude of sins. Both the physical and the spiritual aspects of life are "saved."

From James's perspective, this deliverance or salvation, while already evincing its effects in the believer, is ultimately still in the future.[11] The implanted word, if it is received, has the ability to deliver lives because the development of the word of God within a person removes that person from the power of evil and produces, in place of the abundant harvest of evil, the abundant harvest of good fruit (cf. Matt. 13:23).

The entirety of 1:21 bears a strong resemblance to 1 Pet. 1:22–2:2, which likewise compares the word of God to seed that produces godliness and which likewise enjoins the response of "putting off" evil by laying hold of that word. And the end result in both passages is "salvation." As a result, this one verse packs within it a large amount of gospel teaching: the necessity of (1) repudiating the abundance of evil within, (2) humble recognition of need of help in doing so, (3) decisive response to the gospel, and (4) recognition of the power of the gospel to rescue the believer. All of these are, of course, necessary aspects of genuine faith.

In 1:22–25 the "quick to hear" part of the wisdom saying of 1:19 is fleshed out. Being "quick to hear" means not just quickly hearing what is said, but quickly acting on it. Genuine faith acts. Although γίνεσθε (*ginesthe*) often is translated "become," the ongoing character of the progressive imperative is closer to the English imperative "be" than "become."[12] The latter implies a definitive change at a particular moment, but James is characterizing "word-doing" as an ongoing pattern of life, not a conversion experience or even an ongoing decision. The lack of an article before λόγου (*logou*) does not indicate that James is considering words in general; this is an adjectival genitive to "doers," and its qualitative force is uppermost. Something like "word-doers" captures the idea.[13]

1:22–25

---

11. Note the reference to the implanted word's being "able to save," which implies that the saving is anticipated, not something already in hand. As already noted, the last verse of James (5:20) expects future salvation. James 4:12 also identifies saving as one side of God's judging action (the other side being destruction).

12. In addition to James 3:1, see Luke 6:36; Eph. 4:32; Phil. 3:17. The NT has no second-person plural imperative of εἶναι (*einai*, to be); γίνεσθε often serves for it, as does the future indicative ἔσεσθε.

13. "Word-doer" in secular Greek literature ordinarily would refer to an orator or speechwriter, but James is here reflecting a Semitic idiom (Dibelius 1975: 114).

The injunction sounds very much like Paul in Rom. 2:13–16, where he contrasts the doers of law with the hearers of law,[14] and it echoes Jesus's comments in Matt. 7:24–27 and the beatitude of Luke 11:28 (see also 1 John 3:18). The contrast echoes Ezek. 33:31–32, which warns about the hypocrisy of hearing but not doing.

Scripture was regularly read in the synagogue and subsequently in the church assemblies, but those who only hear the word and fail to act on it in faith derive no benefit (cf. Heb. 4:2) and, indeed, delude themselves. The word "delude" (παραλογίζομαι, paralogizomai) also means "to defraud, cheat" or "to mislead through false inferences" (BDAG 768). The point is that being a hearer only and not a doer leads a person to a false self-reckoning. A concrete example comes in James 1:26: to fail to control one's tongue is to deceive one's heart.[15]

James often speaks of the danger of deceiving oneself (1:16, 22, 26). This quandary has bothered philosophers since before Christ. To deceive someone entails deliberately misleading that person, so a deceiver must know that what the victim is being led to believe is false. But how, then, is it possible to mislead oneself, since one already knows that the error being perpetrated is untrue? Yet it happens with astonishing regularity.

In the latter part of 1:23, James introduces the analogy of a mirror. James contrasts what is looked at (a mirror versus the perfect law), how people look at it (looking and leaving versus gazing intently), and the result of looking (forgetting versus actively doing).[16] Note that James does not think that believers are supposed to find resources within themselves to become perfect, obedient, active doers; James's confidence rests not on human abilities for keeping laws, but on the life-generating power of the "word of truth."

The metaphor of a person[17] looking in a mirror[18] and subsequently forgetting what he or she looks like corresponds to "not doing," because in hearing

14. Outside of James, Rom. 2:13 is the only place in the NT where the word ἀκροατής (akroatēs, hearer) occurs. Mayor (1897: 67) points out that the word is used of those who attend lectures but do not become disciples of the lecturer.

15. A different word for "deceive" (ἀπατάω, apataō) is used in 1:26, but the concept of self-deception obtains in both places.

16. Moo (2000: 90) has a sentence similar to this, but he presents it in terms of having to choose among the three aspects. In subsequent pages he minimizes the first and second contrasts in favor of the third.

17. Although James's word here is ἀνήρ (anēr, man) rather than ἄνθρωπος (anthrōpos, human being), his use here (and elsewhere in the letter) is not gender specific or at least is not singling out males as opposed to females (see L&N 1:104; see also the second additional note on 1:8 and footnote 24 of that unit above). I once heard a well-known preacher observe that James uses the word ἀνήρ here and conclude that this verse does not pertain to women, because just as women are more likely than men to pay attention to their image in mirrors and not forget what they look like, so also women are more likely to avoid the pitfalls of being a hearer only. Whether or not this is true of women, it certainly misses James's point, since nothing in the context suggests that his purpose is to distinguish between male and female proclivities to certain kinds of sin.

18. James's choice of illustration is interesting because, in ethical philosophy, gazing into a mirror was a metaphor for gaining self-knowledge (Dibelius 1975: 147; Denyer 1999) and thus

the word, one gets a glimpse of truth about oneself, but failure to then do the word makes the encounter purely momentary and external—a mere reflection, not the real thing. For most people in the ancient world, mirrors were not everyday objects, and those that did exist were highly polished metal surfaces (Pilch 1998),[19] not the silvered plate glass of modern mirrors. Most people therefore were generally unfamiliar with their own faces. When they did look in a mirror, they realized, of course, that they were looking at their own image, but a onetime exposure to a blurry and slightly distorted image does not give most people a deep and lasting awareness of what they look like. And even modern mirrors show only the external appearance.

"Natural appearance" is literally "the face of his origin" (τὸ πρόσωπον τῆς γενέσεως αὐτοῦ, to prosōpon tēs geneseōs autou). In 3:6 the word γένεσις (genesis) means "existence" or "nature," and Dibelius (1975: 116) therefore rightly understands 1:23 as referring to "natural appearance." Mayor (1897: 68) also notes the connection to 3:6, but compares James's use with its occurrence in Jdt. 12:18 ("all the days of my γένεσις") and concludes that it means "fleeting earthly existence," though even in the Judith passage life's transitoriness lies not in the word γένεσις but in the context. Laws (1980: 86) suggests "face he was born with," pointing out that in 3:6 the word γένεσις occurs in the odd phrase ("cycle of γένεσις"), which some have taken to mean "cycle of birth [death, rebirth, etc.]." If "existence" or "nature" is the meaning of γένεσις here in 1:23, as seems most likely, the focus nevertheless is on the πρόσωπον (prosōpon, face, visage); it is the visage of one's natural earthly existence/origin that stands in contrast with the "visage" or appearance of the soul (i.e., personal identity) in the light of Scripture.

Here James may be continuing with reproductive language, or, given the contrast with the gazing into the law in 1:25, it is arguable that James has in mind the original image of God of Gen. 1:26–27 (so Hort 1909: 39), which is recognized but immediately forgotten. This might fit very well with the difficult expression τὸ πρόσωπον τῆς γενέσεως (to prosōpon tēs geneseōs) in 1:23. But 1:25 does not make anything of one's recognition of the true image of God through the law, and therefore to find it there probably is to overread the analogy.

To "forget" (ἐπιλανθάνομαι, epilanthanomai) refers not just to failing to remember, but to allowing something to escape by inattention or neglect (BDAG 374), to leave it disregarded (cf. Tabula of Cebes 24). The rendering "No sooner has he gone away than he has forgotten what he looked like" is an attempt to express James's unusual use of tenses. Translated literally, the

for moral improvement through self-contemplation, though as Mussner (1975: 105–6) points out, James's purpose in the illustration is "not self-contemplation as in Seneca but the momentariness with which anyone sees his image in a mirror." Johnson (1988) takes the connection with Greco-Roman moral philosophy further and concludes that James is saying that the Torah is the more reliable and permanent guide to moral improvement.

19. Compare Sir. 12:11. See also kataptron in PW 21.29–45. Denyer (1999) sees a parallel regarding mirrors and self-awareness in Plato's Alcibiades 132c–133c, but there it is another person's eye that is the mirror, and the similarity is superficial.

sentence might read, "He observed himself, and has departed, and immediately forgot. . . ." The aorists κατενόησεν (*katenoēsen*, he observed, contemplated) and ἐπελάθετο (*epelatheto*, he forgot) are usually taken as "gnomic" aorists, expressive of general truths. But gnomic aorists typically are used in axioms, whereas these verbs are more illustrative than axiomatic. Further, ἀπελήλυθεν (*apelēlythen*, he is departed), which is perfect, not aorist, does not fit the characteristic of normal gnomic perfect.[20] The conundrum can be resolved by taking the unexpected aorists as further indication of the author's Semitic background, and the aorist verbs as vividly presenting a common general situation, with the perfect used to indicate a condition after the observing but antecedent to "he forgot." This stresses the immediacy of the forgetting, as I have tried to reflect in my translation.

The one who looks at a mirror forgets what he or she looks like partly because the image is unclear (in ancient mirrors) and partly because the image is so rarely encountered. James wants his readers to contrast this with the image of God that can be seen by looking into the perfect law and continuing to do so. In 1:25 the word "continue" (παραμένω, *paramenō*) refers to abiding or continuing in some capacity (BDAG 769), that is, "stick to a task." The one who looks at a mirror may briefly see the reflection of a human being created in God's image, but the one who steadfastly gazes into God's law sees the much clearer image of God constantly and remembers because it is firmly implanted in his or her mind.[21] Further, God's word also reveals how far the reader is from what the image of God should be.

"Gaze intently" (παρακύπτω, *parakyptō*) is the verb used in Luke 24:12 and John 20:11 to refer to disciples peering into the empty tomb. According to 1 Pet. 1:12, the angels desired to "gaze intently" into things (Scripture?), trying to understand the gospel that was coming. It therefore probably refers not to a quick glance (contra Laws 1980: 86), but to looking at something with intense interest and attention. It is this intense and constant looking into the law that, unlike looking in a mirror, is transformative, and thus can the law be seen to be a "law of freedom."

Why the shift from mentioning God's word (1:21) to God's law (1:25)? They actually refer to the same thing (see Ropes 1916: 173, 177; Laato 1997: 50–51). The word νόμος (*nomos*, law) is the Greek equivalent of Torah, and Torah comprises not just legal statutes and mandates; it is the teaching of Scripture. Thus, to equate word and law is by no means to limit the word to God's moral demands; rather, it equates the law of God with the totality of his saving revelation through Scripture. The reason for the shift in terms is

---

20. BDF §344 indicates the presence of "gnomic" perfects in the NT in expressing the (future) results of a general or imaginary condition (see, e.g., James 2:10: "Whoever keeps the whole law but fails at one point has become [γέγονεν, *gegonen*] guilty of all of it"), but in James 1:24 the perfect ἀπελήλυθεν expresses not the future result, but an additional condition.

21. The passage has certain similarities to 1 Pet. 1:23, where the regenerative word is said to be "living and abiding," but there it is the living word, or perhaps God himself, that abides. Here it is the one who studies the law intently who abides.

the new focus on the instructional character of the λόγος/νόμος, because it makes a reader aware of who he or she is and who God is. The "perfect law of freedom" is therefore the same as the word of truth, the gospel, which is instrumental in the bringing forth and maturation of believers.

The association of word of truth and perfect law in Jewish thought goes back at least to Ps. 119:43, which refers to the Torah as "the word of truth." But, just as in Ps. 119, the "law" is not some legal code; it is the transformative and living speech of the living God, with whom one has a relationship. So here the "gazing into the perfect law of freedom" is not a scholastic analysis of a legal text independent of its author; it is a listening to the redemptive story because it is the living speech of the author.

It is called a "perfect" (τέλειος, teleios) law (cf. Ps. 18:8 LXX [19:7 ET]) possibly because it is without error or deceit, in contrast to polished metal mirrors with their blurs and distortions. It probably also carries with it the connotation of the whole and indivisible law, since James later points out, "Whoever keeps the whole law but fails at one point has become guilty of all of it" (2:10). But it is also a perfect law because it is now a completed law. Given James's close relationship with the Gospel of Matthew, it is not too much of a stretch to see the perfect law of freedom not just as the Torah interpreted and supplemented by Christ (so Mussner 1975: 241–42; Davids 1982: 99–100; Moo 2000: 94), but as Torah that has reached its ultimate redemptive purpose (Matt. 5:17). James later calls it the "royal law" (2:8), which is best understood as the Torah of the kingdom of God proclaimed by Jesus (see the commentary on 2:8, which I take to be not simply a reference to the specific law of Lev. 19:18, but the kingdom Torah as summed up in that text). It is "the law of freedom," the law that liberates (ESV: "law of liberty"), because looking into the christologically completed Torah enables a person to become an active doer and receive its blessing. Even if James did not consciously have the christological dimension in mind, in the story of Israel the law was given at the occasion of Israel's exodus and delivery from slavery, and properly he understands the law as that which flows forth from God's work of liberation. As it is a word of both judgment and salvation, it is a Jacobean equivalent to the gospel (Cantinat 1973: 110). There may also be something here of the Jewish belief that only in obeying God can a person truly be free (cf. Rom. 6:16).[22]

One may still ask how the gospel, the story of Christ's bringing salvation to his people by his death and resurrection, could be called the "law," whether perfect or not. And it also may appear on the surface to be radically opposed to Paul's notion of law as that which enslaves and condemns. But that law which Paul places in opposition to faith is only a particular approach to law. Paul indicates that the law itself bears witness to the necessity of faith (Gal. 4:21–31) and, like James, associates the law properly used with freedom (Gal.

22. Compare *m. 'Abot* 6.2 (commenting on Exod. 32:6), "None is free but the child of the law." The entire tract by Philo titled *That Every Good Person Is Free* is essentially an exposition of the same idea.

5:13–14; cf. 1 Tim. 1:8).[23] More importantly, however, James almost certainly is not restricting the meaning of "perfect law of freedom" to the OT, although of course the OT is part of the story. It is, above all, the story of Jesus's fulfillment of the law, and the new life that issues from that fulfillment, that brings freedom (see Davies 1964: 402–5).

A "forgetful hearer" is literally a "hearer of forgetfulness" (ἀκροατὴς ἐπιλησμονῆς, *akroatēs epilēsmonēs*), another Semitic genitive of attribution or quality, describing the one who hears but does not pay any attention or allow it to change behavior patterns. Most parents know how adept their children are at being "forgetful hearers," but it is a malady to which all are prone and requires the remedy of constant, continuous attentiveness to the word of God. Throughout the Bible "forgetting" the covenant is characteristic of unbelief; faith, on the other hand, remembers.

In contrast to the "forgetful hearer" stands the "active doer," or literally "doer of work" (ποιητὴς ἔργου, *poiētēs ergou*). Although the latter makes sense as an objective genitive ("someone who does deeds"), probably, like "hearer of forgetfulness," it is a Semitic genitive of attribution. Biblically attentive doers will be blessed in the doing; that is, their deeds will have genuinely good effects, and they themselves will be regarded favorably by God (see the commentary on 1:12).

The use of the future "will be" (ἔσται, *estai*) may be simply a gnomic future (stating a general truth).[24] In this case, the meaning is "If someone is a doer, [then] he is blessed" (cf. John 13:17: "If you know these things, blessed are you if you do them"). However, this use of the future is rather rare,[25] and given James's eschatological orientation elsewhere (e.g., 1:11–12; 5:7), it is more likely that James sees the basis for the blessedness of the one who obeys God's word not only in the prospering of one's activities now but much more in the future approval of God at the judgment. This eschatological subnote can also be seen in the verses following (1:26–27), with their echo of the judgment of the nations (Matt. 25:31–46), which is based on their response to the needs of the destitute "least ones." Whether or not the future tense is deliberately eschatological, blessedness in James's purview is ultimately eschatological, as we have seen in James 1:12.

The prepositional phrase "in his doing" could simply mean "in the context of his doing." If this is the force of the preposition, then the αὐτοῦ (*autou*, "of it" or "of him") could be read as an objective genitive referring back to the "work" (ἔργου, *ergou*)—"will be blessed in the context of doing *it*" (the work)—though more likely James's focus remains on the character of the person hearing and doing rather than on the deed. Alternatively, the phrase

23. On James's relation to Paul, see views 1 and 2 under "Four Views of Author and Date" in the introduction, excursus 2, and also the commentary on 2:14–26.
24. Wallace (1996: 571) states that "the future is very rarely used to indicate the likelihood that a *generic* event will take place."
25. Wallace (1996: 571) and other grammars typically refer to Matt. 6:24; Rom. 5:7; 7:3 as examples and very little else (cf. MHT 3:86; Burton 1892: 36).

could mean "he will be blessed *because* of his doing" (Moo 2000: 95), or it could be read with an instrumental force: "*by means of* his doing he will be blessed." Since this blessing comes upon one who gazes intently into the law, the phrase may very well be a deliberate echo of the blessed person of Ps. 1:1–3, who "prospers in all that he does" because "he meditates on God's law."

Additional Notes

1:19. The word ἴστε (imperative of οἶδα, and here translated as "be aware") occurs in virtually all the best and oldest manuscripts, but the Majority Text and many other witnesses read ὥστε rather than ἴστε and then either eliminate δέ or substitute a καί for it. This smooths out the sentence and makes ἔστω the main verb (reading the καί not as a conjunction but as adverbial). The sentence would then read, "So then, my dear brothers, everyone be quick to hear. . . ." However, not only is this poorly attested, but also this smoothing out of the strangeness results in an important feature of James's unique concerns being overlooked. It is by *knowing* the word of truth that people are able to be quick to hear and so on.

1:19. When James uses the vocative ἀδελφοί, usually it is accompanied by or associated with either an imperative verb (11 or 12 times out of 16 occurrences) or a rhetorical question implying an imperative (3 or 4 times),[26] leaving only one indicative (3:10), and that too is an implied imperative ("My brothers, these things must not to be so!").

1:19. Usually, εἰς τό with infinitive expresses purpose (as in 1:18), but here εἰς has the meaning "toward" or "with respect to," as in Rom. 16:19: θέλω δὲ ὑμᾶς σοφοὺς εἶναι εἰς τὸ ἀγαθόν. Thus, the phrase simply limits the adjective, and James's injunction is to be quick with respect to hearing and so on (see MHT 3:143).

1:21. The participle ἀποθέμενοι (laying aside, putting off) could be causal ("because you have laid aside all filth") or in some other way antecedent. Or the participle is possibly instrumental ("receive the word by putting aside filth"), but it may be best simply to take the participle and verb as semantically commensurate and to translate paratactically: "put aside filth and evil and receive the word."

The language of "putting off" leads Mussner (1975: 101) once again to see a baptismal formula: "Therefore . . . put off everything . . . receive." But I agree with Davids (1985: 93) that, given the absence of reference to baptism and the total absence of any concern with initiation or ritual of any sort in James, it is a case of overreading the metaphor to see baptism here.

1:21. The phrase "in meekness" is adverbial. As noted above, it can be taken either with the participle "lay aside" or with the verb "receive." Most editions and translations put it with "lay aside," but the attribute of meekness seems more appropriate as a way of receiving the word than of laying aside of filth and evil. Whereas one certainly can receive the word meekly, how does one meekly lay aside filth? But since "lay aside" is itself adverbially related to "receive the word," it does not greatly change the meaning one way or the other.

1:22. In nonbiblical Greek ποιητής means "maker, composer," and hence a "word-doer" or "word-maker" would, in a non-Jewish context, refer to an orator or a rhetorician (LSJ 1429; it could also mean "poet"). This, among other things, led Scaer (1983) to propose that the entire letter of James is written to church leaders (teachers and preachers), not to Christians generally, and indeed this almost works at points (especially with James 3). However, a better approach is to recognize that the influence of the Hebrew *ʿāśâ* (do, make) is at work here, and the term is a favorite with James, as

26. James 2:1 can be taken either as an imperative or as a question.

is its companion ἀκροατής, since they vigorously capture the contrast between the noncommittal entertainment of ideas and a committed, life-altering response to the word of God. Compare the Hebrew expression *'āśâ hattôrâ* (to do the law), which means to obey it (e.g., Deut. 28:58, reflected in Paul's expression ποιητὴς νόμου in Rom. 2:13).

1:22. Romans 2:13 is probably the source of the occasional scribal substitution of νόμου for λόγου (C[2], 88, 621, et al.).

1:22. The noun upon which the participle παραλογιζόμενοι depends, ἀκροαταί, is anarthrous, making it formally uncertain whether the participle is adverbial or adjectival. In context the participle seems more likely to be specifying what kind of hearers are in view, or what characterizes these hearers, rather than specifying in what way "you" (James's audience) might be hearers only, and thus I have rendered it attributively with "who deceive themselves" in the translation.

1:23. Some important manuscripts (A, 33, and by implication some versions) omit the word ὅτι, but 1:23–25 clearly is giving reasons why the readers must be doers and not just hearers, and the ὅτι is broadly supported.

E. True Religion (1:26–27)

James's reference to being a "doer of work" (1:25) that flows from the implanted word invites interest in what kind of work is in view. The last two verses of chapter 1 both summarize the preceding material and effectively encapsulate the concerns for "word-worthy" and "faith-ful" behavior that occupy the remainder of James's letter: (1) wise use of speech, (2) integrity in social responsibility, and (3) personal holiness. But although his concern is highly practical, James, unlike many of his later interpreters, does not lose his grounding in the gospel. Pure and undefiled religion is possible because God is Father, particularly a father for the fatherless, who brought forth his people by the word and continues to implant that word which produces the good works in view. This is what constitutes true religion that is acceptable to God.

James, like the other NT authors, is relatively uninterested in religiousness as personal piety. Even his exhortations to prayer are directed largely toward prayer for one another in the community (5:13–18). It is the ethical reflection of the character of God—his wisdom, his fatherhood, his purity—that constitutes true and "undefiled" religious expression, both in personal life (keeping oneself pure) and in communal responsibility (visiting widows and orphans).

Exegesis and Exposition

²⁶If someone thinks of himself as being religious ⌜ ⌝ and yet does not have control of ⌜his⌝ tongue but deceives ⌜his⌝ heart, such a person's religion is void. ²⁷Religion that is pure and undefiled in the sight of ⌜the⌝ [one who is] God and Father is this: to look after orphans and widows in their distress, and to ⌜keep oneself unstained by⌝ the world.

The verb δοκέω (*dokeō*) can mean either to "seem (to others)" or "to think (to oneself)." The following phrase "he deceives his own heart" clearly favors the latter. The adjective "religious" (θρησκός, *thrēskos*) is found only here in the NT; the corresponding noun "religion" (θρησκεία, *thrēskeia*) appears only four times in the NT, two of those here in James 1:26–27. In Acts 26:5 Paul is reported to have used the word to refer to the strictness of his Jewish practice. In Col. 2:18 it is used of the worship of angels (cf. Wis. 14:18, 27, where it refers to the worship of idols). It thus may be closer to our words "religiousness," "piety," or even "religiosity,"[1] although 4 Macc. 5:7 uses it to refer to the Jewish religion in a general sense.

1:26–27

---

1. For Josephus (*Ant.* 17.9.3 §214) it signifies religious activity or cultic ritual, as it does for Herodotus (*Hist.* 2.18; 2.37); and the verb θρησκεύω (*thrēskeuō*) means "to perform religious observances" (Herodotus, *Hist.* 2.64).

Human speech has enormous capacity for harm as well as good, and it is easy to say things that one will later regret. The OT, especially Psalms and wisdom literature, is full of comments about the requirement of keeping close watch over what one says (see, e.g., Ps. 34:13), and the failure to do so runs counter to genuine service to God. James will develop this further in James 3.[2] It is noteworthy that in James's summary of piety, a prime requirement of faithful behavior is control of the tongue.

The form of the first sentence sounds odd. We might expect "he deceives his heart" to go with the apodosis (the "then" part of the conditional sentence), thus reading "If someone thinks of himself as being religious and does not control his tongue, [then] he deceives himself, and his religion is void." But James puts "not controlling the tongue" and "deceiving the heart" in parallel, both as evidence for the vanity of such a person's religion, perhaps because deceiving the heart is a verbal activity. In Rom. 16:18, Paul warns against those who "by smooth talk and flattery . . . deceive the hearts of the naive." An unbridled tongue can deceive even the tongue's owner. Self-deceit, then, is a corollary to failure to control the tongue, just as in 1:22 it is the corollary to being a hearer only. Speaking and not doing is the complement to hearing and not doing (cf. 2:16).

Further, James wants to stress that just as one is responsible for failing to control the tongue, one also is responsible for deceiving oneself. Allowing oneself to be deceived and not controlling the tongue are passive decisions, but passivity does not remove responsibility. This may be why James stresses actively doing work here and in James 2. His hearers were in danger of thinking that as long as they did not actively break commands they were off the hook. But a passive religion, an inactive religion, a simple assertion of faith, is worthless and void.

When James says that this religion is "void," he is echoing the judgment of Jeremiah (2:5; 8:19; 10:15; 51:18 [28:18 LXX]) against idolatrous religion. In James's eyes, uncontrolled speech and self-deception put a person's religion in the same class as idolatry.

"Pure and undefiled" in 1:27 probably is a hendiadys, using two words to express the same thing, in this case positively and negatively. In context, it refers not to the ritual purity of the OT cultic requirements, but to ethical purity (although, of course, ethical purity extends to behavior in worship assembly, as is clear in 2:1–4).

True religion must be pure in the sight of[3] the one who is God and Father.[4] Although the OT and other Jewish materials occasionally speak of God as Father, the concentrated interest in God as Father is distinctively Christian,

2. James uses the same word for "control" in 3:2 as he uses here in 1:26, χαλιναγωγέω (chalinagōgeō, literally "to bridle"). In 3:2 the one who does not stumble in speech is mature indeed, able to "control" the entire body.

3. "In the sight of" renders παρά with the dative case in accord with its context. See BDAG 757 (definition B.2).

4. For the translation "the one who is God and Father," see the first additional note on 1:27.

stemming from Jesus's characteristic and frequent reference to God's father-hood. James has already picked this up in saying that God "brought forth" his people and that he is the "father of lights." But in the OT God is especially a father to the fatherless and a protector of widows (Ps. 68:5; see also, among many other OT examples, Ps. 10:14, 18). Hence, those who are genuinely re-ligious and bear the character traits of God will also take a special interest in orphans and widows (cf. Sir. 4:10 NRSV: "Be a father to orphans, and be like a husband to their mother; you will then be like a son of the Most High"). It is thus that human beings who have become children of God are to reflect his character and do the works of God (cf. Ps. 72:4; see also especially Ps. 82:3, where the preceding verse also condemns showing partiality, as does the very next verse in James).

The verb "to look after" (ἐπισκέπτομαι, *episkeptomai*) carries several pos-sible connotations. In the Greek OT it was used to translate the Hebrew *pāqad*, which could mean "to visit" or "to bring justice to," and both these meanings can also be found in the NT (e.g., Luke 1:68; Acts 15:36). It can also mean "to care for" (Heb. 2:6) or "to seek out" (Acts 6:3) or "to concern oneself with" (Acts 15:14).[5] Any of these meanings work well here. The most common meaning in the NT is "to go see a person with helpful intent" (BDAG 378). It is the motive of helpful intent, the objective of giving aid, or undertaking to look out for the interests of someone that is operative here. Given James's concern that people do things for the needy rather than just say things to them (2:16), it is unlikely that James has only visitation or an intellectual interest in mind here.

The word for "distress" (θλῖψις, *thlipsis*) is the one commonly used in the NT for the pre-eschatological trials experienced by the faithful (Matt. 24:21; Rom. 5:3), but although James does connect suffering and patient endurance with eschatological hope (1:12; 5:7), here he probably is simply speaking of the economic and social distress that widows and orphans commonly experience, a distress that those whose faith is real are called to alleviate.

The requirement to keep oneself "unstained" or "spotless" (ἄσπιλος, *aspilos*)[6] from the world is again an aspect of the imitation of God. In 1 Pet. 1:19 Jesus is the "spotless" lamb. James 1:27 has close parallels in 2 Pet. 3:14 and 1 Tim. 6:14. In James the adjective probably has special reference to purity of speech, since 3:6 marks the tongue as "that unrighteous world that stains [σπιλοῦσα, *spilousa*] the whole body."

The term "world" (κόσμος, *kosmos*) is used in various ways in the NT. Here, as at 3:6 and 4:4, it signifies the human environment standing in opposition to God, which acts as a corrupting agent (as also in, e.g., John 12:31; 1 Cor. 1:21). Therefore, to keep oneself unstained from the world is not to withdraw

5. In the LXX, it often means "to examine, inspect" (Lev. 13:36), "to make a record of" (over forty times in Num. 1–4), and even "to bring judgment against" (Ps. 58:6 [59:6 MT; 59:5 ET]; Jer. 5:9).
6. On the variant reading here, see the second additional note on 1:27.

from the world, but to avoid being unduly influenced by the world's values (Bauckham 1999: 145–46).[7]

This verse is not meant as an exhaustive list of what pleases God; rather, it describes by practical example the behavior patterns exhibited by a person whose character is being shaped by "true religion," that is, genuine faith. Both personal holiness and social responsibility are manifestations of the character transformation that genuine faith effects. It is noteworthy that James includes both here, because it is difficult to be involved in the ills of the world without getting entangled in its idolatries, and it is difficult to cultivate holiness without cutting oneself off from the exigencies of the world. Ultimately, however, to be truly effective in dealing with the ills of the world requires personal holiness (cf. 3:17), and genuine personal holiness entails involvement in dealing with the world's ills.

Additional Notes

1:26. The Majority Text adds ἐν ὑμῖν after εἶναι, making it less of a generalized saying. But its omission is supported by better manuscripts and a wider geographic distribution, and James punctuates his letter with similar apophthegmatic and generalized proverbial material.

1:26. Several manuscripts have ἑαυτοῦ instead of αὐτοῦ after γλῶσσαν or καρδίαν or both. This would have little effect on the meaning.

1:27. Some important manuscripts, and the original hand of ℵ, omit the article before θεῷ. A corrector of ℵ, along with 𝔓⁷⁴ and most older manuscripts, includes it. The presence of the article with the two singular nouns in the same case connected by καί makes clear that "God" and "Father" are referring to the same person (though even without the article the context would suggest this), and the translation given above ("the [one who is] God and Father") attempts to render this. The literal rendering "the God and Father" in English puts too much stress on the article, while "God and the Father" in English suggests two different entities.

1:27. The verbs of the second half of 1:27 exhibit some variety in the manuscript tradition. A handful of manuscripts (614, 1505, 2495, and a few others) have second-person plural imperatives instead of infinitives (ἐπισκέπτεσθε . . . τηρεῖτε) and correspondingly change the singulars ἄσπιλον ἑαυτόν to the plurals. Like the addition of ἐν ὑμῖν in 1:26, this would make the verse a more direct exhortation rather than a generalized statement. But although James has no lack of direct exhortation, here he is making a general comment that he will proceed to apply in the chapters following.

𝔓⁷⁴ has a unique reading. Instead of ἄσπιλον ἑαυτὸν τηρεῖν ἀπὸ τοῦ κόσμου (to keep oneself unstained from the world), 𝔓⁷⁴ has ὑπερασπίζειν αὐτοὺς ἀπὸ τοῦ κόσμου, which perhaps could be translated "to protect them [i.e., the widows and orphans] from the world." Roberts (1972: 216) argues that this should be the preferred reading, in spite of the testimony of all other Greek manuscripts, because the usual reading "is not in keeping with the thought of the Epistle of James," which advocates involvement in the world, not keeping away from it to avoid being soiled (see also Trudinger 2004). Johanson (1973) effectively counters this argument by pointing out that "from the world" goes with "unstained" rather than "keep,"[8] and that James elsewhere (3:6)

7. See further the exposition on 4:4.
8. Of the five other occurrences of ἀπό with genitive in James, it twice means "by" rather than "from" (1:13; 5:4). Failure to recognize this usage of James has led to confusion in those verses too.

uses the notion of "staining" and "world" together in a negative sense (with respect to the tongue). But decisive is 3:17, where James declares that the wisdom from above is "first of all pure," then peaceable, sincere, and so on. Purity, that is to say, moral or ethical purity (not ritual purity), is a significant concern for James.[9]

9. The lack of concern for ritual purity and the separation of Jew from Gentile is, contra Dibelius 1975: 122, no indication that the author was not James of Jerusalem; rather, it is an indication of an early acknowledgment by the disciples that Jesus had put purity concerns on different ground (cf. Mark 7:18–23).

III. First Discourse: Faith and Behavior (2:1–26)

James 2 begins in earnest the author's appeal to genuine faith. It consists of two parts: (1) a vigorous diatribe against showing favoritism, which stands as a denial to both faith in Christ and the liberating and perfect law (2:1–13); (2) a sharp rebuke to the notion that a faith that does not produce good works can have saving value (2:14–26). The latter section is the best-known part of James because it appears, at first glance, to contradict Paul's declaration "One is justified by faith apart from works of the law" (Rom. 3:28). As we shall see, however, James is simply reinforcing the teaching of Jesus that hypocritical "faith" is not true faith and in fact is deadly.

Many scholars (e.g., Dibelius 1975: 124–25) notice a style change beginning in James 2. Dibelius recognizes 2:1–13 as a coherent unit having the marks of a treatise with characteristics of both diatribe and sermon. Whereas James 1 floats around several items of concern, introducing in broad strokes the general concerns of the letter, James 2 begins a series of more extended diatribe-like segments dealing with particular issues, extending at least through most of James 4.[1] As noted in the introduction (see "Structure"), each of these diatribes is marked off by an opening rhetorical question or prohibition (2:1; 2:14; 3:1; 3:12a; 3:13; 4:1; 4:11) and closed by a short summary proverb or saying (2:13; 2:26; 3:12b; 3:18; 4:10; 4:12). Further, the larger structure of James 2 and that of James 3 are almost exactly parallel.

An introductory verse introduces two concerns of this chapter: favoritism (developed in 2:2–13) and faith (2:14–26). They are tied together because if the Lord does not play favorites, then for people to do so is unbelief, a lack of faith.

We should note that James is not the first to connect the themes of showing no favoritism, doing righteousness, justification, and the lordship of Christ; these four elements also appear together in Peter's speech to Cornelius in Acts 10:34–36.

---

1. Except for the interjected oracle of 4:13–5:6, this pattern may even be considered to continue through to the end of the epistle. See "Proverbs as 'Closers'" and "The Parallel Structure of James 2 and James 3" in the introduction.

A. Part 1: Faith, Favoritism, and Law (2:1–13)

Believers, as God's offspring through the word (1:18), are presumed to exhibit God's character. God shows no favoritism to those of high societal status, and so his children must do likewise. This equality of people before God is even more evident in the new covenant than in the old, as Jeremiah prophesied (Jer. 31:34).

The first half of James 2 sets the stage for the attack on dysfunctional, hypocritical "dead faith" that James will develop in 2:14–26. Here is addressed a specific problem, hinted at in 1:9–10: wealth can get in the way of genuine faith. Some in the community of believers apparently have been dealing, or have been tempted to deal, with people according to their economic and social status. This makes a mockery of their averrals of faith, for God shows special interest in the poor, and it is the poor who will inherit the reign of God. Indeed, the wealthy are those who typically inhibit and resist the gospel and are persecuting those who have received the word.[1]

The theme of the first half of James 2, on showing favoritism, is announced in 2:1 and then developed in two thought units, the first (2:2–7) focusing on the folly of favoritism, and the second (2:8–13) on its being contrary to God's commands and character.

---

1. Kloppenborg Verbin (1999) sees this passage as specifically targeted against the practice of patronage in the Greco-Roman world. This certainly is a viable application of James's concerns in 2:1–13 and may have been included in James's purview, but the tendency to show deference to the rich, with its attendant disrespect of the poor, is not unique to that world, and the passage's concerns are broader than patronage as such.

1. Faith and Favoritism (2:1–7)

The opening verses of James 2, dealing with "favoritism," begin with a prohibition followed by a series of rhetorical questions. Wachob (2000: 63) sees here a deliberate rhetorical progression, 2:1 being the thesis, 2:2–4 the reasoning (*ratio*), and 2:5–7 the proof (*probatio*). However, James is not simply making a rational disputation. The mandate in 2:1 is not a thesis needing to be proved; it is a general statement that the readers would have trouble disagreeing with, and it becomes the basis for an accusation and a call for behavioral change. The whole passage has substantively more in common with OT prophetic calls than with Greek rhetoric.

Whether taken as a rhetorical question (so NRSV) or as an imperative (so most translations and commentaries), 2:1 sets the nature of the concern: incompatibility of favoritism based on wealth or social status with genuine faith. The verses of 2:2–4 comprise one long sentence that unpacks that concern by presenting an extended condition, concluding with another rhetorical question that acts as an indictment: "Have you not discriminated?" This sets the stage for James's observations on the incompatibility of such favoritism with the kingdom of God and on the foolishness of pandering to the wealthy (2:5–7), all expressed as rhetorical questions except for one indicting indicative: "You dishonor the poor."

Exegesis and Exposition

¹My brothers, you must not show favoritism if you have faith in our ⌜glorious⌝ Lord, Jesus [the] Christ. ²For if some man comes into your gathering with gold rings on his fingers and dressed in fine clothes, and at the same time a poor man dressed in filthy rags comes in, ³if you pay attention to the one wearing fine clothes and say, "Take this good seat here," and then you say to the poor man, "You stand over there," or else, "Sit⌜ ⌝⌜below⌝ my footstool,"⁴have you ⌜not⌝ discriminated among yourselves and have you not become judges rendering perverse verdicts?

⁵Listen, my dear brothers, has not God chosen the poor ⌜in worldly things⌝ to be rich in faith and heirs of the ⌜kingdom⌝ which he promised to those who love him? ⁶You, however, have dishonored the poor man. Is it not the rich who oppress ⌜you⌝, and are they not the ones who drag you into court? ⁷Are they not the ones who blaspheme the good name which has been invoked upon you?

2:1 Most translations and commentaries, like the translation given here, treat 2:1 as a prohibition (e.g., ESV: "Show no partiality as you hold the faith in our Lord Jesus Christ"). However, the verse also could be read as a question

(NRSV: "Do you with your acts of favoritism really believe in our glorious Lord Jesus Christ?").[1] The vocative "my brothers" in James usually occurs with an imperative (1:2, 16, 19; 3:1, 10; 4:11; 5:7, 9, 10, 12, 19), but 2:14 and 3:12a address rhetorical questions to "my brothers," the latter being quite similar in form to 2:1 (μή with indicative).[2] Given the author's penchant for rhetorical questions in this opening part of James 2 (2:2–4, 5, 6, 7 are rhetorical questions), 2:1 could well be such a question. However, the formal similarity between 2:1 and 3:1, and the fact that 3:1 is much less likely to be a rhetorical question, favor reading this verse as an imperative. This requires that the force of the prohibition be placed not on the verb but on the prepositional phrase "in favoritism" and that another verb be supplied to go with it, as I have done in the translation at the top of this section.

"To have faith" (ἔχειν πίστιν, *echein pistin*) in the LXX means "to be faithful, trustworthy" (see, e.g., Jer. 15:18 LXX: "like a false spring that does not keep faith"). In the NT it generally is equivalent to "to believe" (e.g., Matt. 17:20 NASB: "If you have faith the size of a mustard seed . . ."). Hence, James is referring to his hearers' faith in Jesus Christ as being incompatible with showing favoritism. However, since only in the opening verse and here in 2:1 does James name Jesus Christ specifically, some have seen a reference here to "faith in Jesus Christ" as unlikely, taking this as a reference not to the audience's belief in Jesus but rather to the example of the faithfulness of Jesus Christ, or Jesus's own belief and trust in God.[3]

Only in Mark 11:22–23, however, is there an exact parallel to the phrase found here (ἔχειν πίστιν + genitive), where Jesus commands his disciples to "have faith of [i.e., 'in'] God"[4] and contrasts that action with doubt. And James's reference to Jesus Christ as "our Lord" and the addition of the genitive "of glory," however it is rendered, are patent evidence that James regards Jesus not just as an example for faithfulness, but as the Master to whom one must give allegiance. Finally, note, in a literal rendering, what James writes: "not in favoritism should you (or do you) have faith." As the "faith of/in Jesus Christ" is something that

1. Mayor (1897: 76) refers to some older commentators, such as R. Stier, M. Schnecken-burger, and A. R. Gebser, who rendered 2:1 as an interrogative, but Mayor himself argues for the imperative.

2. James 2:5 is both imperative and rhetorical interrogative: "Listen, my dear brothers, has not God chosen. . . ."

3. For a defense of the view that here James is referring to Jesus's own faith in God, see Wachob 2000: 64–65. Wachob argues that "faith" in the Epistle of James always signifies believing in God, not Jesus, and it is the pattern of Jesus's faith that is being set forth as determinative for the readers (see also Hartin 2003: 117). This presupposes that James had no cognizance of Jesus's divinity; however, here the very phrase "our glorious Lord, Jesus [the] Christ" suggests that James had at least some awareness of Jesus as the focus of Christian allegiance.

4. Use of the genitive to express the object of faith is not uncommon. Acts 3:16 describes a healing as occurring ἐπὶ πίστει τοῦ ὀνόματος αὐτοῦ, where ὀνόματος can only be an objective genitive. Likewise, Eph. 3:12 and Phil. 3:9 uncontestably use "faith of" to mean "faith toward" or "faith in." The genitives in Rom. 3:22 and other texts are controversial, but they too probably are objective genitives. For more on the meaning of Paul's phrase πίστις Ἰησοῦ Χριστοῦ, see Silva 2004.

the audience is said to "have," a reference to the example of Christ's faithfulness seems out of place.[5] Believers do not "have" the faithfulness of Christ.

The words "belief" and "faith" in these passages and elsewhere in the NT signify more than the loose idea that often characterizes our use of them. The NT use of "faith" is rooted in the Hebrew *ʾĕmûnâ*, which connotes both faithfulness and truth, as well as trust and belief. In 1 Tim. 1:19 "having faith" means "holding on to faith" (NIV), remaining faithful to Christian commitments (cf. 1 Tim. 3:9). A "faith" that is only loose belief receives ridicule from James later in this chapter (2:14): "If someone says he has faith but does not have works, can that faith save him?" There can be no separation between the trust component of faith and the faithfulness component, because to trust an authority entails a commitment to it. This is not to turn faith into some kind of work, but to point out that faith is a matter of commitment to relationship, not just the acceptance of some intellective truth.

Thus, the fact that some in the community of believers apparently are showing favoritism is a serious breach of their faith and calls into question its viability (as will be expounded more in 2:14–26). Favoritism (προσωπολημψία, *prosōpolēmpsia*, literally "face-taking,"[6] sometimes rendered "respect of persons" or "showing partiality")[7] is a breach of faith not just because it makes one a transgressor of the law of love (2:9), but because it is inconsistent with God's own character. That God is no "respecter of persons," that he does not judge people by extrinsic considerations but instead looks on the heart, is a commonplace in both Judaism and Christianity (Deut. 10:17; 2 Chron. 19:7; Sir. 35:12–13; Acts 10:34; Rom. 2:11; Gal. 2:6; Eph. 6:9; 1 Pet. 1:17). Ethics for James is largely a matter of *imitatio Dei*, which he no doubt acquired from Jesus (e.g., Matt. 5:48). Thus, faith *in* Jesus Christ will necessarily eventuate in a reflection of the character *of* Jesus Christ.

James's extensive title for Jesus is noteworthy. In the sequence of genitives in Greek (τοῦ κυρίου ἡμῶν Ἰησοῦ Χριστοῦ τῆς δόξης, *tou kyriou hēmōn Iēsou Christou tēs doxēs*), almost certainly τοῦ κυρίου Ἰησοῦ Χριστοῦ is a single genitive entity, that is, "the Lord Jesus Christ," the object of the phrase "have faith in."[8] Both "Lord" and "Christ" are not names but meaningful titles.[9] To

---

5. Note that in 2:14 James speaks of the one who "says he has faith but does not have works," indicating it to be a worthless faith. This is not saying that a person claims to be holding on to the example of someone else's faith (or has someone else's faithfulness).

6. Although the Hebrew expression *nāśāʾ pānîm* (literally, "lift up faces") is sometimes in the OT taken in a good sense of "looking favorably on someone" (e.g., Deut. 28:50), when it was adopted into Greek in the LXX (e.g., Mal. 1:9; 2:9) and the NT (e.g., Luke 20:21), it took on the consistently negative connotation of making judgments on the basis of a person's status, appearance, or other external matters unrelated to the merits of a case—in other words, being prejudiced.

7. James somewhat unexpectedly uses a plural form, perhaps suggesting that he is not speaking hypothetically but has heard of some actual cases.

8. It is quite unlikely that the object of faith is the "glory of Jesus." See Dibelius 1975: 127.

9. The earliest believers understood "Christ" as a title, "the Anointed One." The translation "the Christ" makes the titular character of "Christ" clearer in English, even though the article is not in the Greek text.

call Jesus "our Lord" is an acknowledgment not just of the general sovereignty of Jesus, but especially of his lordship of his people (and hence the necessity of their obedience to his teaching); and "Christ," of course, refers to his Jewish messiahship. Clearly, James assumes that the people to whom he is writing are believers in Jesus, those who acknowledge him as the Lord and the Christ, or at least those who claim to be.

"Of glory" most likely reflects James's Semitic phraseology and should be read as simply a genitive of quality: "glorious Lord" (as in 1 Cor. 2:8)[10] or possibly "glorious Christ" (Dibelius 1975: 128; Mussner 1975: 116; Davids 1982: 106).[11] Compare "glorious Father" in Eph. 1:17, "glorious name" in Neh. 9:5 LXX, "glorious throne" in Wis. 9:10, and "glorious robe" in Sir. 6:29. Since the one article τοῦ seems to group κυρίου ἡμῶν Ἰησοῦ Χριστοῦ into a single entity, "glorious" modifies the entire noun phrase ("our Lord Jesus Christ"), not any particular one of the nouns. Much less likely is the suggestion by Hort (1909: 47) and Mayor (1897: 77–78), recently supported by Laws (1980: 95–96), that "glory" is in apposition to "Lord Jesus Christ," thus reading "the one who is 'the glory'"; in other words, Jesus is the manifestation of God's character. Although Jesus is indeed the manifestation of the glory of God (Heb. 1:3), the bare term "the glory" is nowhere else used as a title for Jesus,[12] whereas, as noted already, the qualitative genitive is not uncommon.[13]

But even if "the glory" is not a title, "glory" in biblical literature refers to a manifestation of attributes, importance, and honor, particularly of God. In calling Jesus "glorious Lord," James effectively ascribes the divine attributes and importance to Christ. Since he does not do so in 1:1, one may ask why he does so here. Perhaps he does so, first, because here he spells out that Jesus is the object of faith (the one in whom believers trust), and, second, because in speaking against showing favoritism he wishes to remind his hearers that faith in the glorious Christ must exhibit his divine character, which plays no favorites.

The situation presented in 2:2 is presented as hypothetical (ἐάν [*ean*] + subjunctive), but the specificity of the example (such as the law courts in 2:6) and

2:2–4

10. Bauckham (1999: 139) suggests that both James 2:1 and 1 Cor. 2:8 are derived from the christological exegesis of Ps. 24 and observes that James 4:8 appears to allude to Ps. 24:3–4 (23:3–4 LXX).

11. Reicke (1964: 27, 65n13) takes "of glory" as qualitative ("glorious"), but understands it as modifying "faith" rather than "Lord Jesus Christ," yielding "not in favoritism should you have the glorious faith of our Lord Jesus Christ." However, nowhere else in the NT or the LXX is πίστις called "glorious," and πίστις is farther away than the nouns "Lord" and "Christ," with which "glory" often goes (e.g., 1 Cor. 2:8), so Reicke's suggestion seems highly unlikely.

12. All the examples given by Mayor (1897: 78) are either cases where δόξα is further qualified in some way (e.g., 2 Pet. 1:17, "the majestic glory") or are debatable (e.g., Col. 1:27, "the riches of the glory of this mystery which is Christ in you," where probably not just "Christ," but "Christ in you," is equated with the entire preceding phrase, not with just "glory").

13. The suggestion by Calvin (1948: 301), following Erasmus, that τῆς δόξης refers not to the glory of Christ but rather to the esteem involved in showing favoritism is grammatically possible, but is unlikely, given both the distance of τῆς δόξης from προσωπολημψίαις and that in the NT δόξα rarely means "esteem" or "opinion."

the use of the plural προσωπολημψίαις in verse 1 suggest that it may reflect actual events as well (contra Dibelius 1975: 125). As Laws (1980: 98) says, "For the example to convey his message it must presumably bear some relation to his readers' experience, and portray a situation which either has [obtained] or could obtain for them." However, James typically addresses issues by way of concrete examples, some of which are drawn from Scripture (see the commentary on 5:6) and may only be analogous rather than literal representations of events in the communities to which the letter is directed.

"Your gathering" (literally "your synagogue") is often taken as evidence either of a Jewish audience or that the church members are still meeting with non-Christian Jews for worship. But James calls it "your" synagogue and refers to actions within the synagogue as a whole (such as discriminating "among yourselves" in 2:4), not a subgroup within the meeting. James is referring to a Christian gathering, to which visitors rich or poor may come.

If James is an early letter (prior to the completion of the rift with Judaism), then "your synagogue" is perfectly understandable as a reference to an early Christian church's local gathering for worship,[14] in echo of synagogue worship in Judaism generally. It might be expected that the early Christian gatherings borrowed much of the terminology as well as the structure of Jewish gatherings for worship and hearing of Scripture. "Church" (ἐκκλησία, ekklēsia), as a translation of Hebrew qāhāl, would more properly apply (as it does in 5:14) to the body of Christian believers than to a worship gathering. No doubt, if James is early, it is also true that the makeup of the audience is likely to be largely ethnically Jewish, but it need not be exclusively or even predominantly so. And the Greek word συναγωγή (synagōgē) had a perfectly ordinary use as "gathering" or "assembly" long before Judaism gave it a technical meaning, and it was used by the church even into the second century to refer to Christian gatherings for worship[15] (see Dibelius 1975: 132–34).

"A man with gold rings on his fingers and fine clothes" (literally "a gold-fingered man in shining raiment") might imply someone from the equestrian class,[16] who would have the status of a rich merchant, but whether or not James refers to that specific class, the term indicates someone making an ostentatious display of wealth, which tends to elicit deference and special treatment from others, not unlike many symbols of status and wealth today (Rolex watches and Armani suits). It is not surprising that the world pays deference to the bearers of such symbols, but it is tragic and incompatible with faith for Christians to do so.

The unusual term ῥυπαρός (rhyparos, filthy) used to describe the poor person's garments is almost unique in the NT (the only other occurrence is

14. Ward (1969) argues that this is not a regular church gathering, but a judicial assembly (see note 20, below).

15. See, for example, Ign. Pol. 4.2; Justin, Dial. 63.14; Herm. Mand. 11.9–14.

16. But Jews also wore rings (Luke 15:22), and gold was commonly used for ornament and a show of wealth, then as now. Judge (1960: 53) likens the person in question to a "big business-man," who could of course be either pagan or Jewish.

1. Faith and Favoritism

Rev. 22:11). It is a term that evokes revulsion. James is not making it easy for his readers. Many people would say that even saying "Sit below my footstool" is a magnanimous gesture toward someone whose clothes are filthy and who could very well be exuding unpleasant odors, but James says that such persons must be treated with respect equal to anyone.

Paying attention to outward appearance is one of the primary ways of showing partiality. The sense of the latter part of 2:3 is perfectly clear: the rich person is offered a seat of honor, whereas the poor person is disdainfully tolerated. But the translation is difficult because the idioms are strange to us. The rich man is told, literally, "You, sit here, well," which is fairly easily understood: it is an offer to sit in either a good seat or an honorable one, most likely both.[17] But the poor person is told either "Stand over there" (out of the way, where he would not be seen, presumably) or "Sit [here][18] under my footstool." This probably means not literally under the footstool,[19] but below it, on the floor, out of the way and placed to underscore the unimportance of the person sitting there. Since "under the feet" or "as a footstool" was idiomatic for a recognition of subjugation, there may also have been a connotation that the poor person must acknowledge subservience to the one giving the place to sit, introducing a hierarchicalism directly contrary to Jesus's teaching (Matt. 23:8–9). The point is at least that there seems to be an attitude of not particularly wanting the poor to be there and sending both them and the world a message to that effect, or that they are wanted only as long as they "know their place." The people of God, however, are to be distinguished from the world particularly in this very matter.

In 2:3 we can observe a strong similarity to a rabbinic saying preserved in Sipra (on Lev. 19:15), which, in referring to fairness in the tribunal, says, "You must not let one stand and another sit." This similarity leads Ward (1969), taking "synagogue" to indicate a judicial assembly, to think that James is referring to a poor person and a rich person appearing in ecclesial court.[20] Even if James had intended some allusion to Jewish legal tradition, however, this does not imply that he is addressing Christian ecclesial court cases; rather, he is saying that what is true for a court in Jewish law certainly is applicable to the Chris-

17. The RSV translates καλῶς (*kalōs*) here with "please" (supported by Zerwick and Grosvenor 1979: 694). That makes for idiomatic English: "Sit here, please." But surely James is contrasting the seat offered to the wealthy in the sharpest way with that offered to the poor, and καλῶς is identifying the former as one of honor or advantage. The RSV obscures this contrast.

18. See the second additional note on 2:3.

19. Compare Exod. 19:17: the Israelites stood ὑπὸ τὸ ὄρος (*hypo to oros*), "below" the mountain (i.e., at the foot of the mountain), not "under" it.

20. Ward bases his argument on some rabbinic parallels and on the presence of judicial imagery in 2:4–7. But the judicial imagery in 2:4 is illustrative, and that in 2:6–7 is outside the gathering of believers. Further, Ward must suppose that both the rich and the poor persons are already members of the community coming to it for judgment, but the natural way of reading the text is to suppose that they are visitors. Ward's hypothesis is therfore both problematic and unnecessary, and it obscures the actual focus of the passage.

tian assembly, a community where the law of love (2:8) is expected to prevail in welcoming outsiders, both rich and poor (see Dyrness 1981: 13).

"Have you not discriminated" (2:4) is οὐ διεκρίθητε (*ou diakrithēte*). The verb is the aorist passive of διακρίνω (*diakrinō*), which here differs in meaning from the use of this verb in 1:6, where it means "to doubt" in the sense of inconstancy. One might try to read "doubt" here ("If you show favoritism, have you not doubted . . .") in order to maintain a uniform meaning of διακρίνω throughout James. As is the case with πειράζω, however, it is pedantic to insist that James must always use the same meaning of a word. After all, the letter by Jude (identified in Jude 1 as the brother of James) uses two different meanings of διακρίνω within a few verses: in Jude 9 it means "to argue or contend" (it can hardly mean "to doubt"), but in Jude 22 it can hardly mean "to argue" and almost certainly means "to doubt." The context here in James 2:4 easily determines the meaning in view: "to discriminate, make distinctions." However, discrimination, like doubt, still stands opposite to faith, and readers may have picked up on the wordplay. Just as doubt undermines faith, so too does discrimination on the basis of worldly wealth or any other source of class distinction.

James's addition of the words "among yourselves"[21] brings home that it is not just visitors who are affected by such discriminatory behavior. The very class distinctions that Christian faith is supposed to transcend have insinuated their way into the worship service and into the social fabric of the church.

"Judges rendering perverse verdicts" is literally "judges of evil disputations" or "judges of evil thoughts." The phrase "evil disputations" is a characteristically Semitic genitive of quality (BDF §165). This might mean "having evil motives," but BDAG (232) notes that the word διαλογισμοί (*dialogismoi*, disputations, thoughts) is commonly used in legal contexts to refer to judicial rulings, which certainly suits the context here (see the second additional note on 2:4). James likens discriminatory behavior to that of corrupt judges who are biased or bribed and give rulings in preference to rich clients, and who then justify their rulings by specious reasoning. In the ancient world, as is still to an appalling degree the case in the modern world, the application of justice in the civil and criminal courts quite often was a function of the economic resources and social status of the litigants. But Judaism, and Christianity with it, insisted that God gave real justice; he cannot be bribed (Deut. 10:17), and his judgments are based not a whit on whether the person in the dock is king or pauper, movie star or farmhand (see Job 34:19). Thus, equity is also required of human judges, and inequity is roundly condemned in the OT (e.g., Lev. 19:15; Deut. 16:19; 27:19, 25; Ps. 82:2; Mal. 2:9). James points out that discriminatory seating is of a piece with the perversion of justice that all too frequently occurs in secular courts, and thus it is an implicit denial of faith in the God who shows no partiality (see

---

21. The phrase ἐν ἑαυτοῖς (*en heautois*) could either mean "among yourselves" or "(with)in yourselves" (see BDAG 326–27), but the contextually more likely reference is not to the individual's internal reasoning processes (as Mussner 1975: 119 thinks), but to discriminatory activity within ("among") the community of believers (Dibelius 1975: 136; Davids 1982: 110).

2 Chron. 19:7). Since the following verses bring up the subject of lawsuits that the rich are bringing against Christians, this is a shocking judgment indicating that when believers show favoritism, they class themselves with the corrupt judges who are giving unfair verdicts against them when they are accused in court.

"Listen, my dear brothers" has the same form as 1:16 and 1:19 and functions in the same way, introducing what follows (2:5–7) with a call to attention that links to the preceding material (2:1–4). The form of the rhetorical question expects a positive answer. James expects his readers to know very well that God has chosen the poor in worldly things[22] to be rich in faith and be heirs of the kingdom. It is, after all, a *verbum Christi* (cf. Matt. 5:3; Luke 6:20)[23] and is also found in the OT (1 Sam. 2:8; Isa. 14:30; 61:1). There is, however, no inherent virtue in poverty that simply translates into faith. It is rather that God's choice makes one rich in faith, and God has chosen to grant faith to those of low estate in worldly matters.

The double accusative following ἐξελέξατο (*exelexato*, he chose) implies a predication: God chose the poor to be rich in faith, just as God chose lowly Israel to be his people (Deut. 7:7). Note that it is faith that is key to inheriting the kingdom, and it is God's choice that grants this faith.

To be "rich in faith" (i.e., "rich in matters of faith," thus parallel to "poor in matters of the world") simply means to know God well. The poor with respect to worldly things have lots of practice in relying on God and thus often have, in general, a deeper knowledge of God than those who are not so poor. Of course, as is clear from the context, the poor can be tempted to show favoritism as much as the rich, and economic poverty alone does not guarantee wealth in respect to the things of God, but the appeal of a future kingdom will naturally be much greater for those who have none at present.[24]

"Heirs of the kingdom" is rooted in the beatitude already noted (Matt. 5:3; Luke 6:20). The "kingdom of God" is in the Gospels a rubric for the content of Jesus's eschatological announcement that defines his ministry (Mark 1:15; see Ridderbos 1962: especially xi). It is a Jewish term for the expected restoration of God's righteousness on earth, and it implies also the overthrow of wickedness and the restoring of God's people to a subordinate sovereignty (McCartney

22. The phrase πτωχοὺς τῷ κόσμῳ (*ptōchous tō kosmō*) perhaps could mean "poor in the eyes of the world" (Dibelius 1975: 137; Davids 1982: 112; Moo 2000: 107; similarly Mayor 1897: 82: "in the world's judgment"; cf. Cantinat 1973: 126), but since it is juxtaposed with "rich in [i.e., with reference to] faith," it seems better to take it as meaning "poor with reference to worldly things." However, I concur with Davids (1982: 111–12) that the term "poor" here no doubt has both a spiritual and a material sense, and certainly it is true that those who are poor with respect to worldly things are also poor in the world's eyes.

23. According to Deppe (1989: 89–91), almost all studies of this verse agree that it is an allusion to a saying of Jesus.

24. Wachob (2000: 140–43) understands this verse to be indicative of a major rhetorical purpose of the letter. Further, he takes "rich in faith" to allude specifically to the pre-Synoptic form of the Sermon on the Mount/Plain, and since he sees a subjective genitive in 2:1, the "faith *of* Jesus Christ," he takes the verse to be commending the poor as having the same faith that Jesus himself had. See the commentary on 2:1.

1994), sharing in the rule of God on earth. The phrase thus summarizes the eschatological hopes of Israel, which the NT writers typically focus on Jesus. James makes no explicit christological identification of this kingdom, though neither does anything in James dechristologize it. The "heirs" of the kingdom refers to those to whom subordinate sovereignty is restored. They are further identified, like the recipients of the crown of life in 1:12, as "those who love him," a phrase commonly used to refer to true believers who keep faith with God (cf. Rom. 8:28). Note that in Greek "those who love" is a progressive participle, implying a continuous, ongoing love for God.

In 2:6a James delivers a stinging indictment: "You have dishonored [ἠτιμάσατε, *ētimasate*] the poor man." According to Prov. 17:5 (cf. Prov. 14:31), to dishonor poor people is to dishonor their maker, so this discriminatory conduct not only is a behavior of unbelief, it is an insult to God. The word "you have dishonored" is in Greek an aorist indicative. This cannot be a general or gnomic aorist, for it is not stating an axiom, and it is in second rather than third person. The aorist indicative implies that at least some of James's readers have in fact shown such favoritism, and James points out that in doing so they are in opposition to God, who has chosen the poor.[25] Those who have shown partiality to the rich may have been unaware that they were dishonoring the poor, but that is the end result nevertheless.

2:6b–7 The rich can oppress the poor in many ways, and "drag you into court" could refer to the common experience of a rich creditor hauling a poor debtor into court. The echo in 2:13 of the warning implied in the parable of the unforgiving steward (Matt. 18:23–35) may support that this is what James has in mind here. But "oppress you," "drag you into court," and "blaspheme the good name" (2:7) are in parallel construction, and it is probably best to read all three as activities directed against those who believe in Jesus Christ (see commentary below on 2:7; and cf. 1 Pet. 4:14–16), as Jesus predicted would happen (Matt. 5:11; 10:17–18).

The verb for "oppress" (καταδυναστεύω, *katadynasteuō*) is quite rare outside biblical literature, and James probably has in mind its meaning in the LXX, where it is used to refer to the oppression of the Israelites in Egypt (e.g., Exod. 1:13) and the tyrannizing of the poor (Amos 8:4).

The "blaspheming" in view in 2:7 could simply refer to slander, but usually it has a religious nuance, involving the profane abuse of sacred things, especially impious speech (cf. 1 Cor. 10:30). Here the rich are not just defaming the poor themselves, but are blaspheming the "good name" invoked upon them, which further establishes the religious nuance of the word here.

25. The sentence might still be presumed hypothetical if one takes 2:6 as harking back to the condition of 2:3 ("*If* you say to the poor man, 'Stand there . . . ,' then you have dishonored him"). But even if this opening condition is strictly hypothetical, an apodosis already appears in the question of 2:4, and the opening vocative of 2:5 ("Listen, my dear brothers") seems to have moved away from this conditional statement and on to real events, such as rich people hauling some believers into court and blaspheming the name (2:6b–7). Actually, the reality of the poor person of 2:6a gives further support to the reality of the condition of 2:2–3.

"The name invoked upon you" is the name by which believers are called and recognized. Here it can signify no other than the name of Jesus Christ. Dibelius (1975: 23, 140–41) points out that the "name" can be neither "God" apart from Christ nor "Judaism" because these would not set the name-bearers over against the "rich" who come into the assembly. This is therefore incontrovertibly a mark of the Christian provenance of James.

That the name of Christ "has been invoked upon" them means that they are "named" as those who belong to and acknowledge Jesus as Lord and Christ (2:1), even as children bore the name of their fathers (cf. Gen. 48:16), or slaves were named according to their owners' household. In the OT the idiom was used particularly to indicate God's special possession. Thus, the ark and tabernacle are "named" as the Lord's (2 Sam. 6:2), but more importantly, Israel as God's people is called by the name of the Lord (Deut. 28:10; 2 Chron. 7:14; Isa. 43:7; Jer. 14:9). This "naming" that is blasphemed by the "rich" refers to the poor believers being identified as belonging to Jesus, even as God said of Israel, "All the peoples of the earth shall see that you are called by the name of the LORD" (Deut. 28:10). This could be a reference to baptism, therefore, as in Acts 2:38; 10:48 (Mayor 1897: 85; Mussner 1975: 122; Davids 1982: 113; Laws 1980: 105), but this is neither demonstrable nor important to James's immediate concerns. It is more likely that the phrase evokes the notion of election. The Greek translation of Deut. 28:10, speaking of Israel's election, uses the same words for "to invoke the name upon" (ὄνομα ἐπικαλεῖν, *onoma epikalein*). In James's encyclical letter recorded in Acts 15, James, in broadening the understanding of God's election to include Gentiles, quotes from Amos 9:11–12 and comments that God's promise of rebuilding the tent of David is so "that the remnant of mankind may seek the Lord, and all the Gentiles who are called by my name, says the Lord" (Acts 15:17). There too the phrase seems to refer not to baptism, but to election or to God's claim of ownership of his people generally. In any case, James's irony is sharp. Those who show favoritism to the rich are siding with the people who oppose the elect of God and speak against his Christ.

Additional Notes

2:1. Some scholars (e.g., Spitta 1896; Massebieau 1895) who suggest that the Epistle of James originally was non-Christian Jewish material have difficulty here. The reference to Christ is so integral to 2:1, and 2:1 so inseparably integral to what follows, that only by seeing radical editing can the letter be taken as having been non-Christian in origin. And in 2:7 "the good name by which you have been called" can hardly be anything other than the name of Christ. It cannot be the name of God, because the rich coming into the synagogue would not deny the name of God (cf. 1 Pet. 4:14, where the ὄνομα in which the recipients are reviled is χριστός). Even if portions of James have origins in non-Christian Jewish wisdom, it is still very much a Christian letter.

Further, the specificity of this command and the vividness of 2:2–4 make it difficult to suppose that James is addressing people only in generalities. Although the examples are presented as hypothetical, the problems such as favoritism and strife that gave rise to James's letter were real, and the letter is a real letter, albeit of an encyclic epistolary style (see "Is James a Real Letter?" under "Genre and Purpose" in the introduction).

2:1. Both the noun προσωπολημψία in 2:1 and the verb προσωπολημπτέω in 2:9 are based on the Semitic idiom appearing in the LXX (Lev. 19:15; Ps. 81:2 [82:2 MT]; Mal. 2:9; 1 Esd. 4:39; Sir. 4:22) as λαμβάνειν πρόσωπον, literally "to take a face" (see E. Lohse, *TDNT* 6:779–80). It refers to basing a judgment on a person's social position, connections, or status rather than on the merits of the case. Paul uses the noun in Rom. 2:11 to refer to God's showing no favoritism between Jew and Gentile. It is interesting that a condemnation of favoritism and an adage about "not hearers but doers" also occur together in Rom. 2. Peter in Cornelius's house recognizes that οὔκ ἐστιν προσωπολήμπτης ὁ θεός (Acts 10:34) because God also receives Gentiles who believe in Jesus. In 1 Pet. 1:17, eschewing partiality appears to be virtually an article of Christian faith linked to God's fatherhood of believers.

2:1. The placement of the negative particle μή before the prepositional phrase "with favoritism" is unusual and may have the force of "Surely not with favoritism do you have faith in Christ, do you?" or if, as argued above, 2:1 is to be read as an imperative, then "Not with favoritism must you have faith in Christ."

2:1. A very few manuscripts (33 and a few others) omit τῆς δόξης (here translated "glorious") from the end of 2:1, but both the older manuscripts and the Majority Text include it.

There is no manuscript evidence at all for the omission of "Jesus Christ," as Spitta (1896: 3–8) proposes. For a critique of Spitta's view that James was originally a purely Jewish document, see "Was the Audience Christian or Jewish Non-Christian?" in the introduction.

2:3. This verse has several minor textual variants, mostly of a stylistic nature. One variant is noteworthy: several manuscripts, including some important ones, read ἐπί instead of ὑπό before τὸ ὑποπόδιόν μου. The ὑπό is the more difficult reading—it is difficult to see how someone could sit "under" a footstool—and it is more likely that ὑπό was changed to ἐπί than vice versa.

2:3. A more difficult decision involves whether the word "here" (ὧδε) is original in the words to the poor person, "Sit [here] below my footstool." It has excellent external support (𝔓74 [probably], ℵ, a corrector of C, K, P, and a range of other witnesses including the Majority Text and some versions) that may even be slightly superior to the reading without ὧδε. But it is likelier that ὧδε was added due to the influence of the "sit here" early in the verse than that it was accidentally omitted.

2:4. The omission of οὐ by a few manuscripts is due to a failure to recognize that 2:4 is a rhetorical question.

2:4. The word διαλογισμός is a verbal noun formed from διαλογίζομαι, which in turn is a causative verb formed from the noun διαλογή, which was used to refer to accounts, estimation, monetary reckoning, or reasoning. The verb thus commonly means "to calculate, compute," but in a legal context it can mean "to weigh arguments," "to debate," or even "to hold court." Likewise, διαλογισμός can mean simply "thought" (as in Matt. 15:19), but in legal settings it refers to debate, argument, or judicial inquiry, the processes by which a legal decision is reached. See LSJ 402.

2:5. The Majority Text has the genitive τοῦ κόσμου, but the oldest and best manuscripts modify πτωχούς with the dative τῷ κόσμῳ, probably a dative of reference: "the poor with reference to worldly wealth." The rare reading ἐν τῷ κόσμῳ almost certainly is a smoothing of the simple dative and/or a conforming to the following ἐν πίστει.

2:5. For βασιλείας the original hand of ℵ and A have ἐπαγγελίας, but this is a geographically isolated reading and probably is under the influence of Heb. 6:17.

2:6. The occurrence of ὑμεῖς with ἠτιμάσατε is not tautologous; with the δέ it stresses the "you" in contrast with God. Likewise, the emphatic αὐτοί[26] in 2:6–7 stresses the subject: "Is it not *they* who . . . ?" or as I have phrased it, "Are *they* not the ones who . . . ?"

2:6. A few important manuscripts (𝔓[74], original hand of ℵ, A) have the accusative ὑμᾶς as the object of καταδυναστεύουσιν instead of the genitive ὑμῶν. This does not affect meaning.

---

26. On James's use of emphatic third-person nominative pronouns, see footnote 3 of my comments on 1:13–18.

2. Faith and Law (2:8–13)

James's indictment of the showing of partiality by those who claimed faith in Christ is continued here. Showing favoritism is set over against the "royal law," particularly the great command to love one's neighbor. If it were not clear enough already, 2:9 makes it crystal clear: showing favoritism is sin, and it makes the one who shows such favoritism just as much a lawbreaker as the adulterer and murderer. This section concludes with two reminders: first, speaking as much as doing is not neutral ethically, and people will be held accountable for words as well as deeds (2:12); second, in the gospel mercy is of greater weight than judgment, and as God is merciful, those who expect to receive mercy must likewise exhibit mercy (2:13). The first of these will be developed at length in James 3, the second in James 4–5. Once again the behavior of faith is expected to exhibit the characteristics of the one in whom one's faith is placed.

James's references to the law and judgment are reminiscent of Matthew's record of Jesus's instruction. In Matt. 22:39 (and pars.) Jesus quotes as the second greatest commandment Lev. 19:18, and James reminds his hearers that this love command, the centerpiece of the "royal law" (see exposition below), summarizes a series of commands in Leviticus that includes a prohibition against showing partiality (Lev. 19:15). James 2:10, which points out that to transgress one part of the law is to transgress the whole, echoes Matt. 5:19. The concluding verses of this half of the chapter (2:12–13) state that mercy is (only) for the merciful, an echo of the beatitude of Matt. 5:7 as well as of Jesus's parable in Matt. 18:23–35. Also, 2:13 serves as a bridge verse to the following section, where James attacks the notion that faith without works can avail anything by reminding the readers that the law's liberating aspect, the aspect that will lead to eschatological deliverance, is bound up with the requirement and blessing of being merciful, even as God is merciful.

Exegesis and Exposition

[8]If indeed you fulfill the royal law, in accordance with the scripture "You shall love your neighbor as yourself," you do well. [9]But if you show favoritism, you commit sin and are proven by that law to be a lawbreaker. [10]For whoever keeps the whole law but stumbles at one point has become guilty of all of it, [11]because the one who said, "Do not commit adultery," also said, "Do not murder." So if you do not commit adultery but you do murder, you have become a ⌜lawbreaker⌝.

[12]So speak and so act as those about to be judged by the law of freedom, [13]for

judgment is merciless to those who show no mercy; [but] mercy ⌜triumphs⌝ over judgment.

The "royal law" refers to the law of God generally, as summed up in the com- **2:8** mand of love. Some commentators (e.g., Laws 1980: 108–9) take "royal law" to refer specifically to the Lev. 19:18 command, which Jesus made the center-piece of ethical behavior between humans (Matt. 22:39). And indeed there are several points of contact between Lev. 19 and James (Johnson 1982; Laato 1997: 57–59). But James is hardly setting one part of the law over against the rest (2:10–11), and "law" (νόμος, *nomos*) generally refers to God's instruction as a whole rather than a specific commandment, for which ἐντολή (*entolē*) is normally used (Ropes 1916: 198). It is better to say that Lev. 19:18 gives expression to a controlling and central principle of God's ethical imperative for human conduct (cf. Gal. 5:14) and serves as a framework for understand-ing its parts.[1] This law summarized in love is "royal" (βασιλικός, *basilikos*) because it is the "law" of the kingdom (βασιλεία, *basileia*) of God (Johnson 1982: 401), the kingdom promised to the poor who love him (2:5).[2]

James refers to "fulfilling" or "completing" (τελέω, *teleō*) the royal law rather than using a more customary expression such as "keeping" or "obeying" it. This verb occasionally is used to refer to fulfilling an obligation, including carrying out the commandments of the law.[3] But given James's frequent use of the τελε- stem (1:4 [2x], 17, 25; 2:8, 22; 3:2), its use here may be a deliberate emphasis of the comprehensive nature of biblical ethics (2:10–11). For James, "fulfilling" or carrying out the royal law is of a piece with fulfilling or carrying through on faith by works in 2:22, where law is not set over against faith, but rather law and faith together are fulfilled or made complete by obedient ac-tion. Further, 2:8 connects with the fact that the law is a complete and perfect (τέλειος, *teleios*) law (1:25), and it therefore does not admit of partial obedience (2:10), because all parts of the law come from one source (2:11).

Here James possibly is being somewhat sarcastic when he says, "If indeed you fulfill the royal law in accordance with the command 'Love your neighbor

1. It may to some be tempting to speculate on what James would have said about those aspects of the law now regarded as "ceremonial," but there is little indication in the letter that such questions are any concern to him. All of the ethical focus in James is on the broad issues of faithfulness to God and the responsibilities of love to one another, and these matters are indisputably applicable to Christians.

2. So also Johnson 1982: 401. Calvin (1948: 305) considers the law royal because like a royal highway (cf. Num. 20:17 LXX) it is straight and level as opposed to the sinuous roads of local provenance. Similarly, Philo (*Posterity* 30 §§101–2) compares the royal road (king's highway) of Num. 20 to the law of God.

3. BDAG 997. The other NT texts that use "fulfill" the law as a term for obeying it are Luke 2:39 (where Joseph and Mary complete the requirements for Jesus's circumcision) and Rom. 2:27 (which speaks of Gentiles "fulfilling" the law even though they are not circumcised). But in Matt. 5:17 Jesus is probably claiming more than just that he observes the law, especially since it is not just the law but the Law and the Prophets that he fulfills (cf. Guelich 1982: 162–63; Schnackenburg 2002: 52).

as yourself,' you are doing well" (cf. 2:19, which also could have some irony in it), because although the readers may assert that they are trying to "love neighbor" as Jesus commanded, showing favoritism completely belies that assertion. Selective love of neighbor is not love at all; it is a cover for the attempt to gain advantage or benefit.

2:9   So, says James, to show favoritism is to commit sin, and no matter how people may try to hide their pandering to the rich behind the screen of "love," the ones who do so stand convicted as lawbreakers by the law that they profess to keep.

Because the law is a perfect, complete law, selective obedience of it is disobedience. Thus, the one who keeps the whole law save in one respect is a transgressor. This may seem harsh, but at issue is not the totaling up of merits and demerits, where one demerit then wipes out all the merits, but an attitude toward God's law. Violation of even one of its tenets bespeaks the attitude of the doer toward the law: it is an attitude of rebellion. The unity of the law is based on the unity of the lawgiver (James 4:12), and therefore "disregard to a single point is disregard to the Lawgiver" (Mayor 1897: 86). James's application here, of course, is first of all that someone who "loves" wealthy people more than the poor is not truly obeying the command of love. However, the principle is more far-reaching. It undercuts any notion that keeping most of the law most of the time has any value at all, and it should give the lie to the theory that James is advocating the acquisition of merit by obedience.

James's use of terms for "doing sin" is instructive. Literally, those who show favoritism "work" (ἐργάζομαι, ergazomai) sin. Works can be sinful as well as faithful. What marks the Christian is not works per se but works of faith, such as those done by Abraham and Rahab (2:21–25).

2:10–11   James's comments about keeping the whole law are sometimes compared with Paul's similar statement in Gal. 5:3 that the one who is circumcised is then obligated to keep the whole law. Paul and James certainly agree that the law has an indivisible integrity, but whereas James is concerned with the self-delusion of selective obedience, Paul's concern in Galatians is with the believer's way of relating to God, so that when Gentiles become circumcised, they symbolically attach themselves to the law as the means of relating to God rather than depending on Christ, and hence it is not just to circumcision that they are then obligated but to the whole law in every detail. The way Paul concludes his paragraph in Gal. 5:6 shows his essential commonality with James: "Neither circumcision nor uncircumcision counts for anything, but only faith working through love." Paul also concurs with James that the whole law is truly fulfilled by obedience to Lev. 19:18 (Gal. 5:14).

James's word for "stumble" in 2:10 (πταίω, ptaiō) is interesting in that in 3:2 he makes the comment that "we all stumble [πταίομεν, ptaiomen] in many ways," and yet those who stumble can also be "perfect" if they control their speech. James is quite aware that no one can completely keep every commandment in the whole law, and, as he will say in 2:13, mercy is a necessary

2. Faith and Law

component of anyone's relation to God, but he does not allow anyone to pretend that it suffices to keep only most of the law. Relationship to God is the goal, not some abstract obedience to a collection of discrete commands. This is why breaking even one command is breaking the whole. "The one who said . . . also said . . ." emphasizes that the unity of the law lies in its personal character (see Johnson 1982: 232). The law is not an abstract social contract; it reflects God's character and is thus bound up with the relationship of God with his people.

The general principle that to keep the law means to keep it in its entirety is known not only by Paul and James, but also broadly in early Judaism (e.g., 4 Macc. 5:20–21; 1QS 8.16) as well as elsewhere in the NT (Matt. 5:18–19). It may also have been partly recognized in the Gentile world (O'Rourke Boyle [1985] refers to Seneca's *De beneficiis*, which says, "He who has one vice has all"), although its opposite is better known, that the one who has one virtue has them all (see the many references in Dibelius 1975: 145n114). But these "total virtue" or "total vice" comments in paganism do not operate from the notion of revealed law, and thus they are only superficially comparable.

In 2:12 the adverbial demonstrative οὕτως (*houtōs*, thus, so) can refer either to the preceding, "*because* it is true that any transgression of the law makes one a transgressor, speak and act as those about to be judged," or the following, "*because* you are about to be judged, speak and act accordingly" (see Mayor 1897: 91). Given the close parallel in 2:17, where οὕτως appears to pick up on the preceding as that which leads to the conclusion that follows, the former is preferable. The οὕτως probably means that 2:12 is a conclusion to be drawn from 2:8–11.

Throughout the Epistle of James, words and actions are the foci of the ethical ellipsis, and therefore speaking, as well as doing, must be in the purview of the one who lives by the law of freedom. Bringing actions into line with ethical mandates is the more obvious requirement, and people often make free with words, thinking that these are less harmful than physical deeds. But elsewhere in the letter (3:1; 5:9) the focus is on the liability to judgment for sins of speech. This concern echoes that of Jesus (e.g., Matt. 12:36: "I tell you, on the day of judgment people will give account for every careless word they speak"). Words such as "You, go sit on the floor below my footstool" can do more damage than a blow with a fist.

Here in 2:12 the "royal law" of 2:8 is called, as it was in 1:25, the "law of freedom." James has described the law as "perfect law" (1:25), "royal law" (2:8), and "law of freedom" (1:25; 2:12) not because there are three different laws, but because the law of God is complete, kingly, and liberating. The liberating law of the kingdom (i.e., Jesus's view of the law), by which believers are to reckon that they will be judged, is also the law into which the godly gaze (1:25) and remember to do.

As God's law, it is the criterion for the eschatological judgment, and the word rendered "about (to be)" (μέλλοντες, *mellontes*) reminds the reader of the imminence of that judgment. But this law has a mercy principle as well as a judgment principle, and hence it brings ethical freedom (see the commentary on 1:25), not bondage to guilt, even though stumbling at one point makes one guilty of the whole. It builds on the presentation of justice in Jer. 34, where Zedekiah's republication of God's law resulted in a proclamation of liberty (and the people's subsequent reenslavement was decried as a rebellion against God's law). Thus, to behave as those about to be judged by the law of freedom is to remember mercy and justice and thereby to proclaim liberty. God is merciful and just; therefore, Christians must be merciful and just.

2:13   In 2:13 James offers two aphoristic wisdom sayings juxtaposed with no conjunction: "Judgment is merciless to those who do no mercy. Mercy triumphs over judgment." Such joining without an expected conjunction (a technique known as asyndeton) often is used with axioms or sayings and "provides solemnity or weight to the words" (BDF §462; see also BDF §494). The two phrases juxtaposed here provide a context for the eschatological expectation expressed in 2:12: "about to be judged by the law of freedom." Mercy could be seen to triumph over judgment partly because it comes after the judgment and is the last word in the judicial process. However, it also triumphs over judgment because the quality of mercy exercised by the believer is the quality of genuine faith; it is the quintessential "work" that manifests true belief in the God of mercy. The saying therefore serves as a preparation for 2:14–26.

The focus of the word "mercy" here in a judicial context certainly would include mercy as loving-kindness in spite of moral failure or deficiency in the person being shown mercy, but it may also include kindness despite the recipient's incapacity to repay. Thus, the notion of mercy as simple kindness to the needy (as in 3:17) certainly is present and probably provides the link to the example that will follow in 2:15. In fact, James's use of the term "mercy" may be invoking the OT concept of ḥesed, the word commonly translated in the LXX with the Greek word used here (ἔλεος, eleos). The word ḥesed has a range of applications, but encompasses steadfast covenant love and kindness, especially God's faithful, gracious, and compassionate love of his people (see R. Bultmann, *TDNT* 2:479–80; for a fuller discussion, see H.-J. Zobel, *TDOT* 5:44–64). The same covenant love that God shows to his people he expects his people to show to each other.

The triumph of mercy over judgment, therefore, specifically shows the relation between God's mercy in judgment toward people and the mercy of those people, who will be judged. The fact that in the context James has been speaking of human rather than divine mercy in the first part of the verse might suggest that the mercy that triumphs over judgment is the believer's acts of mercy, which in judgment "will count as evidence of the presence of Christ within us" (Moo 2000: 118) and so evoke God's verdict of "righteous in Christ." However, that reads too complicated a theological construction into James, who is simply echoing the words of Jesus found in Matt. 7:2 ("For with the judgment you pronounce you will be judged, and with the measure you use it will be measured to you"). It is a principle repeated by Jesus in many contexts that it is the forgiving who may expect forgiveness, and those who are forgiven are expected to forgive (e.g., Matt. 6:12, 14–15; 18:33).

It may seem incongruous for James to interject a word on mercy here, because the theme up to this point is that a certain kind of behavior is lawbreaking and is liable for judgment. As a result, some have read this verse as suggesting that God's mercy "trumps" or overturns his justice. But although from a certain point of view God's mercy and his justice may seem to be opposed, with God's mercy "trumping" his justice, James does not see mercy as being opposed to law or justice; rather, mercy is one of the aspects of the law's application. James may very well have in the back of his mind Zech. 7:9, "Render true judgments, show kindness and mercy to one another," which Zechariah goes on to connect with not oppressing the widows and the poor. Since both justice and mercy are traits of God,[4] the one who has faith in Jesus (2:1) must also evince both justice (by showing no favoritism) and mercy (by refraining from judgment [4:11–12], by restoring a wandering believer [5:19–20], and by providing for the needy [1:26–27]).

The connection with judgment underscores the fact that favoritism based on economic status is not the only form of favoritism; there is also the danger of "virtuistic" partiality, a favoring of those who keep themselves clear of those sins that a particular society regards as especially degrading. In Jesus's culture tax collectors and prostitutes were especially despised as "sinners," yet Jesus showed them mercy, and when he did not show the favoritism to the "virtuous" Pharisees that they expected, they were deeply confused and offended. Perhaps this "virtuistic" favoritism is even harder for Christians to resist than the economic or ethnic variety.

The verb for "triumph over" (κατακαυχάομαι, katakauchaomai) is unusual, occurring elsewhere in the NT only at James 3:14 and Rom. 11:18 (2x), and in both of these places it appears to mean "boast." English common parlance might paraphrase with "mercy crows over judgment." The proverb is not speaking in particular of God's mercy triumphing over God's judgment (though that very well could be in view [cf. 4:6]), nor is it saying that a person who has a history of showing mercy has something to boast about at the time of judgment. It simply considers mercy abstractly as being of greater power and glory than judgment, even as "love covers a multitude of sins"

4. The juxtaposition of mercy and justice as attributes of God, which at first might appear to be contradictory but in fact indicates an alignment, is a theme of OT theology. When God reveals himself to Moses in Exod. 34:6–7, God gives his name as "The LORD, the LORD, a God merciful and gracious, slow to anger, and abounding in steadfast love and faithfulness, keeping steadfast love for thousands, forgiving iniquity and transgression and sin, but who will by no means clear the guilty, visiting the iniquity of the fathers on the children and the children's children, to the third and the fourth generation." A marvelous example of God's mercy triumphing over justice is seen in the story of Ruth. Ruth was a Moabite and therefore under a curse (Deut. 23:3); nevertheless, when she clings to the true God (Ruth 1:16), not only is she shown mercy, but also she becomes an ancestor of the Messiah (Matt. 1:5).

(1 Pet. 4:8, citing Prov. 10:12 in a non-LXX form apparently also known to James [5:20]).[5]

Additional Notes

2:8. The rare conjunction μέντοι could be either adversative-disjunctive ("although") or emphatic-continuative ("indeed, really, of course"; LSJ 1102; BDAG 630). Elsewhere in the NT (mostly in John) it is always adversative or concessive, and if that is James's use here, it yields something like "Admittedly, if you fulfill the royal law . . . you do well." But 2:8 appears rather to set the contrast with 2:9 (μέντοι . . . δέ), and thus the context in James favors the emphatic meaning: "If indeed, on the one hand, you fulfill . . . but, if you show favoritism. . . ."

2:9. The verb "show favoritism" (προσωπολημπτέω) is found only in Jewish Greek literature; it appears to be a back formation from the noun form προσωπολημψία found in 2:1 and also in Rom. 2:11; Eph. 6:9; Col. 3:25. As noted above, the concept in the Greek OT appears as two words, λαμβάνειν πρόσωπον (reflecting the Hebrew idiom nāśāʾ pānîm and found in the LXX at Lev. 19:15; Ps. 81:2 [= 82:2 MT]; Mal. 2:9; 1 Esd. 4:39; Sir. 4:22).

2:10. The phrase ὅστις τηρήσῃ presents a general condition ("whoever keeps"), and the perfect γέγονεν expresses a future result contingent on it ("will have become"). It is an example of the rare "gnomic" use of the perfect (BDF §344). Fortunately, the English perfect can also serve this way, so "whoever keeps . . . has become" corresponds well.

2:11. Most commentators feel obliged to offer explanations as to why the order of the commandments here listed reverses that in the Masoretic Text, often delving into the problematic manuscript tradition, the history of the LXX, and the variations in order in other NT texts (e.g., Luke 18:20; Rom. 13:9). But this is a pointless exercise because although it is quite possible that James, like Paul and Luke, is following a form of the LXX text that reverses the order from the MT, he is neither prioritizing nor even enumerating commandments but is pointing out the unity of the whole.

2:11. Once again manuscript 𝔓⁷⁴, this time also supported by A, exhibits an unusual reading, here having ἀποστάτης instead of παραβάτης (thus reading "you have become an apostate from the law"). Kilpatrick (1967) defends ἀποστάτης as the more difficult reading, but given its singular character and the somewhat idiosyncratic character of 𝔓⁷⁴ (the apparatus of NA²⁷ lists nine noteworthy unique readings for 𝔓⁷⁴),[6] his argument is unconvincing.

2:12. The two verbs λαλεῖτε and ποιεῖτε could be read as indicatives rather than imperatives; however, the whole tone of the section is not commending the readers for a good job, but rather is admonishing them to obey God in speech and action. Doing and saying represent the spectrum of human ethical activity.

2:12. The distinction sometimes made between judgment "through the law" and judgment "according to the standard of the law" (Hort 1909: 56; Ropes 1916: 201; Laws 1980: 116) puts too fine a point on the preposition. It probably is motivated by the perceived difficulty of speaking of the law of liberty as a criterion of judgment. But James is speaking of the law as the expression of God's ethical will for human behavior, and the NT consistently indicates that conformity to God's will is the standard for judgment (e.g., Matt. 7:21; 25:31–46; Rom. 2:13). Although such a standard sometimes may appear

---

5. The form of the proverb in both 1 Pet. 4:8 and James 5:20 more closely resembles the Masoretic Text and probably was introduced into the Christian tradition independently of the LXX at an early stage. See the commentary on 5:20.

6. For description and dating of 𝔓⁷⁴, see Kasser 1961.

to be restrictive, in James's mind it is liberating because it shows a human being how to be most human.

2:13. A few Alexandrian manuscripts (A, 33, et al.) have the third-person imperative κατακαυχάσθω (may it triumph), but the better Alexandrian witnesses (א, B) and most of the rest of the tradition have the indicative κατακαυχᾶται.

B. Part 2: Faith and Works (2:14–26)

The latter half of James 2 comprises the most extended development of a single subject in the letter.[1] It is also the best-known part of the letter because at points it appears to directly contradict the teaching of Paul that believers are justified by faith apart from works. The exposition below demonstrates that the contradiction is superficial and results from Paul and James having different concerns, different backgrounds, and different audiences with different problems. But for all these differences, the concern for "works" here is part of James's overall concern for faith. Faith is no less important to James than it is to Paul, and it is precisely because faith is so important to James that he harshly condemns a false variety of it. As Verseput (1997b) points out, James, like the OT prophets, condemns not faith, but a hypocritical faith that fails to produce righteous behavior. The preceding material in 2:1–13 condemns the prejudicial treatment of people not just because it is evil, but also because it is radically incongruous with faith in Jesus as Lord (2:1).[2] Likewise, because of his concern that faith in Christ be a true faith with integrity, James in 1:6–8 condemns the double-minded person who waffles between God and something else. And in James 3 it is James's expectation that the confession of God as Lord and Father have integrity that results in his denunciation of any use of the tongue that is incongruous with that confession (3:9–10).

This passage contains many marks of the type of Greek discourse known as *diatribe*, especially the use of rhetorical irony, hyperbolic examples, colorful metaphors and analogies, and a hypothetical interlocutor (see Ropes 1916: 12–16; Burge 1977; see also the various rhetorical observations in Dibelius 1975: 124–206).[3]

This particular diatribe comprises three subsections: (1) inactive faith is useless and dead (2:14–17); (2) two types of false faith: that which separates

---

1. James 2:14–26 follows on the first half of James 2 not because, as Ward (1968) thinks, the underlying concern of both is hospitality, but because James's dominant concern is that faith eventuate in appropriate actions. But Ward rightly sees the diatribal address of 2:14–26 as following naturally from 2:12–13.

2. Peter, in his sermon to Cornelius, likewise connects God's lack of favoritism with his acceptance of everyone who "fears him and does what is right" (Acts 10:35), effectively a parallel with the "synergism" of faith and works in "justification" in James 2:22.

3. Ropes understands the entire Epistle of James to be of the diatribe genre. However, the beginning and end of the letter only weakly evince the generic markers of diatribal form, as Dibelius has amply shown. Burge (1977), noting a parallelism in the two halves of this section (2:14–17 and 2:18–20 being parallel to 2:21–24 and 2:25–26), has alternatively suggested that this has the form of a synagogue homily. Since synagogue homilies themselves no doubt were influenced by Greek rhetorical traditions, we need not decide between them.

faith and works and that which confuses faith with intellectual assent to a creed (2:18–19); (3) two examples of genuine faith: Abraham and Rahab, concluding with a reiteration of the principle that inactive faith is dead (2:20–26).

Exegesis and Exposition

[14]What good is it, my brothers, if someone claims to have faith but does not have works? Can that faith save him? [15]If a brother or sister is without clothing and lacks daily food, [16]and one of you tells them, "Go in peace, be warmed, be filled," but does not give them anything for their bodily needs, what good is that? [17]So, too, that [kind of] faith by itself, if it does not have works, is dead.

[18]Now someone will say, "One has faith, another works." [But I say,] "Show me your faith without works, and I will, by my works, show you [my] faith." [19]Do you believe that ⌜God is one⌝? That's good! Even the demons believe that, and tremble.

[20]Would you understand, vain human, that faith without works is ⌜useless⌝? [21]Was not Abraham our father justified by works when he brought Isaac his son to the altar? [22]You see that faith ⌜worked together⌝ with his works, and by works his faith was brought to completion, [23]and the scripture was fulfilled that says, "Abraham believed God, and it was reckoned to him for righteousness," and he was called God's friend. [24]So you see! By works a person is justified and not by faith alone. [25]Likewise also Rahab the ⌜prostitute⌝, was she not justified by works when she received the messengers and sent them out by another way? [26]For just as a body without a spirit is dead, so also is a faith without works dead.

As noted above, 2:14–17 introduces James's main theme for the second half of the chapter: inactive faith (i.e., a nonworking faith) is ineffective, dead, and worthless.

2:14–17

The sharply ironic opening and closing words "What good is it" serve to tie 2:14–16 together. But although the irony is sharp, James also reiterates his connection with them as the people of God by addressing them as "my brothers."

James does not say, "If someone has faith but has not works . . ."; he says, "If someone *claims* to have faith but does not have works. . . ." The claim to faith is not the same as faith. The article before the second occurrence of "faith" probably is an article of previous reference (see Moo 2000: 123; Mayor 1897: 93 traces the observation back to Bede). It cannot mean "Can *the* [Christian] faith save him," nor is it likely to be an abstraction ("Can faith abstractly considered save him"); instead, it is referring to the specific kind of "faith" of the person who claims to believe in God but has no commensurate deeds. James, in other words, is asking, "Can *that* [inactive] kind of faith save him?"[4] James does not at all reject the notion of "saving faith," for in 5:15 he avers

4. Dibelius (1975: 152) objects to giving the article a demonstrative force, but his objections primarily seem to focus on the opposition of "this faith" to some other faith, that is, Christianity as opposed to some other religion, and he rightly rejects that notion as being in James's mind. But although one ought not place too much meaning in the article alone, its context here seems

that the prayer of faith saves the ill person, a saving that includes forgiveness of sin. What James rejects is the notion that inactive faith saves.

The "saving" in view may be broadly considered. Although in 5:15 it refers (at least on one level)[5] to deliverance from physical illness, in both 1:21 and 5:20 James refers to the salvation of "souls," and this is the salvation spoken of here.[6] It refers to the deliverance from eschatological judgment (Dibelius 1975: 152) and hence deliverance from death, and the reception of the "crown of life" (1:12) from God. Without "faith-full" behavior, the claim to have faith will not itself eventuate in deliverance from judgment, because it is an invalid claim.

The "works" that James has in view are "faith-deeds," the kind of actions that are as endemic to and characteristic of faith as heat is to fire or as breathing is to life for human beings, as James will make clear in 2:20–26.

In 2:15 James points to the care of needy fellow believers (brother or sister) as a basic faith-deed. The main point is to draw an analogy. Just as saying "Shalom" to a desperate brother or sister without doing anything to meet his or her need is a meaningless blessing, so too faith that does no deed is empty faith. But the very nature of the analogy also points to an endemic manifestation of deedless "faith": the neglect of fellow believers in need. Martin (1988: 84) goes so far as to think that James is addressing an actual situation known to him. However, the form of James's comment is too generalized and hypothetical to allow for that conclusion. On the opposite end, Dibelius (1975: 152–53) goes to some length to try to show that the situation of 2:15 is only an analogy, purely hypothetical and not representative of any real or potential situation; it is purely a parabolic analogy to a faith being empty and of no value. On this view, then, James could just as easily have said, "If someone dug a well, but there is no water in it, what good is that?"

It is true that James is making a comparison, but two little words make it clear that this situation is not simply a parabolic analogy. James says, "If someone *from among you* [ἐξ ὑμῶν, *ex hymōn*] says" (2:16). If he were only making a comparison, he simply would have said, "If someone says," not specifying "from among you." Further, the extensiveness and detail of the hypothetical instance are evidence that such neglect of the poor has at times been a real problem. Dibelius is correct that the example is stylized and hyperbolic, but, like 2:2–4, it almost certainly reflects real possibilities in the community. The neglect of the desperately poor in the church is an egregious fault, but it does happen, and when it does, it sharply erodes the credibility of the claim to have faith.

As a unit, 2:15–16 lays out the extended hypothetical situation, just as in 2:2–4. In this first example of a nonworking faith, James is particularly concerned for poverty within the community. Two exemplary needs within the community of believers ("brother or sister" denotes fellow believers) are

---

to suggest a reference to the faith claimed, that is, to the specific faith of the one claiming it. The translation above uses the English demonstrative to bring this out.

5. See, in excursus 1, "Salvation Is by Faith."

6. Although "soul" (ψυχή, *psychē*) can refer to one's life, the contexts of both 1:21 and 5:20 clearly encompass the person's identity and individual integrity.

presented: lack of adequate clothing (the term in question, γυμνός, *gymnos*, literally means "naked," but it could be used to describe inadequate dress or the lack of an outer garment) and lack of daily food (probably referring to habitual hunger rather than just a lack for one day; Adamson 1976: 122). Note how it is connected with 2:14 in that someone *says*, "Go in peace. . . ." "Go in peace" is the blessing of *šālôm* with which Jews greeted and said farewell to one another (1 Sam. 20:42; 2 Kings 5:19; Judg. 18:6) and that early Christians borrowed (Eph. 6:23; 1 Pet. 5:14b; 3 John 15; cf. Mark 5:34; Luke 7:50; 10:5; Acts 16:36; and the many compound "grace and peace" greetings in Paul's letters). That, together with "be warmed, be filled" (which in modern English idiom might be something like "stay warm, and eat well"; see the additional note on 2:16) would be mockery in a real situation. This is a sober reminder that pleasant but inactive "well-wishing" in effect mocks fellow believers in need. True faith responds to need to the extent that it is able.

Thus, the faith-deed of provision for a fellow believer's hunger or nakedness is a particularly apt example, not only because it emphasizes the necessity of love of neighbor in the church, but also because the needy person receives no benefit from nice words, just as the professing Christian receives no benefit from inactive faith. And there is an echo here of Jesus's words in Matt. 25:31–46, where Jesus's verdict to the Gentiles is based on their response to the nakedness, hunger, and imprisonment of Jesus's "little ones."

So too, *that* kind of faith (2:17),[7] the kind that is unaccompanied by appropriate deeds (faith "by itself"), shows itself to be dead. In other words, its inaction is a mute but powerful testimony to its deadness (dead bodies do nothing), and it shows itself to be a false faith by the way it responds to the needy brother. So James is telling his hearers, "If your faith does not benefit others, it will not benefit you either."

Indeed, such a faith is less than worthless; it is repulsive. James pulls no punches here: this faith devoid of deeds is not just sick or in danger of dying; it is νεκρά (*nekra*, dead), a corpse (an evaluation repeated in 2:26). Religious Jews, for whom contact with a dead body imparted ceremonial pollution, would have regarded such an image as especially repugnant, but dead bodies are repulsive to Gentiles as well.

2:18–19 In the brief paragraph comprising 2:18–19 James deals with two misconceptions about faith, or two dimensions of false faith. First, he attacks the supposition that faith is somehow opposed to works, or that there are two different ways of approaching God, some people coming by faith and others coming by works. Second, he repudiates the notion that faith consists solely in believing certain doctrines to be true.

In general, 2:18 is not difficult to understand, but it is notoriously difficult to identify precisely how it should be construed.[8] The first clause of 2:18

---

7. As in 2:14, the article is an article of previous reference.
8. For lengthy discussions of the critical problem, see Ropes 1916: 208–14; Dibelius 1975: 154–58.

may be rendered literally as "But someone will say, 'You have faith, and I have works.'" James clearly means to deny the notion that it is possible to have faith without works. This he does by means of a hypothetical conversation. Interaction with a hypothetical interlocutor is a common technique in Greek rhetoric, used to anticipate and preempt possible objections. But James appears to have made the hypothetical interlocutor say the opposite of what was intended. One would have expected "But someone will say, 'You have works, but I have faith,'" which James would then answer with "Show me your [so-called] faith without works, and I will show you [genuine] faith by means of my works." This difficulty has led to several suggested solutions.

1. One approach is to emend the text. At least two conjectural emendations have been suggested. Pfleiderer (1911: 4.304n1) suggests that the original text was in fact "You have works, but I have faith." Another suggestion (Spitta 1896: 78) is that the interlocutor's statement somehow got dropped, leaving only James's response. But such conjectural emendations, being devoid of evidence, should only be a last resort when no other acceptable solution presents itself, and even then they remain dubious.
2. Some (e.g., Mayor 1897: 96; Adamson 1976: 124–25; Mussner 1975: 136–38) suggest that the interlocutor is an ally, not a hypothetical opponent, who says, in support of James, "You have faith, and I have works." The problem with this view is the introductory words: "But someone will say," which elsewhere always set up an opposing point of view in order to shoot it down (cf. Paul's similar use of "You will say" in Rom. 9:19; 11:19; cf. 1 Cor. 15:35). Further, James's stinging words at the end of the exchange in 2:20 ("O foolish man") do not suggest that the interlocutor is an ally. The only natural way of reading 2:18 is that James is introducing a possible objection to his view.
3. Another suggestion (Hort 1909: 60–61) is that the hypothetical interlocutor's words stop with the first few words of 2:18, which should be read as a question:

   Interlocutor: Do you have faith?
   James: I have works. Show me your faith without works, and I will show you my faith by works.

   This almost convinces, but in the context, James is not trying to justify his own working faith; rather, he is challenging the validity of a faith without deeds. Furthermore, the contracted conjunction (κἀγώ = καὶ ἐγώ, *kai egō*, and I) between "you have faith" and "I have works" makes this solution unlikely.[9]

9. Compare the exactly parallel form of expression in Theophilus, *Autol.* 1.2: δεῖξόν μοι τὸν ἄνθρωπόν σου κἀγώ σοι δείξω τὸν θεόν μου ("Show me your man, and I will show you my god"), where clearly the two halves function together.

4. Going the opposite direction, Donker (1981) suggests that all of 2:18–19 represents the opponent's viewpoint, that opponent being a "Paulinist." The interlocutor's question is asking whether the Jewish Christian author believes anything more than Jewish monotheism. Despite Donker's attempt to support this suggestion with a structural analysis, however, 2:20 does not seem to be in contrast with 2:19, and introducing the (Pauline) interlocutor's objections then seems to be a distraction from James's main point, that faith without works is dead.

5. Zahn (1909: 1.97–98) presents a view somewhat similar to that of Mayor, but he understands the opponent/interlocutor as articulating a Jewish non-Christian viewpoint, not as fully allied with James. Zahn reads the interlocutor's comments as running all the way through 2:19 and expressing the viewpoint of the unbelieving Jew who is critiquing Christian reliance on faith. Thus, the interlocutor is only partially an ally. James resumes speaking then with 2:20. But it is hard to see how an early reader of James could have figured this out. More importantly, as Ropes (1916: 214) notes, there is no evidence that Judaism ever rejected faith or that Christianity rejected works such that they became a "faith" party and a "works" party, and monotheism certainly was a faith commitment of both.

6. Somewhat similar to Zahn is Hodges (1963), who, in addition to taking the interlocutor's words through 2:19, argues for following the Byzantine Text, reading "by works" instead of "without works" in the first sentence. This results in the following reading:

Interlocutor: You have faith and I have works. Show me your faith by your works, and I will show my faith by my works. You believe that God is one. You do well. The demons also believe and tremble.

James: Do you want to understand, vain man, how hollow faith is without works?

Hodges, then, is suggesting that James's dialogue partner is ridiculing the notion that someone could demonstrate internal faith through external works. But this solution appears to make for a very unnatural reading even of the Byzantine Text and also appears to miss entirely James's main point in the passage as a whole.

7. A seventh possibility is that James simply mixed it up, as public speakers frequently do, and any attempt to resolve it grammatically is doomed to failure, but since the mix-up does not make the passage impossible to understand, we need not worry about it. This is in some ways the easiest solution,[10] but the fact that we are dealing not with extemporaneous

10. I do not think that this view necessarily disrespects the authority of James's letter. Such an "error" would be of a piece with grammatical mistakes such as disagreement of subjects with verbs or the use of the nominative case for a direct object. Since they do not affect the

speech but a written letter, especially if it is an encyclical letter (as suggested by 1:1), makes it unlikely that this kind of "mistake" would survive a first copying. Hence, a solution needs to be sought elsewhere.

8. The most common approach among recent commentaries, and the one adopted here, is to treat the hypothetical interlocutor's comment not as specifically identifying his own faith as opposed to James's works, but as using the "you" and "I" as a way of saying "One person says this, another that." Thus, the position James is setting himself over against is the notion that works and faith are somehow separable, and either faith or works is a viable approach. James insists that faith and works are inseparable. Although this suffers from poor attestation of such use of "you" and "I," it is the solution that does the least violence to natural use of language.[11]

Thus, the second half of 2:18 is the key to understanding James's point. "*Show me*," James says, "and I will *show* you."[12] One cannot show faith by any means other than works, and thus faith and works cannot be separated.

In 2:19 James challenges another false notion, that faith is simply the acceptance of doctrine. Probably the central defining teaching of both Judaism and Christianity in the context of the Greco-Roman world was the doctrine that there is only one true God. For Jews it was encapsulated in the Shema, found in Deut. 6:4 and reiterated by Jesus as the opening to the greatest commandment (Mark 12:29–30): "Hear, O Israel: The LORD our God, the LORD is one."[13] This, of course, is not a distinctively Christian doctrine, since non-Christian Jews and even some Gentiles accepted it, but nevertheless it is a commendable belief so far as it goes: "That is good," says James (literally "You do well," which might be mildly ironic [cf. 2:8]). But the specific doctrine in question is not the main issue; rather, it is that bare knowledge of theological truth is something that even demons share, but it hardly benefits them.[14] Believing *that*

---

meaning of what is said, they are not communicating untruth. However, as indicated, I reject this view on other grounds.

11. Although the roots of this interpretation can be traced earlier, its definitive presentation was Ropes 1908 (cf. Ropes 1916: 211–12), and most commentators since that time have adopted Ropes's solution (see especially Dibelius 1975: 156–57). McKnight (1990: 355–64) provides a good summary of the problem and its proposed solutions and offers a slightly nuanced version of Ropes's approach.

12. Moo (2000: 130) points out that "show" here means to demonstrate or prove, not simply "allow to be seen."

13. The Shema itself was at times regarded as having almost magical power. That it was possible for Jews to believe in a quasi-magical power of the Shema is evinced in *b. Ber.* 15b. See especially the reference to Rabbi Hama b. Hanina saying, "If one in reciting the Shema pronounces the letters distinctly, hell is cooled for him" (translation in Epstein 1948: 92).

14. Given James's predilection for classical words, there is a remote possibility that the δαιμόνια (*daimonia*) here is a reference to the lesser gods of paganism (as in Acts 17:18 and in most nonbiblical Greek literature). But the reference to them "shuddering" and the general usage in Judaism favors the notion of them as evil supernatural beings. Laws (1980: 126–28) even argues for a background in the practice of exorcism.

there is one God (intellectual acknowledgment) is different from believing *in* (εἰς, *eis*, into) the God who is one.

Moo (2000: 131) points out the possibility of some irony here. At least the demons have the sense to shudder, which suggests that their "faith" has more reality to it than the faith of those who claim to believe but do not do the deeds of faith.

In 2:20–26 James presents two examples of genuine faith: Abraham and Rahab. But Abraham and Rahab are not just "illustrations" in the sense of making more vivid what has already been shown. The examples of believer Abraham and believer Rahab themselves have probative force, and they help to define the nature of genuine faith. This is especially true of Abraham, whom James calls "our father" (2:21). Just as ethnic Judaism regarded Abraham as the progenitor of the Jewish race, Christians understood Abraham as the progenitor of the spiritual race that encompassed many nationalities (cf. Rom. 4:16, which harks back to Gen. 17:5).[15]

2:20

Another rhetorical question begins 2:20, this one addressed to the hypothetical interlocutor as "vain human." A certain play on words is evident in Greek because the word for "vain" (κενός, *kenos*) also means "empty." The one who claims to separate faith and works is an "empty human" because he or she has an empty faith, just as a body without a spirit is empty (2:26). Further, even with his "empty" concept of faith, the interlocutor does seem to value "knowledge," so James ironically asks whether the interlocutor wants to *know* that faith without works is useless. And the word for useless (ἀργή, *argē*, idle, ineffective, useless) further represents wordplay because it is a contracted form of α + εργος, that is, "no work." Hence, "Faith that doesn't work doesn't work" (Moo 2000: 132). James may also be recalling Jesus's word in Matt. 12:36 that people will have to give an account on judgment day for every "empty word" (ῥῆμα ἀργόν, *rhēma argon*), since claiming to have faith while having no faith-deeds is the ultimate in empty words.

In 2:21 James brings into play the issue of Abraham's "justification," and this has generated much discussion since the Reformation. In dealing with the issue, it is helpful to remember James's main point in the latter half of James 2: faith without works is nonviable and ineffective, and faith therefore needs works in order to be regarded as viable and effective. This main point is directly stated at least four times in this discourse: at the beginning (2:14), middle (2:17, 20), and end (2:26).

2:21–24

James's concern is thus different from Paul's interest in Galatians and Romans.[16] Paul's interest is in one's legal standing before the eschatological

15. In Luke 16:24–30 and John 8:39 Jesus is already putting the fatherhood of Abraham on a different basis than a racial one. As Hort (1909: 63) points out, it is as father of those who show faith that Abraham is invoked, because his faith was a true and active one.

16. See excursus 2, "Faith, Works, and Justification in James and Paul." Here it should suffice simply to point out that Paul agrees with James that the believer's works must be in concert with his or her profession. Titus 1:16, for example, refers to people who "profess to know

tribunal of God (or as some scholars have recently argued, one's inclusion in the covenant people).[17] He is interested in how God can rightly give a verdict of "just" for a sinner (the answer being through union with Christ) and how one appropriates that verdict and union (by faith, not by "works of the law"). James, however, is interested in the legitimacy of active faith, as over against the emptiness of an inactive "faith."

Hence, James's recounting of Abraham's and Rahab's "justification by works" is not presenting the process by which a sinful human being can obtain the verdict of righteous, much less a theory on how one becomes a child of God; rather, it is part of the argument to demonstrate that faith cannot be divorced from works—they necessarily go together (2:20). His concern is not the *ordo salutis* (order of salvation), but consistent Christian behavior.

That said, what James means by "justified" remains difficult to identify. There are five possible meanings of the word δικαιόω (*dikaioō*, justify) in biblical literature:

1. "To *give justice* to someone; to correct a wrong" (Ps. 81:3 LXX [82:3 MT]).
2. "To *declare* someone righteous (generally) or in the right (on a specific issue); to render a verdict of 'innocent'; to vindicate or acquit (and thus the opposite of condemn"; see, e.g., Matt. 12:37; Rom. 8:33–34). This is by far the most common biblical usage, both in the Greek OT and in the NT. This meaning is related to the first, in that giving a verdict of "righteous" to the right party is also providing justice for that party. Sometimes this juridical justification simply establishes one party as being righteous or in the right as compared with another; it is not a general statement of someone's overall virtue (e.g., Gen. 38:26; Luke 18:14).
3. "To *prove* or *demonstrate* that someone is righteous or in the right" (Jer. 3:11 LXX; Matt. 11:19; Rom. 3:4; 1 Tim. 3:16).[18] This clearly is the meaning when it is God who is justified (e.g., Ps. 50:6 LXX [51:6 MT; 51:4 ET]). Proving someone to be righteous can also be related to meaning 2, of course, because giving a verdict of "righteous" in court entails

---

God, but they deny him by their works [ἔργοις]." Even those who think that Paul did not write Titus should note that in Gal. 5:21 Paul says that those who do wicked deeds will not inherit the kingdom of God. For Paul, ultimately the issue is not works versus faith, but law-works (whereby one tries to gain or retain God's approval) versus faith-works (which flow out of an already extant approval in Christ; Gal. 5:6).

17. In my view, people on both sides of the "new perspective on Paul" debate have made far too much of this. Certainly, inclusion in the covenant people is an aspect of justification, especially in Galatians, but the word *justification* and its use in Romans suggest that broader issues are at stake for Paul, namely one's standing before God and eschatological destiny.

18. This meaning could be further subdivided into "to prove righteous" and "to prove to be in the right" (i.e., correct or wise), the former being moral and the latter intellective, but the key distinctive of this meaning is "proof" or "demonstration," and a biblical line between moral righteousness and wisdom is difficult to draw.

the legal demonstration or proof of a party being righteous generally or being in the right on a specific issue.

4. "To *clear a debt* obligation, either by forgiveness or by the debt being paid off" (Sir. 18:22; Rom. 6:7; possibly Acts 13:38).

5. "To *cause* someone to behave righteously." This meaning is quite rare and indeed appears to be operative only once in biblical literature, in Ps. 72:13 LXX (73:13 MT), which literally reads, "All in vain have I justified my heart."[19]

We may first dispense with a couple of other suggested meanings that have no basis in Greek lexicography. First, we have no evidence to support that the word ever means "to show someone to have been declared righteous." Calvin (1948: 314) touches on this idea in one sentence, but he mainly presents James as using the word in the sense of "prove righteous" (meaning 3). Second, "justify" cannot mean "to show that one has faith." Although either of these would fit quite well and harmonize James and Paul nicely, there is no usage elsewhere in Greek literature to support such meanings for the Greek word δικαιόω.

Neither meaning 1 (give justice) nor meaning 4 (clear a debt, forgive) fits the context in James. Meaning 5 (cause to behave righteously) is barely possible, but that meaning is extremely rare. More importantly, James appears interested not in how one becomes upright, but in the consistent living of the life of faith and thus in the connection between faith and action. Further, meaning 5 is hard to fit with any construction of James's quotation of Gen. 15:6.

This leaves either the juridical meaning 2 (vindicate, declare righteous) or the demonstrative meaning 3 (show to be righteous or prove to be in the right). Since James does refer to the future judgment by God (3:1; 4:9; 5:8), here he may be thinking of God's ultimate future verdict for Abraham and Rahab (meaning 2), or he may simply be thinking of God's approval of their actions at the time they were performed (also meaning 2). However, James is also concerned with the believer enduring tests and demonstrating faith in action, so justification as the demonstration of righteousness (meaning 3) also fits with James's concerns.

Many commentators, from Calvin to the present, have opted for meaning 3. Abraham's obedience recounted in Gen. 22 demonstrated his righteousness. It manifested his righteousness and thus brought to fruition God's declaration of Abraham's righteousness that occurred several years earlier in Gen. 15. On this view, the offering of Isaac was not the basis for Abraham's righteousness or even for God's recognition of Abraham as righteous; rather, it was the necessary and proper outworking and manifestation of Abraham's inward righteousness that came by a working faith, so that his faith and works together resulted in a genuinely righteous life. But it is the works, especially

---

19. Compare the Hebrew רִיק זִכִּיתִי לְבָבִי (*rîq zikkîtî lēbābî*, in vain I have kept my heart pure).

the obedience in offering Isaac, not a bare claim to faith, that demonstrated Abraham's righteousness.[20]

The offering of Isaac, commonly known as the Aqedah (binding), was the subject of much discussion in ancient Judaism. It was regarded as the greatest test that Abraham faced (Jub. 17.17; 1 Macc. 2:52; Pirqe de Rabbi Eliezer 26–31) and as the clearest evidence of his total commitment and love for God. It became a pattern for Jews facing persecution (e.g., 1 Macc. 2:52). But whether James knew of or accepted this tradition is irrelevant to his purpose here. The Aqedah is not given any particularly redemptive force in James, nor is it developed as anything more than a classic example of how Abraham's faith was not something apart from his obedience, and how the incredible deed of obedience in offering Isaac "justified" Abraham, that is, demonstrated that he was righteous and that his faith was genuine, without indicating how he came to be righteous.[21]

On this view, therefore, James's justification by works (a manifestation of righteousness by obedience) is seen to be something completely different from the justification by works that Paul rejects (a verdict of God's acquittal based on conformity to law). For James, "justify" is a synonym not for "save" (cf. 2:14) but for "show" or "prove" (2:18).[22] James is not saying that Abraham, by offering Isaac, is for that reason declared righteous (as Paul uses the word),[23] nor is he saying that Abraham makes himself righteous before God by his action (this meaning of "justify" is exceedingly rare), for as Calvin (1948: 316) points out, the scriptural quotation from Gen. 15 recounts an event several years before the offering of Isaac. Thus, the forensic declaration of Abraham's righteousness (justification meaning 2) long preceded the demonstration of it (justification meaning 3), and although the former is brought to fruition in the latter, they are different.

20. In Calvin's words (1948: 316), "Man is not justified by faith alone, that is, by a bare and empty knowledge of God; he is justified by works, that is, his righteousness is known and proved by its fruits."

21. Nor should being called "friend of God" be seen as Abraham's reward for the Aqedah. Dibelius (1975: 172–73) cites Philo, *Abraham* 46 §273, and Jub. 19.9 to argue that James was building on the Jewish notion that Abraham's faith, especially in the Aqedah merited God's friendship. Apart from the question of whether James's contemporaries thought that Abraham merited a reward, James's own focus is on Abraham's behavior exhibiting the reality of a relationship (i.e., "faith"), which God then acknowledged (Abraham was "justified" and called "friend of God").

22. Moo (2000: 130) makes a distinction between "showing" and "proving," but although the latter may be slightly more emphatic and forensic, they are synonymous, and one word, δείκνυμι (*deiknymi*), covers both nuances in Greek.

23. Paul's use of "justification" is further complicated by his linking of faith in Christ to a devolvement of righteousness upon believers that is not inherent in them but rather is acceded to them by virtue of their covenantal union with Christ (e.g., Gal. 2:17). Although recently the language of "imputation" has been questioned in some quarters, it should at least be clear that for Paul, a believer receives the verdict of "righteous" before God by virtue of what Christ has done, not what the believer has done (e.g., Rom. 3:22–25; 4:5). This is because Paul is dealing with the issue of how a sinful person, Jew or Gentile, may hope for a favorable verdict from a holy God who does not clear the guilty. But this issue is not the issue that James is dealing with, and James should not be read with these questions in mind.

This view also works well for the example of Rahab. Her sheltering of the spies was clear and probative evidence of her belief that the God of Israel would enable Israel to conquer her Canaanite city (Josh. 2:9–11). She too gave evidence of her inward righteousness by her outward act of giving succor to the people of God, and later by doing as she had been instructed (Josh. 6:22–25). And James's summary statement in 2:24, "A person is justified by works and not by faith alone," is simply saying that faith without works cannot demonstrate a person's righteousness, because faith without works is as useless as a corpse.

Several commentators, however, and indeed almost all recent scholarship on James, favor meaning 2. They point not only to the predominance of the meaning "vindicate" or "declare righteous" in the biblical literature generally, but also to the fact that James begins this diatribe in 2:14 with the question "Can that (workless) faith save him?" At issue in the passage is what counts with God (cf. the parable of the tax collector and the Pharisee in Luke 18:9–14), not how faith or righteousness is displayed. Since "save" refers to divine acceptance or deliverance from condemnation, the assumption is that James contrasts a nonworking, inactive faith, which cannot save in the judgment, with a working faith, which can save in the judgment, not because faith itself saves, but because it is the kind of faith that God accepts.

Further, it seems too obvious to say that faith alone does not demonstrate a person's righteousness. Faith (as belief) is internal, whereas demonstration by its very nature must be external and visible. But someone very well might mistakenly think that a deedless belief could be the basis for salvation.

On this view, therefore, the "justifying" in James's purview refers either to (1) God's future verdict of "righteous" that will be uttered for people who, like Abraham and Rahab, do faith-deeds (e.g., Moo 2000: 135; Beyschlag 1897: 132–33), or to (2) God's commendation of Abraham (Gen. 22:12) and salvation of Rahab (Josh. 6:25) in the events that followed their righteous acts (e.g., Davids 1982: 127; Dibelius 1975: 162), or to (3) God's acceptance of Abraham and Rahab as righteous because they behaved righteously.[24] On this understanding, the fact that God's pronouncement of Abraham's faith as his righteousness happened many years prior to the binding of Isaac is not determinative for James, because Gen. 15:6 was simply anticipatory of the later obedience.

Although James certainly is aware of the future judgment and bases certain exhortations upon it (3:1; 5:8), his grammar involves some difficulties for the "future verdict" view. First, both Abraham and Rahab "were" justified (ἐδικαιώθη, edikaiōthē). If James has the future final judgment in view, why does he not say "will be" justified (δικαιωθήσεται, dikaiōthēsetai), as in 3:1

---

24. Davids (1982: 127), following Ward 1968, thinks that the righteousness of Abraham in view was his works of hospitality recounted in Gen. 18, an idea developed and amplified in Second Temple Jewish literature. But James breathes not the slightest allusion to Abraham's hospitality. It is not necessary to go to Gen. 18 to find Abraham's righteousness; for James, it lies explicitly in the intertextuality of Gen. 15:6 and Gen. 22:12. See the additional note on 2:21.

he says that teachers "will" receive (λημψόμεθα, *lēmpsometha*) the greater judgment? The second difficulty is the aorist participles accompanying the justification: "having offered" and "having received." If these participles are to be taken as temporal, they imply that the "justifying" took place shortly after their faith-deeds occurred. Even if not temporal, they likely are instrumental, and the offering of Isaac and the receiving of the spies were the means by which they were justified, and once again eschatological judgment seems too remote. Third, if future judgment is in view, then the connection with James's citation of Gen. 15:6 is obscure. How can Abraham's justification have been "fulfilled" (also in the aorist tense) by the offering of Isaac if the justification has not yet occurred? Fourth, James indicates that a person "is" justified (2:24) by works and not by faith alone, which again is not a future tense but this time a general present.[25] And again, the passage at this point is concerned not with how one may stand in the judgment, but with present Christian living.[26] Of course, present obedience is not irrelevant for future justification, but it seems unlikely that Abraham's justification and the justification of the one who works are regarded as different things to James.

James's meaning still could be a reference to God's verdict of "righteous," however, in that in Gen. 22:12 God says to Abraham, "Now I know that you fear God," and Josh. 6:25 indicates that Rahab and her family were saved by virtue of her action; these are functional equivalents of God's approval, that is, a verdict of "righteous." James is, however, ultimately concerned not with the historical justifications of Abraham and Rahab (James never mentions or alludes specifically to Gen. 22:12 or Josh. 6:25), but with how a person generally is recognized as righteous: by works and not by faith alone. It is the acts of Abraham and Rahab that are mentioned as instrumental in the "justifying." However, although James makes no mention of God's later commendation of Abraham or Rahab's protection in the fall of Jericho, he does refer to an actual declaration by God of Abraham's righteousness: Gen. 15:6. As noted already, surely James knew the Abraham story in Genesis and that the declaration of Gen. 15 occurred long before the Aqedah. But Dibelius (1975: 162)

25. This probably is a gnomic present tense that expresses a general truth, and thus the present tense is not necessarily indicative either of action "in the present time" or of "ongoing" action (Moo 2000: 140). A general truth about the future judgment more likely would be expressed with a future tense, as in 3:1.

26. Paul, it is true, makes reference to the future judgment and treats it as having occurred already in Christ's death and resurrection, so that the believer stands already justified in view of his or her connection to Christ, the already justified one. Paul therefore sometimes can speak of the believer's justification in the past tense (Rom. 8:30; 1 Cor. 6:11; but notice the future tense in Rom. 3:30; Gal. 2:16) because of the "already" dimension of God's verdict for those who are in Christ. But James is concerned not with the "already/not yet," nor the inbreaking of the eschaton, nor the believer's preexperience of judgment by faith through union with Christ, but with a practical matter, the dangerous notion that a nonworking faith is of any value. Paul's complex covenantal recasting of the tenses, where God's future verdict of "righteous" is proleptically applied to the believer by virtue of his or her union with Christ (Rom. 4:23–5:1), is outside James's purview.

and many others have pointed out that in the general Jewish interpretive milieu in which James lived, the story of Abraham was taken as a whole, as a supreme example of a "righteous life" climaxing in the Aqedah, and thus the historical distance between Gen. 15 and Gen. 22 was irrelevant. All that mattered was that Abraham lived a righteous life and therefore was accepted by and named as a friend of God.[27] This is particularly evident in 1 Macc. 2:52 RSV: "Was not Abraham found faithful *when tested*, and it was reckoned to him as righteousness?" The author of 1 Maccabees apparently regarded the Aqedah as the basis for Abraham's justification by faith. That James shared this viewpoint is indicated, it is argued, in his reference to Abraham as "our father," in the linkage of the offering of Isaac and the pronouncement of Gen. 15, and in James's concern, shared with 1 Maccabees, with faithfulness under duress. Further evidence is James's use of the moniker "friend of God," a title not found in the Genesis story but commonly applied to Abraham in Second Temple Judaism. Indeed, Jub. 19.9 refers to Abraham as "reckoned" as God's friend (thus providing a common link between Gen. 15:6 and "friend of God," just as in James), thus placing James's use of the Abrahamic tradition firmly within that milieu. Hence, one cannot draw any conclusions from the fact that the events of Gen. 22 occurred several years after those of Gen. 15.

Further, the declaration of Gen. 15, as well as the promises of Gen. 12, is not unrelated to Gen. 22, as Heb. 11 points out. The promise that Abraham believed, which belief gained him God's verdict, was the promise of the coming of Isaac and Abraham's destiny as father of countless descendants. Hence, the belief in the promise could be seen as bound up with the faithful offering of Isaac, which, says Hebrews, was implicitly a belief in the resurrection power of God. The historical distance therefore is irrelevant; the justifying word of Gen. 15 was an anticipatory acquittal, integrally connecting Abraham's faith in the promise with his obedient offering of Isaac in Gen. 22. Even within Gen. 22 itself, when God reiterates the earlier promises of seed and blessing, God says that it is *because* Abraham did not withhold his son that the blessings of Gen. 12 and Gen. 15 will ensue (Gen. 22:16–18).[28]

Despite all of this, certain items in the text of James suggest that he was not so historically oblivious as Dibelius and others suggest. The fact that Abraham's faith was made complete by his works, along with the reference to the Scripture being fulfilled, indicates that James indeed was aware that the

---

27. Dibelius (1975: 162) argues extensively that in Jewish thinking about Abraham the acts and faith of Abraham became "timeless" in their exemplarity. Particularly in 1 Macc. 2:52, Abraham's being found faithful was the result of his passing the test, and God's declaration of Abraham's righteousness was the reward for his faithfulness in offering Isaac. Dibelius attributes a similar lack of historical consciousness to James and argues that it was precisely the offering of Isaac that constituted his "faithfulness" and resulted in God's declaring him righteous.

28. Thus, it appears that the blessing of Abraham is prior to and not contingent on Abraham's obedience (Gen. 12; 15), and yet at the same time it is indeed contingent on his obedience (Gen. 17; 22). There is no getting around the mystery of the relationship between divine grace and human responsibility.

offering of Isaac occurred as the eventuation of, and thus at least logically subsequent to, Abraham's justification. But whether or not James was conscious of the historical development, we must remember that his overarching purpose here is not to set forth a soteriology, but to deny the viability of faith without works, to deny that a workless faith can save. Unlike Paul, for whom God's justification of the ungodly is a key to understanding the gospel and why Jesus died, James's concern with justification is subsidiary to the practical concerns of genuine Christian life, a theme that he invokes to show the emptiness of a nonworking faith. Hence, it may be most faithful to James to suppose that he would not have drawn a sharp line between the notions of a demonstration of righteousness and God's verdict of righteousness. There is the element of God's approval of Abraham's and Rahab's righteous faith-deeds and his consequent saving acts on their behalf, and also the element of these faith-deeds being demonstrations of Abraham's and Rahab's righteousness. The Aqedah both demonstrates Abraham's righteousness and elicits God's commendation and renewal of the promise (Gen. 22:16–18) that connects with Gen. 15:6. God's statement in Gen. 22:12, "Now I know that you fear God," may be viewed as a verdict, but it also may be viewed as God's acknowledgment that Abraham's commitment to God has been conclusively demonstrated. And note that what is demonstrated is that Abraham "feared" (i.e., believed) God.[29] Likewise, whereas no "justifying word" was uttered by God over Rahab in the book of Joshua,[30] she, like Abraham, feared God (Josh. 2:9–11; cf. Heb. 11:31, which sees her fear as equivalent to faith) and acted on that fear/belief by sheltering the spies, and as a result she was "justified" in that she was rescued from the destruction of Jericho.

To the quotation of Gen. 15:6 James adds the title "friend of God." As noted already, Second Temple Judaism was fond of this term for Abraham (Philo, *Sobriety* 11 §55; Jub. 19.9; 30.20; T. Ab. *passim*; cf. *m. ʾAbot* 5.4).[31] It is based on the fact that already in 2 Chron. 20:7 and Isa. 41:8 Abraham is "beloved" (so MT and LXX) of God. James may intend to evoke thereby that Abraham stood over against the friendship with the world decried in 4:4 (see Johnson 1985), although 4:4 follows 2:23 by quite a few verses, making it doubtful that many of James's original readers would have caught the

29. Even Dibelius (1975: 165) gives tacit acknowledgment to this dimension when he says that "Jewish exegetes quite universally saw the main evidence of Abraham's faith in his offering up of his son."

30. According to the article "Rahab" (*JE* 10:309), some traditions in later Judaism did describe Rahab as someone whose righteousness was given express recognition by God. But such traditions are ambivalent and late (cf. the description of conflicting traditions about Rahab in *EncJud* 17:66). Although there is a small possibility that such a tradition was known to James, this argument from some late Jewish sources is weak, and even if James knew of some "justifying word" of God to Rahab, his focus still is on her "faith-deeds," not the process by which Rahab was pronounced righteous.

31. The cognomen passed into Christian usage (1 Clem. 10.1; 17.2; Tertullian, *Adv. Jud.* 2.7; Irenaeus, *Haer.* 4.14.4) and also into Islam, where Abraham still is often referred to as *El Khalil*, "The Friend (of God)."

connection. Perhaps more significantly, according to Wis. 7:27, it is wisdom that makes one a friend of God. If something of the material of James 3 is already in James's mind, Abraham's faith is seen to have made him a doer of the wisdom from above.

In 2:22 James draws the practical conclusion from Abraham's justification: his faith "cooperated," "worked together with" (συνήργει, *synērgei*) his works,[32] and faith is "completed" (ἐτελειώθη, *eteleiōthē*) by works, just as sin is completed by death in 1:15. This sounds at first like "synergism," but again we must remember that James is talking not about how one obtains a relationship with God, or how a sinner may hope to receive a verdict of "not guilty" in the final judgment, but about the necessity of faith being completed by works. Thus, the "synergism" in view is far from the notion that humans cooperate with God in their salvation. James rather is speaking about a person's faith operating in synergy with his or her works as an unfolding of the righteous life.

That faith is "completed" by works is to say that it comes to its fruition. The verb τελειόω (*teleioō*), like its cognates in James 1:4, has to do not so much with perfection (as Davids 1982: 128 posits) as with maturity, fruition, or completion. Just as sin, when completed (ἀποτελεσθεῖσα, *apotelestheisa*), brings forth death (1:15), so faith finds its completion in works. Moo (2000: 137) notes that James's use of the word is quite similar to 1 John 4:12 NIV: "If we love one another, God lives in us and his love is made complete in us."[33] Clearly, 1 John is not claiming that our love makes God's love "perfect" in the sense of "flawless," for God's love is always flawless, but our love does bring God's love in us to its fruition. Similarly, works do not make faith flawless; they bring faith to its proper completion.

Hort (1909: 64) summarizes the verse's intent well: "The works received the co-operation of a living power from the faith: the faith received perfecting and consummation from the works into which it grew."

James says that the Scripture that speaks of Abraham's justification by faith (Gen. 15:6) was "fulfilled" by the offering of Isaac (2:23). This phraseology is consistently used throughout the NT to refer to the realization of the redemptive promises made in the OT by the events of Jesus Christ and of the Spirit, sent after his resurrection. Such fulfillment often is understood to be simply a coming to pass of things predicted, but "fulfill" in the NT involves more the notion of "full realization" than simply connecting a NT event to an OT prediction. This is particularly true here. James is saying not that God predicted that Abraham would be righteous, which then came to pass at the Aqedah, but that the friendship and the right relationship with God that were accounted to Abraham in Gen. 15:6 resulted in, were brought to completion at, the Aqedah.

---

32. Dibelius (1975: 163) and Davids (1982: 128) read συνήργει as "assisted." But this puts the works as primary and the faith helping out with whatever is lacking in the works, a notion that does not fit the context.

33. Compare, however, the ESV's "his love is perfected in us," which I think is misleading.

James's addition to the quotation of Gen. 15:6 in 2:23, "and he was called the friend of God," could be read as simply attached to the quotation, or as connected back with the two previous aorist passive verbs, or most likely both, forming a chain of aorist passives:

Faith was completed [ἐτελειώθη, *eteleiōthē*] by works (2:22).

Scripture was fulfilled [ἐπληρώθη, *eplērōthē*] that says . . . (2:23a).

It was reckoned [ἐλογίσθη, *elogisthē*] to him as righteousness (2:23b).

He was called [ἐκλήθη, *eklēthē*] God's friend (2:23c).

Such a series of aorist passives seems to have a somewhat confessional tone to it. Compare 1 Tim. 3:16 NASB:

By common confession [ὁμολογουμένως, *homologoumenōs*], great is the mystery of godliness:

He who was revealed [ἐφανερώθη, *ephanerōthē*] in the flesh,
Was vindicated [ἐδικαιώθη, *edikaiōthē*] in the Spirit,
Seen [ὤφθη, *ōphthē*] by angels,
Proclaimed [ἐκηρύχθη, *ekēruchthē*] among the nations,
Believed on [ἐπιστεύθη, *episteuthē*] in the world,
Taken up [ἀνελήμφθη, *anelēmphthē*] in glory.

The conclusion to the Abraham example comes in 2:24. As noted earlier, "justified" in James probably means both "shown to be righteous" and "vindicated (by God) as righteous." Thus, James invites the reader to conclude ("You see!") that a person is justified (δικαιοῦται, *dikaioutai*) in the sight of both God and people by works and not by faith only.[34] Thus too, it is clear that for James faith is not simply another work, as some in Judaism apparently thought, but something that operates along with works (2:22).[35]

Although this verse looks like a direct contradiction to Paul's statement in Rom. 3:28 ("one is justified by faith apart from works of the law"), the different context of their statements and the difference in meaning of the terms "faith" and "works" indicates that the contradiction is superficial (see excursus 2, "Faith, Works, and Justification in James and Paul"). On the other hand, this

---

34. The use of the present tense (or better, progressive aspect) is gnomic (expressing a general truth), but since James did not use the perfect tense (which would mean that a person "stands justified" or "is in a justified state") or the "gnomic" aorist of axioms, the present tense may also have something of the progressive force in it, declaring that a person is continually shown to be right by works. However, this cannot be pressed; Paul uses the present passive of the same word to deny that someone "is justified" by works of the law (Gal. 2:16).

35. Once again Dibelius (1975: 174) is forced by his interpretation to admit an inconsistency in James's use of Gen. 15:6, because on the one hand, according to Dibelius, Abraham's faith is one of his works that justify, but on the other hand, faith is something other than works that goes together with works. I would respond that this perceived inconsistency is a clue that Dibelius misunderstands James rather than that James misunderstands Genesis.

verse is also a reminder that Paul's doctrine of justification by faith does not gainsay the general teaching of the OT (e.g., Gen. 18:25; Ps. 7:8; 96:13), found also in the teaching of Jesus (e.g., Matt. 12:36), elsewhere in the NT (e.g., Rev. 20:13), and even in Paul (Rom. 2:2, 13; 2 Cor. 5:10), that God judges people according to their actions. As Calvin (1948: 317) puts it, "We, indeed, allow that good works are required *for* righteousness; we only take away from them the power of conferring righteousness, because they cannot stand before the tribunal of God" (italics mine).[36] Thus, Calvin does not divorce God's verdict of "righteous" from the righteous deeds of the justified ones (cf. Rom. 8:4).

In 2:25 James presents another example that, although much briefer, helps clarify **2:25** what kind of "work" he has in view. What a remarkable example is Rahab! A prostitute and a Canaanite, she nevertheless became a great exemplar of faith (see Heb. 11:31).[37] The example of Rahab should put to rest the idea that James thinks of Abraham's justification as a reward for the Aqedah, for no "justifying word" was spoken to Rahab, yet her faith was demonstrated and she was "justified by works" (shown to be, and accepted as, righteous) by receiving (ὑποδεξαμένη, *hypodexamenē*) the Israelite spies, which is exactly the point that Heb. 11:31 makes: "*By faith* . . . [she] did not perish with those who were disobedient, because she had received [δεξαμένη, *dexamenē*] the spies in peace" (NRSV). Her "justification" is marked by the fact that she is spared. Here in James the spies are called "messengers" (ἄγγελοι, *angeloi*), probably because they were a means of Rahab's discovering more about God and his intentions. Rahab's justifying works in view, then, are not a righteous life generally, but those acts based upon her recognition (i.e., nascent belief)[38] that the God of Israel was the true and mighty God, and that her Canaanite society was doomed. Thus, like Abraham, she was justified by her faith-deed and the events that followed.[39]

36. The translation by A. W. Morrison in the Torrance edition (Calvin 1960) misleadingly renders the italicized phrase with "required *of* righteousness," but Calvin's Latin cannot mean that: "Fatemur quidem requiri *ad* iustitiam bona opera" (italics mine).

37. Hebrews 11:31 likewise identifies her as Rahab the prostitute.

38. The fact that Rahab's knowledge of the particulars of revealed religion at that point was extremely minimal is an indication that "faith," properly understood, is not an acceptance of intellectual content, but a conviction that generates actions. Rahab's faith was more the fear of God than the acceptance of a set of propositions about God.

39. The early church's allegorizing of Rahab's scarlet thread (1 Clem. 12.7; Justin, *Dial.* 111) to represent the blood of Christ may indeed read too much into the text of Joshua, but it is not as far off the mark redemptive-historically as the frequent ridicule that it has received might suggest. In the original story the scarlet cord was, after all, a "sign" (Josh. 2:12). And some elements of the story in Josh. 2 and Josh. 6 appear to echo the story of Passover and the exodus. Note especially how Rahab is instructed to gather her whole family into her house and is warned that anyone who leaves the house is no longer under protection (cf. Exod. 12:22). In addition, the word for "cord" in Josh. 2 is *tiqwâ*, which is not the usual one (*pātîl*); most commonly in the OT *tiqwâ* means "hope." It is this crimson *tiqwâ* bound on the outer window that is called a "sign," just as the blood on the lintel was a "sign" to the destroying angel in Exod. 12 (note again that James refers to the spies as ἄγγελοι). Furthermore, when Rahab testifies to her nascent faith in God (which was essentially the fear of God; see Josh. 2:9–13), she recounts the exodus and the plagues of Egypt, the climax of which was the destruction of the firstborn.

James, then, is not raising the issue of how God can save the ungodly, nor is he asking how Abraham and Rahab became righteous; he simply sets forth Abraham and Rahab as examples of righteous people who were proven and acknowledged by God as righteous through their deeds of faith, thereby obliterating the entirely mistaken and dangerous notion that a faith without deeds has any value or power. He was incited to use such language as "not justified by faith alone" in response to a vapid notion of "faith alone" (either a perversion of Paul's teaching[40] or, more likely, a syncretization of Jewish monotheism with pagan religiosity)[41] that resulted in people claiming to believe in Christ but giving the lie to that claim by their lack of faith-deeds. James asserts that such a claim is self-delusional, and that is his only interest at this point.

2:26   In 2:26 James reiterates the observation made earlier (2:17) that, just as a body without a spirit is a corpse, faith without works is a corpse, devoid of life. The analogy should not be pressed too hard; it is unnecessary to conclude that just as the spirit is what makes a body a living body, so too that which energizes faith is works. Here the word πνεῦμα (*pneuma*) does not have its theologically loaded meaning "spirit," but simply its common Hellenistic meaning "breath" (Laws 1980: 139). Breath, of course, is the quintessential evidence that a body is alive, even though it does not constitute that life. But it is not evident that first-century readers would have put so fine a point on it or understood that breathing is only one among many subsidiary requirements for life; for them, it virtually *was* life, or at least the most characteristic manifestation of life (cf. Luke 23:46). Hence, perhaps better than "breath" is "vital principle by which the body is animated" (Ropes 1916: 225).[42] James's principal point is not in doubt, in any case: that which distinguishes living faith from dead faith is works of faith. By no means does any of this suggest that one could create genuine faith by works, any more than an effort at mouth-to-mouth resuscitation could revitalize a corpse.

Additional Notes

2:15. The middle (or perhaps passive) participle λειπόμενοι is active in meaning in James. See the second additional note on 1:4.

I think that it is arguable that the book of Joshua presents Rahab's cord as the equivalent of the Israelites' blood on the lintel—it was Rahab's "passover." If Christian interpreters can regard the Passover lamb's blood as a type of Christ's blood, then it is at least possible that Rahab's cord is also typologically connected to the blood of Christ. Even if this is not the case, the cord certainly was a confirming indicator of Rahab's fear of the Lord, and thus it was the means of salvation for her and her house.

40. Note that Paul never uses the phrase "faith alone." The closest he comes is Gal. 5:6, where he declares, "For in Christ Jesus neither circumcision nor uncircumcision counts for anything, but *only faith* working through love," but there Paul makes it perfectly clear that this faith is not "alone" in the sense of being without works.

41. For the argument for a pre-Pauline date and occasion for James, see view 1 under "Four Views of Author and Date" in the introduction.

42. In 4:5, whatever that obscure verse means, πνεῦμα obviously means something more than our word "breath," because it "longs" for something.

2:16. The imperatives θερμαίνεσθε and χορτάζεσθε could be middles, which might be rendered "Keep warm, eat well!" (even as passives, the force of the verbs could be rendered idiomatically into English this way). But χορτάζω is poorly if at all attested in the middle voice, and so the passive is preferred. The passive is also retained in my translation because the passive imperative conveys the wish for God[43] to clothe and feed destitute fellow believers without acknowledging one's own responsibility in the matter.

2:17. In the phrase καθ' ἑαυτήν the κατά functions to isolate or separate, yielding the meaning "by itself" (BDAG 511 refers to Thucydides 1.138.6: οἱ καθ' ἑαυτοὺς Ἕλληνες ["the Greeks by themselves"]; cf. Mic. 7:14; Zech. 12:12–14; Acts 28:16). Moo (2000: 126) suggests faith "in itself" is dead and refers to Mayor (1897: 95), who says that it is "not merely outwardly inoperative but inwardly dead." I could find little lexical support for this. James's point is this: faith that is alone is dead.

2:18. The hypothetical interlocutor may or may not be representative of an actual position in James's audience. Dibelius (1975: 156) treats not only the interlocutor but also his position as purely hypothetical, presented only as a foil to James's own position. One might, however, question why James would so vehemently attack a position that no one had ever heard of. But Dibelius may be correct that the interlocutor's position is stylized and drawn in much sharper relief than was held by any people whom James may have been addressing.

2:19. The verse might be taken as a question (as in the Westcott-Hort Greek Testament), but is better understood, like the preceding σὺ πίστιν ἔχεις, as a simple statement (Mayor 1897: 97).

2:19. The phrase εἷς ἐστιν [ὁ] θεός may be rendered either "God is one" or, if the article is not original, "There is one God." The manuscript tradition contains much variation in regard to the order of the words and whether θεός has an article. This is possibly because this most basic creed of Judaism from the Shema (Deut. 6:4) has a variety of possible renderings from the Hebrew (yhwh 'eḥād).[44] Here the Majority Text (ὁ θεὸς εἷς ἐστιν) probably is conforming to Gal. 3:20 and the similar form in Rom. 3:30. Codex Vaticanus and some others read εἷς θεός ἐστιν ([Only] one is God), which is closer to 1 Tim. 2:5 and Eph. 4:6, which have simply εἷς θεός. I prefer the reading found in NA[27] (εἷς ἐστιν ὁ θεός), mainly because it best serves to explain the other readings (see Dibelius 1975: 158n50). It is not crucial to resolve this issue, however, because all the various permutations are at least asseverations of theological truth, and James's point is the same whether this bare kind of faith is a belief in the unity of God or an acceptance of monotheism.

2:19. The word φρίσσω occurs only here in the NT. It literally means "to have one's hairs stand on end" (LSJ 1955; cf. the Franco-English word *frisson*), but, along with its cognate noun φρίκη (whence the English word *fright*), which occurs in Job 4:14 and Amos 1:11, it commonly refers more generally to the physical responses to terror. The terrified response (shuddering) of the demons to the saying of the Shema or to the power of the divine name is reflected in the magical papyri (Laws 1980: 127–28).

2:20. The most extensive manuscript tradition (including the basis for the KJV) says that faith without works is "dead" (νεκρά) rather than "useless" (ἀργή), almost certainly having been assimilated to

---

43. The use of passives when the subject of the implied action is God, particularly when imperatives are used, is quite common in Jewish literature, including the NT (e.g., Acts 1:20, citing Ps. 69:25 [68:26 LXX]) and the first three petitions of the Lord's Prayer in Matt. 6:9–10 (cf. Matt. 26:42). In Mark 5:34 Jesus says, "Go in peace, and be healed," although there he is also doing something about the problem.

44. Many modern scholars take the Hebrew of Deut. 6:4 originally to have meant neither "Yahweh our God is one" nor "There is only one God, our God Yahweh," but "Yahweh alone is our God" (cf. the New Jewish Publication Society translation: "Hear, O Israel! The LORD is our God, the LORD alone"). But in NT times it was universally understood to be an expression of exclusivistic monotheism (Rainbow 1991).

2:17 and 2:26 by early copyists; ἀργή is the superior reading and is more interesting because of the wordplay (of which James is fond). As in 1:27 and elsewhere, manuscript 𝔓⁷⁴ goes its own unique way, here reading "empty" (κενή), making a nice pairing with the "empty" person who holds such a faith, but the isolation and idiosyncratic character of 𝔓⁷⁴ make its reading improbable.

2:21. The aorist participle ἀνενέγκας is best read as instrumental, the tense indicating not antecedent but simultaneous action: Abraham was justified by works, specifically *by* offering up Isaac. Thus, he is shown righteous and approved by God by means of his faith-work. This is relevant for consideration of the proposal by Ward (1968) that the ἔργα of Abraham are not the offering of Isaac, but his acts of mercy and hospitality. The Aqedah, then, is only the climactic test and acquittal, the imprimatur, as it were, of God's approval of Abraham as one who showed mercy. But although hospitality might be seen as the ground for the justification of Rahab, of whom James said ἐξ ἔργων ἐδικαιώθη ὑποδεξαμένη τοὺς ἀγγέλους, no mention is made of Abraham's hospitality; rather, Abraham ἐξ ἔργων ἐδικαιώθη ἀνενέγκας Ἰσαάκ. This makes things quite difficult for Ward's view, and a few commentators (e.g., Davids 1982: 127; Hartin 2003: 160–61) do not commonly follow Ward on this score.[45] Even Rahab, however, was not justified by her hospitality; rather, her "justifying" deed was her rescue of the spies by "sending them out another way," which was an act of faith in the God of Israel.

2:22. Some manuscripts (ℵ [original hand], A, 33, 630, and the Old Latin ff) have the present συνεργεῖ instead of the imperfect συνήργει, easily understandable as an error of the ear. However, James is referring here, as in the last part of the verse (πίστις ἐτελειώθη), to the specific case of Abraham.

2:23. James here may be seen to follow a well-known Jewish exegetical tradition in expounding one text by means of another (Davids 1982: 129; cf. Longenecker 1975: 32–38). As such, the secondary text (Gen. 15:6) is taken as elucidating the primary (Gen. 22:12). Since James does not quote his ostensibly primary text (Gen. 22), it might be argued that this is a case of modern scholars trying too hard to make things fit neatly into rabbinic interpretive categories. But it seems undeniable that James is taking Gen. 22 as that which clarifies the meaning of the faith of Abraham noted in Gen. 15:6 (cf. Sir. 44:20–21; 1 Macc. 2:52).

2:23. The phrase "it was reckoned to him as righteousness" occurs also in Ps. 106:31 (105:31 LXX), which says that Phinehas, on the occasion of Israel being stricken by plague for idolatry, intervened, and it was "reckoned to him as righteousness from generation to generation forever."[46] This is difficult on two counts: not only is Phinehas's faith not mentioned in Ps. 106, but also Phinehas's means of intervention—slaughtering the chief leaders in Israel's idolatry movement—hardly appears to be in line with the gospel's emphasis on the availability of forgiveness or with James's insistence on mercy (2:13). It thus does not appear to be an act in accordance with faith.

In the context of Ps. 106, however, Phinehas's act most certainly was an act of faith: it is not the form of Phinehas's intervention that is mentioned in the psalm, but that he stood up and intervened (the LXX uses ἐξιλάσατο, meaning "he made propitiation"). The killing of the idolaters is seen in the psalm as a means of preventing the destruction of the whole of Israel and thus as a quintessential demonstration of belief in God's promises of judgment against idolatry, in God's power, and in God's holiness.

Still, this could be taken as evidence that the OT already understood the "offering up" of idolaters by Phinehas as parallel to the offering up of Isaac by Abraham and thus as evidence that Judaism saw

45. I suspect that the early church's references to Rahab's hospitality (e.g., 1 Clem. 12) are motivated less by a concern for hospitality as the supremely justifying work and more by the desire of both Jewish and Christian interpreters to soften the force of πόρνη (see the additional note on 2:25).

46. Psalm 106 is not in James's purview, but it does give some indication of the way the phrase "credited for righteousness" was used in the Hebrew Bible.

the Aqedah as the justifying act of Abraham rather than his belief in the promise of progeny in Gen. 15. But even if this is so, we must remember that the Aqedah itself is an act of belief in the Gen. 15 promise of progeny, because the killing of Isaac would appear to have made the completion of the promise humanly impossible, and it is precisely this belief that Heb. 11:17–19 identifies as effectively a belief in the resurrection. It is only an idle, impoverished, intellectualized notion of faith (condemned in 2:19) that generates problems for the reader of James.

2:24. "You see" (ὁρᾶτε) could be either imperative or indicative. There is little semantic difference between them, and the translation given above could represent either. If imperative, it commands the readers to acknowledge the conclusion; if indicative, it invites them to do so. In 2:22 the unambiguously indicative βλέπεις is used (it is also singular, being addressed to the imaginary interlocutor), and since the conclusion addressed to the readers in 2:24 is parallel to the earlier one spoken to the interlocutor, the likelihood is that this too is indicative.

2:25. Sometimes Rahab was described not as a prostitute but as an "innkeeper," a tradition found in Josephus *Ant.* 5.1.7 §30 and the Palestinian Targum on Josh. 2:1. This is an attempt to sanitize Rahab, but such whitewashing detracts from the power of Rahab's example. Although she was a prostitute and a Canaanite, she was justified and rescued from destruction because of her faith-deeds. There is gospel in the story of Rahab.

2:26. The articles with σῶμα and πίστις are generic rather than particular (MHT 3:180; BDF §252), and therefore here they are translated with an indefinite rather than a definite article.

IV. Second Discourse: Faith, Wisdom, and Speech Ethics (3:1–18)

In James 3 the author returns to a concern initially voiced in 1:19 and 1:26, that of the "unbridled tongue." Jesus says in Matt. 12:34 (also Luke 6:45), "Out of the abundance of the heart the mouth speaks." Speech, metonymically referred to in James as "the tongue," is the vehicle for wisdom and instruction, and for blessing. But it also is capable of enormous evil, sometimes done deliberately and sometimes simply by lack of control, and is more commonly in the employ of the evil world than of righteousness. Hence, it is risky to be a teacher, someone whose profession is the use of the tongue.

Like James 2, James 3 has two parts. The first half deals with speech ethics generally; the second half touches on the contrast between earthly and heavenly wisdom. The two halves of this chapter are related because wisdom is effectively a speech matter. The ultimate wisdom in Judaism was Torah, God's speech, and human wisdom is wise to the extent that it mirrors the divine wisdom.

Most translations and commentaries divide the chapter between 3:12 and 3:13. Inasmuch as the end of 3:12, contrasting sweet with bitter water, seems to answer the rhetorical question of 3:11 and thus continue and conclude the issue of speech control, this is logical. However, there is some ground for instead dividing the chapter a verse earlier. If divided between 3:11 and 3:12, then, like 2:1–13 and 2:14–26, the first segment begins with a general imperative addressed to "my brothers" (3:1) and ends with a proverb (3:11); the second begins with a rhetorical question addressed to "my brothers" (3:12) and ends with a proverb (3:18). Also, if "my brothers" in 3:12 is simply emphatic, then the doubling of the emphatic vocative in 3:10 and then again in 3:12 seems overdone. This awkwardness is relieved if 3:12 begins a new section, since the reiteration of "my brothers" would be marking a new division. This also would obviate the criticism, often made, that the end of 3:12 seems lame and out of place, prompting some (e.g., Laws 1980: 158) to suggest that a later copyist may have added it.

Further, if 3:12 goes with 3:13, it means that the proverb about the fig tree and olives introduces the theme of wisdom and works. This fits better in some ways than with the duplicity of the tongue, because the knowing of a tree by its fruits (cf. Matt. 7:16) applies very well to the distinguishing of wisdom from above from earthly wisdom (3:15); it applies less well to the incompatibility of cursing and blessing in the same mouth or the taming of the tongue.

However, the close flow and connectedness of 3:11 and 3:12, and the fact that 3:13 seems to mark a clear departure, naturally produce the impression of a logical break between 3:12 and 3:13. Therefore, 3:12 may be best understood as having a bridging function, connecting the theme of tongue control in 3:1–11 with wisdom in 3:13–18, much like 1:12 bridges 1:2–11 to 1:13–15.

A. Part 1: Teachers, Tongues, and Turmoil (3:1–12)

James 3 opens with a general warning to teachers (3:1), but then seems to shift gears to address the evils of the tongue in 3:2–12. There seems at first glance, then, to be little relationship between 3:1 and what follows. In James 2, by contrast, the first verse announces a theme (showing no favoritism) that then is expounded in what follows. The similar structure of James 3 would suggest that therefore 3:2–12 is somehow further addressing the issue of teachers. But unless the tongue is being regarded as a metaphor for teachers, which is unlikely (see comments on 3:3–5a below), this connection is unclear.

Recently, some efforts have been made to identify the relationship in terms of Greek rhetorical structure. Watson (1993b) proposes that 3:1–12 comprises a structured argument: 3:1 contains both the theme or *propositio* (few should be teachers) and the initial reason or *ratio* (teachers will receive greater judgment), 3:2 the proof or *confirmatio* (we all stumble in many ways), 3:3–10a the embellishment (it is difficult to control the tongue), and 3:10b–12 the conclusion. This analysis is interesting, but the fact that other attempts to identify such a structured argument come out somewhat differently[1] suggests that if James intended to build such a careful structure, he did not do it carefully enough for modern scholars to agree on its boundaries, let alone for his original readers to perceive it, and hence identifying such structure probably is of little importance for discerning his meaning. The key connection is that since teachers use the tongue, they are engaged in a dangerous enterprise, and only the mature person of humility, purity, gentleness, and sincerity (3:17) should engage in it.

Exegesis and Exposition

[1]Not many of you should be teachers, my brothers, inasmuch as you know that we [who are teachers] will receive a more severe judgment. [2]For we all stumble in many ways, and if someone does not stumble in [matters of] speech, he is a mature man [indeed]. Such a person ⌜is able⌝ to bridle his whole body. [3]⌜If⌝ we put bits into the mouths of horses to make them obey us, we can direct their whole body at will. [4]Look also how ships, though they are huge and driven by harsh winds, are by a tiny rudder

---

1. Hartin (2003: 181–82) takes all of 3:1 as the theme, 3:2 as the causal reason, 3:3–5a as the proof, 3:5b–10 as the embellishment, and 3:11–12 as the conclusion. For more on the rhetorical analysis of James 3, see "Structure" in the introduction.

directed wherever the pilot wishes. [5]So also the tongue is a little body part, but it makes great boasts. Look how so tiny a fire sets ablaze so great a forest. [6]And the tongue is a fire! The unrighteous world is established in the midst of our members as the tongue, staining the whole body, and setting on fire the whole course of life in this age, as it itself is set on fire by hell. [7]For all kinds of animals and birds, reptiles and sea creatures, are being tamed and have been tamed for humankind, [8]but the tongue no one can tame; it is an ⌜unstable⌝ evil, full of death-dealing poison. [9]By it we bless the ⌜Lord⌝ and Father, and by it we curse human beings who were made in God's likeness. [10]Out of the same mouth come blessing and curse! My brothers, it must not be this way! [11]Can a spring gush [both] sweet and bitter from the same opening? [12]My brothers, can a fig tree produce olives, or a grapevine figs? ⌜Neither⌝ can salt water yield fresh.

James moves from the specific (wanting to teach) to the general (control of the tongue). In 3:13 he will return to the matter of teaching when he contrasts godly wisdom with that of the world. As is his custom in beginning a new section, James reminds his readers of their relationship to God and to himself by addressing them as "my brothers."

3:1

"Teachers" might refer to a specific office in the church, such as those called to a specific ministry in distinction from apostles and prophets (as in, e.g., Eph. 4:11), but in the context of speech ethics it addresses anyone involved in or considering teaching ministry in the church. The verse has some affinity with Jesus's warning in Matt. 23:9–10 against acquiring or using titles such as "father" or "teacher," but the concerns are not quite the same. Jesus's concern has more to do with the problems of pride and hierarchicalism; James, however, is dealing with the specific issue that, since all verbal activity is potentially dangerous, teaching is especially so, for the teaching of error has the potential not only to destroy the teacher, but also to harm the students. The potential error is, however, not so much doctrinal as moral. Jesus said that teachers who "devour widows' houses" would receive greater judgment (Mark 12:40). Similarly, teachers who slander, who make reckless accusations or verbal attacks, who grumble and quarrel (cf. 4:1; 5:9) will naturally cause greater damage to the community by virtue of their position and implicit authority than those who are not teachers. It is also consequent upon their wider influence that they will be judged more strictly: "From everyone who has been given much, much will be required" (Luke 12:48b NASB). One can see a sad example in Moses, the great teacher of Israel, who received a severe judgment when he failed to do exactly as he was told, striking the rock instead of speaking to it (Num. 20:11–12). Hence, James's command that few should be teachers[2] stands as a warning that the vocation of a teacher is dangerous.

"Greater judgment" can be taken in two ways, as involving either a greater punishment (Laws 1980: 144) or a higher standard of judgment (Ropes 1916:

---

2. "Should" translates the third-person imperative (see the second additional note on 1:5).

227). As Hartin (2003: 173) says, it may be unnecessary to choose between them, since a more rigorous application of law will naturally result in infringements being punished more severely.

3:2 The word "for" begins 3:2. Although the verse appears to be a change of subject from the peril of being a teacher to the perils of speech, the two things are related as specific to general. Hence, the "we" of 3:2 is not limited to "we teachers" (as Wandel 1893 suggests), as though James is saying that teachers all stumble in many ways. But teachers are ministers of the word, and so the consequences of stumbling "with respect to speech" are greater for a teacher. Sin is universal, and the sins of the tongue are the most difficult to avoid; hence, teachers run the greatest risk.

The adverbial "in many ways" (πολλά, *polla*), which connects as a catchword to the "not many" (μὴ πολλοί, *mē polloi*) of 3:1, can also mean "many times, often." The resultant meaning is similar. Everyone stumbles or gets tripped up (see BDAG 894) frequently and in many different kinds of circumstances. Those who reach a point in their life where they rarely stumble in their speech are mature indeed, because it is the epitome of maturity to have self-control even over that most difficult aspect of life to control. Thus, the point is not that a person who controls the tongue is totally and perfectly blameless,[3] or that such a one has achieved total moral perfection. That would either contradict the previous clause ("we all stumble") or be purely hypothetical. James's meaning is that such a person has become truly "grown up" in faith, behaving in accordance with adulthood (see the commentary on 1:4), in distinction from children, or childish adults who have yet to achieve self-mastery.

The observation that the most common sins, and the most difficult to overcome, are sins of speech is commonplace in Jewish wisdom (e.g., Sir. 19:16b NRSV: "Who has not sinned with his tongue?"; cf. Prov. 10:19). Here James uses it specifically to underline why few should be teachers.

"With respect to speech" is literally "in word." It is in a grammatically emphatic position: "But if *in word* someone does not stumble, such a man is τέλειος [complete, mature, whole]." One of the principal marks of maturity is self-discipline, and self-discipline with regard to one's speech is rare. Hence, few should be teachers. Further, the "word" that teachers ought to bring is the word of truth that gives new birth and brings salvation (1:18, 21); it is the word that people are to do, not just hear (1:22). Therefore, it is all the more incumbent on teachers that their own lives exhibit the wholeness and integrity that the word they teach is expected to engender.

---

3. If James does mean "morally perfect," then the sentence could imply that since the control of speech indicates that a person is "perfect," and since there is only one perfect person, Jesus, only he can truly control his speech, and the rest of us are in need of constant forgiveness for our sins of speech. But nowhere else in the letter does James draw this kind of theological connection to Jesus, and as noted already, τέλειος (*teleios*) for James has more the force of maturity and wholeness than moral perfection (see the first additional note on 1:4); hence the translation "he is mature indeed." James's point here is not so much ethical purity in general (contra Ropes 1916: 228) as maturity in self-control, particularly with regard to speech.

The verb "to bridle" is the closest English can get to the Greek verb χαλιναγωγέω (*chalinagōgeō*), meaning "to control by means of a bit in the mouth," a verb unique to James, introduced in 1:26, and in 3:2 providing a connection to the "bits" (χαλινοί, *chalinoi*) in the illustration in 3:3. Leading a large animal by putting a bit in its mouth is a common metaphor for speech control in many languages. Wisdom literature the world over knows of the problems that uncontrolled speech generates and therefore sees that the control of one's own speech must be as rigorous and unremittant as the control of a recalcitrant and unruly large animal.

It sometimes is suggested that James is doing more here than generalizing about the difficulties of minding one's speech. In particular, Reicke (1964: 37) and Martin (1988: 103–7) suggest that the "whole body" that the mature person guides by speech refers to the church. If so, the verse would be indicating that the mature or "perfect" teacher who does not stumble in teaching is able to guide the whole church well. James has warned that few should be teachers. In this context, the person who, by not stumbling in speech, directs (μετάγω, *metagō*) the "whole body" might refer to the teacher who rightly steers the course of the church. Paul's notion of "the body" is not explicit in James, but the phrase "in your members" in 4:1 could mean "among the people in the church," so there is an implied "body" of believers. Add to this the fact that the early fathers often depicted the church as a boat or ship (e.g., Clement of Alexandria, *Paed.* 3.2 [PG 8:633]; Tertullian, *Bapt.* 12 [PL 1:1214]; see also 1 Pet. 3:20, and possibly Matt. 8:23–26),[4] and the suggestion gains more credence.

If in fact the church is the referent of "body" in 3:2b–12, several interesting results follow:

1. The disconnection among the verses 3:1, 2, 3 is overcome. If 3:2b means no more than that the one who can control the tongue can control the whole body, then apparently it is not very closely related to the subject of 3:1–2a, which is the danger of being a teacher. But if 3:2b also refers to the guiding of the church, then 3:1–3 fits together quite well.

2. The structural similarity between James 3 and James 2 is better maintained. Both 2:1 and 3:1 begin with a general ethical admonition not to do something. This is immediately followed by a "for" verse giving specific illustrative material to elucidate why that admonition is important. Both James 2 and James 3 also close with a broadening out to more general ethical concerns (true versus false faith in James 2, growing out of 2:1; true versus false wisdom in James 3, growing, perhaps, out of 3:1). The structural clues thus seem to nudge the reader toward reading 3:2–12 as somehow related to a concern with teachers, and hence "the body" is that which teachers may influence and direct for good or ill.

4. If Bornkamm's (1948) observations about Matthew's recasting the story found in Mark 4 are sound, then Matthew was drawing an analogy between Jesus's disciples in the boat fearing the storm and his own contemporaries in the church fearing persecution.

3. The illustrations in 3:3–5 work better. One's control of the tongue does not produce control of one's own literal body, and control of one's own body does not require control of the tongue. Likewise with ships, where the added details of "driven by harsh winds" and "directed wherever the pilot wishes" do no more than add color if only an individual's self-control is meant. But things fit quite well if the illustrations and comments that follow (to 3:6 anyway) operate not just on the personal level, but also on the level of church life. The speech of teachers steers, for good or ill, the church as a whole. If the tongue is uncontrolled, either because of doctrinal unsoundness or, as in James, because it sows bitterness and rancor (cf. 4:1–12), it not only consumes an individual, but also initiates a cycle of evil (see 3:6) motivated by hell that can destroy a church or vitiate its effectiveness for generations. The warning to teachers is thus doubly severe, for their speech failings can have unanticipated consequences and repercussions.

4. The whole of 3:1–12 is then more closely related to the theme of the one who would be wise and understanding (3:13–18).

However, several things in the text stand against this approach:

1. What in the text would have clued the original readers to the notion that the "body" of the horse now represents the church? The evidence that James could have thought of "the body" as a metaphor for the church in the way Paul did is restricted to only one questionable datum: the expression "in your members" (4:1), which might mean "among the people in the church."

2. The examples of "ships," as also "bits in the mouth of horses," are in the plural. If the illustrations represented the church, one would expect the singular. The plural implies only a general resemblance, not an allegorical correspondence. It is only the remarkable power-versus-size differential between the ships and their rudders, or between horses and bits, that is given point, as also with forest fires.

3. Decisive is 3:6. If the tongue represents teachers, then why suddenly are they regarded not just as potentially dangerous, but as "a fire" that inflames the course of life of this age and is inflamed by hell? And why are teachers now regarded as the representatives of the wicked world (literally "world of unrighteousness") within the church?

4. In 3:7–8 the tongue is said to be untamable and an unstable evil. If the tongue simply signifies an individual's speech, then this is comprehensible (if hyperbolic), but it is unlikely that James, who classifies himself as a teacher (3:1), would say that teachers as a class are untamable and an unstable evil, even if he were speaking hyperbolically.

Hence, we must conclude that James is simply making comparisons to the outsized power of speech and warning of its susceptibility to wickedness and the consequent necessity of guarding it closely. Teachers must be especially careful because their speech is especially important, but such advice is applicable not just to teachers. The horses and ships are only illustrations; they are not intended to be metaphors for the church.

Several commentators note that the images James uses here—bridling a horse, controlling a ship by a rudder, and even the wildness of fire—not only are commonplace illustrations in the Greco-Roman world, among both Jews and Gentiles, but often appear together.[5] Indeed, there are so many instances of these very images (horses, ships, fires) being used together that if James did borrow from a particular source, it would be quite difficult to identify with any certainty. The illustrative material was "in the air." However, while some of these images run parallel to James, as Dibelius (1975: 190) points out, the metaphors in the background regard that which guides, controls, and has power as either a human being (pilot, charioteer, commander) controlling conveyances (ships, animals, armies) or the mind controlling the body or the person. James, on the other hand, "has changed the emphasis of the metaphors: the one who is steering is not the human being, not reason, but the tongue" (Dibelius 1975: 190–91). If James did borrow, he made radical alterations for his own purposes. Further, as Davids (1982: 139) points out, horses and ships basically constituted the sum total of things that people steered in the first century, and the imagery is common enough that we need not postulate James deliberately borrowing from a specific source for these verses. Thus, whether or not James is borrowing from a particular source or adopting a common grouping of metaphors from his general speech environment, his meaning is likely to be elucidated not by identifying his source(s), but by attending to how he uses the metaphors.

Horses and ships are large things of great power that are nevertheless controlled by human will and by means of very small items. The controlling verb is the same (μετάγω, metagō); they are directed or steered. The horse example is interesting because the literal mouth is the means of control; the ship is interesting because it harnesses great powers outside of itself that are then directed by means of the small rudder. Both examples emphatically illustrate the power of speech: if it is controlled well, its effect is wonderful, but if uncontrolled or controlled poorly, the disaster can be enormous. Particularly in the case of the ship, if the rudder is uncontrolled in the presence of a strong wind, the ship can run aground or spin across the wind and capsize. Even if the ship is controlled, a misguided rudder can send it to the wrong place.

Thus, the tongue "makes great boasts" or "boasts of great things" (ESV). The saying is an echo of Ps. 12:3, where the boasting tongue is also identified as a lying and a flattering tongue, by which the "double-hearted" oppress the poor and needy:

> Everyone utters lies to his neighbor;
>   with flattering lips and a double heart they speak.

5. Sometimes the correspondence is remarkable (see the additional note on 3:3–4).

May the LORD cut off all flattering lips,
    the tongue that makes great boasts,
those who say, "With our tongue we will prevail,
    our lips are with us; who is master over us?"
"Because the poor are plundered, because the needy groan,
    I will now arise," says the LORD;
    "I will place him in the safety for which he longs." (Ps. 12:2–5)

Although in James the emphasis is not on the tongue's pride as such but rather on its vast power, the close resemblance to Ps. 12 probably points both to the tongue's great capacity for damage and to its choice as a tool for wickedness.

Assuming that the "whole body" is not a metaphor for the church, we should not press the imagery in 3:3–5 very far. One's speech does not direct one's literal body, although it does direct the course of one's life, and a loose tongue can send shock waves into the future for its owner as well as for those around the owner. The point of the ship illustration, like that of the horse and also the forest fire, is that the tongue's effectual power is grossly out of proportion to its size. Huge ships and the harsh winds that drive them are ruled, as it were, by a tiny rudder.

The phrase that James uses, here translated "directed wherever the pilot wishes," is awkward in Greek, reading literally "wherever the impulse of the pilot wishes." The word "impulse" (ὁρμή, *hormē*) could refer either to external or internal pressure (Mayor 1897: 107). Hence, it might simply be a redundant way to refer to the pilot's wishes ("where the intentions of the pilot intend"), or more likely it could refer to the pressure of the pilot's hand upon the tiller that accomplishes his intentions.

An interpreter inclined to wax allegorical at this point might say that the pilot is Jesus, whose pressure on the teacher (whose tongue is the rudder) directs the course of the church in its journey to maturity not just through, but even by means of, the harsh winds of persecution. But it is probably wise not to press the illustration in this way, and the conclusion is general: the tongue is little but lays claim to much, and it is especially capable of evil. It is also doubtful whether one should press the details of the illustration for more information about the tongue being directed by a human decision (Dibelius 1975: 189–91).

3:5b–6 In 3:5b–6 James warns against the tongue run amok. The imagery is vigorous and hyperbolic[6] in order to make the warning against the undisciplined tongue as sharp as possible. Flames are called "tongues" in many languages because they resemble tongues; they flicker and make noise, and above all they do damage (Ps. 120:3–4 compares the deceitful tongue to hot coals). The tongue, as the instrument of speech, can set the heart aflame with fury,

---

6. James does, after all, recognize both a positive role for speech at some points and the possibility of a person being mature enough to control the tongue (3:2).

or patriotic fervor, or courage, or love, or hate, and it can inflict damage that goes on for generations. James here reflects a wisdom theme found also in Prov. 16:27 NRSV: "Scoundrels concoct evil, and their speech is like a scorching fire."

"So tiny [a fire]" and "so great [a forest]" in 3:5b represent the same Greek word, the correlative adjective ἡλίκος (*hēlikos*), which refers to remarkable size in general. It therefore can mean either "how small" or "how large," depending on the context. A more literal translation reads, "Behold what size of fire ignites what size of forest."

The word for "forest" is literally "wood" (ὕλη, *hylē*) and can refer to a stack of cut wood as well as a forest (as in the NEB). But the commonness of references in the ancient world to the great damage caused by forest fires and other wildfires,[7] and proverbial reference to the fact that they can start with only a small fire, suggest that James has nothing in mind so controlled or tame as a bonfire.

A series of nominatives begins 3:6, making it difficult to differentiate subjects from appositives or predicates. Add to this the fact that several of the words or phrases can be taken in more than one way, and we have one of the most problematic verses in James. The diversity of options can be seen in the variety of translations, a few of which I reproduce here:

> And the tongue is a fire: the world of iniquity among our members is the tongue, which defileth the whole body, and setteth on fire the wheel of nature, and is set on fire by hell. (ASV)

> And the tongue is a fire, a world of unrighteousness. The tongue is set among our members, staining the whole body, setting on fire the entire course of life, and set on fire by hell. (ESV)

> And the tongue is a fire, a world of iniquity: so is the tongue among our members, that it defileth the whole body, and setteth on fire the course of nature; and it is set on fire of hell. (KJV)

> And the tongue is a fire, the very world of iniquity; the tongue is set among our members as that which defiles the entire body, and sets on fire the course of our life, and is set on fire by hell. (NASB)

> And the tongue is in effect a fire. It represents among our members the world with all its wickedness; it pollutes our whole being; it keeps the wheel of our existence red-hot, and its flames are fed by hell. (NEB)

---

7. For data on ancient literature's fondness for the illustrative value of forest fires, see Ropes (1916: 232–33). Elliott-Binns (1955: 48–50) suggests that the image in view is the wild-fires among the scrubby brush on Palestinian hillsides, which can engulf a hill in flames very quickly. Given the paucity of trees of any size in first-century Palestine, this may be correct, but any Palestinian author capable of writing the Greek prose of this letter probably knew about forest fires too.

The tongue also is a fire, a world of evil among the parts of the body. It corrupts the whole person, sets the whole course of his life on fire, and is itself set on fire by hell. (NIV)

The tongue is a flame too. Among all the parts of the body, the tongue is a whole wicked world: it infects the whole body; catching fire itself from hell, it sets fire to the whole wheel of creation. (NJB)

And the tongue is a fire. The tongue is placed among our members as a world of iniquity; it stains the whole body, sets on fire the cycle of nature, and is itself set on fire by hell. (NRSV)

The main questions to be resolved are these:

1. Where is the sentence to be divided: after "fire," after "world of unrighteousness," or after "among our members"?
2. Is "fire" an appositive or a predicate to "tongue"?
3. What is the meaning of "world of unrighteousness"?
4. What is the function of the article with "world"?
5. Is the verb in the second half (καθίσταται, *kathistatai*) to be translated "is established," "is appointed," or "sets itself up as"?
6. What exactly is established, appointed, or set up, and what is it established/appointed/set up as?
7. What is the meaning of the phrase translated variously as "cycle of generation," "course of life," "course of nature," "wheel of creation," and so on?

Several of these are, of course, interdependent. The place to begin to sort it out is the phrase "world of unrighteousness," which Ropes (1916: 233) declares impossible to interpret satisfactorily. Some Greek commentators[8] understood the term κόσμος (*kosmos*, world) in the sense of "ornament." Thus, the tongue was said to be that which makes unrighteousness look attractive; polished rhetoric can make evil sound good. This makes good sense, but this meaning for κόσμος is quite uncommon in the NT, and it does not correspond to the other uses of "world" in James (1:27; 2:5; 4:4), all of which are negative and represent humankind in opposition to God. Hence, few modern translations or commentators (with the notable exception of Chaine 1927: 81) support this view.

Some commentators (e.g., Calvin, Erasmus, and most nineteenth-century scholars) follow Bede (PL 93:27) in understanding "world" in the sense of "the whole." The NASB ("the very world of iniquity") probably reflects this view. Thus, the tongue is the "whole" or "totality" of iniquity. This preserves the article, but like the first view, it suffers from the fact that in James the word

---

8. This interpretation appears as early as Isidore of Pelusium (d. 435), *Epistle* 4.10 (PG 78:1057). See Mayor 1897: 110.

"world" is not a neutral term, but a consistently negative one, and "totality" does not work elsewhere in James. Of even greater difficulty is the weak evidence in Greek sources for κόσμος meaning the "whole" or "totality," confined indeed to one passage in the LXX (Prov. 17:6b).[9]

Many modern translations follow the lead of Oecumenius (PG 119:488) in taking "world" as a way of saying "much" or "in large quantity." Thus, the tongue is "a world of unrighteousness" in that it is full of wickedness or brings with it a great deal of wickedness. This preserves the negative force of the word in James, but it ignores the article. As Mayor (1897: 110) illustrates, one may speak of "a world of cares" as a way of saying "many cares," but to speak of "*the* world of cares" says something about the world.

Therefore, as Moo (2000: 157), Hort (1909: 71), Mussner (1975: 162–63), and Hartin (2003: 177) argue, the phrase probably is best taken to mean "the unrighteous world." "Of unrighteousness" is, then, a simple qualitative genitive (the genitive noun serves like an adjective), a common Semitism,[10] which we have seen operative elsewhere in James (1:25; 2:1; compare "steward of unrighteousness" = "unrighteous steward" [Luke 16:8], and "mammon of unrighteousness" = "unrighteous mammon" [Luke 16:9; cf. 16:11]). This translation is partially reflected in the NJB, but the presence of the article specifies that the tongue is not simply "*a* whole wicked world," but "*the* whole wicked world." Also, the NJB translation seems to have combined the qualitative genitive approach with the "totality" view.

A second preliminary item to be resolved is whether καθίσταται should be taken as a reflexive middle, meaning "sets itself up as, appoints itself," or as passive with the force "is appointed" (as in Heb. 5:1; 8:3), or as a passive having the force of "is made, becomes, is established" (as in Rom. 5:19). The passive "is appointed" raises the question as to who does the appointing of the tongue to be "the world of unrighteousness" in our members. It is unlikely that James would say that God appointed the tongue to be the wicked world in our members (cf. 1:13). Further, the same verb occurs at 4:4, where "is appointed" works poorly (the friend of the world probably is not *appointed* to be the enemy of God, but is *made* an enemy by that friendship with the world). Laws (1980: 149) and Moo (2000: 158) therefore argue for the reflexive middle,[11] which fits quite well at James 4:4 (the friend of the world "sets himself up as" the enemy of God). However, the reflexive middle of καθίστημι (*kathistēmi*) is difficult to substantiate anywhere else in Greek literature.[12] Hence, the best

9. Proverbs 17:6b LXX reads, "The faithful man has the whole world of wealth [τοῦ πιστοῦ ὅλος ὁ κόσμος τῶν χρημάτων], but the faithless not even a penny." Thus, even here it is the word ὅλος, and not the word κόσμος by itself, that has provided the sense "whole."

10. Recently, grammarians have pointed out that this qualitative or simple attributive genitive is not uncharacteristic Greek, but it is infrequent except in Greek stemming from Jewish sources (see Wallace 1996: 86n44).

11. Dibelius (1975: 194), who suggests "presents itself as," may be classed here as well.

12. Rarely does the NT use the middle voice of nondeponent verbs. But more importantly, where the middle voice of καθίστημι in the sense of "appoint" does occur in Greek literature, it

option is the well-substantiated meaning "is made, becomes, is established" (LSJ 855), which also works well in 4:4 ("the friend of the world [thereby] is made an enemy of God"). Mayor (1897: 111) assigns the verb a place between simple "is" and "becomes."

These issues being resolved, where do we divide the series of predicates? In terms of semantic result, it probably matters little.[13] Clearly, James wishes to identify "fire" and "the wicked world" and "staining the body" as predicable of the tongue and also to place this not outside ourselves but within us, "among our members." Most translations and commentators take the second occurrence of "tongue" as also a subject ("the tongue becomes as . . ."), either with "the wicked world" as the predicate (the tongue becomes as the wicked world, staining the whole body) or, if "wicked world" is taken as the predicate of the first "tongue," with the participle "staining" as the predicate (the tongue becomes that which stains).[14] Mussner (1975: 163) thinks that the first occurrence of "tongue" is the subject, and the second is simply a reiteration, yielding "The tongue, as a fire, indeed as the unrighteous world, the tongue stands forth among our members." All these options make the restating of the noun "the tongue" otiose. But the reiteration of "tongue" might serve to indicate a shift in its grammatical function, from subject to predicate, with "world" the likely subject of "is established." Hence, the first predication is "And the tongue is (indeed) a fire"; the follow-up is "The wicked world is established among our members as the tongue."

This has presupposed that "among our members" goes with the verb "is established" rather than with the first "tongue" or as modifying the phrase "wicked world." Most translations agree, though some (e.g., the NIV) are ambiguous. If "wicked world" rather than "tongue" is, as I have proposed, the subject of the second sentence, this is effectively demanded. But as noted already, the semantic value of the whole is little affected whether it modifies "wicked world" or "is established."

Thus, James is saying that the wicked world establishes a presence in the body (either the individual or the church) by way of the tongue (speech), which not only can spoil one's integrity (it "stains," and remember that James indicated in 1:27 that true religion must keep itself "unstained") but also keeps the spoiling active; it starts a process that generates evil over and over again. Just as was the case with Adam, speech is the primary point of entry for the evil world and its worldly "wisdom" (3:15) that disrupts and destroys.

---

does not mean "to appoint oneself," but "to appoint *for* oneself," that is, "to choose" (LSJ 855) refers to Xenophon, *Anab.* 3.1.39).

13. S.-J. Austin (2009) argues convincingly that the apparent lack of clear order in the series of nominatives may be explained as a deliberate patterning on Semitic poetic structure.

14. Since both κόσμος (*kosmos*) and γλῶσσα (*glōssa*) have the article, the first ordinarily would be the subject. Hort (1909: 71) apparently recognizes the difficulty, since he specifically justifies the subject γλῶσσα being later in order to connect more securely with ἡ σπιλοῦσα (*hē spilousa*).

The phrase translated "course of life" is literally a "wheel of generation" (τροχὸς τῆς γενέσεως, *trochos tēs geneseōs*). Phrases quite similar to this were used in Orphic mysteries and other Hellenistic religious contexts for the "cycle of origin," or the notion of metempsychosis, the recycling of the soul.[15] Other, similar phrases refer to the never-ending cycle of life, death, and new life (perhaps reflected in the NRSV translation: "cycle of nature"). But although the phrase is similar, these ideas are far from James's world of thought,[16] and most commentators rightly look elsewhere for his meaning.

Ropes (1916: 235) postulates a simple solution, that γένεσις (*genesis*, generation) is equivalent to κτίσις (*ktisis*, creation), which he supports by reference to the πρόσωπον τῆς γενέσεως (*prosōpon tēs geneseōs*) in 1:23, which he takes to mean "natural face." Thus, τροχὸν τῆς γενέσεως simply means "the whole world." A clearer direction comes from Hort (1909: 72–74), who insists the solution should be sought in Jewish background, not Hellenistic. Hort's tentative suggestion for "wheel" is that it connects with the Jewish mystical speculations based on the wheel of Ezekiel's vision (Ezek. 10). However, this is hard to find relevant to James's concern, which is that the evil of uncontrolled speech has wide-reaching effects. "Wheel" probably is better related to the Jewish notion of the created world as a circle (e.g., Isa. 40:22 LXX, where God "holds fast the circle [γῦρος, *gyros*] of the earth"). But Hort rightly insists that the key is not the word "wheel" but instead the fact that γένεσις is the Greek word used in the LXX to translate *tôlĕdôt*, a word of many values, often translated "generations," signifying origins or birth or even a period in the story of humankind. Thus, the "wheel of γένεσις" in James could simply be a reference to the entire compass of this place or period of human existence[17] being inflamed by the tongue. Alternatively, James may be referring to the fact that the tongue's fire tends to reproduce itself in

15. Particularly similar phrasing occurs in Proclus Diadochus, *In Platonis Timaeum commentaria* 5.330a–b (available in an edition by Diehl 1903–6: 3.296–97), who speaks of the κύκλος τῆς γενέσεως (*kyklos tēs geneseōs*) as the continuous recycling of souls into this worldly existence from which the rational mind longs to escape. See further Dibelius 1975: 196n79.

16. Ropes (1916: 236–39) discusses the Greek philosophical (Stoic) and religious (Orphic) parallels to "wheel of generation" and rightly concludes, "To think of the tongue as enflaming the wheel of metempsychosis is nonsense; and on the other side, nothing could be more opposed to James's robust doctrine of moral responsibility than the idea of a fatalistic circle" (see also Dibelius 1975: 196–98). The proposal of Reicke (1964: 38) that James is reflecting the Stoic notion of cyclical aeons destroyed by fire, and that the tongue is what proleptically sets the universe ablaze with its final conflagration, is somewhat more likely, since James does expect a judgment and refers to "hell" (gehenna), but nothing about the destruction of the aeons by the tongue is apparent in James's purview, and hell in James 3:6 is not the final destruction of the evil world, but the origin of the tongue's evil, and so Reicke's suggestion too must be rejected.

17. Mayor (1897: 113) cites several examples to demonstrate that for Philo, γένεσις often stood for the earthly sinful created order as over against God (e.g., the merciful God versus the merciless γένεσις, or the stability of God versus the instability of γένεσις). The backdrop of Philo's platonic and de-eschatologized cosmology then yields a physical and lust-filled γένεσις that stands over against a Platonic ideal heavenly existence. This, of course, is not in James's purview, but the meaning of the word itself is not entirely dissimilar.

this age, even from generation to generation, or over and over again (a view apparently taken by the Peshitta [Syriac translation] of James, which reads, "the successions of our generations, which run like wheels" [translation in Ropes 1916: 236]).

The most common approach, however, appears to be to take τροχός (or τρόχος)[18] not as a wheel but in the sense of "course" (as a racecourse or track), and γένεσις as a way of speaking about existence or life, yielding "the whole course of life." This fits both the context and the meaning of γένεσις that I found to be likely at 1:23. At least one LXX use of γένεσις seems to demand the sense of "life span" (Jdt. 12:18 NRSV: "Today is the greatest day in my whole life"). It is unnecessary to make anything more of the "circularity" of the "wheel" than in our expression "circle of friends."

Whatever the origin and precise nuance of James's phrase, it seems to refer either to the whole compass of human life in this age or to the continuing effects of evil speech as one generation passes to the next, not, however, as an unending cycle, but simply as one that continues through time within this order of existence. The main meaning is not in doubt: the tongue's potential for damage, like that of a wildfire, extends well beyond its point of origin, spreading outward in an ever-widening circle.[19]

This depiction would take on an additional reservoir of meaning if it referred to the church (see the commentary on 3:3–5a). In that case, James's point would be that undisciplined and froward tongues of would-be teachers can both despoil the whole church and further set fires that run amok and keep reigniting; no sooner is one put out than three more emerge from the ashes elsewhere. Such is the destructive power of ugly rumor, jealous backbiting, and other forms of verbal warfare (depicted further in 4:1, 11). Even though I am unconvinced that the "body" directly means "church" in James, it is nonetheless clear that the damage done by the tongue is difficult to undo because, like a fire, it spreads, and it affects far more than the owner of the tongue by which it started.

No wonder, then, that James describes the uncontrolled tongue further as "inflamed by hell," literally "gehenna,"[20] the term used by Jesus to refer to the place of divine retribution. Here "hell" is a metonym for its eventual

18. The word τροχος (*trochos*) can be accented on the first syllable, meaning "course" (LSJ 1829). Recent commentators correctly point out that even without the accent change, the word could easily refer to anything circular, such as a racecourse. But the key to the phrase lies in the Jewish background of γένεσις, not τροχος (however accented).

19. The depiction of the axle hole of a chariot wheel catching fire from friction and spreading outward along the spokes of the wheel is colorful but probably far-fetched.

20. Gehenna, or Ge-Hinnom, literally referred to the Hinnom Valley, south of Jerusalem, which became a garbage dump where trash fires burned continuously (as of 1996, it was still a trash dump and perhaps still is). It also was associated with some of the most evil events in the life of Israel (2 Chron. 28:3; 33:6; Jer. 7:31; 32:35) as well as the judgments that they precipitated (Jer. 7:32; 19:6), and thus it was identified not only as the symbolic place of judgment, but also as the symbolic origin of that which brings judgment. James may also be playing on the word's phonic resemblance to γενέσεως (Laws 1980: 151–52).

inhabitant, the devil,[21] or perhaps for evil generally. Although this is apparently the earliest instance of the use of "hell" as representing the source of evil as opposed to its destiny, it would not be difficult to discern the metonymy, and the term is apt, because Jesus calls it the "gehenna of fire" (Matt. 5:22; 18:9). As worldly speech is inflamed by hell, so in 3:15 is worldly wisdom demonic (δαιμονιώδης, *daimoniōdes*).

The word φύσις (*physis*) in 3:7 means "nature" or "kind." The series of kinds of creatures is intended to cover the breadth of what we call the "animal kingdom." All the various kinds of animals are contrasted with the human φύσις, under whom (or by whom)[22] all those animals are tamed, but which cannot tame its own speech. James is claiming not that all the creatures have been tamed, but that representatives from every kind either are tamed or are being tamed. Further, the word for "tame" (δαμάζω, *damazō*) does not mean "domesticate" so much as "subdue" or "bring under control" (BDAG 211; its only other use in the NT is in Mark 5:4, which says of the Gerasene demoniac that no one had the strength to subdue him). James is reflecting on the created order given in Gen. 1:26 ("Let us make man in our image, after our likeness. And let them have dominion over the fish of the sea and over the birds of the heavens and over the livestock and over all the earth and over every creeping thing that creeps on the earth")[23] and then mandated in Gen. 1:28 ("Be fruitful and multiply and fill the earth and subdue it and have dominion over the fish of the sea and over the birds of the heavens and over every living thing that moves on the earth"), thereby granting humankind a dominion, that is, a subordinate sovereignty or vicegerency, over all the other creatures. God also then commanded humankind to realize that dominion,[24] a mandate that humanity is more or less successfully carrying out. He thus contrasts human success in a lesser matter to human failure in a more important one.

3:7–8a

21. Dibelius (1975: 199n87) refers to Apoc. Ab. 14 (usually dated toward the end of the first century AD), which sees Azazel (= Satan) as already in the "inaccessible parts of the earth." Chapter 31 of the same work also refers to the wicked being "burnt with the fire of Azazel's tongue." Whether or not James is aware of such a tradition, "hell" as a metonym for the devil is a natural analog to "heaven" as a metonym for God (as in 5:18).

22. The dative phrase τῇ φύσει τῇ ἀνθρωπίνῃ (*tē physei tē anthrōpinē*) could mean "by humankind," in the sense that humans did the taming. The dative of agency is rare (BDF §191), but occasionally it does occur with a perfect passive verb (cf. Luke 23:15). Wallace (1996: 164) even adduces James 3:6 as a "clear" example of dative of agency. However, it is more likely either a dative of advantage (creatures of every kind are tamed *for* humankind) or a dative of respect, which with verbs of submission indicate to whom the submitting is done (the creatures are subdued unto humankind's control). The instrumental dative ("by means of . . .") certainly does not fit.

23. In 3:9, James will again allude to the first part of Gen. 1:26.

24. James uses both a present tense "are being tamed" and a perfect tense "have been tamed." This is most simply taken as indicating James's awareness that the subduing of the creatures is both a state of affairs and an ongoing process. Moo (2000: 161) points out that this reflects the situation in Gen. 1, where dominion is both an accomplished fact by divine declaration (1:26) and a mandate for humans continually to fulfill.

To heighten the contrast, the tongue is described as an "unstable evil" and "full of death-dealing poison" (an image borrowed from Ps. 58:3–4; 140:3; cf. Sir. 28:18–21; Rom. 3:13). The tongue's instability recalls the double-minded person who is unstable in all his paths (1:8), and it anticipates the instability generated by jealousy and striving (3:16). Many wild animals are unstable, in the sense that they are uncontrollable, but they are not evil. And even the animals that contain deadly poison, such as the adder and the scorpion, are not evil, and they only poison humans when attacked or threatened. Poisonous words, however, do not just kill the body; they can kill the soul or even a church.

Commentators often point out that James seems to be contradicting himself (as well as passages such as Ps. 34:13), because the exhortation in 3:2b implies that at least some people indeed can subdue their own tongues, and the pilot can successfully control the rudder of ships (3:5). But note that here in 3:8 James is speaking broadly; it is the tongue of people generally (ἀνθρώπων, *anthrōpōn*, of human beings; not ἀνθρωπίνη, *anthrōpinē*, human) that cannot be subdued. Hence, the wisdom of humans, earthly wisdom (3:15), does not ultimately bear the fruit of righteousness (3:18; cf. 1:20).

3:8b–10 The undisciplined tongue is pernicious (full of poison) because it hides its evil under the guise of good. It can profess the gospel of Jesus in calling upon God as Lord and as Father (cf. 1 Pet. 1:17) while at the same time cursing another human being. Although the concept of God as a father was nascent in Judaism (1 Chron. 29:10; Isa. 63:16; Sir. 23:1, 4), it was an uncommon appellation prior to Jesus. Hence, it is probably a specifically Christian appellation, and to call God "Lord and Father" performs the highest function to which speech can be put (blessing God). It is all the greater a travesty, then, to give it the lie by cursing those made "in God's likeness" (a phrase rooted in Gen. 1:26, probably indicating sonship; cf. Gen. 5:3, where Adam begets Seth after his "likeness").[25] The result is an intolerable inconsistency, a "double-mindedness," as it were, for "out of the same mouth comes cursing and blessing." James expostulates, "My brothers, it must not be this way!" This might be more idiomatically rendered "This cannot be!"—not that cursing and blessing coming from the same mouth is impossible, but that it is radically inconsistent. Using this rare expression (οὐ χρή, *ou chrē*), James does not claim that such inconsistent speech is impossible, but declares vigorously that it ought not to happen, it must not happen (LSJ 2004).[26] Not only is cursing an insult to the maker of the one being cursed (3:9)[27] and a direct disobedience to the command of Christ (Luke 6:28; cf. Rom. 12:14), but also it is especially a

25. The word for "likeness" (ὁμοίωσις, *homoiōsis*) is found only here in the NT and is rare even in the LXX, making the allusion to Gen. 1:26 almost certainly deliberate.

26. On οὐ χρή, see the additional note on 3:10. The sentence more literally reads, "It must not be, my brothers, that these things should be this way."

27. This connection is made in other Jewish traditions (Mek. Exod. 20:26; Gen. Rab. 24.7–8 on Gen. 5:1; 1 En. 44.1; Sipra on Lev. 19:18; T. Benj. 6).

denial of the truth (3:14) when coupled with blessing God, for the blessing then becomes hypocrisy (cf. 1 John 4:20: "He who does not love his brother . . . cannot love God").

The "opening" (ὀπή, *opē*) through which a spring gushes in 3:11 can refer to   **3:11–12** a hole or cave. Sometimes the word refers to the eye socket; springs are like "eyes" (the Hebrew word for "spring" also means "eye"), and the hole from which water bubbles up is the spring's eye. Springs often are in caves and not uncommonly spring forth from holes or cracks in the rock. Generally, springs may be assumed to hold fresh and potable water, so a fountain or spring gushing water holds the promise of life. But in Palestine, particularly in the Rift Valley, there are springs that are brackish or so laden with minerals as to be poisonous. The point is that at its source, a spring is either one or the other, and it either aids life or inhibits it. A spring that sometimes gives fresh water and sometimes poisonous would be not just anomalous, but dangerous.

As already noted (see the introduction to 3:1–18), 3:12 serves as a bridge verse linking the themes of the tongue's instability and the incompatibility of heavenly and earthly wisdom. It also serves to pull back the subject to those who would be teachers and moves toward the next section (3:13–18), which will remind them that the wisdom from above that mature teachers should dispense is a wisdom characterized by godly life.

Figs, olives, and grapes were and are the primary staples of Mediterranean agricultural life, and the recognition that each kind of plant produces its own distinctive fruit was long proverbial in both Jewish and Greco-Roman sources.[28] The rhetorical question echoes the saying of Jesus that one cannot obtain good fruit from a rotten tree (Matt. 7:16–18; 12:33). Likewise, the fact that one cannot obtain "sweet" (i.e., potable) water from a brackish source illustrates that a teacher living a bad life cannot be the source of true wisdom. By picking up again on the illustration in 3:11 that a single spring does not produce both sweet and bitter water, it further connects with the fact that it is inappropriate for the tongue, the instrument of teaching, to produce both blessing and curse. True wisdom makes for peace (3:18).

Additional Notes

3:1–12. Even more than in James 1, the literary flow of the beginning of James 3 is marked by a chain of catchwords that, though hardly noticeable in English translation, is conspicuous in Greek: πολλοί . . . πολλά (3:1–2); πταίομεν . . . πταίει (3:2); χαλιναγωγῆσαι . . . χαλινούς (3:2–3); μετάγομεν . . . μετάγεται (3:3–4); τηλικαῦτα . . . ἡλίκον . . . ἡλίκην (3:4–5); πῦρ . . . πῦρ (3:5–6); φλογίζουσα . . . φλογιζομένη (3:6); φύσις . . . φύσει (3:7); δαμάζεται καὶ δεδάμασται . . . δαμάσαι (3:7–8). In addition, the phrase ὅλον τὸ σῶμα recurs in 3:2, 3, 6.

28. E.g., Plutarch, *Tranq. an.* 13. For further examples, see Mayor 1897: 120. Seneca (*Ep.* 87.25) makes a comment strikingly similar to James: "Good does not spring from evil, any more than figs grow from olive-trees. Things which grow correspond to their seed; and goods cannot depart from their class. As that which is honourable does not grow from that which is base, so neither does good grow from evil" (translation in Grummere 1920: 337).

The apparent disjuncture of 3:1–2a from 3:2b–12 leads Dibelius (1975: 182) to suppose that 3:2b–12 originally existed separately as a treatise on the problems of control of the tongue, and that the redactor somewhat awkwardly put it here in the context of discussing why few should be teachers. But the catena noted above begins in 3:1, not 3:2b, and one ought not to impose literary criteria of Western logical arrangement on an Eastern Mediterranean document. As noted in the introduction and elsewhere, the structure, like that of 1 John and 2 Peter, is cyclothematic, not linear. Even if Dibelius is right, 3:2b–12 meant something to the final redactor, and it is this final contextual meaning of the extant document, not an "original" meaning of a hypothetical one, that we are seeking.

3:1. The negative particle μή negates the verb γίνεσθε, but it is placed before πολλοί to highlight it (MHT 3:287). The verb γίνεσθε is imperative and equivalent to the command "be" (see the commentary on 1:22–25). Hence, "Not many of you should be. . . ."

"Inasmuch as you know" translates the participle εἰδότες as causal. Compare Hort (1909: 67): "knowing as ye already do." Presumably, it indicates knowledge that the church has as part of its tradition (cf. Rom. 5:3; 6:9; 1 Cor. 15:58; 2 Cor. 4:14; Eph. 6:8).

3:2. The word for "man" here (ἀνήρ) is the term commonly used to mean a male adult. Nevertheless, the opening conditionality "if someone" indicates that James is thinking of persons generally, not just adult males, and other uses of ἀνήρ in the letter confirm this (see the second additional note on 1:8).

3:2. Many important manuscripts (most notably ℵ [original hand], C, and 33 [apparently]) read δυνάμενος instead of the preferable reading δυνατός. The meaning is virtually identical: having the power to control is the same as being able to control.

3:3. The reading εἰ δέ adopted here, as in NA²⁷, is uncertainly attested, as also is the case with the variant reading ἴδε. Both εἰ δέ and ἴδε were pronounced similarly (though with different accentuation), which may account for the variation, and Mayor (1897: 104–6)[29] makes a strong case for the originality of ἴδε based on the reading ΕΙΔΕ ΓΑΡ in ℵ (the γάρ supposedly indicating that ΕΙΔΕ was read as an imperative rather than as two words). However, ἴδε is never used elsewhere in James; he prefers the equivalent ἰδού (3:4, 5; 5:4, 7, 9, 11). Also, since ἴδε is the easier reading, it is more likely to be secondary.

3:3. The singular "their body" in reference to the bodies of horses (plural) perhaps is jarring to English readers, but this distributive use of singular is not uncharacteristic of biblical Greek (BDF §140; cf. Mark 8:17; Phil. 3:21). I preserved the singular in translation because the "body" theme is running through the first part of James 3, and so James's choice of the singular here may be deliberate.

3:3–4. The imagery from these verses, connecting riders steering horses and pilots steering ships, and also the small fire/big forest comparison, were quite common in the Mediterranean literary environment. Two particularly noteworthy examples are found in Plutarch and in Philo. Plutarch (*Adol. poet. aud.* 33F) quotes Menander, "'Tis not the teacher's speech but practice moves," and then comments,

> Yea, rather, say we, both the speech [λόγος] and practice—or the practice by the means of speech—as the horse is managed with the bridle [χαλινός], and the ship with the helm [πηδάλιον]. For virtue hath no instrument so suitable and agreeable to human nature to work on men withal, as that of [speech] [λόγος]. (translation in Goodwin 1906: 2.86)

An even closer parallel is in Philo, *Alleg. Interp.* 3.79 §§223–24:

29. The reading is also supported by Laws (1980: 146) and Ropes (1916: 229), mainly because εἰ δέ makes poor sense.

When the charioteer is in command and guides the horses with the reins, the chariot goes the way he wishes [ᾗ βούλεται ἄγεται τὸ ἅρμα], but if the horses have become unruly and got the upper hand, it has often happened that the charioteer has been dragged down. . . . A ship, again, keeps to her straight course when the helmsman grasping the tiller [πηδαλιουχεῖ] steers accordingly, but capsizes when a contrary wind has sprung up over the sea, and the surge has settled in it. Just so, when Mind, the charioteer or helmsman of the soul, rules the whole living being . . . the life holds a straight course, but when irrational sense gains the chief place, a terrible confusion overtakes it . . . for then, in very deed, the mind is set on fire and is all ablaze, and that fire is kindled by the objects of sense which Sense-perception [αἰσθητά] supplies. (translation in Colson and Whitaker 1929: 176–77)[30]

Dibelius (1975: 185–90), citing these and other parallels in Greco-Roman moral literature, both Jewish and otherwise, therefore claims that these verses in James were borrowed from Hellenistic stock sayings, and the author simply adopted the stock metaphors as a bundle without reference to their original use. This is said to explain the unusual vocabulary and odd transition from ships and horses to wildfire, since James radically redirects the imagery from an original description of the control (or lack thereof) of Reason or Mind over the senses or person to that of the control (or lack thereof) of the person over the destructive power of the tongue. Whether or not James consciously or unconsciously borrowed from such a source, he does not imbue his analogies with precision, nor is he bound by the original purposes of the illustrations, and it is a mistake to press the imagery for too much subtle information.

3:5. The reading μεγαλαυχεῖ (is proud) found in ℵ and the Majority Text involves simply dropping one of the two adjacent *alpha*s in μεγάλα αὐχεῖ and closing up the two words. It also may have been influenced by Ps. 9:39 LXX (10:18 MT) and other OT passages. But although it certainly is true that the tongue is proud and arrogant, James's point here is that the tongue is *not* exaggerating when it makes great claims (μεγάλα αὐχεῖ).

3:6. The complexity noted in the exposition generated a plethora of solutions even in antiquity. The Peshitta, assuming that something had dropped out, translated "the tongue is the fire and the wicked world is the wood," a solution more recently advocated by Adamson (1976: 142). However, solutions to difficulties by way of textual emendation, though easy, are unlikely to be correct.

The progressive participles σπιλοῦσα, φλογίζουσα, and φλογιζομένη should be read as expressing general characteristics of the wicked tongue, not necessarily continuous action.

3:8. James indicates literally that "no one from humans" can tame the tongue, which is an awkward way to say "no one." Augustine (*Nat. grat.* 15) thinks that this is a subtle way of guarding against the conclusion that the tongue absolutely cannot be tamed, for certainly God can tame it. But such linguistic subtlety is uncharacteristic of James, and it is more likely that he is simply contrasting human ability to tame animals with human inability to tame the tongue.

3:8. The phrase ἀκατάστατον κακόν is neuter because it is not modifying "tongue" directly; it is in apposition, either as an abstraction (the tongue is an "unstable evil") or as substantival (the tongue is an "unstable evil thing"; see BDF §137.3). In place of ἀκατάστατον κακόν some texts (C, Ψ, and the Majority Text) read ἀκατάσχετον κακόν (uncontrollable evil), which better suits the context, but for that reason is most likely an error of scribal hearing (ἀκατάστατον could easily be mistaken for ἀκατάσχετον).

3:9. Hort (1909: 76) recognizes that works of Jewish provenance sometimes use ἐν to express instrumentality, but regards it as inconsistent with James's language. Instead of the usual "by it [the tongue] we bless," Hort proposes that James effectively makes the tongue an actual speaker, not just the organ of speech, yielding "in [the person of] the tongue we bless." This seems excessively subtle.

---

30. See also Philo, *Creation* 28 §86.

3:9. As should be clear from the exposition, the "we" in 3:9 refers not to humanity generally (as Dibelius argues) but rather to those who claim God as Lord and Father.

3:9. The Majority Text has "God" instead of "Lord" in the phrase "we bless the Lord and Father," but the latter reading is much better attested (א, A, B, C, P, 33, and most versions), and Metzger (1994: 611) points out that it is much likelier that a scribe would replace the unusual "Lord and Father" with the familiar "God and Father" than the reverse.

3:10. The word χρή is a common classical term that occurs in the NT only here (its only other biblical occurrence is Prov. 25:27). It occupies a place somewhere between ὀφελεῖ and δεῖ, stronger than the former though perhaps not as deterministic as the latter (see LSJ 2004).[31] James is saying not just that believers should refrain from cursing other people, but that such cursing is an intolerable contradiction; it is so contrary to the very nature of faith in God that it effectively denies that faith.

3:11. The article with πηγή is unexpected, leading Hort (1909: 79) to suggest that it represents the human heart. This would then reflect Matt. 12:34: "Out of the abundance of the heart the mouth speaks."

3:11. The word βρύω (here translated "gush") in classical literature is used of a bud bursting into flower. By the first century, it was used of springs to refer to their gushing or pouring forth abundantly from their source (LSJ 332).

3:12. Here οὔτε is used like οὐδέ (this substitution also occurs in Rev. 9:21). The reading οὕτως οὐδέ (א and 33; also reflected in several versions) may reflect a scribal attempt to smooth the awkwardness of this verse, which literally reads, "neither does salty yield sweet water." Commentators point out that strictly speaking, it makes no sense to say that "salty water does not yield fresh water," but as has been observed repeatedly, James often is imprecise in his use of illustrations, and he should not be read in an overly subtle fashion.[32] Most people have no trouble understanding the idea "one does not get fresh water from salty."

---

31. In classical usage it is virtually equivalent to δεῖ, especially in Homer, who only once uses the latter, and who, according to LSJ, consistently uses χρή in the sense of "must" or "is necessary."

32. The NIV supplies the word "spring" here, but since the adjective "salty" is neuter rather than feminine, this is as much a smoothing move as the scribes who changed the verse to read οὕτως οὐδεμία πηγὴ ἁλυκὸν καὶ γλυκὺ ποιῆσαι ὕδωρ (K, L, and the Majority Text).

B. Part 2: Wisdom from Above (3:13–18)

"Wisdom" enters our modern consciousness infrequently, but the desire to avoid its opposite is common enough. No one wants to appear foolish. Sadly, the foolishness that we fear is mostly earthly foolishness. We hate it when our retirement portfolio fares poorly, or when we buy a car that later gets a low rating in consumer magazines, or when we wear inappropriate clothes to a social occasion. Would that we were as concerned about not being foolish with respect to God.

James here in the second part of James 3 gives expression to the same thing that Paul addresses in 1 Cor. 1–3: God's wisdom (in James's terms, "wisdom from above") can look like foolishness to the world, but God's "foolishness" turns out to be mightier than human wisdom (in James's terms, "earthly wisdom").

The parallels between this description of true heavenly wisdom and true faith in James 2 are obvious. Just as genuine faith is distinguished from false faith by works, so also heavenly and earthly wisdom are differentiated by their works. Likewise, the "wisdom" identified as demonic in 3:15 stands as a counterpart to the "faith" that even demons have in 2:19 (Hort 1909: 85). The very term that James uses, wisdom "from above," shows his roots in the OT notion that genuine wisdom comes from God, not from experience (1 Kings 4:29; 10:24; cf. Eccles. 1:13), that this high wisdom consists not in knowing how to get along in this life, but in walking with God (Job 28:28; Mic. 6:8–9), and that therefore the beginning of wisdom is the fear of God (Ps. 111:10; Prov. 1:7; 9:10), a concept not far removed from that of faith (Exod. 14:31: "Israel saw the great power that the LORD used against the Egyptians, so the people *feared* the LORD, and they *believed* in the LORD and in his servant Moses"). Once again James demonstrates his deep concern for a consistent and active faith on the part of his readership. Genuine wisdom proceeds from genuine faith.[1]

Because of his conviction that this section originally was entirely independent, Dibelius (1975: 208–9) misses how 3:13–18 serves: by contrasting God's wisdom with the human wisdom that is at root self-seeking and envious, it moves from the dangers of speech (especially for those who would be imparters of wisdom) to the problems of intracommunity strife found in James 4.

---

1. See further excursus 3, "James and Wisdom."

Exegesis and Exposition

> [13]Who among you is wise and understanding? He must show, by means of his good behavior, his works in humble wisdom. [14]But if you harbor bitter envy and selfish ambition in your heart, ⌜do not boast about it and thus give the lie to the truth⌝. [15]Such "wisdom" is not that which comes down from above, but the kind that is earthly, unspiritual, demonic. [16]For wherever there is jealousy and selfish ambition, there is instability and every base thing. [17]But the wisdom from above is, first of all, pure, then peaceable, considerate, compliant, full of mercy and good fruits, constant, sincere. [18]And the fruit of righteousness is sown in peace for those who do peace.

3:13   James's challenge here, "Who among you is wise and understanding?" is not unlike Paul's rhetorical use of Isa. 19:12 in 1 Cor. 1:20.[2] By it James resumes the concern with those who would be teachers (3:1) and connects it with the practical demonstration of wisdom by good works. The paragraph also links the issues of speech and wisdom with the discussion of faith in James 2. The question serves as a conditional clause (Mayor 1897: 121): those who deem themselves wise and understanding (i.e., have the potential to be a teacher; see Martin 1988: 132) must show their works by good behavior.[3] The works are the same kind of works as were instrumental in the justification of Rahab and Abraham: works of faith. Hence, although James says literally that the wise and understanding must show the works in humble wisdom by means of good behavior, the context makes it clear that, just as in 2:18, the works are instrumental in showing faith, so here works are the key to showing what kind of wisdom one has. Good behavior points to the kind of works that point to humble wisdom. James's point again is that grasping concepts or having worldly success is not what avails either for genuine faith or wisdom from above; what counts is the godly life that results from genuine faith/wisdom.

"Humble wisdom" is literally "meekness of wisdom." Ropes (1916: 244), suggesting that this is simply a general associative genitive, offers "meekness appropriate to wisdom." Similarly, the genitive could be understood (Moo 2000: 170) as a genitive of source ("meekness that comes from [true] wisdom"). But since the adjective "true" is absent, and since the subject in the rest of the paragraph is different kinds of wisdom, with humility being a characteristic of the heavenly variety, it may be better to understand "wisdom" as the principal word and "meekness" as the modifier (Dibelius 1975:

---

2. In 1 Cor. 1:20 Paul also denounces worldly wisdom, asking, "Where is the one who is wise? Where is the scribe? Where is the debater of this age? Has not God made foolish the wisdom of the world?" This echoes the words of Isa. 19:12–13, spoken against those who wanted to turn to Egypt for help (which looked like a wise thing to do from a worldly point of view): "Where then are your wise men? Let them tell you that they might know what the LORD of hosts has purposed against Egypt. The princes of Zoan have become fools, and the princes of Memphis are deluded."

3. For the use of "must" to translate third-person imperatives, see the second additional note on 1:5.

209), or both terms as equally in focus (Hartin 2003: 192). Although this is not a typical Greek construction, the Hebrew construct state, which often is translated by the Greek genitive, sometimes can treat the first noun as the qualifier and the second as the principal; when that is carried over into Greek, it is sometimes referred to as an "attributed genitive" (Wallace 1996: 89–91). The text goes on to describe just this kind of wisdom that is not triumphalist, proud, self-serving, and contentious, but generous, peaceable, and humble. The concept that genuine wisdom is humble is from the OT (e.g., Prov. 11:2: "When pride comes, then comes disgrace, but with the humble is wisdom"). A wisdom stemming from humility stands in contrast to Greek wisdom,[4] the wisdom of power and worldly success, and increasingly in contrast to the "wisdom" of our own day, which regards meekness not as a virtue, but as a mark of servility and obsequiousness.[5] But James's "wisdom from above" is not the wisdom of how to "get ahead" in life or how to achieve worldly success, nor is it special insight into divine secrets; it is about how one displays godly character patterned after the life of the one who identified himself as meek and lowly (Matt. 11:29).

"If you harbor bitter envy [ζῆλος, *zēlos*] and selfish ambition [ἐριθεία, *eritheia*] in your hearts" describes the grasping and self-advancing motivation for the use of the life skills frequently considered wisdom by the world. James's warning reminds readers that it is all too characteristic of the body of believers. The terms recur in 3:16, where James says that they result in instability and every base thing.

3:14

Inasmuch as ζῆλος may also mean "zeal," and ἐριθεία is quite rare and thus of uncertain meaning (see the first additional note on 3:14), several commentators follow Ropes (1916: 245) in arguing that ζῆλον πικρόν (*zēlon pikron*) should be rendered "harsh zeal," inasmuch as it is not personal jealousy so much as the desire to impose one's own opinions on others that James condemns. Thus, James's point would be that although zeal for what one thinks of as truth may have the appearance of wisdom, if such zeal (even if based on truth) introduces discord and instability into the community of faith, it is not true wisdom. Certainly, fractiousness and a self-righteous zeal that exalts one's own opinions in order to increase one's political power in the church are displays of "earthly"

4. The Greek word σοφία (*sophia*) originally meant "skill, craft," but came to signify cunning, craftiness, and the ability to manipulate events and people for one's own ends (LSJ 1621–22; see Herodotus, *Hist.* 1.68). Especially in the Stoic tradition, which exerted much influence in the Hellenistic period, wisdom was the understanding of both divine and human matters (Aëtius, *Placita* 1.2; *SVF* 2.15) that enabled the wise person to control the world (Arius Didymus, fragment 29; see U. Wilckens, *TDNT* 7:473). Likewise, the adjective σοφός (*sophos*, skillful, clever) came to mean "shrewd" (Herodotus, *Hist.* 3.85).

5. The Greek fretting over hubris (as in Sophocles) was not to denigrate the acquisition of power or pride in self-advancement, but to remember the unpredictability of the gods and the foolishness of ever thinking that the gods (or fates) were on one's side, no matter how much success one had in life. This Greek attitude resembles OT humility, but only as superficially as the Greek gods resemble the God of Israel. See the commentary on 1:21.

wisdom (3:15), but James appears instead to be dealing with problems in the heart, whereas "zeal" is more associated with external actions. Also, when in 4:2 James uses the verbal form (ζηλόω, zēloō), it is in the context of coveting and frustrated evil desires, which go with envy more than zeal.

"Do not boast" could be idiomatically rendered "do not crow." This verb (κατακαυχάομαι, katakauchaomai) is used in 2:13, where mercy "triumphs" over judgment, but that meaning does not fit here. Ambitious boasting is another way to evince a false faith and earthly wisdom. Human wisdom seeks self-advancement and is anything but humble, especially when it achieves worldly success. Indeed, Greek wisdom gives advice on being successful *in the world*. But anything that generates, or is generated by, jealousy (envy of someone else's success) or selfish ambition (the desire to achieve one's own advancement at the expense of others) is a denial of the teaching of Jesus, as well as the OT, and hence to boast of that kind of wisdom is to "give the lie to the truth," that is, to the gospel (1:18; cf. 5:19).[6] One form of such ambition is the desire to be a teacher, and certainly the honor of being called "teacher" can have the form of worldly success, but without humility, teaching becomes boasting (Hort 1909: 83).

3:15–17   The two kinds of wisdom are expounded further in 3:15–17. True wisdom "comes down from above," that is, from God, as it is a good thing, and "every good gift . . . comes down from the Father" (1:17). But there is a wisdom that is "earthly, unspiritual, and demonic." That kind of wisdom purports to give worldly advancement, prestige, and success, but in fact it proves unstable and productive of all sorts of evil.

That jealousy and selfish ambition generate instability indicates their incompatibility with genuine faith, for it is the double-minded doubter (the one who has no faith) who is unstable in all ways (1:8). Instability (ἀκαταστασία, akatastasia, disorder) stands in contrast to the peaceableness of true wisdom (3:17; cf. 1 Cor. 14:33: God is the God not of ἀκαταστασία, but of εἰρήνη, eirēnē, peace).

Jealousy and selfish ambition also lie at the root of "every base thing." The word for "base" (φαῦλος, phaulos) generally means "of low moral value or quality" (BDAG 1050) and thus is opposite to what is good and valuable (see Rom. 9:11; 2 Cor. 5:10; Titus 2:8). Their production of "every base thing" might be understood to say that every moral degradation in life is ultimately traceable to jealousy and selfish ambition (Johnson 1983 traces the theme of jealousy as the root of violence in Greek ethical literature), but more probably James is saying that every ostensibly "good" thing that earthly wisdom produces is at bottom morally worthless.

The word ψυχικός (psychikos, "unspiritual") is rare and difficult to put into English. In the NT it is consistently set in opposition to πνευματικός

---

6. This phrase "lie against the truth" is not simply a hendiadys (Dibelius 1975: 210), but means to make the truth out to be a lie. Proudly representing one's envy, contentiousness, and rivalry as though it were wisdom and concern for the truth is a contradiction of the gospel.

(*pneumatikos*, spiritual; 1 Cor. 2:14; 15:44–46; cf. Jude 19). Hence, it is most commonly translated "unspiritual" (e.g., BDAG 1100; NIV; RSV; Moo 2000: 173), though that may be somewhat misleading here.[7] In 4 Macc. 1:32 we read of two kinds of desire: σωματικός (*sōmatikos*, bodily), which presumably indicates those desires rooted in bodily urges, and ψυχικός, those stemming from the will, mind, or conscious self. The context in James is best understood if the word is taken as "having to do with the ψυχή" (*psychē*, self, natural life, or soul),[8] and so we might cautiously translate it "self-ish," that is, focused on the advancement of one's own earthly personal welfare. Earthly wisdom offers a person counsel about self-advancement. It is the kind of "wisdom" retained by fallen angels (demons), who no doubt are very intelligent and apt at advancing themselves (in the short term). As in 1 Cor. 1:21, God's wisdom is different from human, earthly wisdom, because it serves different aims. Envy (often considered the motivation for Satan's rebellion; see Wis. 2:24) and selfish ambition (the desire to advance one's power and influence to the detriment of others) are exactly the kinds of desires that motivate the demons, and so James also terms such wisdom "demonic" (in other words, wisdom that is like the "wisdom" of demons, not wisdom inspired by demons; see the additional note on 3:15). But demonic "wisdom" is no more real wisdom than the "faith" of demons in 2:19 is real faith. In sum, this kind of "wisdom" serves "the world, the flesh, and the devil" (Moo 2000: 173).

It is envy, selfish ambition, and strife that are the problems with "earthly wisdom," not simply intellectual disagreement. It can therefore hardly be said with Dibelius (1975: 212) that James "would rather renounce more lively intellectual activity than pay for it with tensions within the community." Since James himself pulls few punches in his rhetoric, he can hardly be said to be averse to all controversy.

In contrast to earthly wisdom, wisdom "from above" (3:17), a wisdom implied already in 1:5, is one of the gifts, perhaps the principal one, that come "from above" (cf. 1:17). The series of attributes of genuine, godly wisdom listed here recalls Prov. 8:22–36 and perhaps even more so Wis. 7:7–30. In contrast to the selfishness and instability of earthly wisdom, wisdom from above is considerate, peaceable, and so forth. But we should note that just as true religion keeps oneself unstained by the world (1:27), the preeminent attribute of heavenly wisdom, from which the other attributes flow, is that it is pure or holy (ἁγνός, *hagnos*). The purity that comes from belonging to God is the fount from which other goodness flows. These characteristics are, strictly speaking, attributes not of wisdom per se, but of the person who has wisdom, thus answering the question that opened the paragraph at 3:13. As Ropes (1916: 250) observes, they fall into three groups:

7. Even more misleading is the association, made by Dibelius (1975: 211–12), of ψυχικός with the gnostic meaning "bound to earth."

8. LSJ 2027 indicates a general meaning "of the soul," but the word is rare enough that clarity is hard to obtain. It sometimes stands in opposition to σωματικός, and as noted already, Paul contrasts it with πνευματικός.

1. Peaceable, considerate (gentle), compliant (deferent). All three adjectives in Greek begin with the letter ε and have to do with the wise person's disposition.
2. Full of mercy (active compassion, not the emotion of pity) and good fruits (i.e., good works [cf. Matt. 21:43]). Both have to do with the wise person's actions.
3. Unwavering, unhypocritical (sincere). In Greek, both of these begin with the privative α (reflected in the English un- prefixes), and they describe the enduring constancy of the wise person.

The word "unwavering" (ἀδιάκριτος, *adiakritos*), found nowhere else in the NT, particularly stands in contrast with the instability (ἀκαταστασία, *akatastasia*) of earthly wisdom and calls to mind the double-minded, unstable (ἀκατάστατος, *akatastatos*) person of 1:8, whose instability is the result of διακρινόμενος (*diakrinomenos*, doubting; 1:6).[9] Once again we see the connection between wisdom and faith.

We may also detect here again wisdom's functional similarity with the Holy Spirit.[10] As Martin (1988: 133) observes, this list of wisdom's attributes is analogous to the fruit of the Spirit in Gal. 5:22–23. And just as in Paul's letters the *Spirit* is the source of faith (1 Cor. 12:9) and is received by faith (Gal. 3:2, 14), so also for James, *wisdom* and faith are coattendant.

3:18   In 3:18 we have the closing proverb for this section, summing up the relationship of peace, righteousness, and wisdom. It reflects one of Jesus's beatitudes: "Blessed are the peacemakers, for they will be called children of God" (Matt. 5:9 NRSV). It also stands in contrast to the poisonous tongue that breeds contention and bitterness (3:5–6; 4:1–12). It may also link back to 3:1, in that true teachers are those who sow peace by disseminating the genuine wisdom from above.

Once again, James's illustration is imprecise, and it is an exercise in pedantry to insist that it is not fruit that is sown but rather the seed that later yields the fruit, and then to search for complicated special meaning in the proverb. "Fruit of righteousness" (καρπὸς δικαιοσύνης, *karpos dikaiosynēs*) could be "righteous fruit" (as "world of unrighteousness" means "unrighteous world"), but the genitive is here better taken as either source (the reward that righteous behavior produces; cf. Isa. 45:8) or epexegetical (the fruit that is righteousness; see MHT 3:215). Mayor (1897: 128) supports the latter, as do Martin (1988: 135), Davids (1982: 155), and Hartin (2003: 195). Ropes (1916: 250–51) argues that its use in the LXX is consistently "the fruit that righteousness produces," but the texts that he adduces can be read otherwise (particularly Amos 6:12,

---

9. Dibelius (1975: 214) denies any connection between 3:17 and 1:6 (or 2:4), taking ἀδιάκριτος in the sense of "harmonious." But this is due partly to Dibelius's disposition of seeing no thematic coherency in the Epistle of James.

10. James is not unique in this identification of "wisdom given from above" and God's Spirit. Wisdom 9:17 also equates the two. See Kirk 1969.

which works better as an epexegetical genitive), and Ropes acknowledges that the phrase in Heb. 12:11 appears to cast righteousness itself as the fruit.

Laws (1980: 166) identifies "wisdom" as the fruit that righteousness produces, pointing to Prov. 11:30, which describes the fruit of righteousness as a "tree of life," and Prov. 3:18, where wisdom is a "tree of life"; hence, "fruit of righteousness = wisdom." Further, wisdom's paths are peace in Prov. 3:17. The required leaps of intertextuality may be too large to be persuasive, but wisdom certainly is still in view. The epexegetical view best fits James's concerns: "the fruit that is righteousness" is the righteous condition that results from the implementation of genuine, peaceable wisdom. Although jealousy and striving produce instability and every evil thing (3:16), those who are peace-doers sow seed that results in righteousness. The verse also reiterates what James declared in 1:20: human anger does not accomplish God's righteousness.

Although the proverb could refer to the effect that peace-sowers have on others (e.g., Moo 2000: 177), the grammar of the sentence suits better the notion that "righteousness" is the reward or, better, the attribute of those who sow peace. As in James 2, this "righteousness" is not a reference to the Pauline notion of justification, whereby a sinner is forensically declared to be a righteous person, but rather reflects the general biblical notion that God's approval attends those who obey him. James, like Jesus (Matt. 5:9: "blessed are the peacemakers"), wants to apply this approval to peace-sowers, not the belligerent.

Likewise, the "peace" that is sown probably is not Paul's notion of "peace with God" (Rom. 5:1–11; 2 Cor. 5:18–20; Col. 1:22), but rather is peace and wholeness (*shalom*) within the community (Matt. 5:24; Luke 2:14; 2 Cor. 13:11). This is confirmed by the incisive condemnation of altercation and backbiting in the verses following (4:1–12). James's point is that those who do deeds of peace and promote peace thereby plant seeds and create an environment that eventually yields righteousness, not only for the sower, but also for the whole community to whom peace comes (cf. 5:20). The tongue's fire spreads destruction, but the seeds of peace-doing disseminate into a harvest of righteousness.

Additional Notes

3:13. Although this could be a case of substituting the interrogative τίς for ὅστις (BDF §298.4), it is more likely that James is simply using the rhetorical question "Who among you is wise?" as a forceful equivalent to a conditional: "If someone is wise ... he must show it." James also uses rhetorical questions to frame conditional clauses vividly in 5:13–14.

On the use of "must" to translate third-person imperatives, see the second additional note on 1:5.

3:14. The word for "selfish ambition" (ἐριθεία or ἐριθία [different manuscripts show different spellings for the same word]) offers difficulty because it is so poorly and ambiguously attested prior to the NT, though within the NT it occurs seven times (besides here in 3:14, 16, in Rom. 2:8; 2 Cor. 12:20; Gal. 5:20; Phil. 1:17; 2:3). Hort (1909: 81–83), who identifies it as expressing ambition and rivalry, has the most thorough discussion. The Greek commentators of the early church (see especially Chrysostom on Rom. 2:8) regularly saw it as closely related to ἔρις (strife) and understood it as "contentiousness." Dibelius (1975: 210) suggests that it is a particular kind of strife, "party spirit." Most recent translations, however, concur with Hort and translate "selfish ambition." Either meaning works in any of the NT passages where it occurs, though in 2 Cor. 12:20 and Gal. 5:20 ἔρις also appears, suggesting that the two words are not quite synonymous. Although James 4 certainly describes strife, here the emphasis seems to be on the inner motivations of the heart (3:14), not on the outward expressions.

3:14. Several important manuscripts, especially ℵ and 33, read the much less awkward μὴ κατακαυχᾶσθε (κατὰ) τῆς ἀληθείας καὶ ψεύδεσθε ("do not boast over the truth and lie"), thus eliminating the oddly redundant "lie against the truth" and also supplying κατακαυχᾶσθε with an expected object. That alleviates the problem, but is, for that reason, suspect. As indicated in my comments above on this verse, although James's phrasing is unusual, the common reading also makes sense in his context, for in fact people with earthly success do often claim to be "wise" and boast of their "wisdom," and people of jealous and contentious disposition often do make the truth look like a falsehood and present falsehood as truth in order to advance themselves or their cause.

3:15. The word δαιμονιώδης (demonic) is unattested in Greek literature prior to James, but the -ωδης ending attached to other nouns makes adjectives that mean "behaving in a manner characteristic of . . . [the noun]." Thus, μανιώδης in 3 Macc. 5:45 (behaving like a maniac) and θηριώδης in 2 Macc. 10:35 (behaving like a beast).

3:17. James's word ἁγνός is not as common in the NT or the LXX as the close synonym ἅγιος, but it is favored in the wisdom literature (4x in Proverbs; 4x in 4 Maccabees). It is also the word used in Ps. 18:10 LXX [19:10 MT; 19:9 ET]: "the fear of the Lord is ἁγνός." The fear of the Lord is also the foundation for wisdom (Job 28:28; Ps. 111:10; Prov. 9:10; 15:33).

3:18. Reicke (1964: 65) claims that "the translation 'is sown in peace' does not provide a good concrete meaning for the expression." He instead takes the phrase "in peace" epexegetically, to mean "consisting in peace." Reicke (1964: 41) thus translates "the fruit of righteousness, which is peace, is sown by the peaceful." But ordinarily, prepositional phrases are adverbial, and such an epexegetical use of ἐν is hardly common or obvious. Hartin (2003: 195) suggests the more probable "sown by means of acts of peace," though a simple adverbial "with peace" or "in peace" also suffices.

Hartin goes on to argue that the phrase translated above as "for those who do peace" should be taken as a dative of agency: "*by* those who make peace." But this is tautologous, and the simple dative rarely indicates agency (BDF §191 claims that there is only one genuine dative of agency in the NT, in Luke 23:15, and even that one is textually uncertain). In James, the only other dative that possibly could be read as expressing agency is φύσει τῇ ἀνθρωπίνῃ in 3:7, and as noted above (see the unit on 3:1–12, note 22), that too is probably a dative of advantage.

V. Third Discourse: Strife in the Church as Lack of Faith (4:1–12)

The section that I identify as the third discourse, unlike the other discourses in James, does not begin with the expected vocative ἀδελφοί (*adelphoi*, brothers), causing some commentators (e.g., Moo 2000: 179) to suggest that the first part of chapter 4 is a continuation of the material in 3:13–18. I addressed the issue of structure more thoroughly in the introduction (see "Structure"), but here we may note that like other segments in James (2:14; 3:13), 4:1–10 begins with a rhetorical question and ends with summarizing proverbial material, this time in a series of wisdom imperatives (4:7–10). The brief subsequent paragraph (4:11–12) begins with a prohibition (like 3:1 and 2:1) and ends with a proverb also, though James has added a rhetorical question as an application to the end of the closing proverb in 4:12.

The subject matter of this discourse does, however, flow naturally from the material of James 3, which warned against the danger of the tongue, especially for teachers in the church, and against the danger of self-seeking, boastful "wisdom," both of which lead to strife and contention. Contentiousness stands in contrast with the faith that asks (compare 4:2–3 with 1:5–6) rather than seeks to obtain by violence, that looks for friendship with (4:4) and draws near to God (4:8) rather than to the world, that seeks to be a doer of the law rather than to slander or judge fellow believers (4:11), especially in fulfilling the love command (4:12, echoing Lev. 19). The material of this section, along with the harsh "woe oracles" that follow in 4:13–5:6, draws together and applies the ethical discourses of the earlier chapters.

A. Part 1: Lusts and Repentance (4:1–10)

Here we have a blending of several themes already introduced: the destructive power of speech (especially slander), doubters who have not because they ask not, the eschatological casting down of the proud and exaltation of the lowly, the worldliness that sets itself over against God, the strife that comes from self-interest and arrogance rather than from true wisdom, which is humble and considerate and thus peaceful, and the relation of the Christian to the law. In all of these matters genuine faith and its fruits are contrasted with selfish unbelief and its fruits.

Exegesis and Exposition

[1]Where do the wars and fights among you come from? Is it not from this, from your [desire for] pleasures that wage war among your members? [2]You desire and you do not have; you murder and envy and you are unable to obtain; you fight and make war; you do not have because you do not ask; [3]you ask and you do not receive because you ask from evil motives, to squander [what you ask for] on your pleasures. [4]You ⌐ ⌐ adulteresses! Do you not know that friendship with the world is enmity with God? Whoever therefore intends to be a friend of the world is [thereby] made an enemy of God. [5]Or do you think the scripture for no good reason says that God jealously yearns for the Spirit that he caused to dwell in us, [6]although the grace he gives is greater [than his jealousy], for it says, "God resists the proud, but he gives grace to the humble."

> [7]Submit, therefore, to God,
>   and resist the devil, and he will flee from you.
>   [8]Draw near to God, and he will draw near to you.
> Purify your hands, you sinners, and sanctify your hearts, you
>   double-minded.
>   [9]Abase yourselves and mourn and weep.
> Turn your laughter into mourning, and your joy into gloom.
>   [10]Be humbled before the Lord, and he will lift you up.

4:1–3   Since true wisdom is known, shown, and grown in peace (3:17–18), the "wars" going on in the community are out of place. In contrast to the peace that true wisdom and righteousness sow, 4:1 speaks of the power struggles and back-biting, contentious jostling for position and murderous desire that are to be expected of the world but here are plaguing the church.

Battles and fights are outward manifestations of what is in the human heart, particularly selfish desires. "From this" refers to a person's own desires (cf.

1:14). The English phrase "desire for pleasures" in 4:1 (cf. 4:3) represents a single word in Greek, ἡδοναί (*hēdonai*, pleasures), whence comes the English word *hedonism*. In both Greek and Jewish moral literature, "pleasures" came to be used metonymically for the unrestrained desire for pleasure (as in 4:1)[1] or for illicitly desired pleasure (as in 4:3), usually of a sensual kind. Its use here is thus more or less synonymous with ἐπιθυμία (*epithymia*, desire; Dibelius 1975: 215). James is using it broadly, including the desire not just for physical pleasures but also for the headier wine of power and honor.

These pleasures, or the desire for them, wage war "in" your members, which may be understood as internal (within a person) or external (among members of the community). Those who see the horse and ship of James 3 as metaphors for the church, and the tongue as the teacher, no doubt will favor the latter view. On the other hand, James's concern appears to be to trace the external conflict to evil internal motivations (1:14), and hence the predominance of external conflicts in the church could be seen as, in effect, an indication of a lack of genuine faith within the individuals in it. Good arguments therefore can be made for either reading, but although the war taking place inside the Christian individual is a common theme in the NT (Gal. 5:17; 1 Pet. 2:11; and perhaps Rom. 7:15, 23), James seems more concerned with actual expression than with inward conflict, and so it seems more likely that his concern here is that selfish desires produce conflict between people. In any case, it certainly is true that the faithless/unbelieving internal war of covetousness and frustrated desires generates faithless/unbelieving outward conflict, jealousy, and even murder among people. This has been true in the world at large since the time of Cain and Abel; James's concern is that this ought not to be characteristic of the church, which should operate by God's peaceable wisdom.

The question and the answer set out in 4:1 are further developed in 4:2. The verb ἐπιθυμέω (*epithymeō*), like the English word *desire*, can be neutral, though it frequently, as here, refers to desire for the wrong things (cf. the use of the noun form ἐπιθυμία, *epithymia*, in 1:14). Despite the suggestion by Martin (1988: 144) that James is specifically addressing zealots who may actually have committed murder (see also Thompson 1976), "murder" (φονεύω, *phoneuō*) here almost certainly is hyperbolic or metaphorical, just as the "battles" (πόλεμοι, *polemoi*) of 4:1 are not real battles in which people are trying to kill one another.[2] But James (as also in 4:4 with the term "adulteresses," which Martin

1. Philo (*Decalogue* 28 §143) shows how this developed: "The appearance of what is at hand and regarded as good rouses and wakens the resting soul, and raises it to a state of great excitement, like a light flashing upon the eyes. This delight [ἡδονή] of the soul is called passion." Pleasure was seen to generate desire, which then produces sin (cf. James 1:14). The English word *lust* took a similar path. Originally, it meant "pleasure" or "delight" (cf. the German word *Lust*), but it came to mean "desire for pleasure" and then particularly "illicit sexual desire." In any case, 4:2 unambiguously identifies desire as the problem.

2. Erasmus conjectures that the text originally read φθονεῖτε (*phthoneite*, you envy) instead of φονεύετε (*phoneuete*, you murder). The two words sound quite similar, and φθονεῖτε suits the context better. It also then would echo a phrase in 1 Macc. 8:16, which fantastically describes preimperial Rome as having "no jealousy or envy [φθόνος οὐδὲ ζῆλος] among them." There is,

1988: 148 does not suggest is literal) probably intends some shock value to this: party spirit, contentiousness, and ambitious striving are not minor problems; they rank right up there with murder as a manifestation of evil.[3]

Animosity escalates when desire is frustrated. The structure of 4:2–3 is a series of short comments without conjunctions that seems to reflect this frustration and escalation and also to root it all in selfish desires and envy. It can be structured in a variety of ways, any of which can illustrate this principle:

> You desire and you do not have;
>> (so) you murder and envy
> and you are unable to obtain;
>> (so) you fight and make war;
> you do not have because you do not ask;
>> you ask and you do not receive because you ask from evil motives,
>>> to squander [what you ask for] on your pleasures.[4]

Although James does not include the word *so*, the structure seems to suggest that murder, jealousy, fighting, and war are derivatives of these self-centered desires, and that even good desires can become evil if motivated by the wrong reason.

"To squander" is expressed with ἵνα (*hina*) plus a subjunctive verb, which ordinarily expresses purpose. Here it might have more of a resultative force,

---

however, no textual basis for reading φθονεῖτε, and James elsewhere is not averse to hyperbole. It also comports with Jesus's declaration that wrath and disrespect are tantamount to murder (Matt. 5:21–22). See also the next note.

3. This is not the first time James connects murder and adultery. Schmitt (1986) points out that James may be picking up on 2:11, where to keep the commandment against adultery means nothing if one is violating the command against murder. It is interesting that in both 2:11 and 4:2–4 James's audience is firm on keeping the seventh commandment, but appears oblivious to the fact that their treatment of one another is in violation of the sixth commandment. Apparently, the problem of stressing sexual ethics and overlooking the ethics of interpersonal responsibility has been around for a long time.

4. Dibelius (1975: 218) has a similar structure, but bases it on the repetition of καὶ οὐ(κ) with a second-person plural verb ("and you do not . . ."):

> You desire—*and you do not* have, so you commit murder.
> You are jealous and envious—*and you do not* obtain.
> You fight and strive—*and you do not* have because you do not ask.
> You ask—*and you do not* receive because you ask with wrong motive.

But this plays loose with James's own placement of καί in other places in the sequence. Other commentators have suggested a 3-3-2-3 verbal structure:

> You desire, and do not have, so you commit murder.
> You are jealous and do not obtain, so you fight and strive.
> You do not have because you do not ask.
> You ask but do not receive because you ask with wrong motive.

The difficulty of resolving the question may itself indicate that James was not attempting to write poetically balanced lines, but simply was heightening the rhetorical effect by a series of statements juxtaposed without conjunctions (asyndeton; see BDF §494).

meaning "with the result that you squander on your pleasures." But it could also be specifying the evil motives for asking: "The reason your asking is evil is that you ask in order that you may squander it on your [illicit] pleasures." Asking for personal gratification is not asking in faith (1:5–6), and so the one asking cannot expect to receive (1:7).[5] James uses the evocative "squander" (δαπανάω, *dapanao*, spend freely, use up, destroy; BDAG 212) to remind readers that gratifying one's desire for pleasure does not build a person up, but instead works to the detriment of the squanderer.

The "world" in 4:4, as in 1:27, refers to the "system of human existence in its many aspects" (BDAG 562), in particular the sphere of desires, influences, and structures that draw a person's attention away from God. The "world" here is neither the physical universe per se, which is God's creation and therefore good,[6] nor human beings per se, who are made in God's image and whom God loves (implied by 3:9), but the ethos of life in opposition to, or disregard of, God and his kingdom. Thus, the problem for God's people is neither delight in the physical world nor love for humanity in its fallenness, but an attitude toward either the physical or the social world that puts it in the place of God.

4:4–6

Hence, the intention to be a friend of the world makes a person an enemy of God[7] because it puts the world in the place of God; it submits to the world's ethics and values instead of God's, desires the things of the world instead of God, and exalts the creature over the creator. James's application is that both those who have resources but spend them on their own "pleasures" and those who have not but want them for "pleasures" are indicted as "friends of the world," spiritual profligates.

The word for "friendship" (φιλία, *philia*) ordinarily means simply "affectionate regard" (LSJ 1934), but it can slide over into the semantic range of sexual love (cf. Prov. 5:19 LXX). Hence, when James berates the world's would-be "friends" as "adulteresses,"[8] he implies that flirting with the world is akin to spousal unfaithfulness.[9] In the OT idolatry sometimes was called "adultery" because Israel was represented as God's bride (especially in Hos. 1–3; but see also, e.g., Isa. 62:5; Ezek. 16:32; 23:45), and, like marriage, Israel's covenant relationship with God demanded exclusive fealty. Although James does not spell it out, he no doubt shares the conviction of other NT writers (e.g., John 3:29;

---

5. Augustine (*Tract. John* 73.1 [on John 14:10]) refers to James 4:3 and points out that if someone asks for something wrongly, God has mercy and withholds what was requested.

6. As God's creation, it remains good as such even after the fall, even though humankind's sin now sets the world askew (Rom. 8:19–22) and renders it inhospitable.

7. The friend of the world literally "is established" (καθίσταται, *kathistatai*) as God's enemy (see the commentary on 3:6).

8. The majority of manuscripts read "adulterers and adulteresses," presumably because a good number of James's readers could be assumed to be male; however, James is accusing his readers not of literal adultery but rather of spiritual unfaithfulness, and in the spiritual realm the people of God are his bride.

9. Another possibility is that James is evoking the image of the "adulterous woman" of Proverbs, particularly Prov. 30:20. See Schmitt 1986.

Eph. 5:28–32; Rev. 21:2) that the present-day community of faith, the people of God, is the bride of Christ, and hence idolatry or covenantal unfaithfulness of any kind is tantamount to adultery.[10] Coziness with the world and its values is not unknown in the church of our day either, and such coziness should be named for what it is: a manifestation of unbelief (nonfaith).

The word "intends" represents the verb βούλομαι (*boulomai*), which sometimes is translated "to wish" or "to want" (see BDAG 182, definition 1); but most often in the NT it has the force of purpose or intention (BDAG, definition 2).[11] James is referring not to a pensively wished-for friendship, though that would be bad enough. It is the outright intention to be the world's friend that makes a person God's enemy. Nevertheless, intentionality often begins with a wish, and even wishing to be friends with the world is as dangerous and stupid as a married person wishing to flirt with someone other than his or her spouse. Those who would be friends with the world thus stand in opposition to Abraham, whose faith made him a friend of God.[12]

We find 4:5 difficult for two reasons: first, its meaning is ambiguous; second, it appears to offer a quotation from Scripture, even though nothing quite like "the spirit that he caused to dwell in us yearns jealously" (or any other meaning that can be construed from the Greek) corresponds to any known text, canonical or otherwise. If we knew what text James had in mind, the ambiguity of the statement no doubt would be more easily resolved, but without a known context for reference, the meaning of the verse stands very much a mystery.

In terms of meaning, six issues need to be resolved:

1. How should the prepositional phrase πρὸς φθόνον (*pros phthonon*, for envy) be taken? Can God be said to do anything πρὸς φθόνον?
2. Is the "yearning" a virtuous longing or a vicious lusting?
3. Is the "spirit" the human spirit neutrally considered (breath of life, as in Genesis), a negative spirit active in humans (as in Eph. 2:2), or God's Spirit?
4. Did the original text read κατώκησεν (*katōkēsen*, he dwelt) or κατώκισεν (*katōkisen*, he caused to dwell)?
5. If causative, is God or the Spirit the subject of "yearns"?

---

10. Likewise when Jesus refers to "this generation" as "adulterous" in Mark 8:38 (see also Matt. 12:39) he marks their sign-seeking as a form of unfaithfulness, a departure from genuine faith.

11. Only rarely in the NT does it mean "to wish" or "to desire" (for which, usually θέλω, *thelō*, is used). Of the four instances (out of thirty-seven) in the NT for which BDAG gives the meaning "to wish," only one (Acts 25:22) is unambiguous. More importantly, James's own earlier use (1:18) clearly refers to God's intention, not his wishes. The noun form βουλή (*boulē*) always means "purpose, intention, resolution, decision," never "wish" or "desire" (BDAG 181–82).

12. See Johnson 1985. The notion that to be friends with the world is to be an enemy of God is rooted in the Jewish "two ways" tradition seen in the moral exhortation known as the Tabula of Cebes, and more importantly in the teaching of Jesus (Matt. 7:24–27), and in the early Christian discipleship manual the Didache (Did. 1–6).

6. How should the verse be punctuated? In other words, does πρὸς φθόνον begin a separate sentence, or does it delineate what the Scripture says?

These questions are interconnected, of course. The one easiest to deal with is the textual problem. The causative κατῴκισεν (*katōkisen*, he caused to dwell) is much likelier than κατῴκησεν (*katōkēsen*, he dwelt).[13] Although the Majority Text has the latter, the best, oldest, and most diverse groups of manuscripts have the causative. In addition, the earliest-known probable use of this passage in James by the early church is in Herm. *Mand.* 3.1 (see "External Indications and the Church's Reception" in the introduction), which has κατῴκισεν. Further, the verb is aorist in either case, and if not causative, then the aorist (the S/spirit that "dwelled" in us) seems out of place; we would expect either a present (the S/spirit that "dwells" in us) or a perfect (the S/spirit that "has taken up abode" in us).[14] Hence, "he has caused to dwell" almost certainly is what James intended.

This narrows the field of possible resultant meanings to basically the following five options:[15]

1. "The Spirit that God has caused to dwell in us [believers] yearns jealously" (i.e., God the Holy Spirit does not tolerate his people trying to be friends with the world).[16]
2. "God yearns jealously regarding the (Holy) Spirit that he has caused to dwell in us" (i.e., the threat of withdrawing the Holy Spirit hangs over those who want to become friends of the world; NASB).
3. "God yearns jealously regarding the breath of life that he has put within us" (i.e., God vehemently desires fealty from his human creatures generally; NRSV, ESV).

---

13. The κατῴκησεν/κατῴκισεν variation is partly due to the fact that they would have sounded almost identical, and the causative κατοικίζω is a much less common word. Since the latter is much better attested and much likelier to be changed to κατῴκησεν than the other way around, "caused to dwell" is the preferred reading. See Metzger 1994: 612.

14. Given the fading of the classical usage of the perfect tense in the Hellenistic period, this is not an ironclad argument, but James does know how to use the perfect (see, e.g., 5:2–4), so the aorist here contributes to the stronger probability of κατῴκισεν being original.

15. Laws (1980: 178) offers a sixth option, suggesting that 4:5 consists of two rhetorical questions, resulting in the following paraphrase: "Does scripture mean nothing? Is this (according to scripture) the way the human spirit's longing is directed, by envy?" The suggestion is interesting, but probably is impossible from a grammatical point of view, because the second question of the set, if it were a question, would be introduced by the particle μή (Davids 1982: 147), as James consistently does elsewhere. The counterargument, that the opening question of 4:5, however far it extends, also expects a negative answer but does not have μή, is irrelevant because the second-person verb in that case, δοκεῖτε (*dokeite*, do you think), carries with it a rhetorical interrogative force already. The third-person verb in the alleged question of the second half (ἐπιποθεῖ, *epipothei*, he yearns) does not.

16. This rendering would make the verse parallel to Gal. 5:17, which says that "the desires of the Spirit are against the flesh" (τὸ δὲ πνεῦμα [ἐπιθυμεῖ] κατὰ τῆς σαρκός, more literally rendered in the KJV as "the Spirit [lusteth] against the flesh").

4. "When the (human) spirit that God has caused to dwell in us yearns (for the pleasures of the world), envy (and thus fighting) is the result."

5. "The (human) spirit that God has caused to dwell in us yearns (for the world) enviously" (NIV).[17]

For making a choice among these options, the following considerations are relevant:

1. The context is that of decrying friendship with the world. God demands from his people an exclusive relationship, like that of a spouse, and if they seek to be friends of the world, they may be called "adulteresses." The first part of 4:5, "Or do you think the Scripture for no good reason[18] says . . . ," presents the second part of the verse as support for the warning against spiritual adultery. This would favor an approach that sees God's jealousy in view. On the other hand, the subject of humans lusting for the pleasures of the world, lust that leads to envy, certainly fits the verses leading up to 4:4.

2. The word for "yearn" (ἐπιποθέω, epipotheō) ordinarily refers to a virtuous emotion. It occurs nine times in the NT, each one carrying a positive connotation (e.g., longing for spiritual milk [1 Pet. 2:2]; longing to see someone [Rom. 1:11; 1 Thess. 3:6; 2 Tim. 1:4]; yearning for someone [Phil. 1:8; 2:26]).[19] Probably in view, then, is not a lust, but a virtuous desire.[20] Thus, it is not unlikely that God (or his Spirit) is the one who yearns, though in only one other place in the Greek Bible (Jer. 13:14) is God the subject of ἐπιποθέω, and it is a context of denial ("I will not yearn, says the Lord").

3. On the other hand, φθόνος (phthonos) ordinarily has negative connotations, being connected with the destructive attitudes of covetousness or envy. Johnson (1983: 334–41) insists that the word can have nothing other than a vicious meaning and therefore is inappropriate as a divine attribute. Although to a large extent φθόνος and ζῆλος (zēlos) are interchangeable

17. The NIV takes a somewhat paraphrastic approach. For "the spirit yearns enviously," the NIV reads, "the spirit . . . envies intensely," thus taking the verb ἐπιποθεῖ as functionally the modifier and πρὸς φθόνον as having the controlling verbal force. Such a grammatical transplacement certainly is defensible in light of James's penchant for Semitic constructions, but I think that the approach is wrong for other reasons.

18. The phrase "for no good reason" represents the single Greek word κενῶς, sometimes translated "vainly" or "in vain." It is the adverbial form of the adjective used for the vain or "empty" man in 2:20.

19. Ordinarily, ἐπιποθέω occurs with a dative or a prepositional phrase to indicate that which is longed for, but sometimes, as here, it occurs with an accusative in that capacity (e.g., Ps. 118:174 LXX [Ps. 119:174 MT]).

20. Of the dozen occurrences in the LXX, only in Sir. 25:21 and Ps. 61:11 (62:11 MT; 62:10 ET) do we find a somewhat negative use (yearning for a woman in Sirach, yearning for riches in the psalm), and even there it is not the word that carries the negative force, but that which is longed for.

and appear as synonyms (e.g., 1 Macc. 8:16), the former never occurs elsewhere as a term referring to God's jealousy.

4. We may note that James often is imprecise in his use of words. We have seen that in 4:1, 3 James uses the word ἡδοναί (*hēdonai*) in a way somewhat loosely related to the more precise meaning "pleasures." James employs phrases such as "cycle of generation" without regard to their technical meanings, sentences such as "He must show by good behavior his works in meekness of wisdom" that do not reward overly exact analysis, and illustrations such as "brackish water does not make sweet" and "where the will of the pilot wishes" that resist being pressed for precision. Therefore, the ordinary connotations of ἐπιποθέω and φθόνος are not decisive considerations.

5. The phrase πρὸς φθόνον (*pros phthonon*) may be read as adverbial and thus translated as "[he yearns] with envy" or "[he desires] jealously," or it may be understood as indicating where yearning leads, "to envy." If God or his Spirit is yearning, then the adverbial reading (God yearns jealously) is less awkward, but if the human spirit's envious desire is in view, then probably it is better read as pronouncing envy as the result of such desire, a pronouncement that connects well with 4:1–3.

6. The subsequent sentence "But he gives greater grace" assumes God as the subject, and for that reason, other things being equal, God, or possibly his Spirit, would be assumed also to be the subject of "yearns." If it were the human spirit longing, then one would have expected James to identify the new subject "God" in 4:6a. Once again, since James's language is imprecise, this should not be given too much weight, but when added to the other considerations, it favors God as the one who is "yearning."

7. As already noted, at issue is the danger and folly of wishing to be friends with the world. This is relevant only for those who would think of themselves as friends of God, that is, believers, and indeed James hints at this when he refers to God causing the S/spirit[21] to dwell "in us."[22] This nudges us either to God's S/spirit yearning for our fealty with jealousy or, better, to God yearning for the Spirit that he gave us. The former makes good

---

21. The ancient Greek manuscripts admitted of no capitalization to mark off the Spirit (Holy Spirit) from the general notion of spirit, which could be anything from a spirit of wisdom from God (which would, of course, be quite close to the notion of the Holy Spirit), to an evil spirit (a demon), to a "spirit of contentiousness" (i.e., a contentious attitude). The occasional use of the awkward "S/spirit" in succeeding paragraphs is an attempt to preserve this ambiguity of reference.

22. Admittedly, this is not decisive, since the "we" in 3:9 could be understood as humanity generally, and the "spirit" that he caused to dwell in us could simply be the "breath of life" that God puts into humans to make them alive. In support of the latter, one could point to the fact that the only other occurrence of "spirit" (*pneuma*) in James (2:26) is this "breath of life" without which a body is dead. But the problem here in James 4 focuses on the relation of God and believers. The problem in 3:9 likewise lies with those who claim to be God's children, who are both blessing God and cursing people. Those of the world on the outside, who make no claim to know God, do not "bless the Lord and Father."

sense, but although the latter appears unclear at first, I think that it is the correct approach.

The Holy Spirit is mentioned nowhere else in James, but Kirk (1969) has shown that in James "wisdom" functions similarly to the way πνεῦμα (*pneuma*, S/spirit) functions in Paul (see also excursus 3, "James and Wisdom"). More important, perhaps, is that James's Jewish environment frequently spoke of God's Spirit as the source and culmination of wisdom (Isa. 11:2; Dan. 5:14 Theod.; Wis. 7:7; 9:17; Sir. 39:6; Ps. Sol. 18.7; cf. Acts 6:3, 10). At Qumran, likewise, wisdom comes from having the S/spirit (1QS 9.14–15; 1QHᵃ 6.12–13 [García Martínez and Tigchelaar 1997–98: 1.153]), and since the S/spirit is the possession of those who enter the community, only its members can truly possess wisdom (1QS 11.5–6; CD-A 3.12–16). It is inconceivable that James, a Jew living in the first century, was unfamiliar with the concept of the S/spirit so prevalent in his Jewish thought world, a world that he is patently familiar with. Finally, although no passage in Scripture resembles James's text in 4:5b, a passage in Philo has certain similarities. In *Virtues* 39 §§215–19 Philo praises Abraham for panting after fellowship with God, who in reward gave him the Spirit, so that Abraham "was indwelt in his soul by the divine Spirit who was breathed down on him from above."[23] This S/spirit from God is the dispenser of ἀκήρατος ἐπιστήμη (*akēratos epistēmē*, pure understanding).[24] One can see several points of contact here. This S/spirit comes from above, is "breathed down" by God, and indwells in the soul and dispenses ἐπιστήμη, a lexical stem used only by James in the NT and appearing earlier in this context (3:13).

Hence, in my judgment, the "S/spirit he caused to dwell in us" is a reference to the divine S/spirit considered not as the person of the Holy Spirit but as the presence of God in divinely given wisdom and understanding, or what the OT called the "spirit of wisdom" with which the Messiah was to be anointed (Isa. 11:2) but that had already been given to leaders such as Joshua (Deut. 34:9) and even artisans such as Bezalel (Exod. 35:31). The jealousy with which God yearns over it reflects the common Jewish understanding that in order to keep the S/spirit, one must remain in submission to God (James 4:7), and that the divine S/spirit is unavailable to the proud.[25]

23. The Greek text reads as follows: τοῦ θείου πνεύματος ὅπερ ἄνωθεν καταπνευσθὲν εἰσῳκίσατο τῇ ψυχῇ (Philo, *Virtues* 39 §217). Although I am unable to reflect it in the translation, the operative verb, εἰσῳκίσατο, is causative, like κατῴκισεν. Abraham was caused to be indwelt by the S/spirit.

24. Dibelius (1975: 224) notes that in Hermas the holy πνεῦμα in a person is a "righteous" spirit that is pure and seeks meekness and peacefulness, and when this spirit withdraws, only evil spirits remain (Herm. *Mand.* 5.2.7). Dibelius connects this to the dualism of evil and good inclinations (*yĕṣārîm*), but James does not set some other "spirit" in opposition to the one that God put in humans.

25. This is also in line with the OT presentation in 1 Samuel of Saul, who received the divine S/spirit of power but did not retain it, largely because of pride. The concern of James, however, has to do with the more restricted matter of the impossibility of God's spirit of wisdom coexisting with the world's friendship, and thus he does not directly address the questions of whether a

Therefore, 4:5b basically reflects, as it were, an implied threat of withdrawal of the spirit of true wisdom. But James does not just utter threats; along with the threat, he reemphasizes God's grace. The grace that God gives is superior to the threat of withdrawal (cf. 2:13: "mercy triumphs over judgment"). The focus on God's graciousness as opposed to his wrath is picked up in a subsequent exhortation, "Draw near to God, and he will draw near to you" (4:8).

But why does James seem to indicate that this is something that Scripture says? One approach is to conclude that James thought that he was quoting an OT text but either remembered a text incorrectly or quoted a text that is no longer extant (Davids 1982: 164; Dibelius 1975: 223–24; Bauckham 2004: 277–81).[26] Those who take this approach sometimes admit that it is generated by the conclusion that no other option is viable. The aforementioned similarity to a sentence in Philo, which might itself be based on some traditional Jewish material, might give more credence to this approach, though still it should be a last resort.

A second approach, one that is available to those who think that 4:5b is speaking of God's jealousy, is to identify the quotation as a paraphrase of the explanation attached to the second commandment, "I the LORD your God am a jealous God" (Exod. 20:5), or other similar texts (e.g., Ezek. 8:3).

A third possibility is that James (or a source that he depends on) has heavily garbled a text that has the lexical elements of 4:5b but means something quite different. One possibility is Eccles. 4:4 in the Hebrew.[27] The second half of this verse has all or most of the necessary lexical components of James 4:5—envy, spirit (wind), vanity, desire—and the context in James is one of the linkage of envy and love of the world, which is similar to that of Eccles. 4. Perhaps James knew a garbled translation of the Hebrew, but at best this can only be conjecture, as no extant Greek translation of Ecclesiastes comes close to James 4:5b, and the similarity is only at the word level, not a similarity of meaning.

A fourth solution, proposed by Brosend (2004: 114), is that James is citing an otherwise unknown saying of Jesus, given that James has a fluid notion of γραφή (graphē, scripture). But although James extensively taps the material of the Jesus tradition, he never elsewhere calls it "scripture" or even indicates

temporarily disobedient but genuine Christian can "lose" the Holy Spirit, or whether hypocrites can have the Holy Spirit, or whether a true believer can lose salvation. These questions must be addressed from other passages of Scripture.

26. Ellis (1992: 153n67) suggests that James is alluding to an unknown Christian scripture. This is very unlikely if the Epistle of James is early, and even if it is late, there are no other indications that James knew of any other Christian writings (as opposed to traditions), unless it is so late that it is dependent on Hermas rather than the other way around (see footnote 40 in the introduction). But even if this were true, none of James's actual points of contact with Hermas is ever referred to as "Scripture" by James.

27. This verse is usually translated something like "Then I saw that all toil and all skill in work come from a man's envy of his neighbor. This also is vanity and a striving after wind" (ESV). The LXX also translates along these lines, and neither comes anywhere near the meaning of James's verse.

that he is quoting. There is no evidence that James's knowledge of the Jesus tradition comes from any written source that he might call "scripture," whereas twice he cites the OT and calls it "scripture" (2:8, 23) or otherwise indicates that he is citing (2:11; 4:6).

A fifth approach is not to take 4:5b as a quotation at all, but to put a full stop (in this case a question mark) after λέγει (legei, says; RV, ASV; see Laws 1973: 214; Johnson 1995: 280). The "scripture" in view, then, is not the clause "jealously he yearns for the S/spirit," but the Scripture quotation in 4:6. The first part of 4:5 is simply a general question, hence this reading: "Or do you think that scripture speaks for no good reason? The spirit that he caused to dwell in us yearns with jealousy, but the grace that God gives is greater, for it says, . . ."; or as Laws (1980: 178) has it, "Does scripture mean nothing? Is this (according to scripture) the way the human spirit's longing is directed, by envy?" This makes excellent sense, for the Proverbs quotation (Prov. 3:34) covers both the arrogant, who lust enviously, and the poor, to whom God gives grace. But can λέγει be rendered simply as "speaks"? In point of fact, James uses λέγει, or some form of it, twelve other times (1:13; 2:3 [2x], 11 [2x], 14, 16, 18, 23; 4:6, 13, 15), and every single one of these introduces either direct or indirect discourse. Add to this the fact that nowhere else in the NT is λέγει easily rendered "speaks," and whenever ἡ γραφὴ λέγει or its equivalent occurs, it is followed by a direct quotation (the one exception is John 7:38, where apparently it is an indirect quotation). Further, the technique of juxtaposing two Scriptures to elucidate an issue, or using one Scripture to interpret another, is a typical Jewish exegetical approach, already seen in James 2:21, 23, which juxtaposes Gen. 22:1–18 and Gen. 15:6, and which we will again see in 5:4–5 and 5:20. All of this certainly gives the reader a strong impression that James 4:5b is understood to be something from Scripture.

Johnson (1985: 280) resolves the issue by concluding that "the reference for this speaking is taken to be the explicit quotation in 4:6 from Prov. 3:34," and so "scripture says" eventually does connect with an actual quotation. However, this is not a natural way of reading λέγει. The natural reading of the verse is that 4:5b expresses the content of what "scripture" says.

Carpenter (2001) offers a more persuasive variation of this approach. He agrees with Johnson that the "scripture" in question is the upcoming citation in 4:6, the two halves of which encompass both the "longing jealously" and the "giving more grace."

4:5b–6a	4:6b (= Prov. 3:34)
Jealously God yearns for the Spirit	God resists the proud
but gives greater grace	but gives grace to the humble

The key is the first word in 4:6—in the Greek text μείζονα (meizona, greater)—and James's point is that God's jealousy is surpassed by God's grace. Thus, 4:5b is not just an intervening parenthetical remark; it is an applicational reference to the first part of the citation of Prov. 3:34, just as 4:6a is an applicational reference to the second half of the citation. Such a paraphrasing of content for applicational purposes is known elsewhere in the NT. The aforementioned John 7:38 apparently is a reflective comment on an extrapolation or application of a Scripture that John did not quote, since no actual text says, "Out of his heart will flow rivers of living water."[28] Thus, James 4:5b is not a quotation, but an interpretive gloss on "God resists the proud."

Admittedly, this does not solve all the problems, but it does have the fewest difficulties and directs attention away from a hypothetical document and toward James's interpretive use of the OT. I would offer only one alteration to Carpenter's analysis. As already indicated, I think that instead of the created "spirit" or natural life of humans, James has in mind the spirit of wisdom (the "from above" type of wisdom), which God gives to the humble who ask (cf. 1:5) and withholds from the proud.

James concludes this first section of the third discourse with a series of imperatives, all of a wisdom type, that unpacks the application stemming from the citation of Prov. 3:34.

4:7–10

First, if the humble are the recipients of grace, it is imperative to submit to God (4:7) and be humbled (4:10) before him. As God resists the proud, so believers are to resist the devil (cf. 1 Pet. 5:8–9),[29] the quintessential architect and archetype of pride. It is the devil who fosters jealousy and ambition, offers a fake wisdom and a false faith, and brews a broth of discord and contention and murderous envy to sap the church's vitality and undermine its integrity. The appropriate response to the demonic urge is to not give in to it. Since the gift of grace is greater than the threat of withdrawal, if we draw near to God, he will draw near to us. Further, as a practical matter, it is by drawing near to God that one can successfully dispense with the motivation to achieve success at the expense of others. One can ask rightly instead of from evil motives (4:3) and can set aside the bickering and bellicosity that so easily undermine the faith of the community (4:1–2).

Submission to God is impossible without resistance to the devil, and probably James is intentionally connecting these things. Submission to God involves two actions:

1. Resist the devil, and (i.e., with the result that)[30] he will flee from you.
2. Draw near to God, and (i.e., with the result that) he will draw near to you.

28. Carpenter (2001: 201) also refers to Jude 17–18, where Jude appears to be summarizing and applying the content of apostolic teaching rather than citing some source.
29. The necessity of resisting the devil is found elsewhere in Judaism as well (T. Iss. 7.7; T. Dan 5.1; T. Naph. 8.4). Also, T. Dan 6.2 has the injunction "Draw near to God."
30. The καί in 4:7b and 4:8a, as well as in 4:10, occurring between an imperative verb and a future indicative verb, expresses what will result if the imperative is obeyed. Thus, "[If] you resist the devil, [then] he will flee. . . . [If] you draw near to God, [then] he will draw near. . . . [If] you are humbled before the Lord, [then] he will exalt you." This idiom is the same in English as in Greek and needs no further comment, except to note that such construction is more typical of axiomatic sayings than of discourse generally. See BDF §442.7.

This prepares the reader for the call to "sinners" and "double-minded" (δίψυχοι, *dipsychoi*) to purify their hands and sanctify their hearts, that is, to repent (4:9–10). As noted earlier in 1:8, double-mindedness basically is unbelief, and it stands in contrast to wholeness (being τέλειος, *teleios*, perfect). The demand for the "double-minded" to sanctify (make holy) their hearts recalls here the command in Deut. 6:5 (cited by Jesus as the greatest commandment; Matt. 22:37 and pars.) to love God with the whole (i.e., undivided) "soul" (ψυχή, *psychē*).

In 4:9 we have an echo of Jesus's warning in Luke 6:25 NAB: "Woe to you who are filled now, for you will be hungry. Woe to you who laugh now, for you will grieve and weep."[31] Luke 6:26 NAB continues with "Woe to you when all speak well of you. . . ." It is quite possible James has this word of Jesus in mind, since this paragraph in James is addressed to the "two-souled" (cf. 1:8), those with divided loyalties, who "sit on the fence," unwilling to make a wholehearted commitment to God,[32] that is, those without genuine, active faith. Further, the people of whom, in Jesus's words, "all men speak well" typically are the wealthy or those with worldly power. But James holds out hope for even such (4:10). Thus, the call to "abase yourselves" is not just a rhetoric of anger, but a genuine call to repent, because such repentance and self-humbling will eventuate in God's lifting up of the sinner who repents. Indeed, all genuine faith begins with repentance (Matt. 4:17; Acts 17:30). This again suits James's emphasis that God's grace surpasses his threats, just as his mercy triumphs over judgment (2:13).

Additional Notes

4:1. The word πόλεμοι refers to larger military engagements (battles or wars), whereas μάχαι typically refers to engagements between individuals or smaller groups (fights, contests). A sword fight between two individuals is a μάχη; an engagement of two armies, or even a full-scale war, is a πόλεμος. The use of both terms may indicate that conflict in the churches involves both individual animosities and party antipathy. The two terms may correspond to the two characteristics of earthly wisdom noted in 3:14 (jealousy triggers individual conflict, and ambition generates party strife), but this may be pressing the precision of language beyond what James customarily employs.

4:4. As mentioned above in note 8, some scribes (a corrector of ℵ, P, Ψ, the Majority Text, et al.) added "adulterers and," apparently believing that James was speaking of literal adulteresses and thinking it strange that only women were mentioned.

4:5. The ingenious but unlikely suggestion by Spitta (1896: 121–22) that the "enviously the spirit longs" quotation is from the lost book of Eldad and Modad is based on a connection between the Lord giving greater grace (4:6) and the situation in Num. 11:24–29, where after the Spirit is given to the seventy elders outside the camp, and to Eldad and Modad inside it, Moses warns the accusers of Eldad and Modad against "jealousy." This complicated hypothesis, being impossible to disprove (barring the rediscovery of the lost book in question), carries little conviction.

31. Moo (2000: 195) observes that this call to repentance may also be an echo of Joel 2:12.

32. Oecumenius, in *Commentary on James* (PG 119:497), points out that James's term "double-minded" describes people who do not wish to live committedly.

4:6–10. Based on the quotation of Prov. 3:34, this section is closely paralleled in 1 Pet. 5:5–9, which likewise links humility before God and resisting the devil, suggesting that this moral application of Prov. 3:34 was a Christian or Jewish homiletic commonplace.

4:9–10. Grammars, especially older ones (e.g., MHT 3:76; BDF §337.1), sometimes press the aorist tense of the imperatives here and identify these as ingressive: "become wretched . . . begin to mourn . . ." and so on. One must be cautious about putting too much weight on the aorist tense as such (see Stagg 1972), but it is true that here James is calling for a change from the current state to a new one.

4:9b. "Turn your laughter into mourning" is in Greek another third-person imperative (see the second additional note on 1:5). The force of the imperative is ambiguous, however (cf. the parenthetical sentence in Wallace 1996: 486n97). It could be pronouncing a condemnation, and in that case the English third-person imperative works: "Your laughter be turned into mourning." Given that the context is condemning the "double-minded," James here may be anticipating the upcoming woe oracles of 4:13–5:6. This approach also corresponds more closely to the dominical woe upon which it may be based (Luke 6:25). However, since 4:9b occurs within a series of second-person imperatives, and since the context is one of urging people in the community to repent, not the pronouncing of doom upon the faithless, I have taken it as equivalent to a second-person command (cf. NIV: "Change your laughter to mourning").

B. Part 2: Defamation and Censure (4:11–12)

The next brief paragraph continues the discourse on strife, but from a different angle. The desire for the world is not the only cause of dissension; there is also the matter of defaming and censuring one another. Here we face again the evil capacity of speech, and thus we return to the concern introduced in 3:1–12. James echoes the teaching of Jesus (as well as that of Paul) in warning against slander and judging. It appears to be a problem endemic to the Christian community.

Exegesis and Exposition

¹¹Do not slander one another, brothers. The one who slanders a brother, or judges his brother, slanders the law and judges the law. But if you judge the law, you are not a doer of the law but a judge. ¹²There is one lawgiver ⌜and judge⌝, who is able to save and to destroy. But who are you to judge your neighbor?

4:11–12   James does not give up on his hearers. Despite the preceding rhetoric in 4:1–10 castigating people for being "adulteresses" and "double-minded," he returns to calling them "brothers" in 4:11. This is not an indication of shift of audience; it simply marks the speech of a pastor reminding his flock that despite his strong rhetoric, he acknowledges them as his siblings in the Lord. And so should they regard one another as brothers and sisters and act accordingly, with concern but not judgment and certainly not slander.

The word rendered "slander" (καταλαλέω, *katalaleō*) is commonly used in the LXX, as well as in other Second Temple Jewish literature (e.g., T. Gad 3.3), to describe both public false accusation or disparagement and more private or covert grumbling (Johnson 1995: 292–93; Dibelius 1976: 228; but see Laws 1980: 186–87). Slander and judgmentalism are close cousins. Many slanderers probably are unaware that they are spreading falsehood; they believe their negative accusations and censorious remarks to be reasonably well founded, and they may even see themselves as having a special calling to inform the world of someone's evil or to preserve a church's purity by excising its less-than-perfect members. To spread accusations or publish unproven allegations is, however, in effect to act as a sentencing judge, but without authorization and probably also without adequate information. Slander indirectly imposes censure because the wider community is implicitly being encouraged to ostracize the accused person, who may very well be innocent. But the more important issue is that no individual in the community is in any position to judge the spiritual condition of another.[1] This does not mean that one should never denounce sin or criticize fellow believers (cf. Moo 2000: 198)—here James himself is doing so—but that one should not spread abroad accusations, cast aspersions, or defame or denigrate persons or their motives.

Why does James say that judging a fellow believer is judging the law? Because a judge, by applying law, effectively makes law. Human judges apply and make human law, but who is authorized to apply and make divine law? There can be only one judge of divine law because only he can "save and destroy," that is, carry out the sanctions of divine law.

But how is slandering a fellow believer slandering the law? It does what the law specifically prohibits.[2] To set one's own judgments over the law is implicitly a denigration of the law. This should be a sobering thought because those within the church who slander their brothers and sisters often see themselves as upholding and safeguarding the word of God.

In 4:12 we come to the closing proverb for this section, with a rhetorical question attached. The "one lawgiver and judge" is in Jewish theology the Lord himself, who gave the law through Moses, and who one day will judge all the people of the earth. God stands at both the beginning and the end of redemptive history; his justice is both the standard of, and the motivation for, obedience. The sober reminder that God is the one judge who can save and destroy calls to mind Jesus's admonition "Fear him who can destroy both soul and body in hell" (Matt. 10:28).

In the Christian context this judge is Jesus (see James 5:9), and we have already seen how frequently Jesus's lawgiving activity so apparent in Matthew is reflected in James. In this very context, by using πλησίον (*plēsion*, neighbor) as the one who ought not to be judged, instead of ἀδελφός (*adelphos*, brother) as in the previous verses, James probably is alluding to Jesus's declaration of Lev. 19:18 to be the "second great" commandment (Matt. 22:39). Johnson (1982: 397) observes that the love command as found in Lev. 19:18 itself specifically forbids judging and slander: "You shall not take vengeance or bear a grudge [slander?] against the sons of your own people, but you shall love your neighbor as yourself: I am the LORD."

Additional Notes

4:12. The majority of manuscripts lack the words "and judge," but all the best and earliest manuscripts except for 𝔓[74] include it, and the context of James seems to demand it.[3]

---

1. Here James is not concerned with how the community as a whole may deal with a member who has trouble with some sin, but in 5:19–20 he does recognize a place for correcting a fellow believer. Rebuking and correcting someone because of love is quite different from slandering and judging, which are generated by different motives, usually jealousy or ambition.

2. Here James echoes a theme found elsewhere in Jewish wisdom literature. Sirach 28:7, for example, equates the judgment of one's neighbor with a disavowal of the commandments.

3. Only one additional uncial, 049 (ninth century), omits "and judge," though a majority of the minuscules do so.

4:12. The articular participle in the phrase ὁ δυνάμενος σῶσαι may be taken substantively, in apposition to lawgiver and judge ("the lawgiver and judge, [namely] the one who is able to save and destroy"), or, as rendered in the translation above, as attributive to νομοθέτης καὶ κρίτης, whether or not the latter has an article[4] (BDF §412.3).

4. 𝔓⁷⁴, B, P, and some others omit it, but ℵ and most other manuscripts include it. Its presence or absence has no significant effect on the sense.

VI. Interjection: Two Oracles of Warning (4:13–5:6)

With his return to the "evils of speech" theme in 4:11–12, James has concluded the discourse on strife within the church. Whereas all the major discourses in James are explicitly addressed to "brothers," the next two paragraphs, introduced with "Come now" (4:13–17; 5:1–6), are not. Although these two sections are distinct, they expound the same theme: the foolishness of selfish, earthly "wisdom" that pursues wealth and success by worldly means, ignoring God's ethical imperatives. Both sections thus serve as examples. The merchant who is self-reliant instead of having faith in God, and the landowner who is self-indulgent rather than faithful (showing faith) in dealing with fellow human beings, are paradigms of unbelief (lack of true faith). Both fail to look to God for life, wisdom, and security.

The lack of a specific address to "brothers" does not resolve the question of the identity of addressees of the oracles. As part of this letter, the intended hearers are those who claim faith in Christ. Does this passage condemn outsiders (non-Christians) at a distance as a means of comforting believers by reminding them that their rich oppressors are going to get their comeuppance? Or are there in fact some rich Christians in the community whom James is sternly warning? Whether or not James had in mind specific landowners or merchants who claimed to be Christians, both this passage and 5:1–6 function rhetorically. Although certainly there was no shortage of arrogant merchants and oppressive landowners, these are presented primarily as foils in contrast with genuine lives of faith. James's intent is not so much to blast particular wealthy people as to encourage poor believers, reminding them that the time of eschatological reversal is coming, and that those self-sufficient merchants and rich landowners whom the Christians may be tempted to envy or, worse, emulate are teetering on the brink of destruction. On the other hand, those who claim faith in Christ and are merchants or landlords should take great care that they not find their own behavior described here.

These two paragraphs are typical of OT "woe" oracles (see, e.g., Isa. 5:8–23; Amos 5:16–20; 6:1–7; Hab. 2:6–19), a form that Jesus also used (e.g., Matt. 23:13–29). Note especially the parallels with the oracle of Amos 8:4–6:

Amos 8:4–6	James 4:13–5:6
Hear this	Come now
you trample the needy	you defraud your workers
you bring the poor to an end	you murder the righteous

Amos 8:4–6	James 4:13–5:6
in the land	[you take pleasure] on the earth/land
you cannot wait to go make money	we will go make money
using deceitful scales and measures	defrauding the laborers

But the closest to an actual quotation in this section, in James 5:4, is the Greek translation of Isa. 5:9: "These things were heard in the ears of the Lord of hosts" (NETS; the Hebrew is slightly different).[1] Isaiah 5 is also a woe oracle or series of oracles that, like the James passage, berates the deceitful acquisition of wealth and property, the oppression of the poor, and a general disinterest in what the will of the Lord is.

Such oracles tend to utter broad condemnations using specific representative illustrations; hence, although James could have had in mind some real people (ambitious merchants and oppressive landlords were no more scarce in the ancient Mediterranean region than they are today), it is more likely that he is using types that are broadly representative of the set of attitudes that characterizes successful people such as merchants and landowners. Hence, these warnings are applicable to more than self-made merchants who think that they have control of their lives or to rich landowners who are tardy in paying wages. Anyone who pursues a career or runs a business without reference to God's will, or who controls property or makes investments without reference to God's ethical concerns and in defiance of his principles of equity, is subject to James's opprobrium. James delivers an illustratively dressed censure of all spiritually blind or socially oppressive behavior as part of a reminder that God's judgment is real.

However, the primary intention of the passage is, as already noted, not to upbraid godless merchants or unjust landowners, but to encourage and instruct believers. These oracles serve as a reminder that human life and wealth (and poverty too) are transient, and that God is aware of the plight of the poor. He is a God who helps the poor, and the day of reversal is at hand (this is made explicit in 5:7). Wealth and power are both nugatory and dangerous, because wealth and power, by facilitating self-reliance and self-indulgence, tend to run contrary to faith.

---

1. Both James 5:4 and Isa. 5:9 LXX use the phrase εἰς τὰ ὦτα κυρίου σαβαώθ, which does have a counterpart in the MT.

A. Oracle 1: Warning to Merchants (4:13–17)

The first group to be addressed is merchants or businesspeople. Whereas 5:1–6 appears in an entirely negative light, 4:13–17 might be understood as addressing Christians. Some commentators (e.g., Moo 2000: 201) have argued that 4:15, which indicates what merchants ought to do, makes no sense if addressed to non-Christians, and therefore 4:13–17 is speaking to Christian merchants. Others argue that the scathing indictment of oppressive landowners in 5:1–6 would be appropriate only if speaking of unbelievers, regardless of their professed faith, and the close parallelism of 4:13–17 and 5:1–6, plus the fact that in these sections James does not address his target as "brothers," suggest that James does not think of the merchants in 4:13–17 as Christians either.

Whether or not James has in his purview actual Christian merchants, it is true that today there are merchants who claim to be Christians, and they may very well need to be reminded of the tenuousness of life and transitoriness of wealth. Planning for the future is wise, not evil, but planning without acknowledging or consulting God, or without reference to his ethical precepts, or, even worse, boasting of one's independent planning (4:16) is both foolish and wicked. So even if James is not urging actual merchants (or actual landowners in James 5) to repent, any merchants and landowners who regard themselves as Christian but fit the description need to apply his words that way.[1]

Exegesis and Exposition

[13]Come now, you who say, "Today or tomorrow we will go to some city or other, stay there a year, and do business and make money." [14⌜]You do not know what your life will be like tomorrow. For you are but a wisp that appears briefly and then disappears.⌝ [15]Instead you should be saying, "If the Lord approves, ⌜ ⌝ we will live [this way] and do this or that." [16]As it is, you glory in your arrogant acts. All such glorying is wicked. [17]Therefore, if someone knows a good thing to do and does not do it, to him it is sin.

"Come now" is an interjection that James seems to use with the force of an upbraiding call to attention (see the additional note on 4:13). Each of the two sections (4:13–17; 5:1–6) is introduced with this call, with a vocative, very

      4:13–14

---

1. Perhaps "instead you should be saying" could be regarded as a call to repentance, but the focus of the passage is simply on rebuke, not exhortation.

much like Jesus's woe oracles in Matt. 23:13–29 and Luke 11:42–52.[2] In no way is James mincing words in these paragraphs.

Ordinarily, the success of merchants lies in their ability to travel, negotiate for the purchase of goods where they are plentiful and cheap, and take them somewhere else where they are rare and expensive, thus not only covering travel expenses, but also making a profit. Planning is of the essence of such activity. But James, as a wisdom teacher, calls merchants, along with anyone else who makes plans, to remember the tenuousness of life and the uncertainty of all plans, and to acknowledge God as the ultimate source of any good that one might receive. Thus, there is no room for merchants or other planners to boast in their acuity.

The force of τήνδε τὴν πόλιν (*tēnde tēn polin*), translated here as "some city or other," is closer to "this or that city" (NIV) than the more common English translation "such and such a city" (Ropes 1916: 276; cf. ESV, RSV, NASB). The translation given here preserves both the indefiniteness and the plurality of possible places for doing business, just as "today or tomorrow" expresses the indefiniteness and plurality of possible times.

The first part of 4:14 sometimes is understood as a comment, "You do not know what tomorrow will bring," followed by a rhetorical question, "What is your life?" (cf. RSV, ESV, NIV). The translation given here takes "what your life is" as the object of "you do not know" and "tomorrow" as adverbial. The original text had no punctuation, making it difficult to tell. In favor of the former is the second half of 4:14, which appears to be answering the question "What is your life?" which would expect the answer "It is a wisp." But James does not say, "It [your life] is a wisp"; he says, "You are a wisp."[3] In any case, James is calling attention to the uncertainty of life and the consequent foolishness of making plans apart from God, because no one knows the future.

The word for "wisp" (ἀτμίς, *atmis*) is as ambiguous in Greek as "wisp" is in English. It can refer to smoke, as in Gen. 19:28, but the more specific word for *smoke* is καπνός (*kapnos*), so sometimes the Greek OT refers to an ἀτμὶς καπνοῦ, a wisp or cloud of smoke (Joel 3:3 LXX [2:30 ET]; cf. Acts 2:19). The word ἀτμίς in the plural is used in Sir. 43:4 to refer to the hot "vapors" (NETS) emanating from the sun, or it can sometimes refer to breath (Wis. 7:25). James's use of the word points to the evanescence of human life and resembles Hos. 13:3, which describes the fate of the idolatrous Ephraimites: "Therefore they shall be like the morning mist or like the dew that goes early away, like the chaff that swirls from the threshing floor or like smoke [ἀτμίς in the LXX] from a window." James's point is that since human plans and even their own existence in this world are nugatory and quickly disappear,

---

2. Even though Jesus directly addresses those upon whom these woes were coming, their inclusion in the written Gospels gives them the same kind of character as James's words; such oracles both warn and encourage believers by reminding them of God's judgment, which for them is an event both sobering and desired.

3. This assumes that the original text read ἐστε, which is uncertain. See the additional note on 4:14.

merchants, as well as everyone else, ought to take thought for larger matters, matters having to do with faith in and subservience to the will of God, who lasts forever (cf. Ps. 37:20). Similar characterization of life, particularly the life of the wicked, is seen in the image of "chaff" in Ps. 1:4; 35:5.

James exhorts his audience to have as a normal attitude a readiness to seek God's will in all actions and plans, that is, to live a life of faith, not autonomy. Such an attitude is not just a matter of inserting "D.V." (*Deus volente*, God willing) in sentences declaring one's intentions or future plans; it involves the continuing, ongoing recognition (the word "saying" [λέγειν, *legein*] is a progressive infinitive) that all of life's activities have an ethical component, derived from the fact that all human acts are either in obedience or in disobedience to God. 4:15

"If the Lord approves" usually is translated more literally as "if the Lord wills" and often is taken as an acknowledgment of dependency on God's decretive will, whereby God decrees or purposes whatever happens, as though it meant "If God has foreordained it, we will live and do this or that." As the adage goes, "Man proposes, God disposes." Such expressions were fairly common in both Jewish and Hellenistic literature (see the references in Ropes 1916: 277; Dibelius 1975: 233–34). This also appears to be the way "if the Lord wills" is used by Paul in 1 Cor. 4:19 (cf. Acts 18:21). Certainly, a recognition of dependency on God entails a recognition that one cannot do anything unless God intends it to happen.

Rarely, however, does James show any interest in God's decretive will;[4] his primary interest is on obedience to God's revealed ethical will (e.g., 1:25; 2:8). We have seen over and over that James will use a Hellenistic-sounding phrase or illustration not in its usual sense, but with a sense more in line with his Jewish wisdom tradition. And if James were advocating nothing more than a passive acceptance of whatever God sends, it would be out of character of the rest of the letter. More likely, James is indicating that merchants and others need to be conscious of and sensitive to God's declared *ethical* will (i.e., his law) when making plans.[5] Such a consciousness is commensurate with genuine faith. Not all plans are easily identified as either clear obedience or clear disobedience to God's revealed ethical will, but all human actions do have an ethical dimension, and if these actions do not proceed from a faithful

---

4. The one clear instance is 1:18, where God purposed "to bring us forth by the word of truth." One other possible occasion is in 5:11, where the τὸ τέλος κυρίου (*to telos kyriou*, the Lord's goal) might refer to the decretive purposes of God for Job, but even there the interest is not Job's submission to the abstract notion of God determining whatsoever comes to pass, but his endurance in spite of not comprehending what God's purpose was, or not knowing how God would restore justice. Also, as I will argue later, it is more likely that τὸ τέλος κυρίου in 5:11 is not the Lord's purpose in sending the suffering, but rather is the "end of the story that God had in mind," a reference to the conclusion of the matter that occurs at the end of Job.

5. James's use of the word θέλω (*thelō*, wish, desire) rather than βούλομαι (*boulomai*, determine, purpose) here does not prove the ethical reading that I propose, but it does slightly favor it. Note that in 1:18, which does refer to God's intent or purpose, James uses βούλομαι.

intention to obey God, they are sin (cf. Rom. 14:23). This reading fits much better with the summary apophthegm in 4:17 ("*Therefore*, if someone knows a good thing to do and does not do it, to him it is sin"), to which otherwise it is hard to see the connection. Further, the fact that the specific activities of the rich described in the following paragraph (5:1–6) are clearly unethical acts in violation of God's law suggests that the ethical dimension of "if the Lord wills" is at the heart of the matter.

Admittedly, the verb "we will live" (ζήσομεν, *zēsomen*) does not sound at first like an ethical decision or a submission to God's command (see the additional note on 4:15). It may be arguable that James is teaching that the attitude of faith recognizes dependency on both God's decretive and his ethical will, and perhaps the two future verbs reflect these two aspects of God's will: "If God decrees it, we will live," and "If God approves of it, we will do this or that." But the phrase "If the Lord wills, we will live and do" is best understood not as a prediction of future life, but as shorthand for "We will live in accordance with God's righteous revealed will, and in conformity to it we will do this or that." At the very least, the acknowledgment that God is sovereign in life implies not that one should make no plans, but that one should consciously seek to know God's ethical will when making those plans.

Note also that, unlike the generalized "if God wills" that might be comparable to the phrase "if the gods will" found in Greek moralists or the "in shāʾ Allāh" of Islam, James says, "If the *Lord* wills." This marks a difference from the general Hellenistic idea (contra Ropes 1916: 279–80, who regards this verse as "of strictly heathen origin") in that for James it is the personal and unique sovereign God in covenant with his people who wills this or that. Furthermore, for James, "Lord" refers either to the Lord Jesus (1:1; 2:1; and see the commentary on 5:7) or to God the Father seen in terms of his relationship with his people, and in either case the term signifies one to whom obedience is due. It therefore is more likely that the "Lord's will" to which James is referring, the "will" to which merchants or anyone ought consciously to be subjecting their plans, is discerned by reference to the ethical instruction found in the teachings of Jesus Christ, teachings that, as we have noted, are repeatedly echoed in James. This submission to Jesus's instruction is essential to faith (2:1). Further, Jesus himself taught his disciples to pray "Thy will be done" (Matt. 6:10), which is not a resignation to "Whatever will be, will be," but a declaration of submission to the heavenly Father (Matt. 26:42) and a desire that his ethical will be done "as it is in heaven."

4:16　Here James clearly echoes Prov. 27:1: "Do not boast about tomorrow, for you do not know what a day may bring." "You glory in your arrogant acts" is literally "you glory in your arrogances." Some translations understand the phrase "in your arrogances" to be adverbially qualifying the boasting; that is, it describes the boasting as being done in an arrogant fashion. But ordinarily when the preposition ἐν (*en*, in) with the dative follows the verb καυχάομαι (*kauchaomai*, to boast, rejoice, glory), it indicates the object of the glorying or boasting. Thus, in Gal. 6:14 Paul boasts "in the cross"; in 1 Cor. 1:31 and 2 Cor. 10:17, referring to Jer. 9:24, he commands, "Let the one who boasts, boast in the Lord"; and in Rom. 5:11 he "rejoices in God." Hence, the sinful boasting in question here probably is the merchants' glorying in their own arrogant acts, their self-reliant successes in handling their affairs independently from God.

For the verb "glory" (καυχάομαι, *kauchaomai*), see the commentary on 1:9. Note the irony here: the merchants in view are proud when they ought to be ashamed. A mind-set of independence from God is the opposite of faith; it is both foolish and wicked.

At 4:17 we have the closing proverb for the first oracle. It is introduced by "therefore" (οὖν, *oun*), and so presumably it is a conclusion that can be drawn from the preceding verses. However, it is difficult to see how the general truth of 4:17 can be drawn from the exhortation to merchants not to glory in their entrepreneurial ability or independence (Dibelius 1975: 235 regards it as unrelated, the οὖν being a remnant from a different context). But if 4:15 is given the ethical reading suggested above, then the proverb is applicable; James has simply moved from a particular problem to a general principle. The merchants in question ought to know better, and thus they sin when they make plans without reference to God. Certainly, believers know better, yet often they act and plan as though God were not in the picture. It is therefore legitimate to apply the proverb broadly: in every dimension of life, to neglect doing what we know we should do, or to neglect to seek to know what God would have us do, is as much a sin as doing what we already know we should not.

4:17

Additional Notes

4:13. The idiom ἄγε νῦν is reasonably well attested in classical Greek literature, an interjectory expression roughly equivalent to our "Come now!" (LSJ 7). According to BDAG 9, it appears characteristically in the Greek comedies. The similar ἄγε δή ("Come then!") occurs in the LXX (Judg. 19:6 Codex Vaticanus) in the context of an invitation to enjoy hospitality. But "come now" seems somewhat tamer than the tone of the rest of the paragraph, which seems to call for something almost like the "Woe!" (Gk. οὐαί) used by Jesus in his denunciations and calls to repentance. Of course, οὐαί itself is not a Greek word, but a transliteration of the Hebrew אוֹי or הוֹיָה, which sound somewhat like ἄγε.[6] Although the νῦν with ἄγε indicates that James was consciously using the Greek interjectory expression (and he was familiar with the LXX's frequent use of οὐαί), it is possible that, because of its similarity to the Hebrew, he was giving it a force more like אוֹי than the "come now" that occurs in Greek plays, just as he gives other Greek phrases a peculiarly Jewish spin (e.g., τροχὸς τῆς γενέσεως). Note also the shift of number from singular (ἄγε) to plural (οἱ λέγοντες), which suggests that ἄγε is being used as a call to attention rather than an imperative verb proper. I have not, however, translated it "woe," because, at least in the case of traveling merchants, the condemnation is not outright and could be seen as an invitation to merchants to repent, to adopt a different attitude in how and why

---

6. The pronunciation of ancient Greek is debated, but Greek *gamma* (γ) almost certainly was pronounced more like the English *y* than *g*, and vowels in any language are the feature most subject to regional dialectic variation.

they do their business. Further, James's Greek-speaking audience probably would have heard it with its familiar Greek meaning.

4:14. This verse has a complex textual condition, further complicated by the possibility of different punctuations. There are six issues: (1) whether the genitive phrase τῆς αὔριον is preceded by the article τό (ℵ, Ψ, and Majority Text), τά (A, P, 33, and many others), or none (B); (2) whether the interrogative particle ποία is followed by a γάρ (many important manuscripts, including 𝔓[74] and a corrector of ℵ include it, but the original of ℵ and B, along with several other manuscripts and versions, omit it); (3) whether there is a γάρ following ἀτμίς (A, 33, and other manuscripts omit it); (4) the absence of the article ἡ in B, 1739, and others; (5) variation in the verb between ἐστέ, ἔσται, and ἐστίν; and (6) the omission in ℵ of the entire phrase ἀτμὶς γάρ ἐστε. We will take these in reverse order.

The unique omission in ℵ (issue 6) is likely to be accidental. The variations in the verb (issue 5) can be explained by the fact that αι and ε sounded similar; the weight of external evidence is on the side of the second plural, and it is more likely that a scribe would have changed to a third singular than the other way around, since the question "What is your life?" expects the answer "It is a breath" (Metzger 1994: 613–14). The article ἡ (issue 4) that links ἀτμίς and its participle has no great effect on the meaning, but its presence is slightly better attested than its absence. Of the two occurrences of γάρ (issues 2 and 3), the second is better attested, and the first is more likely to have been added later to make it clear that "What is your life?" stands as an independent question rather than depends upon "you understand." The article before τῆς αὔριον (issue 1) probably is τό. Its absence in B (which has a tendency to drop articles) is not widely attested elsewhere, and the plural article, though well attested, looks like an assimilation to Prov. 27:1 (Metzger 1994: 613).

There are a few other text variants as well, all poorly attested.

4:15. The Majority Text of 4:15 continues the subjunctive mood for all the verbs: ἐὰν ὁ κύριος θελήσῃ καὶ ζήσωμεν καὶ ποιήσωμεν, meaning either "If the Lord wills, and (if) we live and do" (which leaves no apodosis) or "If the Lord wills, let us both live and do" (which does not fit the context). But if we read with ℵ, A, and B the futures ζήσομεν καὶ ποιήσομεν, then, since καί can introduce an apodosis (BDF §442.7), the text reads more clearly: "If the Lord wills, [then] we will live and do" (or as Dibelius 1975: 234 and Davids 1982: 173 suggest, "we will both live and do").

4:17. The translation given above for 4:17 requires some comment. As is common in the proverbial sayings in James, its brevity makes exact interpretation difficult. The main sentence, ἁμαρτία αὐτῷ ἐστιν, could mean "sin is to him" (i.e., sin is his [possessive dative] or sin is counted to him; cf. Deut. 15:9) because he does not do what he ought. Or, it could mean "for him the 'not doing' is a sin" (even though in the abstract it may not be sinful not to do something). Compounding the difficulty is that the dative participles "knowing" and "not doing" have no article and could thus be either substantive attributives or circumstantial. If the participles are circumstantial, then the text would read something like this: "Therefore, because he knows to do good and does not do it, there is sin on his record." But probably it is best to read the participles as substantival attributives, because otherwise αὐτῷ has no real antecedent. Hence, it should be understood to mean "For the one who knows and does not do . . . such not-doing is sin." On such a view, sin is just as much a matter of not doing what one should as it is of doing what one should not. This is a reflection of the approach of Jesus, who took the negative "golden rule" that was current in the ancient world and made it a positive obligation (Matt. 7:12). A person of faith is not only forbidden to do evil; he or she is obligated to do good.

B. Oracle 2: Warning to Landlords (5:1–6)

The oracle against oppressive landowners in 5:1–6 is even harsher than the first woe in 4:13–17. Here the language approaches the intensity of prophets such as Amos, who excoriated the wealthy oppressors of the poor. A similarly intense condemnation of oppression appears in Jesus's words in Luke 6:20–26 (see also 1 En. 94–97). In James 3 the author expressed his warnings against the tongue in hyperbolic style (especially 3:6), even to the point of calling the tongue "the world of wickedness in our members," although by no means is he saying that all uses of the tongue are evil. It is the very greatness of the gift of language that makes it fraught with deadly danger. Similarly, James here censures unbridled acquisition and hoarding of wealth. Wealth per se is not evil, but it is so commonly acquired by oppressive means and so often hoarded in selfishness that, like the tongue, it can be poison. And just as "by your words you will be justified . . . [or] condemned" (Matt. 12:37), so by our wealth we will be justified or condemned. Thus, in some ways Davids (1982: 171) is right to call wealth another kind of "test."

Frankemölle (1994: 630–32) argues that not just the merchants of 4:13–17, but even these wealthy landowners, are being regarded as Christians, though obviously ones who need to repent. He points out the parallels with 4:13–17, which would make no sense if addressed to non-Christians because of 4:15. But such a view is difficult to defend (Moo 2000: 209–10). Even to ask the question probably is to run outside James's purview. Here James is presenting not a diatribe against real people, or even caricatures of real people, but a paradigmatic example drawn from OT ethical instruction, particularly Deut. 24:14–15 (see the commentary on 5:4). The entire passage is rhetorical, addressed to wicked landowners in form, but actually written for the encouragement of the oppressed believers (Calvin 1948: 342). The passage assumes that the eschatological judgment will bring about a reversal, the exalted and the humble exchanging places, along lines that Jesus announced in Luke 6:20–26.

Exegesis and Exposition

[1]Come now, you who are rich; weep and wail because of your coming humiliations. [2]Your wealth is rotted and your garments are moth-eaten. [3]Your gold and silver are rusted right through, and their rust will testify against you and will consume your flesh like fire. You have amassed treasure in the last days. [4]Behold, the wages of the laborers who mowed your fields, wages which you have ⌜stolen⌝, cry out, and the cries of the harvesters have reached the ears of the Lord of hosts. [5]You have wallowed

in earthly luxury and have satiated yourselves; you have fattened up your hearts in a day of slaughter; ⁶you have condemned, you have murdered the righteous man, and he does not resist you.

5:1   The address to the wealthy in 5:1 stands parallel, but also in contrast, with 1:10, where the rich man is told to "boast" or "rejoice" in his humiliation. The difference here is that this passage is addressed not to wealthy believers or even wealthy people in general, but to those rich folk who oppress the people who depend on them, the "laborers who mowed your fields," by withholding their rightful wages (5:4). Such people will "wail" (ὀλολύζω, *ololyzō*), a word always associated with judgment warnings in the prophets (e.g., Isa. 10:10; 13:6; 14:31; and others in Isaiah, Jeremiah, Ezekiel, Hosea, Amos, and Zechariah).

5:2–3   The form of the warning in 5:2–3 closely resembles Jesus's warning in Matt. 6:19–21: "Do not lay up for yourselves treasures on earth, where moth and rust destroy and where thieves break in and steal, but lay up for yourselves treasures in heaven, where neither moth nor rust destroys and where thieves do not break in and steal. For where your treasure is, there your heart will be also" (cf. Luke 12:33). The danger of treasure acquired unrighteously or selfishly hoarded is also in other Jewish wisdom literature (Prov. 10:2; 21:6; Tob. 12:8).[1]

    James uses an intensified form of the verb "to rust," in the perfect tense (κατίωται, *katiōtai*), probably meaning "completely rusted" or "rusted right through" (see Ropes 1916: 285), where no integrity to the base metal remains.[2] James here picks up on the irony, seen elsewhere in Jewish wisdom literature (e.g., Sir. 29:10), that objects made of gold, and to a lesser extent silver, actually do not rust. Gold can withstand corrosion and retain its metallic integrity for centuries, and although silver tarnishes on the surface, it too lasts a long time in harsh environments and does not "rust through" the way iron does. Yet here James declares the material that is, from a worldly point of view, incorruptible to actually be, on the day of judgment, not just rusted, but rusted right through—totally worthless.

    Further, James may be making a wordplay to signal that such wealth is not just worthless, but in fact has negative value. The Greek word for "rust" (ἰός, *ios*) is homonymous with the word for "poison" (also ἰός), which James uses to describe the tongue in 3:8. Just as the tongue is likened to both poison and destructive fire, so, in effect, is wealth. Since many types of venom feel like fire in one's flesh, the picture is apt and vivid in both cases. And just as the tongue is a great gift but also a source of great evil, so the gift of wealth often

---

1. See also Prov. 1:18 LXX: αὐτοὶ γὰρ οἱ φόνου μετέχοντες θησαυρίζουσιν ἑαυτοῖς κακά ("For they who partake of murder treasure up evil things for themselves").

2. As Dibelius (1975: 236) points out, the use of the perfect tense does not indicate a present condition; here it is a "prophetic perfect," which anticipates the future state of affairs when the hoarded gold and silver of the wealthy will testify against them.

generates much evil. As with King Midas, whose "boon" became a curse, so too wealth gained through oppression or selfishly hoarded will not only, like rust, corrode to nothing, it will in fact, like poison, turn against the oppressor and hoarder at the judgment.

Rust "testifies" in that it manifests the corrosion or rottenness. When one sees the telltale flaky reddish brown on a used car being considered for purchase, the rust "testifies" against the vehicle by revealing its corroded and crumbling condition. Likewise, hoarded treasure will, on judgment day, testify against its hoarder by revealing what he or she is.

The last sentence of 5:3 is syntactically difficult because the verb used for "amassed treasure" is "to treasure up" (θησαυρίζω, *thēsaurizō*), which ordinarily takes a direct object. This problem leads Ropes (1916: 288) to take "as fire" at the end of 5:3a as the direct object of "treasured" and to read ὡς as meaning "since," thus making 5:3b a further explication of how the silver and gold are going to "eat your flesh." The result is: "They will consume your flesh, since you have treasured up fire in the last days." But Ropes himself acknowledges that the words "as fire" go more naturally with the end of 5:3a, and he resorts to his solution only because he regards leaving "treasured" without a direct object as intolerable. Although it may be unusual for "treasured" to lack a direct object, in this context it is perfectly understandable without one.[3] Here James is picking up on the depiction of judgment as the fiery consumption of one's flesh, evident in Isa. 66:24 and cited by Jesus (Mark 9:48).

Although the wealthy "treasure up" things in order to guard against the future, in reality such hoarding simply increases the weight of judgment against them, for to hoard wealth is to deprive the needy of life (Davids 1982: 176). This verse is not simply observing that the rich are saving for retirement. The phrase "the last days" refers to impending judgment day. The message therefore is like that of verse 5, where the rich "fatten themselves" in a day of slaughter (5:5). The verse is also parallel to Rom. 2:5: "But because of your hard and impenitent heart you are storing up wrath for yourself on the day of wrath when God's righteous judgment will be revealed."

But oddly, James says not that the landowners are amassing treasure *for* the last days but rather *in*, or perhaps *at*, the last days.[4] James speaks as he does because, in common with other NT writers (Acts 2:17; Heb. 1:2), he regards the last days as already present, in that judgment is imminent. Hence, the behavior of these landowners is all the more foolish: they are continuing to hoard even in these last days (Dibelius 1975: 237; but see the second additional note on 5:3). James's words call to mind Jesus's parable of the rich landowner in Luke 12:16–21, which concludes with the words "So is the one who lays up treasure for himself, and is not rich toward God."

3. Note that Luke 12:21, in a parable from Jesus that may have influenced James, also uses θησαυρίζω without an object. See also Ps. 38:7 LXX (39:7 MT; 39:6 ET); 2 Cor. 12:14.

4. Here some translations (e.g., KJV) do render the preposition ἐν as "for," which has little warrant other than the need to make it fit.

5:4 The specific background for 5:4 is the OT principle of prompt payment of wages, found in both Lev. 19:13 and Deut. 24:14–15. The prophet Malachi, not unlike James, berates those who, among other things, "defraud the hired worker of his wages" (Mal. 3:5 LXX).[5] In the introduction (see also Johnson 1982: 391–401) I noted the many points of contact between James and Lev. 19, but a greater similarity with James 5:4 is in this case found in Deut. 24:14–15:

> You shall not oppress a hired servant who is poor and needy, whether he is one of your brothers or one of the sojourners who are in your land within your towns. You shall give him his wages on the same day, before the sun sets (for he is poor and counts on it), lest he cry against you to the LORD, and you be guilty of sin.

James reminds his hearers that such cries "have reached" (literally "have entered") the ears of the Lord of hosts. The designation "Lord of hosts" (i.e., Lord of armies) is used in the OT to depict God as the great warrior, at the head of his armies. God is a warrior who will bring disaster upon those who oppress the poor (Isa. 5:9).[6]

It sometimes is proposed that James is addressing actual situations, such as the large landowners of Palestine who displaced small landowners and turned them into day laborers (so Hartin 2003: 235–36). But one might then wonder why James condemns the wealthy only for withholding of wages and not also the antecedent and precipitating sin of the displacement of the legitimate landowners. Further, for James to use as an example of patience the kind of farmer that the poor laborers used to be (5:8) would surely then be cruel. Instead, as elsewhere in James (see especially 2:2–3), here he uses a concrete but nonspecific example from common experience (landowners withholding wages) to represent a general principle (the rich dealing unfairly with the poor). Inasmuch as this entire section is meant to produce a rhetorical effect rather than actually address rich people, it seems more likely that James is simply using the specific issue of Deut. 24:14/Lev. 19:13 as illustrative of typical unrighteous behavior on the part of the wealthy.[7] It is endemic to human behavior everywhere for the rich to oppress the poor, and the Greco-Roman world was no exception, and James's condemnation applies to every manifestation of greed and the abuse of power, not just the withholding of wages.

---

5. Interestingly, Mal. 3:5 LXX utters a judgment oracle against the faithless Israelites as "adulteresses" (cf. James 4:4) who oppress widows and orphans (cf. James 1:27) and steal wages (ἀποστεροῦντας μισθόν). Like James 5:4, the LXX of Mal. 3:5 uses the verb ἀποστερέω (*apostereō*, to rob, steal), though James may originally have read ἀφυστερήμενος (*aphysterēmenos*, withheld; see the additional note on 5:4).

6. In the LXX of Isa. 5:9 the similarity to James 5:4 is clearer: ἠκούσθη γὰρ εἰς τὰ ὦτα κυρίου σαβαωθ ταῦτα ("For these things were heard in the ears of the Lord of hosts").

7. One might note that this is a typically Jewish device. When dealing with an ethical question not directly addressed in the Torah, a teacher often will refer to something in the Torah that is analogous to the situation in question.

The way the rich "fatten themselves" is by self-indulgence at the expense of others. The first of the two words used here for this self-indulgent living (τρυφάω, *tryphaō*) is used in the LXX positively for enjoyment and delight (Neh. 9:25; Isa. 66:11), without negative connotations. But James probably is taking it in its classical sense of "living luxuriously" (Ropes 1916: 289). The other word (σπαταλάω, *spatalaō*) more consistently suggests self-indulgence and careless luxuriance (see Hort 1909: 107–8).[8] It is not the simple enjoyment of material blessings that James here condemns, but the sybaritic enjoyment of material wealth that has been unrighteously obtained. To withhold wages is to steal from those who are less powerful, and to indulge in luxury with those stolen wages is doubly offensive.

Further, even if material wealth has not been obtained by unrighteous means, it becomes unrighteous if used purely for the extravagant pursuit of one's own pleasure. As with any of God's gifts, if the focus is on enjoying the gift rather than the giver, it becomes an idol; and as Prov. 21:13 points out, "Whoever closes his ear to the cry of the poor will himself call out and not be answered."

The phrase "in a day of slaughter" may be referring to the present day when the poor are being "slaughtered" by the rich oppressors who are fattening themselves at their expense. However, "day of slaughter" is an OT term for judgment day (Jer. 12:3; cf. Jer. 19:6; Isa. 30:25; 34:2). Further, the rich landowners are "fattening themselves," and fattening is what is done to the livestock being readied for the abattoir. Therefore, "in a day of slaughter" probably is parallel to "in the last days" of 5:3, and thus James is (ironically perhaps?) warning of the imminent eschatological day when the oppressors themselves will be slaughtered. If a steer could think, it might regard itself as fortunate to be indoors, surrounded by mounds of hay, no longer having to forage for skimpy grass on the hillsides in the rain or in the hot sun, all the while oblivious to its impending doom.

5:5

The actions of the wealthy in 5:6 parallel 2:6, where the wealthy are the ones who drag believers into court. Here the verb "to condemn" (καταδικάζω, *katadikazō*) specifically means "to sentence to death." It does not refer to statements that disapprove of certain human activity; otherwise, James would be condemning himself by his own act of condemning. But is this intended to refer to actual death sentences?

5:6

As in 4:2, James probably is using "murder" (φονεύω, *phoneuō*) metaphorically, but there could be a quasi-literal dimension as well. Here James reflects the attitude, also seen in Sir. 34:22–26, that the confiscation of someone's property that is necessary to his or her livelihood is tantamount to murder. The initial verb "condemn," along with "murder," may indicate legal action (perhaps recalling those who "haul you into court" in 2:6). The slow deprivation of the means of life by confiscation, or by the withholding of wages, resulting

---

8. There may even be a note of decline, from soft luxury (τρυφάω) to lewdness (σπαταλάω; Ropes 1916: 290).

in the exacerbation of the laborer's poverty, is tantamount to murder. Even when such withholding is not immediately life-threatening, such oppression is a violation of the sixth commandment, in that it does not protect human life but instead destroys it by degrees.

The connection may be intended to call to mind Ahab's treatment of Naboth (1 Kings 21), a scriptural example of a faithless deed, an act of unbelief. Ahab, of course, or at least his wife, literally had Naboth murdered to acquire his vineyard, not because they needed it, but because Ahab wanted a vegetable garden near his palace. If this allusion is intended, once again we see James using a concrete example from Scripture to give expression to the principle that faith entails dealing fairly and generously with the poor. Conversely, oppression of the poor is contrary to faith; it is akin to murder because it condemns the poor to poverty, and extreme poverty is soul-destroying. It defaces the image of God in people and thus insults the poor person's Maker (cf. 2:7; Prov. 17:5).

The Westcott-Hort text punctuates οὐκ ἀντιτάσσεται ὑμῖν (*ouk antitassetai hymin*) as a question ("Does he not resist you?") rather than a statement, a suggestion supported by Ropes (1916: 292) and Davids (1982: 180). But it is unclear how a question would fit rhetorically. Johnson (1995: 305) also reads it as a question, but understands God as the subject: "Does not God resist you?" This links back to 4:6, which uses the same word (ἀντιτάσσομαι, *antitassomai*, to resist, oppose) and identifies the landowners with the proud whom God opposes. More likely, however, the statement "He does not resist you" is meant to emphasize the wickedness of the oppression (because the poor person *cannot* resist) and possibly to draw a connection to the Suffering Servant of Isa. 53 (the righteous one), though since James does not directly refer to this anywhere, it is difficult to prove.

Along those lines, however, a few interpreters have taken "You have condemned, you have murdered the righteous one, and he does not resist you" to be an implicit reference to the death of Christ (Johnson 1995: 304 refers to Oecolampadius and Bede, to which we could add Theophylact, *Commentary on James* [PG 125:1184]; the view has more recently been defended by Feuillet 1964). This could be understood literally, in that Christ did not resist being murdered. But the present tense of "he does not resist" and the context suggest that "the righteous one" is more than a reference to Christ alone, and those who hold this view therefore tend to understand it derivatively, as an extension of the principle that "doing something to the least of these my brethren" (i.e., the poor) is doing it to Christ (Matt. 25:40, 45). This is how Bede takes it (PL 93:37). He sees Stephen's martyrdom as an example of how the opponents of Jesus continue to oppress him and also points to the fact that the rich are those who blaspheme the name (i.e., Jesus Christ) invoked over believers in James 2:6–7. It is, however, more likely that "the righteous one" is simply a generalized reference to the oppressed poor person who trusts in God for deliverance, as in several psalms (e.g., Ps. 34:15–22; 37:12–40) and prophetic writings (Lam.

4:13; Amos 2:6).[9] James, like many other biblical writers, does, however, underscore the fact that God identifies with the poor. Thus, even if James is not specifically calling attention to the death of Christ, it is relevant to note that Jesus the righteous one did in fact suffer death and became the oppressed one for the sake of and in identification with all the oppressed. God's identification with the poor reached its ultimate expression when he himself became poor (2 Cor. 8:9). And thus it is also true that when rich people oppress the poor, they are participating in the attack on God himself that culminated in the cross.

Additional Notes

5:2–3. The use of the perfect tenses in all three clauses here (σέσηπεν, γέγονεν, κατίωται) often is taken in the sense of the prophetic use of the Hebrew perfect, which would indicate not a present state of affairs, but the certainty of the future judgment (so, e.g., Mayor 1897: 154; Dibelius 1975: 236). Moo (2000: 213) on the other hand, following Mayordomo-Marin (1992), points out that the normal meaning of the Greek perfect tense also makes sense: "Although the rich people do not, or cannot, see it, their great wealth has already lost its luster." However, the strong echo of prophetic language in 5:1–6 and the emphasis on coming judgment suggest not that the rich are unaware of their present circumstances, but they are unaware of their future.

5:3. The use of the preposition εἰς with εἰμί (εἰς μαρτύριον ὑμῖν ἔσται) could be an example of the Greek equivalent of a Semitic predicate construction with לְ, but here it is more likely the equivalent of "function as" or "serve for" (BDF §145.1; cf. 1 Cor. 14:22). The translation above turns the awkward "will be as a testimony" into the more idiomatic "will testify."

5:3. As noted above, the rich are said to be treasuring up *in* (ἐν) the last days and (v. 5) fattening themselves *in* a day of slaughter. Dibelius (1975: 237) and Moo (2000: 215) therefore point out that the rich hoarders are being especially wicked and foolish, given that the age of fulfillment and judgment is at hand (Dibelius: "Even in the Last Days, the Eschaton, the rich have collected treasure"), and take the phrase ἐν ἡμέρᾳ σφαγῆς in 5:5 to be the present day when the poor are being slaughtered (Dibelius 1975: 239). However, the OT references to a day or time of slaughter as a metaphor for the coming day of judgment (Jer. 12:3; 19:6; Isa. 30:25, 33; 34:2–8) suggest that James is using the same OT irony: the oppressors are amassing wealth and fattening themselves, but in doing so, they are making their coming doom all the more horrific. Further, the close parallels to James in 1 En. 94.8–9 suggest a similar use of the term "day of slaughter": "Woe to you, ye rich, for ye have trusted in your riches, and from your riches shall ye depart, because ye have not remembered the Most High in the days of your riches. Ye have committed blasphemy and unrighteousness, and have become ready for the day of slaughter, and the day of darkness and the day of the great judgement" (translation in Charles 1917: 135–36). Hence, the "treasuring" is going to redound against the treasurers on judgment day, just as the self-fattening is increasing the horror that they will face.

5:4. The reading ἀφυστερημένος (held back from) is that of the important witnesses ℵ and the original hand of B, and since ἀποστερέω (to rob) is the more common verb in Scripture, it is arguable that James, whose vocabulary is large, originally used the former.

---

9. As such, it has been seen to be applicable to James himself, whom some called "the Righteous," and who was martyred shortly before the Jewish war of 66–70 (Mayor 1897: 155).

On the other hand, the verb ἀφυστερέω, which is unattested elsewhere in the NT and rare even outside it (see Neh. 9:20; Sir. 14:14), may have been an "Alexandrian refinement" (Metzger 1971: 685), and the reading only occurs in those two manuscripts. "Robbed" fits better with the prophetic tradition, as in Mal. 3:5 LXX noted above.

The shift from ἀποστερέω to ἀφυστερέω may also have been to make the following ἀφ' less awkward, though as noted in the commentary on 1:13, James can use ἀπό with the genitive to express agency (probably also 1:27). Thus, the better reading is "wages robbed by you," translated above as "wages which you have stolen." The variation does not greatly affect the sense.

VII. Fourth Discourse: Looking to God (5:7–18)

James here reverts to his usual address to "brothers," and the tone reverts from woe to direct encouragement. The exhortations in this last discourse bring us back to the two concerns with which James opened his letter: the necessity of endurance in the face of testing and the importance of faithful prayer (note especially how 5:11 calls to mind 1:12). The series of imperatives in 5:7–11 is focused specifically on what patient endurance looks like, whereas 5:13–18 deals more particularly with prayer. Not counting for the moment 5:12, which both stands apart from and bridges these two paragraphs, we see that each of these two sections begins with a general imperative (5:7, be patient; 5:13, pray), gives some specifics, and then concludes with an OT example of someone who exhibited that virtue (5:11, Job; 5:17–18, Elijah). Both passages, along with the bridge verse of 5:12, are also tied together in having to do with speaking. In 5:7–11 James warns against evil speech (grumbling), in 5:12 deals with avoiding oaths and telling truth, and in 5:13–18 focuses on the positive command to pray for one another.

A. Part 1: Faith and Patience (5:7–11)

Patient endurance is the response to testing with which James opened his exhortation in 1:2–3. Here he makes explicit the eschatological motivation for endurance: the coming of the Lord in judgment, the time of restitution, is near. Patience is a difficult path, but when one has confidence of vindication and a beneficial outcome (in other words, when one has grounds for hope), one can more readily endure. Ultimately, it once again depends on faith. It is because one believes that the Lord is merciful and compassionate that one can look for the end in hope.

Exegesis and Exposition

⁷Therefore, be patient, brothers, until the arrival of the Lord. Look how the farmer awaits the precious fruit of the land, waiting patiently for it until it receives the early and late ⌜rains⌝. ⁸You too must be patient. Fortify your hearts, because the arrival of the Lord is near. ⁹Do not grumble, brothers, against each other, so that you do not fall under judgment. Look, the judge stands before the doors. ¹⁰Brothers, as an example of patience amid suffering, consider the prophets, who spoke in the name of the Lord. ¹¹Look how we consider blessed those who endured. You have heard of the patience of Job, and you know the result that the Lord brought about, for the Lord is merciful and compassionate.

5:7 "Therefore" (οὖν, *oun*) in 5:7 indicates that this section is the response of faith to the wickedness of the unjust landowner presented in the preceding section. "Patience, not resistance, is the virtue of the poor, for their hope is the parousia" (Davids 1982: 181).

The "arrival of the Lord" is the παρουσία (*parousia*) of the Lord. Here James may simply be expressing the general Jewish conviction that God will come in judgment. But this is the very term used elsewhere in the NT for the return of Jesus Christ in judgment (Matt. 24:3, 27, 37, 39; 1 Cor. 15:23; 1 Thess. 2:19; 3:13; 4:15; 5:23; 2 Thess. 2:1; 2 Pet. 3:4). The fact that James identifies the "Lord" in 2:1 specifically as Jesus Christ indicates that James certainly can understand "Lord" to refer to Jesus. Further, the term *parousia* is not commonly used in other Jewish literature to refer to God's coming in judgment (A. Oepke, *TDNT* 5:864). Its use in the NT seems to be based on its use in general Greek to refer to the presence or arrival of a royal or official personage, such as a king (LSJ 1343). Here, then, it is almost certain that

James, like the rest of the NT, regards the future parousia to be the arrival of Messiah Jesus in judgment.[1] This is reinforced by the next verse.

James's mention of the "early and late [rains]" is an allusion to a climatological phenomenon of Palestine, where the "early rains" of late fall or early winter provide groundwater for the early spring growth and first harvest, and the late rains of late spring secure a good summer harvest. This became a symbol of God's faithful provision (Deut. 11:14; Jer. 5:24; Hos. 6:3). If either the early or late rains fail, a bad year ensues. Since this phenomenon would mean little to those outside Palestine, it sometimes is used as supporting evidence that the author of the letter is of Palestinian origin (see "Internal Evidence: Palestinian Indications" in the introduction). But probably more significant to the author is the allusion to Joel 2:23–24, where the early and the late rains are a harbinger of the eschatological abundance of Israel after its promised restoration. James's point here is that just as the farmer waits patiently for the rains (though with longing), so too the believer waits patiently for the Lord's parousia. Joel 2 was especially significant to the early Christian community. According to Acts 2, Peter quoted it in reference to the phenomena of Pentecost, and James perhaps has already alluded to it in 4:9 (see the commentary).[2] Joel himself also draws an analogy between the two rains and the eschatological harvest. James's allusion to it thus reminds the readers that the Lord has indeed promised, in Scripture, to restore all things in righteousness. Further, the mention of these eschatological "rains" also puts in context the later mention of Elijah's prayers first stopping but then restoring the rains.

5:8 James bases his command[3] "be patient" on the fact that the parousia "is near" (ἤγγικεν, *engiken*), the very form of the word used when Jesus announces that the kingdom of God is near, or "at hand," in the Gospels (e.g., Matt. 4:17; 10:7; Luke 10:9). Three other NT authors use this verb (ἐγγίζω, *engizo*) to speak of the day of judgment or the arrival of the Lord (Rom. 13:12; Heb. 10:25; 1 Pet. 4:7). The power for patience lies in the conviction that the time of judgment is imminent.

To "strengthen" or "establish" one's heart is to stand firm in faith and to not give in to doubt (cf. Ps. 57:7; 112:8; Sir. 6:37; 22:16–17; Rom. 1:11; 1 Thess. 3:13; 2 Thess. 2:17).

5:9 This verse seems to bear some relationship to Jesus's teaching not to judge lest one be judged (Matt. 7:1) and to the Olivet Discourse, where he says that the

---

1. So Dibelius 1975: 242–43; Mussner 1975: 201; Laws 1980: 208–9; Davids 1982: 182–83; Hartin 2003: 242. In recent times only Cantinat (1973: 232) takes it otherwise.

2. See also the allusions to Joel 2:2, 10 in the Olivet Discourse (Mark 13:19, 24 and pars.), Joel 2:4–5 in Rev. 9:7–9, and Joel 2:10–11 in Rev. 6:12–17.

3. "You too must be patient" attempts to render the imperative μακροθυμήσατε (*makrothymēsate*, be patient), which James amplifies by adding καὶ ὑμεῖς (*kai hymeis*, you too). Since English imperative cannot include the pronoun "you" it is difficult to capture the emphasis without paraphrasing.

kingdom is "at the very gates" (Matt. 24:33). Here, however, James surprisingly links it neither to "not judging" (as in Matt. 7) nor to the necessity of "watching" as in Matt. 24, but to the injunction not to "grumble against each other." The Greek word used here for "grumbling" (στενάζω, stenazō) ordinarily has the sense of groaning or sighing (BDAG 942; cf. Heb. 13:17, where people are encouraged to enable their leaders to exercise their pastoral duties with joy rather than groaning). Here, however, the qualifying prepositional phrase "against one another" indicates that the concern is for attitudes and relationships within the church. "Groaning" against one another surely is a reference to complaining about one another, which is in fact a kind of judging, and so this verse is an application of both James's and Jesus's prohibitions against judging each other (James 4:11–12; Matt. 7:1). Grumbling is the opposite of patience and thus also is a mark of unbelief; it is contrary to genuine faith. Further, as Johnson (1982: 397) suggests, we have here another connection to Lev. 19:18 (cited by James earlier), the first part of which commands the Israelites not to bear grudges against one another (though a different word [μηνίω, mēniō] is used in the LXX of Leviticus).

Although grumbling may seem to be a minor offense, James's warning against it is serious. To say the judge is "at the doors" surely is to indicate that the day of judgment is imminent. Despite James's paucity of specific references to Jesus (1:1; 2:1), his overall Christian context suggests that the judge is Jesus (so Davids 1982: 185; Martin 1988: 192). Laws (1980: 213) claims that its close association with James 4:12 ("there is one lawgiver and judge") means that the judge is simply "God." But it is not clear that James 4:12 is not also a reference to Jesus Christ (see the commentary on 4:12), and the fact that James so plainly links the imminence of the parousia of the Lord with the judge being at the very doors (just as Jesus does in Mark 13:29) makes it quite likely that here too Jesus is in view.

5:10–11 The reference to the prophets' endurance amid suffering[4] in 5:10–11 reflects a common Jewish interest in the prophets as martyrs, a tradition seen also in Matt. 5:11–12; Heb. 11:36.[5] One might ask here why James did not refer to the example of Jesus himself (Hartin 2003: 255–56), as 1 Peter does. Dibelius (1975: 247) puts this down to "rigidity of the [Jewish] tradition," but a likelier reason is that James sees Jesus not so much as a pattern to be emulated as a Lord to be obeyed (see the commentary on 2:1). Also, James's interest here is not in the redemptive power of suffering, nor is he interested in martyrology as such; his concern is with the pattern of faith in the face of adversity and

---

4. Literally "suffering and endurance." See the additional note on 5:10.

5. Indeed, James may even be consciously echoing the account of the martyrdom of Eleazar and his sons, one of the best-known martyrdom stories in Judaism (recorded in 4 Macc. 6). The rare noun κακοπαθία (kakopathia, suffering) followed by a reference to endurance is quite similar to a phrase found in 4 Macc. 9:8, where the seven Hebrew brothers declare, "For we, through this severe suffering and endurance [κακοπαθείας καὶ ὑπομονῆς], shall have the prize of virtue and shall be with God, for whom we suffer" (RSV). However, since James here uses μακροθυμία (makrothymia) rather than ὑπομονή (hypomonē) for "endurance," this is uncertain.

pressures toward unbelief, a pattern of faith set by those whom we now consider "blessed." As he has already done in 2:21–25 and will do again in 5:17, James refers to these OT examples of faith to show not how extraordinary people of extraordinary power did marvels, but how ordinary people who shared the common human experience of suffering became extraordinary through their persevering faith in the face of adversity. Thus, the blessedness of the prophets involves not their happiness in their earthly lives, but their wholeness in relationship to God.[6]

James's specific example of steadfastness in suffering may appear a bit odd. For a reader of Job, it may be surprising to hear that Job became a paradigm for patience, since much of the book consists of Job's impatient complaining to God about the injustice of his suffering.[7] However, the kind of patience that James has in mind is not passivity, but perseverance, fortitude in the face of suffering. The analogy in 5:7 of the farmer waiting patiently also points in the direction of yearning for the day of justice, since the farmer waits not with nonchalance, but with longing. Job did not give in to the falsity being suggested by his friends, and he did not give up; he kept clinging tightly and unyieldingly to God as the context of his life, which is the very reason he felt such a cognitive dissonance.

"You know the result which the Lord brought about" is literally "you have seen the end of the Lord." The word "end" (τέλος, telos) can refer to a termination point, a purpose, or a result (BDAG 998), and "the Lord" could indicate either Jesus or God the Father. Hence, the phrase has several possible meanings: (1) the end of the Lord's (Christ's) life and earthly ministry (i.e., his death and resurrection; Augustine, Symb. 3.10 [PL 40:634]); (2) the end of history (i.e., the parousia; Gordon 1975); (3) the end result of Job's story (i.e., God's restoration of Job at the end of the book of Job);[8] (4) God's purpose in subjecting Job to suffering (i.e., the reason for the trials).[9]

Since James does not speak elsewhere of the redemptive significance of Christ's suffering, the first of these is unlikely. If James had the second in view, he chose an obscure way of referring to it, and it does not seem to mesh with

6. Happiness is an emotional and subjective state; blessedness is an objective state of favor with God. See the commentary on 1:12.

7. The roots of the tradition of Job as a model of patient endurance are not immediately apparent from the OT text itself. The LXX translation of Job 7:16 might be seen as contributing to the tradition: οὐ γὰρ εἰς τὸν αἰῶνα ζήσομαι ἵνα μακροθυμήσω ("For I will not live forever, that I might be patient"). However, this in fact presents Job as explaining why he *cannot* be patient: it is because he will not live forever. The earliest extant record of the Jewish tradition of Job as an exemplar of endurance is in T. Job 1.5; 27.6–7. Richardson (2006) proposes that James instead was thinking of the book of Job as exhibiting the endurance of one whose faith is proved by endurance when tested.

8. Mayor 1897: 158; Ropes 1916: 299; Dibelius 1975: 246–47; Adamson 1976: 193; Laws 1980: 216; Moo 2000: 230. Compare the NIV.

9. Martin 1988: 195. Compare the ESV. Mayor (1897: 159) reports that Ewald held this view but gives no specifics (perhaps it is Ewald 1870). A further difficulty with this view is, of course, that in the book of Job God never explains why Job suffered.

the last part of the verse ("the Lord is merciful and compassionate"). The third and fourth options are lexically possible, and both fit the context well. The deciding factor may be the concluding statement, "the Lord is merciful and compassionate," which evokes a common OT refrain (see Exod. 34:6; Ps. 103:8; 111:4) and seems to point to "the end of Job's story," where the Lord's mercy to Job is displayed (cf. Job 42:12 LXX, where the Lord blesses the ἔσχατα [*eschata*, last things] of Job). "The result which the Lord brought about" attempts to render this notion.

Additional Notes

5:7. The word "rains" does not appear in the best manuscripts, but the context makes it clear that the intended reference is to the "early and late rains." Curiously, א adds καρπόν (fruit, harvest), suggesting that in Alexandria the phenomenon of the early and late rains was unknown.

5:9. Some commentators have wondered about the force of the plural "doors." It probably is unnecessary to make anything more out of this than the imagery of a city about to be attacked. Since large fortified cities ordinarily had more than one gate, a city under siege would have enemies outside all its doors. James's use of the image is not to indicate the place of judgment, but to depict its immediacy (Davids 1982: 185).

5:10. The phrase translated "an example of patience amid suffering" literally reads, "an example of the suffering and of the patience," and it is arguable (Moo 2000: 226) that the repetition of the article with both "suffering" and "patience" means that they are regarded as two distinct virtues of Job that should be emulated. But suffering is not, in and of itself, a virtue (cf. 5:13–15, which raises the possibility that someone may be suffering because of sin; see also 1 Pet. 3:17; 4:15). Job is an example to be followed in regard to *how* one should respond to suffering: with endurance in faith. It is more likely that the two genitive nouns are a hendiadys, yielding something like "patient suffering" or "patience while suffering" (BDF §442.16; Ropes 1916: 298). Compare Rom. 2:4, where τῆς ἀνοχῆς καὶ τῆς μακροθυμίας together refer to God's patient forbearance.[10]

5:11. The verb translated "we regard as blessed" is simply μακαρίζομεν, which sometimes has been translated "we bless," but there is no thought here of James or his audience imparting some benefit to the "ones who endured." The Hebrew root (*bārak*) associated with μακαρίζω and cognates sometimes can mean "praise" (e.g., Ps. 103:1), which would make sense here, but the Greek word does not carry that meaning (see LSJ 1073; BDAG 610), and the LXX regularly uses εὐλογέω and cognates for that notion rather than μακάριος/μακαρίζω. Instead, "we bless" here in James means "we recognize the exemplary quality of their faith and their relationship to God" or "we regard them as having God's approval" (cf. 1:25).

10. Ordinarily, the repetition of the article would suggest a separate entity, but several cases suggest that the rule may not be absolutely determinative, and that sometimes a hendiadys may be implied even when both nouns are articular: Exod. 11:9–10 LXX (signs and wonders = wondrous signs); 1 Cor. 7:34 (unmarried woman and virgin); 2 Cor. 11:3 (simplicity and purity); Col. 2:15 and Eph. 3:10 (rulers and authorities); Phil. 4:6 (prayer and supplication); 1 Thess. 5:1 (times and seasons). Of course, each of these is difficult to *prove* to be a hendiadys, but this is true also of most anarthrous noun constructions that are commonly taken to be such.

B. Bridge Verse: Prohibition of Oaths (5:12)

As noted above, 5:12 serves as a bridge between the passive command to persevere patiently without grumbling (5:7–11) and the active command to persevere in prayer (5:13–18). The verse has both a negative dimension (do not swear) and a positive one (tell the truth and keep your promises).

Exegesis and Exposition

¹²And above all, my brothers, do not swear, either by heaven or by earth, or with any other oath. Instead, make sure your yes means yes and your no, no, so that you may not fall under judgment.

The force of the proscription in 5:12 is twofold. The main force, evident from the second part of the verse, is clear: a believer should have such integrity in speech that oaths are completely unnecessary. "Make sure your yes means yes . . ." (sometimes translated "Let your yes be yes . . .")[1] is not suggesting some kind of substitute oath, as though the proper formula for an oath is "yes, yes"; rather, it is instructing people to make certain that their yes is always a true yes. In other words, one should always tell the truth (not just under oath), and one should always keep promises (not just those made with an oath). The second is the implication, also evident in Jesus's proscription in Matt. 5:34–37, that oaths bind their takers in ways that could cause them to "fall under judgment."[2]

    5:12

This close echo of the teaching of Jesus regarding oaths is a teaching somewhat unique in Judaism. The OT (Lev. 19:12) and Second Temple ethical literature condemned the taking of oaths lightly or in vain (e.g., CD-A 9.9–10 warns against compelling someone to take an oath in the open field because of the absence of legal authorities), though rarely does Jewish literature advocate the avoidance of oaths entirely. One apparent exception is Philo (*Good Person* 12 §84), who says that the "sacred volumes" advocate "a careful avoidance of oaths and of falsehood," but even this only advises against oaths; it does not proscribe them. General warnings against taking oaths lightly also exist in non-Jewish Hellenistic literature (for references in Pythagoras and Plutarch, see Kollmann

---

    1. The point, of course, is not "*Permit* your yes to be yes" but "*Be sure* you mean yes when you say yes."

    2. It should be evident that the "swearing" forbidden here is oath-taking, not what is commonly called "cussing." Although profanity too can be seen as faithless behavior because it treats what is holy as common, foul language as such is not James's concern here, though perhaps 3:10–12 is applicable.

1996).[3] James and Jesus, however, not only share the notion that *all* oaths should be avoided, but also say so in a very similar way. A direct comparison of James 5:12 with Matt. 5:34–37 shows their striking resemblance:

James 5:12	Matthew 5:34–37 NIV
My brothers,	But I tell you,
do not swear,	Do not swear at all:
either by heaven	either by heaven, for it is God's throne;
or by earth,	or by the earth, for it is his footstool;
or with any other oath.	or by Jerusalem, for it is the city of the Great King.
	And do not swear by your head, for you cannot make even one hair white or black.
Let your yes be yes, and your no, no,	Simply let your "Yes" be "Yes," and your "No," "No";
so that you may not fall under judgment.	anything beyond this comes from the evil one.

It is difficult to regard the high degree of similarity as accidental. Either James and Jesus (or Matthew or Q)[4] both shared access to some otherwise unknown Jewish traditional teaching (fairly unlikely), or James had read Matthew or perhaps Q (unlikely, contra Hartin 1991), or Matthew had read James (extremely unlikely), or James himself had heard Jesus's teaching and remembered it. Given the close relationship of James's teaching with the teaching of Jesus reported in the Synoptic Gospels, though only in content and not (except for this verse) in vocabulary, it seems best simply to suppose that James either heard this material directly from Jesus or heard the Jesus instruction tradition, albeit in a form prior to its development as is now found in the Gospels.[5]

But why is this snippet from Jesus's teaching found here, between the exhortation to patience in 5:7–11 and the command to pray in 5:13–18? The verse seems isolated from its context, an isolation that is aggravated by the words "above all"—above all in relation to what? The injunction against swearing seems to go with neither patience nor prayer.

3. Ropes (1916: 301–3) goes to some length to demonstrate that the teaching of James 5:12 and Matt. 5:34–37 was common in both Judaism and paganism, but his suggested parallels advise against only frequent or rash oaths. Even if Jesus is not prohibiting all oaths, the form of the prohibition is shared uniquely by James and Jesus.

4. Whether Q was a distinct written source or simply traditional material that Matthew and Luke happened to share is irrelevant for our purpose here, but the similarity of James's material to teaching material found in Matthew and Luke, but not so much in Mark, is striking and surely indicates the existence of some body of either written or oral tradition that preserved material about Jesus, particularly his teaching.

5. The observation by Dibelius (1975: 250) and others that other early Christian authors also refer to this saying, sometimes in form reflecting that of Matthew, sometimes of James, is no argument against its authenticity, especially since the distinctive form of the teaching is not found outside Christian circles. See Justin, *1 Apol.* 16.5; Clement of Alexandria, *Strom.* 5.99.1; 7.67.5. The form of the saying in Epiphanius, *Pan.* 19.6.2, agrees almost exactly with James.

Hence, commentators have identified it as an interpolation (Mayor 1897: 165), or as a quirky remainder of the letter's redactive development (Francis 1970: 125), or simply as evidence of the hodge-podge character of James (Dibelius 1975: 242, 248). Johnson (1982: 397–98) points out that this is one among several of James's links with Lev. 19, which enjoins Israelites not to swear falsely, and thus it has some relation to its context, but its sudden appearance here seems odd nonetheless.

The connection may be more intrinsic than simply being another point of contact with Lev. 19. The exhortations to patience and prayer of James 5 are indications of the right and faithful response of the person of faith to the endurance of suffering, and a forbidding of unfaithful responses, such as grumbling. In 5:12 James commands a faithful response (make sure that your yes is yes) and forbids a response that is not from faith (oaths). Oaths may be taken for a variety of reasons. The reason for Jesus's prohibition of oaths in Matt. 5:34–37 is not simply the customary Jewish reticence to swear an oath without knowing its consequences; he does so primarily because people use oaths to compensate for the lack of truthfulness generally (cf. Matt. 23:16–22).[6] Oaths also serve to secure an action by God. It is worth noting that the "oaths" in view in Lev. 19 are specifically vows, not legal testimony, and vows can bespeak an impatience with God (see Reicke 1964: 56). James, in 5:11 and 5:17–18, puts forward Job and Elijah as examples of perseverance and prayer, and although he has no example to illustrate the importance of refraining from oaths, the negative example of Jephthah (Judg. 11) could have been adduced. Jephthah, seeing the oppression of Israel by the Ammonites, did not wait patiently for the Lord to deliver them and did not pray concerning this condition, but instead he rashly swore an oath as a bargaining chip with God (and paid dearly for it).

The use of oaths, then, is contrary to faith; it marks unbelief. Faith always means yes when it says yes; that is, people of faith have no need of oaths, either to give their words weight or to prompt a solution to suffering; they wait patiently and prayerfully for the Lord and always keep their promises, cognizant that God always keeps his. If oaths stand, in contradistinction to prayer, as an inappropriate verbal response to suffering, then James's concern with them here forms the bridge between the exhortation to patience and the prayer commands that follow. Note again James's use of the vocative "my brothers" in 5:12. We have observed how often this vocative marks the beginning of sections (1:2, 19; 2:1; 3:1; 5:7), but sometimes it serves to mark a bridge. Thus, 1:16 seems to bridge 1:13–15 with 1:17–18, and 2:14 connects the two halves of James 2. Hence, 5:12 is not so isolated after all.[7]

6. Philo (*Decalogue* 17 §84) makes a similar observation: "By the mere fact of swearing at all, the swearer shows that there is some suspicion of his not being trustworthy." But again, the motive for Philo is advice, not mandate.

7. We may also note here that in the Sermon on the Mount the expectation of the kingdom, the importance of prayer, and the relation of prayer to forgiveness are linked in Matt. 6 and that this is at only a small remove from Jesus's prohibition of oaths in Matt. 5:34–37.

We still have not answered, though, why James marks this concern as "above all." Is refraining from oaths more important than waiting patiently for the Lord, or showing no favoritism, or seeking wisdom from above? Or is the "above all" simply a literary device, somewhat like "finally," as Davids (1982: 189), Moo (2000: 232), and Hartin (2003: 258) suggest?[8]

No solution is particularly convincing, but perhaps the difficulty comes from restricting the "above all" to 5:12 alone rather than regarding it as a bridge, that is, an introduction to the second half of this final discourse and a link to the previous. If the "above all" serves to introduce the exhortations to prayer in 5:13–18, then James is pointing out that the most important thing to remember, when facing circumstances requiring endurance, is the power of prayer. Rather than resolving their difficulties by resorting to oaths, people of faith pray, seeking the will of God in the matter and interceding for one another. But what does refraining from oaths have to do with prayer? If oath-taking is an articulation of unbelief and denotes a lack of faith, then prayer is the articulation of faith. The word ὀμνύω (omnyō, swear) refers to a formal avowal, usually with some self-imposed sanction given, either concerning the truthfulness of one's testimony (which then calls into question the truthfulness of everything not said with an oath), or as a promise to do something on pain of divine punishment (which suggests that one's promises made without an oath are given lightly), or, worst of all, as an attempt to deal with suffering by bargaining with God (as Jephthah tried to do in Judg. 11). Outside of certain legal contexts,[9] then, oath-taking runs contrary to faith, whereas sincere prayer is its quintessential expression.

Hartin (1999: 106) also notes that it is a mark of the community that its members need no oaths to trust each other (see also Minear 1971). The people of God are, as the eschatological community, called upon to exhibit the reality

8. Both Davids and Moo refer to 1 Pet. 4:8 as another possible case where πρὸ πάντων (pro pantōn, above all) may simply function as a literary concluding device, but although some have argued that the original form of 1 Peter ended at 4:11, most would hesitate at such a conclusion without any textual evidence. Further, the exhortation in 1 Pet. 4:8 has some claim to be "above all" the other ethical injunctions of 1 Peter, since the verse enjoins believers to love one another earnestly. Johnson (1982: 400), noticing the strong connections of James to Lev. 19:12–18, which Johnson identifies as equivalent to the "royal (kingdom) law," suggests that the "above all" is not saying "this is the most important thing," but is referring to the fact that the warning against oath-taking stands at the beginning of the kingdom law code that James is exegeting. However, given that James 5:12 much more closely resembles Jesus's instruction in Matt. 5 than the code of Lev. 19, and since James gives no specific indication that his letter is an exegesis of Lev. 19, it seems questionable whether James reasonably could have expected his audience to draw such a meaning from the words "above all."

9. Both James and Jesus are speaking against the casual use of oaths. The juridical situations of having to give testimony under sanction, and of giving certain transactions legal weight, are not in view (Hartin 2003: 263). Hence, Paul (e.g., 2 Cor. 1:23) and the OT saints (e.g., Ps. 63:11) are not contradicting Jesus and James. Hartin (2003: 258) gives a long list of examples in the OT where oath-taking under certain circumstances is commended, and even God swears (see Heb. 6:17; 7:21). Thus, the refusal by some Christians to take oaths in court is a misapplication of these verses and a misdirection from their main intent.

of the eschaton in their kingdom life, and in the eschatological kingdom of God everyone tells the truth and keeps promises.

Additional Note

5:12. In accordance with classical usage, the entity by which an oath is sworn, in this case "heaven" or "earth," is in the accusative. This differs from the parallel in Matt. 5:34, which has ἐν with the dative, and also from Heb. 6:13, 16, which have κατά with the genitive.

C. Part 2: Faith and Prayer (5:13–18)

The second half of the discourse on patient endurance is entirely focused on the issue of prayer. Similar to 1 John 5 and Jude 17–23, an exhortation to intercessory prayer serves as the final exhortation. James 5:13 mandates a general overall context of prayer in the believer's personal life, regardless of the circumstances. In 5:14–16 intercession is more in focus, especially with regard to sickness and sin. The example of Elijah in 5:17–18 then reminds believers not only of the effectiveness of prayer, but also that God brings about his intended works by answering the prayers of his people.

This section is closely connected with the first section (5:7–11). Note the vocabulary continuations: the noun κακοπαθία in 5:10 and the verb κακοπαθέω in 5:13 (the noun occurs only here in the NT; the verb occurs elsewhere in the NT only in 2 Tim. 2:9; 4:5), and also both prophets (5:10) and church leaders (5:14) speak "in the name of the Lord." Both 5:7–11 and 5:13–18 are concerned with the Christian's response to the suffering and stress of life, 5:7–11 focusing on the passive attitude of patience and 5:13–18 encouraging active prayer (thus drawing to conclusion the overall concern of the letter, first broached in 1:2–15, of the believer's response to testing). Also note that both passages end with a brief description of an exemplary OT character's manifestation of the virtue in view (Job in 5:11; Elijah in 5:17–18). Finally, note that in both sections the analogy of "rain" (implicit in 5:7; explicit in 5:17–18) is used to refer to the promised eschatological restoration, which must be patiently waited for in faith (5:7–11) and prayed for in faith (5:13–18).

Exegesis and Exposition

[13]Is anyone among you suffering? He should pray. Is anyone cheerful? He should sing a hymn of praise. [14]Is anyone among you sick? He should summon the leaders of the church, and they should pray for him, anointing him with oil in the name of the Lord. [15]And the prayer of faith will save the sick person, and the Lord will raise him up. Even if he has committed sins, he will be forgiven. [16]Therefore, confess [your] sins to one another, and pray for one another that you may be healed.

The prayer of a righteous person is very powerful and effective. [17]Elijah was a human being, like us by nature, and he prayed earnestly that it would not rain, and it did not rain upon the land for three and a half years. [18]And again he prayed, and heaven gave rain, and the land brought forth its fruit.

Exhortations to prayer are a feature of several NT letters (Rom. 15:30–32; Eph. 6:18; 1 Thess. 5:17–18; Heb. 13:18–19), but James's exhortation is notable for its length. Included here is not just the importance of prayer in all circumstances, but also the importance of intercessory prayer and the willingness to request it, the power of prayer, especially its efficacy with respect to sin, the mandate of mutual confession of sins in the context of intercession, and even, by implication, the link between the believer's prayer and the coming eschatological judgment.

In 5:13 James lays out the general exhortation to pray in all circumstances, good and bad, and then in 5:14 he specifically raises the issue of physical illness and its relation to intercession, forgiveness, and confession. The situations of 5:13–14 are translated above as questions,[1] and the imperatival conclusions show that the questions are equivalent to conditional statements: "*If* someone is suffering, he should pray."[2] The question form is rhetorically more vivid because it draws the reader into participating more directly. In most assemblies of believers, a question like "Is anyone among you suffering?" would make a forest of hands go up.

The overall teaching of James on the importance of prayer to the life of perseverance is clear enough, but this brief passage is remarkably full of difficult problems. Virtually every verse either evinces interpretive difficulties or raises complex theological questions.

The two conditions described in 5:13, "suffering" and "cheerful," basically express a range of human experience. As noted above, the word "suffering" in 5:13 has the same (rare) verbal root as the word used in 5:10 to describe the suffering of the OT prophets. It refers not specifically to physical illness (though that would not be excluded), which is the specific subject of the third condition (5:14), but simply to the bad or distressing experiences in life. Here the verb "is suffering," especially in opposition to "is cheerful," probably expresses more the emotional state or mental response to circumstances than the circumstances themselves. James by no means downplays the reality or importance of one's mental state, but he does put it in context. Sufferers are reminded that suffering was also the experience of the prophets, in particular Elijah, who, even after the Mount Carmel incident, did indeed become very glum over Israel's prospects and frustrated by their rebellion (see 1 Kings 19:4), yet responded with prayer. Endurance in prayer is what ties together the example of Elijah, the need for healing, and righteousness (Warrington

1. Dibelius (1975: 241, see also 252) translates them not as questions, but as simple statements—"Someone of you is sick. He should pray"—arguing that this fits the diatribe style. But since James is unlikely to have made such a simple statement of fact that "someone is happy" in 5:13b, the conditions are more easily read as questions. Also, earlier, in 3:13, a question is similarly used to vividly frame a condition, and there it is certain that James is not declaring that "someone is wise."

2. "He should pray," "he should sing," and so on are third-person imperatives in Greek, a form that must be circumlocuted in English, as "he should . . ." or "he must . . ." (see the second additional note on 1:5).

1994). Thus, believers are expected to exhibit the same faithful endurance of the prophets.

The word for "to be cheerful" (εὐθυμέω, *euthymeō*), though common in classical Greek, is found in the Bible only here and in Acts 27:22, 25.[3] Some (e.g., Moo 2000: 175; Hartin 2003: 265) take this cheerfulness to refer to the spiritual joy that comes from knowing God, but here James is contrasting cheer with suffering, and suffering does not stand *opposite* joy, but is to be counted *as* joy in 1:2. Hence, the cheerfulness is better understood as the experiencing of God's goodness in ways that are desirable from a human point of view. At any rate, the appropriate response is not pride at one's accomplishments (like the boastful merchant in 4:16) but gratitude that expresses itself in musical praise to God.

Cheerfulness is therefore not to be despised but is to result in singing of praise. The word ψάλλω (*psallō*), whence comes the English word *psalm*, originally meant "to pluck," and hence it referred to playing a harp or other stringed instrument. Particularly in biblical literature it became associated with playing and singing in the worship and praise of God, and by the time the NT was written, it had more connections with singing praise than with playing a harp, especially in Jewish literature (BDAG 1096). Thus, Paul speaks of "psalming" with his spirit or with his mind (1 Cor. 14:15), and clearly he is including verbal content in this singing. An alternative translation, "he should make music," is acceptable and carries the ambiguity of the original, but it is quite unlikely that James had in mind anything other than vocal singing of praise to God. James's word choice, however, can hardly be used to justify excluding instrumental music from worship or restricting singing in worship to biblical psalms. In any case, here James is dealing directly not with music in formal worship, but with the believer's response to God's goodness generally.

In 5:14 (and 5:15) the particular suffering in view is physiological: "Is anyone sick?"[4] However, the mandated response is somewhat surprising. Rather than say, "He should pray," James says, "He should call the church leaders" (literally the "elders of the church").[5]

---

3. The verb occurs nowhere in the Greek OT. The cognate adjective εὔθυμος (*euthymos*) occurs in 2 Macc. 11:26 and Acts 27:36; and in Acts 24:10, Paul makes his defense "cheerfully" (εὐθύμως, *euthymōs*).

4. A few scholars (e.g., Hayden 1981) argue that the "weakness" in 5:14 is not physical ailment but spiritual weakness, which allows the corresponding σώσει (*sōsei*, it will save) in 5:15 to be given a spiritual significance, thus resolving the problem that God does not always heal following every instance of prayer by elders. Although this reading seems to connect well with the forgiveness of sins that is also promised, the fact that James expresses the latter as a contingency ("*if* he has committed sins, he will be forgiven"), and that the afflicted person is also called ὁ κάμνων (*ho kamnōn*, the sick person), gives this expedient little warrant. Virtually all recent commentators therefore understand the illness in view as physical, or at least physical and psychological together, and not as a metaphor for sin or susceptibility to it.

5. In NT times, "elders" (πρεσβύτεροι, *presbyteroi*) signified not simply the oldest people in the community, but those who were spiritually mature and equipped to give counsel and direction

The specific church in question probably is the local congregation, but it is interesting that James uses a term different from the "synagogue" (συναγωγή, *synagōgē*, gathering) that he mentions in 2:2. James's word for "church" (ἐκκλησία, *ekklēsia*) is the one found elsewhere in the NT. It is derived from the Greek OT's use of the term to refer to the *qāhāl*, the assembly of Israel, gathered for worship, consecration, or instruction (e.g., Deut. 9:10; 18:16). Thus, James probably is not speaking of the "church" as an institution as over against Israel, but thinks of it in line with Jesus's use in Matt. 16:18, where it refers to the "assembly" of God's people that Jesus will build, or, to use Paul's language, the "body" of Christ. Since this assembly is now a scattered one (in "dispersion," according to 1:1), the specific leaders or "elders" summoned by the sick person would, pragmatically, have to be those of the local congregation. That James refers to "church" here rather than "synagogue" is a reminder that the believing Christian community in any location is not an entity of itself; it is a local manifestation of the great assembly of God's people.

These elders are to be called not because they are invested with special powers, but because they represent the church as a whole, and their prayers are an expression of the prayers of the entire congregation or community. Moo (2000: 247) rightly observes, "The power to heal is invested in prayer, not the elder."

This instruction calls to mind the surprising response of Jesus to the bringing of a paralytic for healing (Mark 2:1–12). It was not the paralytic's faith, but that of his friends (Mark 2:5), that prompted Jesus both to declare the paralytic's sins forgiven and to raise him up physically.

These verses therefore push us to recognition of the principle of the corporate nature of faith, the interrelatedness of the believing community, and the necessity of corporate intercession, confession, and forgiveness to produce corporate health. (Hence, it is similar to Paul's observation in 1 Cor. 12:26 that when one member suffers, the whole body suffers.) This theme of corporate prayer continues in verses following.

James's mandate to anoint with oil for healing purposes is unique in the NT, but it has some precedent in the actions of Jesus's disciples, who anointed and healed the sick as well as preached (Mark 6:12–13). Both James and Mark do not use the customary word for "to anoint for the purpose of consecration" (χρίω, *chrio*); rather, they use ἀλείφω (*aleiphō*), which normally means "to rub," and only occasionally is used in the Greek OT to refer to consecration (Exod. 40:15; Num. 3:3). There are, nevertheless, a number of possible meanings to this anointing: (1) a sacrament that effects a spiritual result (unction), especially in the face of imminent death;[6] (2) a medicinal application of oil

---

to the members of the community in their obedience to Christ (see Acts 14:23; Titus 1:5–9; 1 Pet. 5:1). On the role of elders in the early church, see J. H. Elliott 2000: 813–16.

6. This was the implied exegesis of the Council of Trent, session XIV, in its publication *De sacramento extremae unctionis*. But even Roman Catholic scholars have difficulty supporting the sacrament of extreme unction by way of James 5. See Hartin 2003: 279; Brown 1997: 736–39.

(such as could be the case in Mark 6:13; cf. Luke 10:34);[7] (3) an administration purely for physical comfort (because being anointed is pleasurable; cf. Ps. 133:2); (4) a symbol of blessing generally (Ps. 23:5; 141:5; Prov. 27:9); (5) a symbolic representation of prayer; (6) a symbol of sanctification (e.g., Exod. 29:21) or dedication (Gen. 28:18); (7) a symbolic representation of the presence of the Holy Spirit (Isa. 61:1); (8) a stimulus to faith (Tasker 1957: 131; Mitton 1966: 191); (9) a symbolic promise of eschatological life (Collins 1997); (10) a symbol of dedication or consecration.[8] There could be more than one at work here; for example, those who regard unction as a sacrament may also regard views 4, 5, 6, and 7 as relevant, and similarly, views 4, 6, 8, and 9 certainly are compatible with each other.

The problem with the sacramental view (1) is threefold. First, James's context is not that of imminent death. The association of James 5:15 with preparation for death did not develop until the Middle Ages. Second, there is no clear indication in James that anointing has special covenantal significance. Third, James is the only NT writer to mention it. Surely, any religious act of such importance as a sacrament would find more treatment than one obscure reference. The main problems for the medicinal view (2) are that oil is a treatment for wounds, not "sickness," and since the anointing is "in the name of the Lord," it is clear that something other than simply the application of medicinal unguent is in view. Also, neither χρίω nor ἀλείφω is used in the LXX to indicate medicinal application. The "comfort" and "blessing" views (3 and 4) are possible, but the concern of the passage is healing and raising up, not simply the alleviation of discomfort or general blessing (though that might be the case in Mark 6:13). The problem with the "Holy Spirit" view (7) is the lack of references to the Holy Spirit elsewhere in James (for discussion of the "spirit" in 4:5, see the commentary on 4:4–6). View 8 comports with the fact that it is the elders who are called upon to anoint and pray rather than the sick person, but as Martin (1988: 208) points out, there is no evidence that anointing was used as a stimulus to or marker of faith in the early church.

This leaves views 5, 6, and 9, which focus on intercessory prayer, consecration, and eschatology. All of these may be involved. The focus in the entire passage is on intercession. It is prayer that is effective, prayer that responds to suffering, faithful prayer that saves and raises, and prayer for one another that heals. The problem is that nowhere does either the OT or the NT explicitly associate oil or anointing with prayer. However, the anointing here is specifically "in the name of the Lord," implying either the invocation of God's activity, particularly God's blessing (cf. Ps. 45:7), or the recognition of God's presence

7. Wilkinson (1971) supports the "medical" view.

8. Dibelius (1975: 252) regards the anointing and prayer together as an exorcism, but since James says nothing about demons, "driving out," or spiritual powers anywhere in this context, I see this notion as unviable. Hilary of Arles, in his *Tractate on the Letter of James* (PL Supp. 3:81), identifies the oil as a symbol of mercy, but although anointing is an act of mercy in the parable of the good Samaritan, there is little even in Luke 10 to support the suggestion that the oil symbolizes the mercy being shown.

(cf. Gen. 28:18, where Jacob anoints his stone headrest in recognition of God's presence in that place). Both of these constitute a kind of symbolic prayer, as it were. Since anointing was a mark of anticipated future exaltation (as when David was anointed in 1 Sam. 16:13; cf. Ps. 92:10), the oil also could serve as a reminder to the sick individual that he or she is accompanied by God and will be raised incorruptible on the last day.

It is best to take anointing, then, as a symbol of God's blessing attendant to intercessory prayer and possibly as "consecrating" in the sense of reminding the sick that they belong to God. Anointing reminds both them and the community that they are specially "set aside" for prayer (see Shogren 1989; Moo 2000: 240–42) and points to the reality of the future blessing of eschatological life (Collins 1997). Quite aside from the pleasurable physical sensation of being anointed, this would bring comfort and encouragement to the sick, even if the one suffering must await the final resurrection before he or she experiences being "raised up."

Further, James may have in the back of his mind a promise made in Isa. 61, one of the great messianic "eschatological reversal" texts of the OT. There Isaiah says that the Messiah is anointed in order to, among other things, "provide for those who grieve in Zion—to bestow on them a crown of beauty instead of ashes, the oil of gladness instead of mourning, and a garment of praise instead of a spirit of despair" (Isa. 61:3 NIV). If James has this in mind, then just as in 1:2, suffering is linked with eschatological joy.

The "name of the Lord" here evokes the prophetic patience of 5:10 and the prophetic prayer of 5:17–18, and it may be no more than an indication that the anointing and prayer are an act of faith. But the phrasing here is unusual: the elders pray "upon" or "over" (ἐπί, epi) the sick person in the name of the Lord. This makes it likely that James has in mind the "name that is invoked upon [ἐπί] you" in 2:7, which, as we noted, is best understood as a reference to the name of Jesus Christ. Hence, prayer "in the name of the Lord" indicates prayer specifically invoking the name of Jesus, thus carrying forward Jesus's promise "If you ask me anything in my name, I will do it" (John 14:14).

James says that the "prayer of faith" saves. What is the prayer "of faith"? It could be (1) a simple adjectival genitive: a prayer characterized by faith, a "faithful prayer"; (2) a prayer generated by belief on the part of the ones praying that God answers prayer, that is, faith that prayer is effective; (3) prayer that meets with faith in the one being prayed for.

5:15

It may be unnecessary to decide among them. Because of the corporate nature of this prayer, the faith of the one prayed for and the faith of those praying are one, and the community's petition to God for healing is characterized by trust that God is the one who sovereignly acts on behalf of his people.

Faith energizes prayer, but not because faith is some kind of magical power or psychic force that effectualizes the prayer. Faith is that which connects a person to God and characterizes a relationship with God. It is this relationship to the healing God that secures answers to prayer. "The prayer of faith will save" is an abbreviated way of saying that the prayer of the person who stands in a faith relationship with God secures God's response in healing the person who is sick.

But this very idea raises two difficult questions. First, does this guarantee that a prayer of faith will result in healing, and if so, does that mean that if God does not heal it is because of insufficient faith? Second, how is it that healing and forgiveness may depend not on the faith and prayer of the person who is sick or in need of forgiveness, but upon the faith and prayer of someone else?

Again, the answer lies in the corporate nature of the people of God. The prayer of the community for the sick person is itself the prayer of the sick person, because when one is sick, all are sick. Thus too, even the result of forgiveness of sins—if that is the cause of the sickness (note the contingency: not all sickness is due to sin, but some might be)—comes about by the intercession of the church. This is why James goes on to exhort mutual confession and intercession "so that you [Gk. plural] may be healed." The health of the community depends on the health of its members, and the prayer life of one is the prayer life of all.

The parallel with the story of Jesus's healing of the paralytic man in Capernaum is also significant because there too the first result of the "intercession," as it were, of the man's friends is not that he was healed, but that his sins were forgiven (Mark 2:5).

The word "save" can, of course, refer either to physical healing (cf. Luke 8:50, where the faith of a girl's parents leads to her physical resuscitation) or to the rescue of a person from guilt and condemnation (e.g., Eph. 2:5, 8) or to the eschatological salvation in the judgment (e.g., Rom. 5:9–10). The context here in James at least partly has healing in view (Ropes 1916: 308), but the connection with forgiveness of sins (5:16) demonstrates that James has both in mind or perhaps does not sharply distinguish between them,[9] and eschatological salvation certainly is evident elsewhere in James (1:21; 2:14; 4:12). Again, the distinction that we generally draw may be more the product of our dualistic mind-set. The health of the individual, both physical and spiritual, is an element of the health of the community, both present and future (see Hartin 2003: 268–69).

"The Lord will raise him up" appears to be some kind of promise also linked with the future. The key here is to recognize the relationship of this verse with the following one, which links the mutual intercession of the community with the health of the whole community. Once again, with the corporate dimension in mind, it is not necessary to suppose that every instance of physical ailment will be healed, nor is it necessary to spiritualize the text. The Lord will provide deliverance to his people, both physical and spiritual, and it is in this mode that James uses resurrection language. Although James does not develop the

9. As indeed is true of many occurrences in the NT. Compare Acts 4:8–12, where both physical and eternal salvation seem to be in view.

theological implications of Jesus's resurrection in the life of the believer, the OT expectation of the ultimate restoration of God's people (which saw its climactic fulfillment in the resurrection of Jesus) is an ever-present theme in James, and in the OT this expectation is often put in terms of "raising up."

These verses also raise the question of the connection between the illness and sin. Some commentators (e.g., Ropes 1916: 308) assume that James is adopting the widespread notion that illness is, or at least can be, the result of sin, as seen in, for example, T. Reu. 1.6–7. A connection between some illness and sin is recognized elsewhere in the NT as well (Mark 2:1–12; 1 Cor. 11:30; and possibly 1 Cor. 5:5, although the story of the man born blind in John 9 urges caution in any specific case [see especially John 9:1–3]). But note James's use of the conditional, "even if." *If* the sick person has committed sin, he or she will be forgiven. And even if there is sin, James does not necessarily directly connect the illness and the sin. But the intercession of the body of believers on behalf of its members does encompass both the physical and spiritual dimension, at both the individual and the corporate level.

The verse as a whole that connects the Lord's saving and raising up, the removal of sickness, and the forgiveness of sins, is an echo of the eschatological expectation of Isa. 33:22–24, which also interestingly refers to the Lord as "lawgiver and judge" (cf. James 4:12).

5:16 Corporate prayer requires corporate confession, and this produces corporate forgiveness. This is not new to James. Daniel's prayer in Dan. 9:4–10 particularly expresses corporate confession as a prerequisite to corporate forgiveness and a preliminary to corporate intercession. The individual believer who called the elders is a part of the body, and he or she therefore shares in its intercession, confession, and healing.

This verse generates still other questions. How do we apply this expectation of corporate confession to one another? Is it a general mandate? What things are supposed to be confessed? Is it all sins, or only certain ones? How is such confession to be implemented in the church?

One way of resolving these questions is to take James's requirement of mutual confession as no more than the obligation of every believer to confess sins one has committed against another believer to the injured party and to ask for forgiveness. This is not, then, a general exhortation to mutual confession but a practical application of Jesus's teaching in Matt. 5:24 that members of the church have an obligation to be reconciled to one another.

The difficulty here is that James gives no indication of such a restriction, and he makes no mention of mutual forgiveness, which would be more to the point if internecine strife was all that he had in mind. The only forgiveness in view here is God's forgiveness. Hence, the mutual confession is for the purpose of intercession with God, not reconciliation between fellow believers. Again, if we may refer to Dan. 9 as the precedent, both individuals and the community as a whole have sinned against God, and God is the one to whom confession is made and whose forgiveness is sought.

Since James's concern is *mutual* confession, no case can be made here for designating the elders (presbyters, priests) as official hearers of confession and grantors of absolution. Corporate confession is appropriate for corporate sin. In other words, although it may be salubrious indeed for individuals to confess their individual sins to other individuals, James probably is thinking about those sins that involve the whole body, such as the "wars" mentioned in 4:1. If an individual has sinned against the whole body, then confession to the whole body by way of its elders is appropriate, and sins that disrupt the harmony and peace of the community must be dealt with within the community, not by posting them in public, not even by putting them on display before everyone in the church, but by way of the elders who represent the body as a whole.

This corporate confession and intercession is important, in particular "so that you may be healed." Note that in the Greek verb (ἰαθῆτε, *iathēte*), the "you" is plural. Both physical and spiritual illnesses attend the church as a whole. Corporate confession of corporate sins and prayer for one another heals the church's wounds. This is particularly applicable to the situation described in 4:1–2 and 4:11–12 of mutual destructiveness that results from selfishness and judgmentalism.

In 5:16b we have the summary apophthegm for the importance of corporate prayer: the prayer of the righteous person is powerful and effective. The word translated "effective" (ἐνεργουμένη, *energoumenē*) is a participle that could be either passive or middle. If the participle is passive, then it is conditional, and the sentence means something like "the prayer of a righteous person is of great power when (if) it is made effective" (either by faith or by the activity of the Spirit; Mayor 1897: 177–79). But James gives no indication of any thing or person making the prayer effectual, and the stress is not on some unseen agent, but on prayer as having significant power.

Alternatively, "effective" could be understood as modifying the noun "prayer" rather than the verb "has power," in which case James would be saying that it is "effective" prayer that has power. However, this would be tautologous, saying, in effect, that effective prayer is effective. Dibelius (1975: 256) proposes that the participle in context simply means "active" (cf. 2 Cor. 4:12, where the verb ἐνεργέω means "to be active"). This yields "the active prayer of a righteous person has great power." But this would imply the possibility of an "inactive prayer," which seems odd.

It is best to take the participle as modifying "is powerful," explaining not under what conditions it is effective, but in what way prayer has power: it is powerful because it effects change. James's point is that prayer causes things to happen, as the example of Elijah in 5:17–18 demonstrates. It causes things to happen because God responds to it.[10]

5:17–18   We who are accustomed to thinking in the categories of Rom. 3 may at this point wonder who is "righteous" that his or her prayer may be powerful. If no

---

10. This appears to be the direction suggested by Ropes (1916: 309), who translates "when it [prayer] is exercised."

one but Jesus is righteous, is this a convoluted way of saying that only Jesus can pray effectively? Is James hinting at Christ's intercession, as it is developed in the book of Hebrews?

These questions are not, however, in James's purview, as his reference to Elijah demonstrates. In Pauline terms, Elijah was a sinner too, yet here he is presented as an example of a righteous man whose prayer was powerful and effective. It is the faithful person, the person motivated by and oriented to faith and who is righteous in the Lord's sight, whose prayer is effective. Even more to James's point here, it is the faithful *community* whose prayer may be regarded as powerful and effective.[11]

Elijah was regarded in Judaism as second only to Moses as a prophet. The stories in 1 Kings present him as manifesting miracles in ways similar to Moses, and apart from his successor, Elisha (who is like a second Joshua), no other prophet in the OT manifests the power of God's Spirit so prominently. Subsequent Jewish tradition developed the Elijah tradition even further. The closing words of the OT in English Bibles (Mal. 4:5–6) expect a returning Elijah to restore Israel in preparation for the day of the Lord, a tradition carried even further in Sir. 48:10.

The appearance of Elijah with Moses at Jesus's transfiguration (Mark 9:4 and pars.) seems to mark Elijah's importance for the followers of Jesus as well (cf. Rom. 11:2), and the expectation of Elijah's "return" as antecedent to the day of the Lord (based on Mal. 4:5) is regarded by Jesus as fulfilled in the ministry of John the Baptist (Matt. 17:12; Mark 9:13; cf. Luke 1:17).

James can therefore assume that his readers know the story of Elijah. The occasion of Elijah's prayer that the drought would end was right after the Mount Carmel incident (1 Kings 18), which more than any other event in Elijah's life stands as a marker of God's judgment against idolatry and the restoration of righteousness in Israel. (One might also note the astonishing faith that Elijah exhibited in being willing to use up large quantities of precious water to douse his offering prior to its supernatural inflagration.) But Elijah's prayer for returning rains after the prophets of Baal were cut down receives no immediate answer. His servant must go and return from looking out to the sea seven times before he finally sees the little cloud that becomes a great downpour. Likewise, the believer in times of trouble may need to wait and pray patiently for some time before the prayer for God's restoration of righteousness is answered.

James's example of Elijah is more than just an example. It puts things, once again, in an eschatological mode of thinking. Many incidents in the life of Elijah could have been adduced to illustrate the power of prayer, but in choosing this one, James reminds the readers that prayer is the context within which the believer faithfully waits for God's justice. Hartin (2003: 271) makes

11. This is not incompatible with Paul's emphasis on Jesus as the only righteous one, because the church, comprising all the people who have faith, is now the embodiment of Christ, and all believers are righteous in him.

the interesting suggestion that James perhaps presents Elijah as the concluding example of the righteous (i.e., "faith-ful") person because the "twelve tribes" to whom James is addressed are still dispersed (1:1), awaiting restoration. The likelier reason for mentioning the restoration of rains is that it draws another connection between prayer and patience, and again it draws attention to God's promises of restoration (the early and late "rains" in Joel 2:23 echoed in James 5:7). As the eschatological rains must be waited for patiently, so they must be prayed for patiently.

However, James's explicit reason for referring to Elijah is simply the effectiveness of his prayer. James stresses that Elijah was a man "like us by nature." The word translated "like . . . by nature" (ὁμοιοπαθής, homoiopathēs) could mean "like [us] in experience," that is, he underwent the same things we do; but more likely it means, as it does in Acts 14:15 (its only other NT occurrence), "of the same nature" (see BDAG 706). Even though Elijah experienced many things that most people do not, he had no special immunity from the limitations and evils of this life, as is apparent from his doldrums recorded in 1 Kings 19:9–10. But Elijah was a man of faith. The same power of prayer that Elijah exhibited is available to every believer.

Additional Notes

5:13. The commands to pray and sing praise (on third-person imperatives, see the additional note on 1:5) are progressive (present) imperatives that might indicate that James is stressing the necessity of continually or habitually praying or singing (Moo 2000: 236), but caution is generally advisable in inferring too much from the tense of a verb.

5:14. The word "anointing" is an aorist participle (ἀλείψαντες) and may therefore indicate an action prior to that of praying, but it also could refer to anointing as simultaneous with praying (Ropes 1916: 305; Mussner 1975: 219–20) and thus be a symbolic indication of prayer (see the commentary on 5:14).

5:15. Here the word for "prayer" (εὐχή) is not the customary one; it more commonly means "vow" or "oath" (as in Acts 18:18), although occasionally it can mean "prayer" (Josephus, *J.W.* 7.5.6 §155; see BDAG 416). Clearly, it cannot mean "vow" here, especially given the proscription of oaths in 5:12. Possibly, James is using this unusual word because it carries the force of commitment along with prayer. In any case, the phrase "prayer of faith" indicates a prayer stemming from an attitude of trust and commitment. It is not the "prayer that really, really thinks that it will get what is asked for" that will rescue the sick person, but the "prayer that flows from trust and faithful commitment."

5:15. "Even if" (κἄν [= καὶ ἐάν]) takes καί adverbially with ἐάν rather than as a conjunction. If read as a conjunction ("and if"), καί is introducing further information rather than introducing a concessive clause, but in either case, James's point is that prayer is effective not just for physical healing, but also for spiritual restoration.

5:15. The passive apodosis "he will be forgiven" is literally "it will be forgiven to him" (ἀφεθήσεται αὐτῷ), a construction found in the LXX that reproduces literally the Hebrew נִסְלַח לוֹ (e.g., Lev. 4:26), semantically equivalent to "he will be forgiven." The occurrence in James of this frequent phrase of Leviticus may further suggest that intercessory prayer by the elders is analogous to priestly intercessory atonement offerings. Of course, the NT elsewhere indicates that the efficacy of such intercession, either by offerings or by prayer, is only by virtue of the once-for-all atonement of Jesus's crucifixion (see especially Heb. 10:1–10), but the emphasis here is on the relationship of God's forgiveness to mutual intercession and communal faith.

5:17. The Greek for "he prayed earnestly" involves the pairing of a dative noun with a cognate verb, προσευχῇ προσηύξατο, which would be translated literally as "in prayer he prayed" or perhaps "prayerfully he prayed." This is suggestive of Semitic idiom and indeed is a common Septuagintal way of rendering the Hebrew cognate infinitive absolute (e.g., Gen. 2:17, where מוֹת תָּמוּת ["you will surely die"] is rendered into Greek as θανάτῳ ἀποθανεῖσθε). Thus, BDAG 879, most translations, and many commentators suggest a translation such as "prayed earnestly" or "prayed fervently." Since the cognate infinitive absolute was already disappearing from later biblical Hebrew, it may be that the intensive force was forgotten, and James may be focusing not so much on the fervency of Elijah's prayer as on Elijah's choice of the power of prayer as opposed to some other action. However, the occurrence of similar dative noun/cognate verb pairings elsewhere in the NT with an intensive force (e.g., Luke 22:15; John 3:29), plus the fact that the idiom occurs with regularity in the LXX, suggests that intensification probably is intended here as well (see Wallace 1996: 168–69).

5:17. The notation of James that it did not rain for "three and a half years" does not perfectly match with 1 Kings 18:1, which indicates only three years of drought (also, 1 Kings nowhere mentions Elijah praying for the drought to start). The tradition of three and a half years also appears in Luke 4:25 on the lips of Jesus, and James may have shared this tradition. Moo (2000: 248) suggests that the figure "three and a half" years is used in both Luke and James specifically to draw an implicit analogy with the eschatological period of trial noted in Dan. 7:25. James thus may be drawing an additional connection between the believer's experience of suffering and the eschatological hope by reminding his readers that the time of tribulation will eventuate in the fulfillment of promise.

5:18. "Heaven gave rain" is idiomatic for "God sent rain" (1 Kings 18:1 is in view), but there may also be a play on the two parts of creation (heaven and earth) as the means of God's provision: "heaven gave rain, and the land [ἡ γῆ] brought forth fruit."

VIII. Closing Exhortation: Mutual Responsibility and Blessing (5:19–20)

The last two verses of James close both the section on prayer and the letter as a whole (Ropes 1916: 313). It seems to us like a strange way to close a letter, but 1 John, another "homiletical" letter like James, ends similarly.[1] This closing exhortation reminds believers not only of the dangers of wandering from the truth of the gospel (which is as much a matter of ethics as of doctrine), but also of the mercy of God in providing for renewal of faith. It thus puts all the preceding warnings and woes in the context of the gospel of God's forgiveness.

As a conclusion to the section on prayer, it also reminds Christians that intercession on behalf of fellow believers might be a matter of life to them and is of a piece with the great work of salvation wrought by Jesus Christ. What a privilege, not just to carry everything to God in prayer, but by doing so to be a part of God's work of covering a multitude of sins and saving souls from eternal death.

Exegesis and Exposition

¹⁹My brothers, if anyone among you has wandered from the truth, and someone turns him back, ²⁰⌐he should know⌐ that the one who turns a sinner back from his wandering way will save ⌐his soul from death⌐ and will cover a multitude of sins.

5:19–20 James introduces this last section, as he has so many others, with the vocative "my brothers" (here, as in 2:1, standing at the very beginning of the sentence). He thereby reminds them one last time of his effective connection with his readers. He assumes that they are fellow believers, siblings in the family of God, and that they, with him, are "all in it together."

The verb for "turn" which James uses twice in 5:19–20, ἐπιστρέφω (epistrephō), is commonly used to translate the Hebrew šûb, the verb used to indicate a turning away from sin and toward God, that is, to "repent" (cf. Matt. 13:15 quoting Isa. 6:10). We are once again reminded of the teaching of Jesus, who began his ministry by urging people to repent and believe the gospel of God's kingdom (Matt. 4:17; Mark 1:15), and who then instructed his disciples to engage in a similar ministry (Matt. 28:19). Bede (PL 93:40) points

1. James's ending also resembles the ending of Sirach (51:29–30 RSV): "May your soul rejoice in his mercy, and may you not be put to shame when you praise him. Do your work before the appointed time, and in God's time he will give you your reward."

out that whereas in James 3 the author acknowledges the tongue's power but condemns its evil use, here he points to its equally powerful proper use.

The word for "wandered" (πλανηθῇ, *planēthē*) is passive in form and might mean "has been led astray"; however, the emphasis is not on an external cause of the wandering, but (as in 1:14) on the willful action of the person departing from the truth, veering from the true course. It is not unlike the experience of getting lost in the woods. When hikers leave the path, they can get entangled and lost, but if a park ranger leads them back to the path, the lost hikers have been saved from grief and possibly from death.

James refers to the sinner in question as wandering "from the truth." "Wandering" is serious business in the NT (2 Tim. 3:13; 2 Pet. 2:15) and involves not just doctrine, but life. Note too that in the NT "truth" (ἀλήθεια, *alētheia*) is something that one does or obeys as well as knows (Gal. 5:7; 1 John 1:6). Likewise for James (see the commentary on 1:18), the truth from which one has wandered is not just intellective or doctrinal (though that would be involved); it includes the practical righteousness indicated by the Hebrew word *ĕmet*, which the Greek OT usually translates with the word ἀλήθεια. It encompasses both thought (truth) and deed (fidelity). The verse should remind us once again of James's deep concern for faith—a true, active, obedient, and genuine faith.

The verb translated "cover" in 5:20 (καλύπτω, *kalyptō*) also means "to hide, conceal" (BDAG 505), but James's point is not that leading someone to repentance conceals or covers up a sin. "Covering sin" in this case signifies forgiving it, removing it, eliminating its guilt, as it does in Ps. 32:1, "Blessed is the one whose transgression is forgiven, whose sin is covered," and Ps. 85:2, "You forgave the iniquity of your people; you covered all their sin."

This last verse of James is ambiguous in one respect. Whose soul is saved by the action of returning a sinner, and whose sins are covered? The antecedent of "his," the one whose soul is saved, could be either the wanderer who repents or the one who turns him back. Some commentators (Mayor 1897: 231–32; Davids 1982: 201; Martin 1988: 220; Johnson 1995: 339; Moo 2000: 250–51; Hartin 2003: 286–87) suggest that it is the soul of the one who wanders, but others (Cantinat 1973: 262) suggest that it is the one who restores a fellow believer whose life is saved and whose sins are covered.[2]

The root of the idea that those who bring others to repentance have their own sins covered and/or souls saved is in Ezekiel (Ezek. 3:18–21), where the prophet is called upon to warn people of the judgment that will come. God tells Ezekiel, "But if you warn the righteous person not to sin, and he does not sin, he shall surely live, because he took warning, and you will have delivered your soul" (Ezek. 3:21). Since it is Ezekiel's own soul that is saved by this warning

2. This latter approach is seen already in Origen, *Hom. Lev.* 2.4. Not a few commentators (e.g., Dibelius 1975: 258; Ropes 1916: 315–16; Laws 1980: 239; Mussner 1975: 233) divide the verse and thus see the life being saved as that of the repenter, but the covering of sins as the benefit for the rescuer. However, as Hartin (2003: 286) points out, "This solution . . . is confusing, and does not give any reason to explain why James would suddenly jump in the course of this brief verse from one referent to another."

activity, regardless of whether or not the warned person repents, it may be argued that this is what James has in mind (see also 1 Tim. 4:16).

However, two things militate against this view. First, Ezekiel's saving of his own soul is predicated on his obedience in giving the warning, not on the repentance of the persons warned, whereas James is linking the saving or covering to the actual return of the erring believer. According to 1:15, death is the result of sin. This "death" that James has in mind in both places is not physical death, but death that removes one from God, that is, eternal damnation. It seems inherently unlikely that failure to accomplish the erring believer's desired repentance would condemn the one who attempts the rescue, and equally unlikely that success in accomplishing someone else's repentance would be the key to one's own salvation.

Second, given the fact that James's interest in this whole paragraph is intercession and its effectiveness even with regard to sin, an interest predicated on the mutual responsibility and interconnectedness of all believers, it appears more likely that James is pointing to the fact that intervention on behalf of an erring believer can be expected to be effective (the prayer of the righteous person is of powerful effect [5:16]).

Whether it is the wanderer or the rescuer who is saved from death, the concluding statement by James, in the context of the whole paragraph, should remind the reader that the sin of an individual within the church is a sin that the church needs to deal with, a sin for which it is responsible, and a sin about which the whole community must pray. Thus does the church share in the interest of Jesus, who as a good shepherd makes the one wandering sheep a priority concern (Matt. 18:10–20).

The passage assumes the corporate character of the community of faith. The errant believer is not separate from the one who returns him to the path, and saving him from eternal death is also beneficial to the one who returns him. So the argument in the commentaries as to whether the one whose many sins are covered is the wanderer or the rescuer is not crucial to understanding James's point. Restoring an errant believer covers sin within the community, which includes both the wanderer and the rescuer.

This is confirmed by James's probable allusion to Prov. 10:12, a verse more clearly quoted in 1 Pet. 4:8: "love covers a multitude of sins." Returning a wanderer to the right path is an act of love. On the cross, Jesus not only has removed sin, covered it, and forgiven it, but also thereby has secured the means of returning the sinner to the path of righteousness. Again, for James, as for Jesus: if no fruits, then no roots. The sinner must repent and believe, not just "believe" in the narrow sense of intellectual acknowledgment (cf. 2:14, 19). For the sinner, repentance (i.e., a return to obedience) and faith are inseparable, and there is not one without the other. The question that we might want to ask, "Which comes first?" is of no interest to James, at least not in this letter. What is of interest to James, as has been evident throughout the letter, is that neither obedience nor faith is optional. And so this final apophthegmatic summary, although to our ears it may sound like an abrupt ending, links faith and works, love and atonement, corporate life and individual life, present righteousness and future judgment, intercession and confession. It thus well serves to end James's exhortation.

Additional Notes

5:20. Here the verbs in future tense (σώσει, καλύψει) are, as in 5:15, probably general futures, stemming from the conditional nature of the phrase "one who turns a sinner from error," but an actual future reference to the final judgment is possible.

5:20. Codex Vaticanus (B) and a few other manuscripts read the second-person plural γινώσκετε (probably still to be understood as an imperative) instead of third singular γινωσκέτω. This reading avoids the ambiguity of the subject of γινωσκέτω, and for that reason it is more likely to be secondary.

5:20. The manuscript tradition is sharply divided on the wording after σώσει ψυχὴν. Manuscripts ℵ, A, P, 33, and, implicitly, the Vulgate read σώσει ψυχὴν αὐτοῦ ἐκ θανάτου, but 𝔓⁷⁴, B, and a few others read σώσει ψυχὴν ἐκ θανάτου αὐτοῦ ("will save a soul from his death"). Manuscript Ψ and the Majority Text simply eliminate the αὐτοῦ ("will save a soul from death"). Although UBS⁴ gives the first reading a C rating to indicate uncertainty, it probably is not that uncertain: both the 𝔓⁷⁴/B reading and the Majority Text reading can be explained as attempts to disambiguate the first reading, whereas relocating or adding the αὐτοῦ after ψυχὴν, which makes the verse more problematic, is an unlikely action for a scribe.

5:20. The allusion to Prov. 10:12 in both James 5:20 and 1 Pet. 4:8 relates to the Hebrew MT, not the LXX, which has τοὺς μὴ φιλονεικοῦντας καλύπτει φιλία ("affection covers those who do not love strife"). Ropes (1916: 316) therefore argues that neither James 5:20 nor 1 Pet. 4:8 is directly dependent on Prov. 10:12, and instead he hypothesizes an otherwise unknown Greek aphorism. Given the wide variations in Greek translations of the OT now known to have existed even in the first century, plus the fact that it is not at all uncommon for a NT quotation to reflect the MT rather than the "standard" LXX reading, Ropes's theory is unconvincing.

Excursus 1
Faith as the Central Concern of James

A feature of the Epistle of James frequently overlooked is its concern with faith. Far from being concerned only with "external" obedience, it is precisely because faith is so crucially important that it is necessary to ensure that one has genuine faith. Because James's emphasis is on the believer's manifesting of God's character rather than understanding his nature, faith is primarily set forth not as an acceptance of concepts about God and salvation, but as loyalty to a person.

The Epistle of James, in its concern with faith in Christ (2:1), therefore bears much closer similarity to the rest of the NT than to anything in Jewish wisdom literature. James shares with some wisdom literature, such as Job, a concern about the problem of suffering, but unlike Job, which struggles with the uncertainties of suffering and asks "Why?" James simply exhorts faith and directs the reader to the eschatological hope. James shares with wisdom literature a concern to "get wisdom," but James's answer is not to pursue it by inquiry, but simply to ask for it in faith. A concern with faith runs throughout the letter. James is not about good works as such; it is about true faith.

Faith Is Christological (2:1)

The genitive clause of πίστις κυρίου ἡμῶν Ἰησοῦ Χριστοῦ (*pistis kyriou hēmōn Iēsou Christou*, literally "faith of our Lord Jesus Christ") should be understood as an objective genitive, "faith in Jesus" (e.g., Mayor 1897: 76; Ropes 1916: 187; Chaine 1927: 40), not subjective, "the faith that Jesus believed" (so, among many others, Hartin 2003: 117, 129; Johnson 1995: 220; see the commentary on 2:1 for interaction with the arguments). In the NT the construction ἔχειν πίστιν (*echein pistin*) + genitive means "to believe in." Mark 11:22 is the clearest NT parallel, where Jesus commands his disciples, ἔχετε πίστιν θεοῦ (*echete pistin theou*, have faith in God) (see also Acts 3:16). It is highly unlikely that Jesus was telling his disciples to have "the faith of God," that is, the faith that God has. Nor in context is it likely to mean "hold on to the faithfulness of God," either in James or in Mark. Further, since in James 2:1 Jesus is referred to as "Christ" and "the Lord of glory" (taking τῆς δόξης [*tēs doxēs*] as modifying not πίστιν [*pistin*] but the much more obvious κυρίου [*kyriou*] or possibly χριστοῦ [*christou*]), it is difficult to see this as no more than a reference to "the faith that Jesus had in God as reflected in his teaching" (Johnson 1995: 220).[1]

Backing this up is James's self-identification in 1:1 as "servant of God and Lord Jesus Christ" (no articles in the Greek text). Whether this means "servant of Jesus Christ who is God and Lord" or "servant of God and also servant of Jesus Christ," the running together of the two between Ἰάκωβος (*Iakōbos*, James) and δοῦλος (*doulos*, servant) demonstrates that they are taken as a unit in James's thinking. As servant of both, James is concerned with faithfulness and commitment to both, a relationship of attachment to both as one.

Therefore, this faith in Jesus as the Lord of glory must determine the meaning of all the other references to "Lord," particularly the parousia of the Lord in James 5.

Faith Is Eschatological (5:7–11)

In James the eschatological aspect of faith is an extension of its christological character: 5:7 exhorts believers to be patient until the parousia of the Lord. Since "Lord" refers to Jesus Christ in both 1:1 and 2:1, this whole segment of 5:7–11 (where κύριος occurs five times) is laden with the expectation of the Lord's (i.e., Jesus's) parousia. James reflects Jesus's language here, declaring the parousia to be ἤγγικεν (*ēngiken*, it is near). This is the same verb that occurs in the Gospels when recounting Jesus's preaching that the reign of God is near.

One might argue that this is nothing more than common Jewish eschatological expectation. However, although it has a marked relationship with Jewish eschatology generally, it is also marked by some specifically, or at least notably, Christian characteristics, especially the pattern of referring to God as Father (1:17, 27; 3:9; and implicitly in 1:18) in echo of Jesus's instruction.

Doubting, or "Double-Mindedness," Is the Opposite of Faith

The one who lacks wisdom must ask "in faith" (1:6), which means not doubting. Because doubting is opposite to faith, it is severely condemned:

1:6: "He who doubts is like a wave of the sea, blown and tossed about."

1:8: "A two-souled person is unstable."

4:8b: "Purify your hearts, you two-souled people."

Hence, the one who does not have faith cannot expect to have prayer answered (1:7).

As Martin (1988: 19) observes, "doubting" in 1:7–8 is not so much uncertainty about whether one will get what one asks for as a lack of full commitment

---

1. For a further defense of the objective genitive here and of the implicitly christological (though primitive) character of faith in the Epistle of James, see the commentary. Suffice it at this point to note that even if 2:1 is a reference to Jesus's faith as the pattern, James's concern is that the recipients of his letter exhibit genuine faith.

to God's promises—and a committed awaiting of God's promises is faith (see the commentary on 1:7). Doubting, the opposite of faith, thus "places the character of God in question."

Genuine Faith Has Another Direct Enemy, False Faith, Which Is the Result of Self-Deception

James repeatedly warns against self-deception (1:16, 22) and false or delusional faith. This is seen especially in James 2 but is also implicit in the false wisdom described in 3:15–16, the "doubting" in 1:6–8, and the failure to reckon with God's sovereign disposition in 4:13–17.

The Poor Are the "Rich in Faith" (2:5)

The poor are the ones who are chosen by God, who are heirs of the promised kingdom, and who love God. Note that James does not say "the poor who are rich in good works." We should also connect 2:5 with 1:12, where those who love God are promised the victor's crown of life for their endurance of testing, which is a testing of faith according to 1:3, which leads to that full expression of faith, ὑπομονή (*hypomonē*, endurance). Obviously, here faith signifies more than just being intellectually persuaded by a proposition, but in fact no NT author, including Paul, simply equates having faith with being intellectually persuaded.

Even Wisdom Is Effectively Faith

Note how in 3:13 the relation between wisdom and deeds parallels the relation between faith and deeds in James 2. This reflects the fact that for James, true wisdom, the wisdom "from above" (i.e., from God), exhibits an attitude of dependence on God, that is, faith.

Salvation Is by Faith

James actually comes closer than Paul does to saying that we are saved by faith. James 5:15 indicates that "the prayer of faith will save [σώσει, *sōsei*] the sick person, and the Lord will raise him up. And if he has committed sin, he will be forgiven."

One might at first suppose that the "saving" here simply refers to healing, since the word σῴζω (*sōzō*) basically means "to rescue" (Greeks thus could say, "Asclepius [the god of healing] 'saves'"). However, a connection between the physical illness and sin occurs in the second half of the verse and indicates that the prayer of faith is also instrumental in the forgiveness of sins. Thus, the need for physical healing (physical salvation) and the need for deliverance from sin (spiritual salvation) are not dissociated in James (cf. Mark 2:5, where Jesus, before healing the man of his paralysis, forgives his sins; note that for neither James nor Jesus is the connection direct). Further, σώσει occurs again just five verses later in 5:20, where again deliverance of a sinner from wandering is also the deliverance of his or her "soul/life" (ψυχή, *psychē*) from death.

Therefore, Since Faith Is So Important to James, It Is Crucial to Have the Right Kind of Faith

Thus, the concern in the diatribe of James 2 is not about faith as opposed to works; rather, it is about true faith as opposed to false faith, empty faith (2:20) versus completed faith (2:22), dead faith (2:17, 26) versus active and living faith. Works are the completion of faith (2:22: ἐκ τῶν ἔργων ἡ πίστις ἐτελειώθη, *ek tōn ergōn hē pistis eteleiōthē*). If people say that they have a "working knowledge" of Greek or Hebrew, it means that they know enough to put it to use. But if in fact they never do put it to use, it is hardly a genuine working knowledge. However, the "putting it to use" is not the same as the knowledge; rather, it is what happens when the knowledge is there.

Thus, James's reference to the "faith" of those who claim to have faith but do not have works is one of irony. The article is one of previous reference in 2:14b: "Can that kind of faith save him?" The point is that James only concedes the term *faith* to the nondoers in a loose way, for the sake of argument. Except for the apparent contradiction of 2:24 with Paul ("So you see a person is justified by works, and not by faith alone"), it is hard to see why anyone would ever conceive of James as proclaiming anything other than faith as the necessary way of relating to God.

Some Other Observations on Faith in James

Faith under Duress Works Endurance (ὑπομονή, hypomonē)

The connection of faith with endurance is suggestive. Why does the testing of faith work patient endurance (1:3)? Because faith is a disposition or orientation toward life that permeates every aspect of life, so that when trial comes, believers have something beyond themselves to hang on to. And because faith is antecedent to ὑπομονή, it is, once again, absolutely essential.

Faith Submits to God

In 4:7–8 James urges his hearers to submit to God: "Submit, therefore, to God, and resist the devil, and he will flee from you. Draw near to God, and he will draw near to you. Cleanse your hands, sinners, and purify your hearts, you double-minded [δίψυχοι, *dipsychoi*]." Sinners and δίψυχοι are parallel because being of divided mind (i.e., not having faith) is ungodliness.

Faith Is an Attitude That Is "Quick to Hear"

Hearing (which in this context indicates the response of obedience) is a faith attitude (1:19). It is a disposition, however, not just a string of deeds. This is even clearer from 1:16, where "not being deceived" includes having the right conception of the person of God. Once again, although the focus is on the character of God, not his attributes abstractly considered, James does indicate a cognitive element to faith that is important. James is concerned with more than just works.

And in this same passage (1:21) James exhorts his readers to "receive the implanted word that is able to save your souls." In the parable of the sower, receiving the word is the way Jesus described the response of faith (Mark 4:20), which is active in terms of the human will deciding something, but the activity is one of deciding to be receptive (an active passivity as it were), allowing an implanted word to take root and grow.

Along the same lines (in the same passage) is the command "Know, my brothers . . ." (1:19). Faith, again, includes a cognitive dimension. Even the works in view are works "of the word" (λόγος, *logos*; 1:22). The nondoer of work (1:25) is a nondoer of the word, a person whom James compares to someone who looks at a mirror but then quickly forgets the image there. In other words, such persons fail to appropriate the *logos* into their lives: they hear it, but they do not believe it. Hence, the Epistle of James is properly seen as the epistle of genuine faith, not the epistle of works (see Mussner 1975: 133–36).

Excursus 2
Faith, Works, and Justification in James and Paul

I maintain that the Epistle of James is best read on its own terms, not as a "reaction" to Paul or even to a misunderstood Paulinism. The assumption, so often made, of a polarization between Pauline (Gentile) and Petrine (Jewish) Christianity in the first century, which Acts has glossed over, must be suspended until both Paul's writings and the Epistle of James have been examined on their own terms.[1] It must be admitted, however, that whether or not James is directly or indirectly reacting to Paul, a comparison of James 2:24 with Rom. 3:28 seems to show a conflict between the two authors.

> **Romans 3:28**   "For we hold that one is justified by faith apart from works of the law."
>
> **James 2:24**   "By works a man is justified and not by faith alone."

James's words "not by faith alone" seem to stand in direct contradiction to Paul's formulation, such that many scholars, like Dibelius, regard it as "inconceivable" that James could be anything but a reaction to Paul (or a misunderstood version of Paul). The apparent irreconcilability even led Luther to offer his doctoral hat to anyone who could bring James and Paul into harmony.[2]

Whether or not James is reacting to some form of "Paulinism," a close examination of both will show that no contradiction actually exists between James and Paul himself. They are using the shared vocabulary and examples of Judaism, but in different ways, since they are facing quite different problems. In particular, the texts cited are using the terms "justification," "faith," and "works" somewhat differently. Further, careful attention to the entirety of Paul's letters and the entire message of James will demonstrate that although

---

1. Schlatter (1927: 419) made this point some time ago, and recently Bockmuehl (2006: 121–36) has reinforced it by his challenge to the entire paradigm of a Petrine versus Pauline Christianity.

2. The conversation is recorded in Luther 1914: 3.253, cited in Laato (1997: 44n8). Melanchthon (*Loci Communes* 9.5.12) argued that James was not fighting Paul, but "refuting the error of those who think themselves to be righteous on account of a profession of doctrines." Unfortunately, Melanchthon failed to persuade Luther.

their interests are different, their underlying theological commitments are constitutive of the same basic faith in Jesus Christ.

Before looking at James 2:14–26 in relation to Galatians and Romans, we do well to pay attention to the context leading up to that passage.

As Laato (1997: 47) notes, the introduction to James's concerns in 1:16–25 gives the background for how James understands the law and the necessity of the believer's obedience.[3] Here we see that James shares with Paul the notion of the priority of God's word in bringing salvation. Note the following:

1. James insists (like Jesus in Matt. 7:24, 26) that it is the doing of the word, not just the hearing of it, that leads to blessing (cf. Rom. 2:13).
2. It is, however, the word that is implanted and received that is able to save souls (James 1:21).
3. Further, the effective power of the word to bring life is according to the purpose of God (James 1:18), and this effectual word is the "word of truth" (cf. Eph. 1:13).
4. This word of truth is the source of the "bringing forth" (i.e., birth) of "us" as a "firstfruits" of creation (James 1:18), a reference to the initiation of the promised eschatological age (cf. 2 Thess. 2:13).
5. This birth-giving, fruit-producing implanted word is also the "law of freedom" (James 1:25).[4]
6. All this points to the fact that James has in the background the promise of Jer. 31:31–34 that in the eschatological age the law would be written on the heart (implanted), which constitutes the new covenant (cf. 2 Cor. 3).

Thus, 1:16–25 indicates that for James as much as for Paul, God's word is what makes alive and brings forth new life. That word, the word of truth, the word that is implanted and received, can only be the gospel.

Likewise, 2:1–13 is contextually important for understanding the latter half of James 2. James's concern is the problem of a disconnection between a professed faith and a life of faith, particularly in the problems of showing favoritism. Favoritism is inconsistent with faith (2:1) on many fronts; in particular, it disrespects the poor (which insults God; Prov. 14:31; 17:5) and is a denial of mercy, to which faith lays claim.

This passage also gives indication as to what James's conception of law is. It is, above all, the love command of Lev. 19:18 (cf. 2:8), just as it is for Jesus (Mark 12:31 and pars.) and Paul (Rom. 13:9–10; Gal. 5:14), and favoritism is out of conformity with this central command.

These set the context for James's discussion in 2:14–26 of the problem of a "faith" that is not really faith. If anything is clear from this passage, it is

---

3. This section is much indebted to Laato 1997, although I think that Laato may have made James too much like Paul.

4. Laato (1997: 50–51) shows how in 1:25 the "law of freedom" is the same as the "word" of 1:21–23, which one may either hear and not do or hear and do.

that faith devoid of commensurate actions ("works") is "dead" (2:17, 26), useless (2:16, 20), a bare corpse (2:26). Such faith is given the name "faith" only because it is being claimed as such, not because it is real (2:14).

Thus, "works" are to faith as the breath of life (the "spirit") is to a body. Further, works bring faith to expression and thus "fulfill" it (2:23) and "perfect" or complete it (2:22). Just as a prophecy is "fulfilled" or brought to its expected completion when the predicted event happens, so faith is fulfilled when it eventuates in works. This does not mean that works somehow turn faith into a living faith. It simply observes that living faith lives; it does not just lie there like a corpse.

This is the context for James's specific reference to Abraham. The offering of Isaac, much discussed in Judaism as the manifestation of Abraham's obedience, is the eventuation of Abraham's real faith. Obedience does not produce true faith; true faith produces obedience. So when James says that faith "works together with his works" (2:22), he is speaking not of soteriology per se (since James knew that Abraham was called by God and that promises were given to him, including the declaration of his justification by faith, long before the offering of Isaac), but of the whole manifestation of Abraham's life in God. Faith was "completed" by works, not vice versa.

We also should note that the particular "works" that James gives as examples are not Paul's works of the law (for the Torah had not yet been given);[5] they are works of faith, works that exemplify the fact that Abraham and Rahab trusted God. In the case of Rahab, her "work" was the sheltering of the Israelite spies,[6] a manifestation of her belief that the Lord would do what he promised in delivering the land into the hand of the Israelites (Josh. 2:9).[7] It is interesting that James here refers to the spies as "messengers" (ἄγγελοι, *angeloi*), a term not used in the LXX of Josh. 2, possibly because the spies were, in effect, those who could tell Rahab about God. Whether or not this is in James's purview, Rahab, by receiving and sheltering the spies, in effect treated them in the same beneficent way that Jesus predicted some Gentiles (ἔθνη, *ethnē*, nations) would treat his disciples and thereby be received into the kingdom on judgment day (Matt. 25:32–40; cf. Matt. 10:42).

5. This, of course, is particularly true if Paul's phrase "works of the law" specifically focuses on the "boundary markers" of the people of God, such as circumcision, Sabbath observance, and food laws (as per Dunn 1998: 356). The example of Rahab runs counter to any notion of these, and James, for all his interest in the law, never mentions these things, but only such things as are encompassed in the love command. But James's explicit identification of Rahab as a prostitute should put to rest any suggestion that any aspect of the law as such is a prerequisite of, or constitutive of, faith.

6. The argument by Ward (1968) that both Rahab's and Abraham's "work" was the showing of hospitality not only is unsupported in the text (Abraham's "hospitality" is not even implied and has to be deduced by circuitous means), but also misses James's point, which is not that "hospitality" is *the* ticket to justification, but that genuine faith results in commensurate behavior.

7. One might object here that Rahab's reaction was one of fear more than trust, but a fear that God will execute his promised judgment is effectively a nascent faith.

We are now in a position to examine James's use of the terms in relation to Paul's. First, the so-called faith that James discusses in James 2 is not the genuine faith that Paul makes crucial to one's relationship to God. James, as much as Paul, is concerned that Christians have faith in all circumstances (e.g., 1:3, 6; 2:1; 5:15; but throughout the letter; see "Controlling Theme: Genuine Faith" in the introduction). But James is deeply aware of the possibility of self-deception and hypocrisy, whereby people think that they "have faith" but are deluded. A life that is inherently and endemically out of accord with the faith that one avers is the best indication that no real faith is present at all.

James therefore regards it as obvious that if someone does not do the works of faith, it is a false faith that cannot save. Further, note that James does not even concede the term "faith" to such a position. James does not say, "If someone has faith but has not works . . ."; he says, "If someone *says* he has faith but has not works. . . ."[8] He thereby indicates that the "faith" critiqued throughout James 2 is not genuine.

Paul never directly uses the term *faith* to refer to such a hypocritical and delusional faith.[9] He does come close, however, in 1 Cor. 13:2, where he says, "If I have all faith, so as to remove mountains, but have not love, I am nothing." This is not all that far from James, for whom the "works" in view are manifestations of the love command.

Conversely, the "works" that Paul condemns are not the works that James commends (Machen 1976: 239).[10] Whether or not Paul's concern with "works of the law" is focused primarily on those things that Jews understood to be the "boundary markers" of the people of God, such as circumcision, Sabbath observance, and food laws (so Dunn 1998: 356),[11] he has in mind some kind

8. A detail observed by Cranfield (1965: 185) and much earlier by Calvin (1948: 309–10).

9. Dibelius (1975: 175) also sees Paul and James operating with different meanings for "faith," but he further detects two kinds of faith even within the letters of Paul. One kind of faith is "the acceptance of the marvelous divine decree which justifies the sinner"; the other kind means "Christian convictions." For Dibelius (1975: 178), the apparent contradiction comes because James only sees the latter, or rather sees faith as a general trust in God. Space constraints prohibit a fuller treatment of this here, but in my opinion, Paul's concept of faith even in passages such as Gal. 3:23–25 and Rom. 3–4 includes not just acceptance of divine provision, but also the commitment to the message of the gospel, and it is precisely Paul's christological convictions that stand over against "works of the law" (Rom. 10:4). James, when he is not talking about the pseudo-faith that makes claims but does not act accordingly, thinks of faith in a way not so dissimilar to Paul (cf. 1:3–6, 18, 21 [receiving the implanted word]; 2:1 [faith in Christ], 5; 5:15; see also excursus 1 above).

10. Bauckham (1999: 134) makes a strikingly similar statement: "When Paul says that justification is not by works he does not have in mind at all these works done in faith. When James says that justification is by works he does not have in mind at all the works of self-reliance which compromise faith. Thus, beneath the surface of disagreement, there is a deeper agreement."

11. Dunn recognizes that "works of the law" does not refer exclusively to the "boundary" laws, but he argues that these are the points at issue, not just in Christian circles but for Judaism generally (as is evident in 4QMMT, a Qumran document that specifically talks about "some works of the law"), because they are what gave the Jews their distinct identity and what gave rise to the controversy among the Galatians. See the discussion in Dunn 1998: 354–66.

of actions that people do to establish their own righteousness (Rom. 10:3; Phil. 3:9) rather than accept the gracious provision of God in Christ's work on the cross (Rom. 3:24). This is a much different problem from the one that James faces, where people simply are not doing works (actions) that are the normal and necessary fruit of faith.

Paul, as much as James, is concerned that Christ be obeyed, not simply acknowledged (Rom. 2:8; 6:16; 2 Cor. 10:5), and that Christian faith be lived, not just claimed. Those who live a life of debauchery will not inherit the kingdom of God (Gal. 5:19–21), and the rebellious are "laying up a treasure of wrath for the day of wrath" (Rom. 2:5), very much like James 5:3. The characteristic "fruit of the Spirit" of Gal. 5:22–23 is, on the other hand, quite like what James mentions as true wisdom in James 3:17. Even the problem of a disconnection between faith and life is condemned in Titus 1:16: "They profess to know God, but they deny him by their works." And before Paul is faced with the specific problem of "works of the law," he resembles James in commending the Thessalonians for their "work of faith" (1 Thess. 1:3; cf. 2 Thess. 1:11; and the quotation of Ps. 112:9 in 2 Cor. 9:9).

Further, when Paul addresses the broad issues of law and righteousness, he is completely in agreement with James: in Rom. 2:13, it is not the hearers of the law who will be justified, but the doers—a statement virtually the same as James 1:22–25.

Finally, the "justification" that James has in mind is not precisely the same as the "justification" that Paul has in view (Calvin 1948: 315), although they are related. The meaning of the term as James uses it is taken up in detail in the commentary, but of the possible meanings for "justify," only two are viable here: "to declare righteous" as in a court judgment or to "prove to be in the right" in some regard, that is, "to vindicate."[12] When James says that a person is "justified by works" and refers to Abraham and Rahab as examples, he is referring either to the eschatological confirmation of righteousness at the last judgment (as in Matt. 12:37; Rom. 2:13) or to the effectual proving of righteousness. Jeremias (1954–55: 371) argued for the former (see also Beyschlag 1897: 132–33; Moo 2000: 135). But as argued in the commentary, James's use of the aorist indicatives and the lack of any indication that James is thinking of future justification at this juncture point in the other direction. Just as Abraham and Rahab were vindicated by their works, so too is the person of faith of any age. This is essentially what Jesus says when he declares, "You will recognize them by their fruits" (Matt. 7:20). It also may be that James implicitly includes both meanings (Laato 1997: 69), in that the probative establishment of righteousness by works and the eschatological confirmation of righteous status are closely connected in James.[13]

---

12. The rare meaning "to make righteous" does not come into play in either Paul or James. The meaning "to clear a debt" is irrelevant here, as is the meaning "to give justice to." See my comments on 2:21–24 above.

13. For example, 3:18: "The fruit [RSV: 'harvest'] of righteousness is sown in peace for those who do peace." This, probably an echo of Matt. 5:9, has in view the eschatological harvest.

In any case, there is no indication that James is thinking of justification either as a process or as a juridical declaration by which a person comes into right relationship to God.

It thus appears that whether one adopts the position of the "new perspective" on Paul that the justification in question involves the matter of who is established as a member of God's people, or whether one takes the classical view that Paul is speaking of the believer being accepted as righteous before God (as is usually taken to be in view in Luke 18:14; Rom. 3:28, and similar passages) or being forgiven by God (as in Rom. 4:6–7), James is not directly contradicting Paul, for James is addressing neither of those two issues. For James, "justified" has the same meaning the word does when Jesus, in Luke 7:35, says, "Wisdom is justified[14] by all her children." It simply means "vindicated" by how it plays out.

We need to address one other matter here: the function and place of the law. James simply accepts the normal Jewish understanding of the law as speaking the will of God; it is the "word of truth" that makes believers a "firstfruits," a word that, in accordance with the new covenant expectation of Jer. 31:33–34, is "implanted" in the believer in order to save souls. It is therefore a "law of freedom," a "kingdom law" (royal law) that has its summary expression in the love command of Lev. 19:18. Paul, on the other hand, views the law as bringing slavery and death by "rousing" the flesh (Rom. 7:5). One should remember, however, that Paul's usual and common view of the law is, like that of James, positive. It is the revelation of God's will and character (Rom. 2:18) and is "good" (Rom. 7:12, 16). It is the improper use of the law that makes it not good (Phil. 3:9; 1 Tim. 1:8). When considered as the law of the Spirit, it brings freedom (Rom. 8:2).[15]

But did not Paul say that believers are no longer "under law" (Gal. 5:18)? Did not the gospel "abolish the law" (Eph. 2:15)? Quite apart from the fact that if what Paul meant was that the law of God is defunct, it would put him squarely contrary to Jesus (Matt. 5:17–18; Luke 16:17), a close look at the passages in question shows more clearly what Paul was getting at. In Eph. 2 Paul is specifically dealing with the law of "commandments and ordinances" that separate Jews from Gentiles, and he is indicating that the gospel now obviates the former distinctions. This "dividing wall" (Eph. 2:14) that kept Gentiles at a distance is now broken down. In Galatians Paul deals specifically with the problem of people who want to be "justified" by the law, that is, to

14. In Luke 7:35 ἐδικαιώθη (edikaiōthē, is justified) probably is a gnomic or proverbial aorist (expressing a general truth). James's use cannot be simply axiomatic, however, because he specifies Abraham and Rahab as the subjects.

15. Although some exegetes understand the νόμος (nomos, law) of Rom. 8:2a as the "principle" of the Spirit of life, the same word is used to describe the "law of sin and death." It is much better to understand the contrastive "laws" of Rom. 8 as the law that the Spirit writes on the heart (as in Rom. 2:15; 2 Cor. 3:7–8, 17, which have Jer. 31 in the background) in opposition to the law written externally in stone, which is engaged by the "flesh." The law kills when it is a tool in the hand of sin (1 Cor. 15:56), but as a tool of the Spirit, it liberates.

achieve a status of righteousness before God by obedience to a set of commandments. As in Ephesians, the particular question is that of circumcision, which divides Jew and Gentile; but more broadly, the "Judaizers" at Galatia were, by insisting on circumcision, binding themselves to a fleshly approach to law—they were, to use the vocabulary of Rom. 10:3, seeking to establish "their own righteousness." That use of the law is precisely what makes the law a killer, because if the law is treated as the source of blessing and curse (justification), and the law curses all nonperformance of it, then the result is death. All these questions James never engages.[16] James's problem is not people who are seeking to establish their own righteousness (as in Rom. 10:3; Phil. 3:9), but people who are not behaving in accordance with their professed faith in Christ.

Faith, real faith, for both Paul and James, is not just a verbalization of belief (Rom. 2:13; James 2:14; cf. Matt. 7:21), nor is it just thinking that certain doctrines are true (James 2:19), nor is it performing some assignment such as keeping the Ten Commandments (cf. the rich man in Matt. 19:16–22 and pars.), or going to church, or going forward at an altar call. Effective faith is, instead, a life orientation, an ongoing disposition of the heart toward faithfulness to God or loyalty to his covenant (including its ethical obligations). This is why Jesus (Matt. 4:17) and James (James 4:9), as well as Paul (Rom. 2:4), expect repentance and a change of life at the beginning of faith. It is also why Paul's faith principle does not overthrow the law, but on the contrary is an upholding of the law (Rom. 3:31).

None of this is meant to deny a significant difference between Paul and James. They appropriated the same Jewish heritage, the same vocabulary, and the same story of Abraham, but they have applied it differently, not because they hold essentially different theologies, but because they are struggling with different problems from different vantage points and have different concerns. Only by listening to each man's own voice can we avoid drawing false conclusions from one or the other.

Nevertheless, it may seem surprising that James would express himself in language that appears so contrary to Paul's formulations, and it may provoke many, as it did Luther,[17] to question the value or reliability of James. But let us approach the issue by way of an analogy. Suppose James had said, "What good is it, my brothers, if someone says he has faith but bows down to idols? Can that faith save him?" I doubt that such language would have raised any objections from anyone, even Luther. Some human actions, such as worshiping

16. Bauckham (1999: 151) rightly observes: "In what James says positively about the law there is very striking continuity between James and Paul. It is only in what James does not say that there is discontinuity."

17. Although Luther expressed doubts about James, he shared James's conviction regarding genuine faith, as is clear from his preface to Romans, where he says, "O, it is a living, busy, active mighty thing, this faith. It is impossible for it not to be doing good works incessantly" (*LW* 35:370). For more on this quotation, see note 1 at the beginning of the introduction.

idols, are so inherently contrary to genuine faith that anyone who claims to believe and does them should immediately be seen to be a fake. James says that one of those inherently contrary actions is inaction in situations where a brother's or sister's need is evident. Jesus says much the same thing as James when he declares, "Not everyone who says to me, 'Lord, Lord,' will enter the kingdom of heaven, but the one who does the will of my Father who is in heaven" (in Matt. 7:21).

This highlights James's conviction that genuine biblical faith cannot be a bare acknowledgment of certain facts, not even the acknowledgment of biblical doctrines—for example, that there is one God only—since even demons acknowledge such facts (2:19). The Greek word for "faith" (πίστις, *pistis*), as well as the Hebrew word that it regularly translates (אֱמוּנָה, *'ĕmûnâ*), ordinarily includes a component of commitment and faithfulness as well as intellectual belief. One might envision genuine believers, under threat of death, bowing to an idol and afterward despising their cowardice, but "believers" who do so continually and without compunction make a mockery of their own "faith," and that kind of "faith" cannot justify, in any sense of the word. To put it tautologously: James simply says that any "faith" that does not do the things that faith does is not faith.

Thus, although Luther and many readers since have construed James 2:14–26, and particularly the statement in 2:24, as a challenge to Paul's notion of justification by faith, it is no such thing.[18] It is precisely because James is aware of the importance of faith (see, e.g., 1:6; see also excursus 1, "Faith as the Central Concern of James") that he is concerned that his readers' faith be genuine. And genuine faith is by nature active, doing deeds of faith, as Abraham and Rahab did. What James does challenge is the idea that by simply adopting a creed, saying the right words, or joining a church, one stands in line to inherit the kingdom of God. In a day when people often confuse justification by faith with justification by *profession* of faith, we do well to hear James's concern.

---

18. It may very well be a challenge to a perversion of Paul's doctrine, but it is easier simply to suppose that James is writing prior to the development of Galatians and Romans, and the similarity in terminology is due to a common Jewish environment, which both Paul and James used to answer entirely different questions. See, in the introduction, "Was James a Reaction to Paul (or Later Paulinism)?"

Excursus 3
James and Wisdom

It has long been recognized that James has, among the NT books, a special relationship to the wisdom literature of the OT and intertestamental period. The margins of the NA²⁷ text of James contain more than thirty cross-references to Jewish wisdom literature of the Old Testament or Second Temple period, versus ten to the Pentateuch, eighteen to prophets, and seventeen to psalms (some of which are "wisdom" psalms). But although James clearly was influenced by Jewish wisdom, the nature and extent of that influence is debated. Almost all scholars who have studied James agree that there is some kind of relevant background in Jewish wisdom literature, but some go so far as to call James the "wisdom" book of the NT,[1] and a few even suggest that it was originally a strictly Jewish wisdom text that only later was Christianized (Massebieau 1895; Spitta 1896: 382–91). On the other hand, Ropes (1916: 7) and Dibelius (1975: 1–11) argue that although James seems to be influenced in some way by Jewish wisdom materials, the essential nature of the book is Hellenistic. Most interpreters in the last few decades have landed somewhere in between, recognizing the influences both of Greek rhetorical devices and language and of Jewish material content. Further, even the Jewish influence is not exclusively that of wisdom: the margins of NA²⁷ also reveal that of the eight actual quotations in James, only two are wisdom texts, most citations being from the Pentateuch.

The object of this excursus is twofold: first, to identify more precisely the relation of James to the genres of Jewish wisdom literature, and second, to describe the character of James's particular "wisdom" content. That is to say, we will ask, first, "Can James be called 'wisdom literature' in any sense?" and, second, "What is the nature of the wisdom that James urges believers to ask for?"

James and Jewish Wisdom Literature

Before we can address the first question, we must ask, "What is Jewish wisdom literature?" This is difficult to answer because the books generally identified

---

The material in this section is adapted and abbreviated from McCartney 2000.

1. H. G. Conzelmann (*IDBSup* 960) says that "the entire Letter of James is a wisdom document in parenetic style." Heinrici (1908: 75; cited in Baasland 1982: 123) likens the relationship of James to Jewish wisdom as like that of Revelation to the Jewish apocalyptic tradition.

as wisdom are quite diverse, both in form and in content. Various answers have been given, but there are some broad characteristics that those who have made a study of this body of material mention frequently as distinguishing marks.

First, the term *wisdom* can apply either to certain generic forms that appear in the wisdom literature (e.g., series of aphorisms, instruction books, nature lists, extended dialogic poetry, self-addressed reflection) or to the themes that wisdom tends to address in various forms (e.g., the purpose of life, the problem of suffering, mastery of one's environment, grappling with finitude, and the quest for truth assumed to be concealed within the created order; Crenshaw 1998). Wisdom literature is that body of material that exhibits both formal and thematic wisdom.

Second, wisdom is a practical matter. It is not a quest for knowledge for its own sake or knowledge of abstract truth, but knowledge of how to live. Wisdom "is the reasoned search for specific ways to assure well-being and the implementation of those discoveries in daily existence" (Crenshaw 1998: 24). It also has an appeal to the desire of human beings to have some measure of control over what happens to them. Wisdom's admonitions are expressed not in terms of duty but of advantage (Zimmerli 1976: 177).

Further, wisdom is, at least in its earlier forms, something hidden. Proverbs, Job, Ecclesiastes, Sirach, and Wisdom of Solomon are books that are searching, trying to ascertain "the truth of the matter." Wisdom typically is linked to creational theology rather than covenantal, because wisdom is looking for the inherent order in the world that can therefore enable humans to control their world. But Jewish wisdom books, coming from a cultural environment that depends on God, must further struggle with the tension between the self-reliance implicit in such a search and the dependence on God's mercy and disposition that cannot be controlled by human effort (Crenshaw 1998).

Does James fit this pattern? First, we must note several indisputable points of similarity. Baasland (1982: 123–24), asserting that James is *the* wisdom book of the NT, observes at least eight "wisdom" elements in the letter.

1. James knows and uses Proverbs. James 4:6 cites Prov. 3:34, and James 5:20 at least directly alludes to Prov. 10:12. To this we might add the echo of Prov. 27:1 ("Do not boast about tomorrow") in James 4:13–16 and many other parallels, although these do not necessarily evince direct dependence.
2. James explicitly refers to wisdom in 1:5; 3:13–18.
3. According to Baasland, at least 40 of the 108 verses of James have literary parallels in Jewish wisdom literature.
4. The language and style of James reflects wisdom origins. Baasland refers to the work of Halson (1968: 309), who notes that of James's 67 NT *hapax legomena*, 34 are found in the wisdom literature of the LXX; and of the 21 words that James shares with only one other NT author, 19 occur commonly in the wisdom books.

5. James is fond of using highly pictorial language in ways similar to Sirach and other wisdom writers. Some of this is directly paralleled in Sirach. Compare Sirach's "double-heart" (1:28) and testing by fire (2:5) with James's double-minded doubter (1:8) and the fire of the tongue (3:6). But it is the sheer quantity of these vibrant illustrations that clearly marks James as standing in this tradition. The stream of illustrative examples on the tongue in James 3:3–12 is breathtaking: bits in horses' mouths, great ships and little rudders, sparks and forest fires, the taming of animals, fresh springs and saltwater springs, and fruit trees—all in just ten verses. The reader also encounters dead bodies (2:26), waves and wind (1:6), misty vapors (4:14), mirrors (1:23), fading flowers (1:10), and patient farmers (5:7–8).[2]

6. James, alone among NT writers, specifically names Job as a figure to be emulated.[3]

7. Verses in James that are transitional from one general subject to another typically are drawn from wisdom tradition (1:4–8; 1:27; 4:6; 5:19).

8. Most important are particular themes of James that, though occurring sporadically elsewhere in the Bible, are central in wisdom—for example, the concern for widows and orphans (Fensham 1976), respect of persons, use and misuse of the tongue, and caution regarding future planning.

To this list many other points of contact could be added, especially James's relationship to Sirach. NA[27] notes no fewer than eleven allusions to Sirach in James, compared with six allusions and two citations involving Proverbs. Further, there are some conspicuous shared themes: the danger of the tongue (Sir. 19:6–12; 20:5–8, 18–20; 22:27; 28:13–26; 32:7–9), wisdom as a gift from God (Sir. 1:1–10), the danger of pride (Sir. 10:7–18), the warning against blaming God for sin (Sir. 15:11–20), and the ironic reference to silver and gold "rusting" in the context of hoarding wealth and not caring for the needy (Sir. 29:10).

In addition to these parallels between James and Second Temple Jewish wisdom, there are similarities in their way of thinking:

1. A person's life is lived either in good connections or in bad. An ethical dualism predominates in both James and in Jewish wisdom. Note in particular the contrast in James between sin giving birth to death and God giving birth to "us" (1:15, 18), the father of lights as opposed to the shifting shadow (1:17), the perfect (τέλειος, *teleios*) work of patience

2. Such illustrative language is not limited to Jewish wisdom. James's illustrative repertoire has parallels in Greek moral literature too, leading Ropes (1916: 6–18) and Dibelius (1975: 1–11) to think of James as primarily a Hellenistic Greek work. Nevertheless, it still stands as one more similarity to Jewish wisdom literature, even if not uniquely so.

3. The use of great OT personalities as exemplars is common in Jewish wisdom. See, for example, Sir. 44:1–49:16. The use of Job as an exemplar of patience is seen in the Testament of Job. For an argument that James is referring not to the Jewish traditions of Job but to the book of Job, see Richardson 2006.

(1:4) versus the maturation (ἀποτελέω, *apoteleō*) of sin (1:15), and the single-minded (ἁπλῶς, *haplōs*) giving of God (1:5) as opposed to the double-minded (δίψυχος, *dipsychos*) doubting of human beings (1:8).

2. As in Jewish wisdom literature generally, James has a fairly strong thematic concern that deeds have consequences.[4]

Not only the themes, but also the generic forms of wisdom literature, are evident in James. Davids (1988: 3635) notes that James exhibits an "apparently disjointed and proverbial nature of style." Many of the sayings in James, even though they have contextual linkages within the letter, could easily stand alone. This aphoristic style is one of the most notable features shared by James and Proverbs. Halson (1968: 311) counts twenty-three short, isolated aphorisms. But also like Proverbs, James has a few somewhat longer discourses, of which Halson identifies seven or eight (2:1–9; 2:14–26; 3:13–17; 4:1–6; 4:13–16; 5:1–6; and possibly 5:16b–18; cf. the "my son" discourses in Prov. 1–7, and the "virtuous wife" discourse in Prov. 31:10–31).

Several recent studies have shown James's similarities to specific instances of Jewish wisdom literature. For example, Gowan (1993) shows the similarity of the presuppositions of James 1:2–5 with those of 4 Maccabees, and Verseput (1998) notices the structural similarities with one of the wisdom texts found at Qumran, 4Q185.

But as Verseput (1998: 692) also warns, "The pervasiveness of wisdom elements throughout all the literature of the Second Temple period suggests that the Epistle of James cannot be accurately grouped among the wisdom documents by merely pointing out sapiential motifs or by imprudently associating its structure with wisdom instruction." And indeed, James does have some characteristics that do not fit the wisdom pattern.

First, at the very least, James is incomprehensible apart from certain Christian presuppositions that have no parallel in wisdom literature. Luck (1984) points to such things as God the Father giving birth to us by the word of truth (1:17–18), the implanted word (1:21), the reference to the audience as "beloved brethren" (1:19; 2:5; cf. 2:1, 14), the importance of and nature of true faith (2:14–26), and the "elders of the church" (5:14) as stemming from the unique social environment of early Christianity. These things are thus absent from Jewish wisdom.[5]

Second, James seems less concerned with the intellectual search for wisdom than with moral action befitting true wisdom.[6] Although not unique among

---

4. Baasland (1982: 124) adds a third similarity in thought patterns: a person is not regarded as an isolated entity, but is always part of a given set of social connections. However, I see this as hardly unique to wisdom literature; it runs throughout the Bible, and indeed if anything, is somewhat attenuated in the later wisdom books.

5. Proverbs writes from the vantage point of a father ("my son") rather than of a sibling ("dear brothers"). Ropes (1916: 17) sees James's form of address as being "utterly different" from that of Proverbs.

6. See below, "Wisdom Is Ethical Rather Than Intellective."

his Jewish contemporaries in thinking of wisdom as a moral matter, James, when speaking of wisdom itself (3:13–18), appears to be setting a true, active, socially conscientious wisdom over against a false kind of wisdom that is boastful and abandons social obligations in favor of private, intellectualized concerns (see Bindemann 1995). This contrast of true wisdom and false wisdom is rare in wisdom literature (although it does have an interesting counterpart in 1 Cor. 1–2).

Third, James does not fit into the literary categories of wisdom literature. Crenshaw (1998) discusses eight such categories: proverb, riddle, allegory, hymn, dialogue, autobiographical narrative, noun lists, and didactic narrative. Of these, only the proverb and the dialogue have a generic counterpart in some of James's aphorisms and the literarily constructed interlocution of 2:18. But even these are used differently. Whereas these genres are indigenous and constitutive in wisdom literature, they are only incidental useful tools in James, and the overall arguments of James can be sustained without them. Most of James is imperatival in tone,[7] even to the point of upbraiding the hearers and calling down woes, more like OT prophets than sages.

But the most significant difference is that James appears to be deeply conscious of real existential problems, not just generalized truths. The exhortations to stop fighting (James 4) and to anoint and pray for the sick (James 5) have no counterpart in wisdom literature. And the diatribe against favoritism in James 2 bears the vivid marks of real occurrences. Although the situations may be common enough that James can address them in a circulating letter, they are specific enough to characterize James not as a book of wisdom per se, but as a work that uses the wisdom tradition and forms familiar to his audience as a means of exhortation. Nor can we place James firmly in the camp of Hellenistic diatribes or paraeneses.[8] If nothing else, the passion evident in 2:4, 14–17; 4:1–6; and 5:1–6 ought to clue us in to the fact that James is neither a remote sage in his school nor a Hellenistic preacher uttering generalities. He is a pastor concerned for his people.

Nevertheless, James does recognize that his audience values wisdom, and he offers a picture of what true, godly wisdom looks like. His letter reveals at least five characteristics of such wisdom; it is (1) a divine gift (and therefore related to faith), (2) primarily ethical rather than intellective, (3) eschatologically motivated, (4) spiritual in nature, and (5) the wisdom of Jesus. The first

---

7. These generic differences from other Jewish wisdom texts are precisely why Ropes and Dibelius find James to be generically much closer to Greek forms of hortatory literature.

8. It is curious that even Ropes (1916: 15–16) points out so many marked differences between James and Greek diatribes that one wonders why he stuck with identifying James as a diatribe. Given that Dibelius (1975: 1–11) cannot provide any positive characteristics for an ostensible genre of paraenesis other than the use of *Stichwörter* (catchwords), and the paucity of evidence for paraenesis as a generic form as opposed to a rhetorical device, we must conclude that he too has failed to find any convincing generic model in Hellenism. Dibelius's only other characteristics of paraenesis are negative, such as the lack of organization and of continuity of thought. And as he himself shows, the use of catchwords is so common in much Jewish literature that their use can hardly be seen as evidence for paraenesis being a distinct genre.

three of these have points of similarity with some (though by no means all) other Jewish wisdom; the last two are uniquely Jacobean.

Wisdom Is a Divine Gift

James mentions wisdom twice in his letter (1:5; 3:13–18). In both places the concern is not on wisdom generally, but on true wisdom, which is of divine origin. "If someone among you lacks wisdom, he must ask from God, who gives to everyone unreservedly . . ." (1:5). The notion that wisdom is obtained by asking it of God is rooted in the prayer of Solomon (1 Kings 3), but the relationship between wisdom being a gift and the need therefore to ask for it is much more developed in Wis. 8:17–9:18.[9]

James's fuller discussion of wisdom occurs in 3:13–18. Hartin (1991: 97) regards this as the "very heart and centre of the body of the epistle."[10] Whether or not that is so, James does share the opinion of other Jewish wisdom writers that wisdom is a divine gift and crucial for living.

Also, because true wisdom comes "from above," it is singularly inappropriate to boast about it (3:14), for to do so gives the lie to one's very claim to be speaking the truth.[11] True wisdom is therefore marked by humility.[12]

But James goes further, because wisdom in James is closely related to faith. Baasland (1982), who is willing to identify James as a Christian wisdom book, nevertheless recognizes here a clear distinction from common Jewish wisdom. James's exhortation to wisdom is on the basis of faith (and, according to Baasland, baptism); it is not "clan" wisdom or simply the "Torah" wisdom found elsewhere, but an eschatological, Christian wisdom.

Notice the relationship of true wisdom and false wisdom in 3:15–17, and compare it with true and false faith in 2:14–26. Particularly close are 3:13 and 2:18:

2:18   But someone will say, "You have faith, and I have works." Show me your faith apart from your works, and I by my works will show you my faith.

3:13   Who is wise and understanding among you? Let him show by his good behavior his works [done] in the meekness of wisdom.

9. Indeed, the rest of the Wisdom of Solomon perhaps is intended to be read as the prayer of Solomon. Note the continued use of the second person throughout the book.

10. Although Hartin's chiastic analysis of 2:1–5:6 is somewhat forced, it is true that the gaining of true wisdom from God by humbly asking for it in submission to God is a major concern of James.

11. James 3:14: "But if you harbor bitter envy and selfish ambition in your heart, do not boast about it and thus give the lie to the truth." The implication is that to boast of one's wisdom, to be proud of knowing truth, is to belie the very truth that one professes to know (Mussner 1975: 171), since that truth includes the fact if one has wisdom, it is purely by grace. Teachers in the churches should read this verse twice a day until they take it to heart. Pride in one's knowledge is now, as much as in James's day, the source of much strife and is no product of true wisdom (3:16).

12. Instead of the proud, self-serving wisdom of the guru, James advocates the humble wisdom (Davids 1982: 209) of Jesus, who himself was humble (Matt. 11:29) but nevertheless spoke a wisdom that demanded a great deal of his hearers.

Just as true faith produces good works, so does true wisdom.

In 5:7–11 James contrasts the wisdom of the farmer, patiently waiting for God, with indifference to the poor. This seems an odd juxtaposition, but its oddity shows the connection with faith. Faith also waits in trust, but if it is indifferent to the poor, it is no true faith.

Finally, James says that faith without works is ἀργή (argē, vain, empty). Vanity is a wisdom concern. Ecclesiastes particularly dwells on the emptiness and vanity of life in this world. James seems to pick up on this, so that even a life of faith is vain, empty, and meaningless if it is a "faith" that does not act in accordance with its precepts. True wisdom is true faith.

Wisdom Is Ethical Rather Than Intellective

The "first of all" attribute of wisdom in 3:17 is that it is ἁγνός (hagnē, pure). For James, wisdom is essentially an ethical quality (U. Wilckens, *TDNT* 7:524–25). Knowledge, "savvy," cleverness, and wit may be considered as forms of wisdom, but these are capable of being used for impure purposes and can easily be regarded as grounds for and the means of boasting. But ethical purity, if it boasts, ceases to be purity, and hence a wisdom that is contentious or boastful ceases to be wisdom.[13] Because of this basic quality of purity, true wisdom produces its other ethical fruit: peacemaking, gentleness, and so forth.

Just as faith is associated with ethical behavior, so too is wisdom. Wisdom exhibits good behavior and meekness (3:13) and runs contrary to bitter envy, ambition, boasting, and lying (3:14). At no point in James is wisdom simply a matter of the knowing of facts (theoretical knowledge) or even of know-how (practical knowledge).

In particular, the wisdom of James focuses on two ethical issues: speech ethics and humility. The speech ethics of James is the subject of a special study by Baker (1995), who has given ample evidence for James's roots in the speech ethics of the ancient Near East, particularly as found in Jewish wisdom. But the ethics of humility is a dominant theme in Jewish wisdom as well, and many if not all the economic and social ethical matters in James essentially stem from this matter of humility. The description of wisdom in 3:13–18 is largely a description of humility: it lacks bitter envy, ambition, and boasting and is instead peaceable, gentle, compliant, and full of mercy. And consider the ills that James rails against throughout the book: blaming God for sin (1:13–14; cf. Sir. 15:11–20), favoritism (2:1–7; cf. Prov. 14:21), friendship with the world (4:1–10; including a quotation of Prov. 3:34 LXX and the exhortation to "humble yourselves" in 4:10), judging brothers and sisters (4:11–12; cf. Wis. 1:11), boasting (4:16), and business planning without recognition of God (4:13–17; cf. Prov. 27:1). Pride lies at the root of them all. Even the evils of the tongue may be classified here, since the section in James 3 begins with

13. Laws (1980: 163) points out that James avoids referring to this "earthly" thing as "wisdom." There is only one wisdom, and that which is contentious, self-seeking, and boastful is not it.

the warning that few should be teachers. Apparently, the desire to be called "rabbi" survived in the church, even though Jesus had discouraged it (Matt. 23:7–8).

Of course, the ethical character of wisdom is not unknown in Jewish wisdom. Later Judaism recognized all or almost all the books of the OT as the word of God, and the ethical demands of the Torah stood as the supreme standard of life, so an increasingly revelational notion of wisdom permeated later Judaism. And indeed, much of the later Jewish wisdom literature identifies wisdom with God's law.[14] The identification of wisdom with Torah may have its roots even in the earliest levels of Jewish wisdom tradition. In Prov. 9:10 the beginning of wisdom is the fear of the Lord, and "the fear of the LORD" in Ps. 19:9 appears in synonymous parallelism with the law, the decrees, the precepts, the commandment, and the ordinances of the Lord.[15] The identification of law and wisdom is even more developed in the late Second Temple period, Sirach being the prime example.[16]

Since the Torah is the ultimate source of wisdom, it is a freedom-giving Torah (2:12), but James takes the additional step of referring to this word of God as "implanted" (1:21). Here is another way in which James's uniquely Christian application of wisdom finds expression. For the wise, freedom-giving law of God to be effective, especially the royal law of love (2:8),[17] it must be implanted (1:21; see Luck 1984: 17). Once implanted, it must be received humbly.[18] Sustaining the agricultural metaphor, James affirms that the humble

14. Although this identification is already evident in Prov. 28, its vigorous development is seen in Sir. 24 (especially 24:23–25). Later Judaism adopts this idea generally. For example, *m. 'Abot* 6.7 gives a series of attributes of Torah that in Proverbs are a description of wisdom. Genesis Rabbah (a midrash on Genesis) begins with the words of Prov. 8:30 and applies it to Torah: "By looking into Torah, God created the world." See also Bar. 3:9–4:4.

15. If there is such a thing as a "wisdom" psalm, Ps. 19 surely is it, moving from the creation theology (19:1–6), to the praise of God's law for its guidance and protection (19:7–10), to the warning and safety of Torah, which uncovers what is hidden (19:11–13).

16. On the identification of wisdom and Torah in Sirach, see the comprehensive study by Schnabel (1985: especially 69–92). Schnabel's work also traces the identification of law and wisdom in other intertestamental Jewish literature, including the Dead Sea Scrolls, and in Paul's letters.

17. I take the "royal law" as a reference to the "kingdom law" or Torah summarized in Lev. 19:18, which James quotes (see the commentary on 2:8). The law is royal (βασιλικός, *basilikos*) because it is connected with the kingdom (βασιλεία, *basileia*) of 2:5, which may in turn have roots in Jesus's proclamation of the βασιλεία τοῦ θεοῦ (*basileia tou theou*, kingdom of God). In Mark 12:34, Jesus comments to the scribe who acknowledged this command that he was "not far from the kingdom of God." A passage from the Wisdom of Solomon shows well how Judaism related the notions of Torah, wisdom, and kingdom: "The beginning of wisdom is the most sincere desire for instruction, and concern for instruction is love of her, and love of her is the keeping of her laws, and giving heed to her laws is assurance of immortality, and immortality brings one near to God; so the desire for wisdom leads to a kingdom" (Wis. 6:17–20 RSV).

18. In James 1:21, it seems inherently much more sensible to take ἐν πραΰτητι not with ἀποθέμενοι (as the punctuation in NA²⁷ suggests), but with the following δέξασθε. Thus, the verse is not a tautologous "receive the word that has been implanted" but instruction on the attitude with which one is to receive what has been implanted, a sentiment echoed in 3:13.

response to God's planting of ethical wisdom eventuates in the production of good fruits (3:17). The following verse encapsulates this in what sounds like a wisdom saying: "Fruit of righteousness is sown in peace for those who do peace" (3:18).[19]

Since wisdom is, for James, primarily a moral or ethical entity rather than an intellective or cognitive one, the prayer mandate of 1:5 comes into clearer focus. The lack of wisdom that one should pray to have remedied is not an intelligence gap, but a moral gap. What is to be requested is the moral fortitude to face up to suffering and temptation and thereby become "perfect."

Wisdom Is Eschatologically Motivated

Although the eschatological dimension of the letter, particularly in James's exhortations to patience, are clear enough, some recent study has shown that this dimension of his thought permeates every aspect of the letter, including his notion of wisdom (Penner 1996). Such an eschatological focus is uncharacteristic of ancient Near Eastern wisdom generally and also of older Jewish wisdom, which takes its cue from creation and focuses on God's work and truth in the created order. Eschatology gets its impetus from redemption, stemming from a distrust of this world and a longing for the future overthrow of the present order. In wisdom, the idea is to avoid the natural retributions and seek the natural rewards of this present age; eschatology recognizes that this world is unfair, and thus it seeks reward and punishment in the future.

However, two forces were at work to merge these notions. First, wisdom had to deal with the problem of unjust suffering. Just as Jewish prophets struggled with the cognitive dissonance generated by a belief in Israel's election in the face of Israel's poor political situation, so Jewish wisdom struggled with the more generalized cognitive dissonance of a world wherein traditional wisdom did not always eventuate in a visibly happy life. Hence, Jewish wisdom of the late Second Temple period was drawn increasingly toward the redemptive eschatological framework of the prophets.

Second, and related to this, as awareness grew of a revealed wisdom from God (as opposed to what humans are able to figure out for themselves), the nature of the wisdom concept changed toward participation in God's wisdom, not just in creation, but also in redemption and law.[20] The seeds of this may already be seen in texts such as Isa. 33:6, where wisdom and understanding are eschatological blessings, and Isa. 11:2, where the "spirit of wisdom" is a messianic endowment. In the book of Daniel, wisdom and eschatology were

---

19. It has been suggested that this may be an *agraphon*, a saying of Jesus that was known as such in the early church, but was not written down and specifically attributed to him in the NT. By definition there is, of course, no way of knowing.

20. By the second century BC, all or almost all of the books in the Hebrew Bible were known and regarded as authoritative by all Jews, so that Jewish wisdom teachers such as Jesus the Son of Sirach, Baruch, the author of 4 Maccabees, and Pseudo-Phocylides drew freely not just from the wisdom books, but also from law, prophecy, and apocalyptic as sources for the divine wisdom.

being fused (Daniel was a sage, but his wisdom was supernatural), and Testaments of the Twelve Patriarchs has many instances of both traditional wisdom and eschatological expectation. Eschatology and wisdom come together also in Wisdom of Solomon and 4 Maccabees.

James stands in this stream. As Bauckham (1999: 34) says, "An eschatological orientation is not therefore anomolous; it is to be expected in wisdom paraenesis from the first century C.E." However, although the later wisdom books have an interest in God's judgment and refer to eschatology as a way of resolving certain wisdom questions, the sayings and admonitions of James, like those of Jesus, have an eschatological dimension not found in classical Jewish wisdom material (Hartin 1991: 64–69). This is because James recognizes the fact that the eschatological expectations are already being fulfilled. Although the parousia is still to come (5:7), James knows that the Messiah has already come (2:1). Hence, the divine gift of wisdom is now freely available to all who ask in faith (1:5–6). Above all, the readers are the "firstfruits of his creation" (1:18) who were given birth by the word of truth. The eschatological harvest has already begun.

Wisdom Is Spiritual

Remarkably, James never refers to the Holy Spirit in his letter.[21] Kirk (1969) probably is right in arguing that wisdom functions in James much as the Holy Spirit does in other NT writings. Kirk observes the following:

1. Wisdom in James, like the Holy Spirit in the Gospels, is a good gift that is requested of the Father. James speaks of asking God for the gift of wisdom (1:5) and goes on to speak of it as "every good gift," which comes down from above from a heavenly father ("father of lights," 1:17).[22] This is very much like Matt. 7:11, which speaks of asking the heavenly Father for good gifts, and its parallel in Luke 11:13, which identifies the good gift requested and given as the Holy Spirit.
2. There are some striking parallels between the fruit of wisdom in James 3:17 and the fruit of the Spirit in Gal. 5:22–6:8. (Note again that for James, wisdom is primarily not intellective, but moral and relational.)
3. Several references to wisdom elsewhere in the NT also refer to the Spirit. The most obvious is Eph. 1:17, where the author prays that "the Father

21. While I do take the πνεῦμα (pneuma, spirit) of 4:5 to be God's spirit—as that by which God imparts wisdom and understanding and certain unusual abilities to leaders, judges, and artisans (as in Exod. 35:31; Deut. 34:9; Judg. 3:10; Isa. 11:2; et al.)—this is not yet by James understood to be the person of the Holy Spirit, who is God himself. See the commentary on 4:5 for more.

22. The best explanation for "father of lights" is that of creator of the heavenly lights of Gen. 1. As creator of lights, he is source of all light and thus cannot be shadowed or darkened or mistaken. Referring to the creator as "father" personalizes the creator's relationship even to the nonhuman world, much as God's relationship is personalized in wisdom literature by the personification of wisdom itself.

. . . may give you the Spirit of wisdom" (NIV). The Spirit of wisdom is the Spirit given to the Messiah in Isa. 11:2. In contrast with the Holy Spirit and true wisdom are false wisdom and the spirit of the world in 1 Cor. 2:12–13 (Davis 1984). In 1 Cor. 12:8 the Spirit is identified as the source of the utterance of wisdom. Finally, Acts 6:3, picking up again on the messianic promise of Isa. 11, refers to those qualified to be deacons as those "full of the Spirit and of wisdom."

Kirk found the roots of this wisdom/Spirit identification in the OT and Jewish wisdom literature. Throughout the OT, wisdom and the presence of God's Spirit are closely linked (Gen. 41:38–39; Exod. 31:3–4 [cf. Exod. 28:3]; Deut. 34:9; Isa. 11:2). The activity of the creator Spirit of Gen. 1:1–2 resembles the activity of wisdom in Prov. 8. Likewise, Sir. 24:3–5 portrays wisdom in terms of the spirit of Genesis. In Gen. Rab. 85 Solomon's wisdom is identified as the product of the guidance of the Holy Spirit. And Hag. 2:5 suggests an identification of the pillar of cloud and fire as "my Spirit," the Spirit of God (echoed in Wis. 10:17). Broadly speaking, the functions of the Spirit of God in the OT frequently become, in the intertestamental period, the functions of wisdom (compare 1 En. 5.8–9 with Isa. 11:2–9). In the midst of a prayer attributed to Solomon, Wis. 9:17 even goes so far as to equate the gift of wisdom with the "holy Spirit from on high" (RSV).

Hence, Davids (1982: 55–56) suggests, "If some works have a wisdom Christology, James has a wisdom pneumatology, for wisdom in James functions as the Spirit does in Paul." This perhaps is somewhat overstated, but it does reinforce that James conceives of wisdom not as an abstract intellectual ability or cleverness at manipulating life, but as God's eschatological gift to the believer (the one who asks in faith) that empowers the believer ethically to live rightly and to endure persecution and trials.

Wisdom Is the Teaching of Jesus

The correspondences of James with the teaching of Jesus are numerous. In more than twenty instances, James's teaching reflects that of Jesus. The correspondence with the Gospel of Matthew is particularly high, with as many as fourteen points of contact with the Sermon on the Mount.[23]

Some of these correspondences are found elsewhere in Jewish literature. For example, the notion in James 2:10, that the one who keeps the whole law but stumbles in one matter becomes guilty of all of it, occurs both in Jesus's teaching (Matt. 5:19) and in Jewish teaching (*m. 'Abot* 2.1; Sipre Deut. 96.3.2; see Moore 1927: 1.467–68), although James and Jesus seem to have strengthened this notion somewhat. Similarly, the warning against slander, which James associates with judging (4:11; 5:9), resembles Jesus's warnings against judging in Matt. 7:1–5 and the caution against slander in Wis. 1:11.

23. See "James and the Wisdom of Jesus" in the introduction.

Both Jesus and James reflect Jewish wisdom in the form as well as the content of their teaching. Bauckham (1999: 37–47), referring to the work of Aune (1987) in classifying the aphorisms of Jesus, notes several points where the aphorisms of James, Jesus, and Jewish wisdom literature have formal (not necessarily material) resemblances.

These similarities, among other things, have led to the recent burgeoning of scholarship suggesting that Jesus was a wisdom teacher, a Jewish sage (Witherington 1994: 236–44; Stein 1978: 2–3). But Jesus did not simply echo the traditional wisdom of other Jewish sages. Much of what is found in traditional Jewish wisdom is absent from both Jesus's teaching and James.[24] Further, not only was his overall message of the presence and imminence of the kingdom unique, but also many of his specific ethical instructions were unique, or at least they are unknown elsewhere in Jewish literature. But curiously, some of these in fact are known in James. The preeminent example is the prohibition against swearing (for a comparison of Matt. 5:34–37 and James 5:12, see the commentary on 5:12).

Although some Jewish wisdom warned of the dangers of taking oaths (Eccles. 5:4; Sir. 23:9–13), none prohibited it entirely. Only 2 En. 49.1 resembles the statements of James and Jesus, and most scholars view this as a Christian interpolation.

Baasland (1982: 126) rightly observes that James's wisdom is decidedly drawn from the Jesus tradition. Where James reflects traditional Jewish wisdom, those aspects of Jewish wisdom are found also in Jesus's teaching. On the other hand, wherever James differs from Jewish wisdom tradition, he is demonstrably at one with the preaching of Jesus. As Witherington (1994: 236–47) suggests, James is expounding the peculiarly "subversive" wisdom of Jesus. This is true even though James never actually quotes any saying of Jesus as found in the Gospels.[25] It appears that James is either writing prior to the formal solidification of the Greek tradition of Jesus's words or is paraphrasing and reapplying the ethical teaching of Jesus.

All this is to show that wisdom for James is what it was for Jesus: it involved both the hearing and the doing of Jesus's words. According to Jesus, it is the "*wise* man who built his house upon the rock," who "hears these words of mine and does them" (Matt. 7:24). And this further demonstrates the essential Christianity of James. Whereas Paul refers to Christ himself as the wisdom of God (1 Cor. 1:24, 30), James understands the teaching of Jesus to be wisdom[26]

24. Bauckham (1999: 95) lists several—for example, exhortations to work hard, advice on what kind of friends to have, good and bad wives, and the raising of children.

25. This is one reason why the view of Hartin (1991) that James is directly dependent on an early form of Q (a hypothetical predecessor of a hypothetical document!) is unconvincing. See Bauckham's review of Hartin in Bauckham 1993.

26. This is not necessarily to deny any christological dimension to wisdom in James whatsoever. Vouga (1984: 22) sees the reference to "wisdom from above" in 3:14–18 as a christological allusion. Unfortunately, Vouga does not develop this idea in the introduction or in the commentary.

and Jesus to be the ultimate sage, along the lines already suggested by Matt. 12:42 // Luke 11:31: "The queen of the South . . . came from the ends of the earth to hear the wisdom of Solomon and behold, something greater than Solomon is here."

Conclusion

The goal of wisdom is the formation of character (Crenshaw 1998: 3), and James shares that goal. His unique interest in the practical application of the moral instruction of Jesus, and his frequent use of aphoristic style may well earn him the epithet of "the wisdom book of the New Testament," as long as it is clear that it is a *New Testament* wisdom, and that this wisdom is addressed to real-life church situations, not just hypothetical generic ones. Inasmuch as Jesus himself used Jewish wisdom, both its material and its forms, it is no surprise that Jewish wisdom tradition was taken over by his disciples. Thus, there is no need to suppose that the Epistle of James originally was a non-Christian wisdom piece later Christianized, nor is there good reason to think that the letter lacks any clearly Christian character. True, the great Pauline issues of Christology and redemptive history do not arise in James, but James ought to help us understand what is characteristically Christian. Without James, much of what it means to be a disciple of Jesus might have become lost. James reminds us that the essential matter is not just hearing or understanding the word of Jesus, as vital as that is, but acting on this intelligence and actually doing it. That is his wisdom.

Excursus 4
James and Suffering

Wisdom literature is concerned with the pragmatic questions of how to live and how to understand life, which for the Christian means how to live the life of faith. One of the great questions of wisdom literature is how to deal with suffering, and the experience of suffering causes people to yearn for understanding and wisdom. Thus, it is not surprising that James is concerned with Christian suffering. Indeed, Davids (1980; see also Davids 1982: 28–34) identifies the Epistle of James as being generically an instance of *Leidenstheologie*, a subgenre within the Jewish wisdom tradition. Yet James has no interest in either suffering or wisdom for its own sake. In this letter, the search for wisdom is closely linked with faith. Driving this letter is James's concern that his hearers evince genuine faith (1:3, 6; 2:1, 5, 14–26; 5:15), and suffering is of interest because it calls forth faith.

In this concern with suffering, James resembles 1 Peter. Both letters address the existential concern of why Christians are suffering, and both link suffering to the deepening of faith. However, each letter deals with it in distinct ways. Like Isaiah (and in dependence on Isaiah), 1 Peter links the suffering of the faithful with the redemptive-historical event of the suffering of the servant of the Lord (Christ), thus giving the Christian's suffering a christological meaning. Suffering becomes an experiential outworking of the believer's union with Christ. James, however, has only the slightest traces of this. His focus, like that of Daniel and other later wisdom literature, is on the promise of eschatological reversal and the theme of suffering as opportunity to show faith. For this reason, James has no emphasis on "suffering for the name" as 1 Peter does, and his only reference to "the name" in relation to suffering (2:7) is no more than an aspect of his argument against showing favoritism. It is not suffering itself, but the Christian's faithful response to suffering, that is of interest to James.

The subject of suffering comes up more or less explicitly only in the opening exhortation (1:1–12) and in part of the closing exhortations (5:7–11). Yet wisdom literature frequently uses *inclusio* (the placement of a feature at the beginning and the ending of a text) as a defining device. One can see it in, for example, the book of Job, where chapters 1–2 and chapter 42 frame the long poetic narrative and give it direction. Likewise, Matthew, the Gospel most influenced by the

This excursus has been adapted from McCartney 2002: 477–86.

Jewish wisdom genre (and the Gospel with the closest affinities with James),[1] begins and ends with a reference to God with us (1:23; 28:20) in order to give focus to that Gospel. So here in James the Christian response to suffering, as the framing subject of the letter, appears to be a significant feature.

James's treatment of the topic of suffering has three main interests: (1) suffering is a characteristic of the people of God; (2) suffering is one of the "trials" or tests that are a means to achieving Christian "perfection" or maturity; (3) suffering is a call to faithful living, in response both to one's own suffering and to the suffering of others.

Suffering Is a Characteristic of the People of God

The reference in 1:1 to the recipients as "diaspora," whether or not the term here implies a strictly Jewish audience, immediately emphasizes the suffering character of the people of God as those who are scattered in the world. It also may hint that the scattering/sowing is for the benefit of the world, since the scattering of God's people also scatters the seed of the word that they carry (the theme of word as seed is in 1:18, 21).[2] James thus shares with other NT writers the notion that the suffering of believers benefits others.

James also shares the NT conviction that the eschatological reversal has begun. The community of faith is the community of those who endure in suffering.[3] The people of humility are the people who will be exalted (1:9–10; 4:10).[4]

The notion of the community of faith as the suffering community has roots in the OT. For example, Ps. 86:1 uses "poor" as equivalent to one who depends on God. The Qumran community regarded itself as the community of the poor (1QHᵃ 13.22 [García Martínez and Tigchelaar 1997–98: 1.173]; 1QpHab 12.3, 6, 10; 4QpPsᵃ 2.10; 3.10). Possibly, James also regarded the Christian community as "the poor" (1:9; 2:5 [cf. Luke 6:20]).

1. On the similarities between James and Matthew, see, in the introduction, "James and the Wisdom of Jesus." See also Mussner 1975: 48–50. Hartin (1991) closely examines these similarities and concludes that Matthew and James came from a common environment and had access to a similar form of Q.

2. Hort (1909: 3) regards "diaspora" in James as strictly a reference to the scattering, unconnected with the sowing of the word in the world, because although such an idea does exist in the OT, it never uses the *zr'* (sow, seed) word group in such connections. However, the strong correlation of James with Jesus's teaching in the Synoptic Gospels suggests otherwise, because in those books Jesus frequently uses the imagery of sowing seed to refer to the dissemination of the word in the world.

3. James is concerned with individual response to suffering, but his main interest is in the suffering of the community, or the behavior of individual believers as that behavior affects the community.

4. See the commentary on 1:9–11 in regard to the question of whether the wealthy person in 1:10 is being addressed as a Christian who should rejoice that the wealth is temporary or as a reprobate who should mourn at the prospect of impending destruction. Whichever answer is given, James's main focus is on the eschatological reversal and consequently on a different way of looking at suffering and poverty.

However, economic poverty is not James's main concern. Where the economically poor person is mentioned, this person is not the believer, but rather is someone whom the believer is enjoined to treat with respect (2:2–6).[5] Likewise, although it is true that James has some harsh words for the rich in 5:1–6,[6] the concern is not the fact that they are rich, but that they fail to act responsibly with their wealth and even oppress the poor. It is because economic and social responsibility is indispensable to faith (2:15–16) that James is concerned with such responsibilities. James is interested in the genuineness of his readers' faith. Thus, although the community may have had both rich and poor in it, James is concerned not with the political dimensions of social justice, but with a sense of familial connectedness in the church and the believers' active compassion for those who suffer. Economic poverty, or wealth for that matter, is viewed as another "test" for the Christian, an opportunity to demonstrate faith by being ever cognizant of the eschatological reversal found in the gospel. And this brings us to the second dimension of suffering in James.

Suffering Is One of the Trials That Are Means to Christian Maturity

James has no notion of suffering itself being redemptive, either for the sufferer or for someone else; rather, it is the fortitude displayed in times of trial that is given positive theological value.[7] Again, this is somewhat different from 1 Peter, which focuses heavily on Christ's suffering as redemptive, and where the believer's suffering in doing good is a means of identification with Christ. Endurance in 1 Peter is enjoined because of what suffering does in the believer, uniting the believer to Christ's suffering. James, on the other hand, regards endurance as the primary thing that functions in the believer's life, and suffering is seen mostly as an opportunity to let endurance do its job of "perfecting" or maturing the believer.

This too is more along the lines of wisdom literature (cf. Wis. 3:4–5; Sir. 2:1; 2 Bar. 52.5–6). There, suffering is a test that gives one an opportunity to heroically endure, like Abraham (Jub. 19.8) or Joseph (T. Jos. 2.7) or Job

---

5. Both "the poor" and "the rich" are treated in James 2 in the third person. The "you" are those who react in certain ways to the poor and the rich. There is a diatribe against "you rich" (probably rhetorical), but no corresponding commendation or any kind of address to "you poor." Bauckham (1999: 188) therefore argues that at least the bulk of James's hearers were ordinary working-class people who by modern Western standards were indeed poor, but who in their society were not destitute. They are presumed to have the wherewithal to help the truly poor, the destitute who lack basic means of survival, such as food and adequate clothing.

6. James does not go as far as 1 En. 94–105, which suggests that all the rich are bound for perdition.

7. The term for "endurance" (ὑπομονή, *hypomonē*) is common in Greek moral literature, especially among the Stoics, for whom it refers to patiently enduring whatever comes without allowing distress to influence one's convictions, thinking, or lifestyle (F. Hauck, *TDNT* 4:582). Endurance is a particularly desirable trait for a soldier to possess. James, like Paul, applies the term to the Christian's faithfulness in staying the course in the face of opposition. It thereby is related to the biblical notion of faith.

(T. Job 4.5–6). Joy too is associated with suffering in wisdom thinking. Sirach 40:20 locates joy in wisdom, the path of which involves discipline and testing (cf. Sir. 4:17). James, in line with this tradition, states that trials are to be regarded as all joy (1:2). Although James later gives further reasons for joy in testing (1:12), here he indicates that testings are to be regarded as occasion for joy because they bring opportunities to endure and prove faith-keeping, and because they lead to wisdom. Again, in James it is not the suffering itself that produces maturity, but the faithful endurance within the trial. To put it succinctly, the Christian who endures is the Christian who matures.

James expresses this notion in a sorites, a sequence of causal links, in 1:3–4: trials (πειρασμοί, *peirasmoi*) are the means of testing (δοκίμιον, *dokimion*),[8] which provide opportunity for patient endurance (ὑπομονή, *hypomonē*), which brings one to be perfect or mature (τέλειος, *teleios*). Thus, James regards suffering as something to rejoice in because it moves one toward the eschatological goal of completion or perfection.

The believer's state of being complete or mature (τέλειος, *teleios*) is simply being what God intends one to be, being all that a human being should be, achieving the goal or purpose (τέλος, *telos*) of one's life. The adjective τέλειος, when used of humans, typically refers to their being "full-grown" or mature, though in a few contexts it can mean "perfect" in the sense of "faultless." Reflected here is Jesus's command that his disciples "be perfect" (Matt. 5:48), which echoes throughout the NT (e.g., 1 Cor. 14:20; Col. 4:12; and perhaps Col. 3:14; cf. 1 Pet. 1:16). Endurance under pressure is a means of growth. As bodybuilders like to say, "No pain, no gain."

James's combination of τέλειος with another word for "complete" (ὁλόκληρος, *holoklēros*) in 1:4 may imply another dimension to the imagery, that of sacrifice. In the OT, offerings acceptable to God had to be perfect and whole, that is, without defect. Although James is not speaking in a cultic context here, this may very well have evoked the notion of the believer as, to use Paul's language, "a living sacrifice, holy and acceptable to God" (Rom. 12:1; cf. 1 Pet. 2:5). And James joins Peter and Paul in attesting that trials somehow are necessary to the preparation of believers.

Along similar lines, James's concern that his hearers be "not lacking in anything," or be fully equipped, may also carry forward the priestly notion of proper investiture and preparation. This phrase might, however, be more closely associated with military imagery of being fully armed for battle. Since endurance was the prime virtue of a soldier, this fits. Whatever the particulars of the image in James's mind, the meaning is clear: the strengthening of endurance through trials is an important aspect of Christian life, and without it the Christian is ill-equipped for service to God, whether that service be

---

8. Here δοκίμιον refers not to the process, but to the instrument used for testing, as in Prov. 27:21 LXX, where the furnace is a δοκίμιον for silver and gold (Hort 1909: 5). Thus, it is not the same as its use in 1 Pet. 1:7, where it means "genuineness" (see Davids 1982: 68).

viewed in military, athletic, or priestly imagery (all of which are used in the NT at one point or another).

The sorites of 1:3–4 is echoed in 1:12 in another sorites, this one leading to life: the one who endures trial (ὑπομένει πειρασμόν, *hypomenei peirasmon*) is "proven" (δόκιμος, *dokimos*), which results in the crown of life.[9] Opposite this stands a sorites of death in 1:13–15: testing → desire → sin → death. Again this shows that it is not the trial itself that produces maturity and life, for a trial can also result in failure to endure, in surrender to the desire that gives birth to sin and leads to death; instead, it is faithful endurance in the trial that leads to life.

The life in view is the "crown of life," the victor's crown awarded at the end of the race.[10] In 5:1–11 James puts it in a more clearly eschatological framework. In concord with later Jewish wisdom literature, James sees the final solution to the problem of evil in eschatology, specifically the "eschatological reversal." The rich who oppress the poor in 5:1–6 are harshly warned of the coming wrath, and in fact their future judgment is described as something already in place ("Your wealth has rotted, and moths have eaten your clothes; your silver and gold are corroded," 5:2–3). On the other hand, those who suffer in 5:7–11 are encouraged to wait patiently for the coming of the Lord, as the prophets did.

The eschatological dimension is another reason why the enduring of trials may be counted as joy: they are an indication of the nearness of the eschaton. At the very least, it is a reflection of the biblical hope found in Ps. 126:5: "Those who sow in tears shall reap with shouts of joy!"

What are these "trials" that James's readers are supposed to count as joy? What kind of trial or testing is involved here?[11] The word πειρασμός (*peirasmos*) can mean either "test" in the general sense or the specific kinds of test rendered in English as "temptation." James appears to use the word in both senses. The context of 1:2 makes clear that James is thinking of the various

---

9. Compare the similar sorites in Rom. 5:3–5, though there it is hope that stands at the end of the list rather than "perfection": θλῖψις (*thlipsis*, affliction) → ὑπομονή (*hypomenē*, endurance) → δοκιμή (*dokimē*, character) → ἐλπίς (*elpis*, hope). In both cases the treatment of suffering is driven by christological eschatology (likewise 1 Pet. 1:6–7). This is one of the many surprising points of contact between James and Paul's letters that suggest that the book of Acts is accurate in its portrayal of Paul and the Jerusalem church as ultimately harmonious. Paul, however, completes the sorites by adding the dimension of the Holy Spirit: "And hope does not disappoint us, because the love of God is poured out in our hearts through the Holy Spirit which is given to us." James, on the other hand, with the possible (and, in my view, unlikely) exception of 4:5, never mentions the Holy Spirit (see the commentary on 4:4–6).

10. Could this crown of life be the crown of true wisdom, as in Prov. 4:9? This comports well with the wisdom from above that is to be sought in James 3. But here the image seems to be the gift of eschatological (eternal) life that comes at the end of the human story, not the wisdom that enables one to live in the middle of the story.

11. Many commentators attempt to answer the question of whether these trials or testings are particular and real sufferings that the original hearers were experiencing. Understanding James's meaning does not require this to be answered. All believers eventually experience trials of some sort, and at such times these encouragements apply.

pressures often applied against believers that threaten their well-being and obedience (Martin 1988: 15), which may very well cause believers to doubt the sovereignty of God in their lives. But it would not work to translate here with "temptations." Here the injunction of James is to "think differently," knowing that when faith is tested, it is proven by the test and becomes purer and stronger as a result, and this is cause for joy.

The meaning in 1:12–15 seems to be somewhat different. The context here demands that the noun πειρασμός (*peirasmos*) and the verb πειράζω (*peirazō*) have the sense of "tempting to evil." God does not tempt to evil, because he is not tempted by evil. God is "untemptable" and untestable because that which makes a trial a trial is the evil desire within the person being tested (the pressure to sin comes from within).

Nevertheless, these two senses are not unrelated. Testing by suffering (which is an opportunity to endure) can turn into testing (tempting) to evil, such as quickness to anger (1:19–20) brought on by impatience when faced with testing. But put positively, circumstances of suffering are also opportunities for endurance, or as James puts it in 4:7, for resisting the devil. It is one's response to the *peirasmoi*, "patient endurance" (*hypomonē*), not the *peirasmoi* themselves, that according to James does the work of maturing. Further, the testing in view is not just physical suffering, nor is it only eschatological tribulation; it is any kind of testing (Chester 1994: 31), such as being confronted with the suffering of others (see the next section below) or the need to control the tongue (see James 3).

Thus, James's exhortation is to let patience have its perfect work, or as Dibelius (1975: 74) puts it, "Let endurance do its work of perfecting," that is, its work that leads to perfection or maturity. Trials and testing have a purpose, and the person of faith should not defeat that purpose by impatience, by giving in to wrath, or by abandoning obedience for the sake of comfort.

Suffering Calls Forth Faithful Living (Living by Faith)

The third way James deals with suffering is to note that suffering is a call to faithful living. Adamson (1989: 308–16) points out that in James testing is eschatological, and eschatology is bound up with ethics. Suffering therefore is connected with ethics because suffering drives one to eschatology (see Chester 1994: 16–17, 30–31).

The response demanded of one's own suffering is patient endurance. This exhortation to patience is eschatologically motivated. James compares it to a farmer's patience: "Therefore, be patient, brothers, as you await the coming of the Lord. Look how the farmer awaits the precious fruit of the land, waiting patiently for it until it receives the early and late rains. You too should be patient" (5:7–8). The sufferer now waits patiently, knowing that judgment of the wicked and relief for the oppressed (5:4–5) will occur when the Lord comes

(5:8–9). The response of the prophets, and especially of Job too, to suffering provides the paradigm for believers to be patient in suffering (5:10–11).[12]

But James is even more interested in how the Christian responds to the suffering of others. Because a Christian is a sufferer, he or she is expected to respond to the suffering of others as a fellow sufferer. Hence, James even goes so far as to say that true religion[13] is to care for sufferers (1:27). That is to say that, because real faith (2:14–17) is faith in God's exaltation of the humble, the works that proceed from true faith will involve showing mercy to those who suffer.

Of particular concern to James are the truly destitute (symbolized by "orphans and widows," who in that social environment often were the most marginalized and powerless people). These are the "humble" who will be exalted (1:9). The church is the community that anticipates the eschatological reversal by caring for and respecting the poor.

Therefore, James has no tolerance for favoritism toward the rich. Such favoritism is a major offense for two reasons: (1) it violates the law of love and belies the character of God as one who cares about the poor (note that the context of the law of love in Lev. 19 specifically condemns partiality [Lev. 19:15]); (2) it belies the eschatological character of the community, which ought to echo God's exaltation of the poor. This is the remarkable point of 2:1–13: the poor are not just to be pitied, they are to be respected. For most people who are not poor, this is quite a difficult concept. Suffering, especially poverty and destitution, makes a person repulsive in the eyes of many, which thereby increases the sufferer's distress.

Yet the eschatological reversal proclaimed in the gospel means that it is precisely those who suffer who are to rejoice in trials; it is those who are poor who are rich in faith; it is those who are humble who will be exalted. "Perfection" and wholeness in the gospel run counter to the world's notion of wholeness. As Tamez (1990: 86–87) points out, "For people today, perfection is linked to success, competition, excelling at the expense of others. For James it is the opposite; for him it is to attend to the needy in order to be consistent with what we believe and what we read in the Bible." The world's view of τελειότης (teleiotēs), the goal or telos of worldly life and worldly wisdom (3:15), often is "success" and the achievement of domination. However, the wisdom from above is good behavior in a humble wisdom (3:13).

12. Anyone who has read the book of Job may find this example odd because Job was hardly a model of what we typically regard as patience. The tradition of Job as an exemplar of patience first appears in Jewish literature in the Testament of Job, so James is following an already existing Jewish wisdom tradition; however, true patience, as James sees it, is not passive acceptance, but an unremitting appeal to God for help and the certain hope of eventual vindication. See Martin 1988: 16.

13. The term used here for "religion" is θρήσκεια (thrēskeia), which usually refers not to one's overall faith commitments, beliefs, or doctrine, but to the expression of "religiosity," that is, religious practice, acts of piety, or cultic activity. But James, like the rest of the NT authors, is relatively uninterested in religiosity; his religion is far more than external cultic acts (Ropes 1916: 182).

Finally, suffering calls forth prayer, both by the sufferer and for the sufferer. In 5:13 James says to his hearers, "Is anyone among you suffering? He should pray." And in 5:14 he expands this responsibility for prayer beyond the sufferer to church leaders, for whom intercessory prayer is a major calling. The anointing of the sick commanded here is not the establishment of some sacrament of unction, nor is it simply medicinal anointing; it is symbolic of the anointing with the oil of gladness. Isaiah 61:3 is one of the great prophecies that speak of the messianic "eschatological reversal." There we are told that one purpose for which the Messiah is anointed is to "provide for those who grieve in Zion—to bestow on them a crown of beauty instead of ashes, the oil of gladness instead of mourning, and a garment of praise instead of a spirit of despair" (NIV). It is once again, as in James 1:2, linking suffering with joy. Sickness, like other forms of suffering, is a trial, and trials are opportunities for endurance, which leads to maturity.

Conclusion

James's concern with suffering arises from his concern with genuine faith. Suffering is a test of faith, demonstrating both whether one really has faith and what kind of faith it really is. Faith shows no favoritism, and especially it does not despise those who suffer from poverty or experience any other kind of suffering. Faith, when it encounters the suffering of others, does not simply utter pious wishes of health; instead, it looks to the interests of the sufferers, especially the destitute such as widows and orphans. Faith, when it encounters one's own suffering or other form of testing, does not doubt (is not double-minded); instead, it waits patiently for the coming of the Lord.

A crucial aspect of the life of faith is one's attitude toward things in life and one's response to events. We usually have little control over our environment and what happens to us, but we can control how we think about it and react to it. Knowing how to interpret events and actions is a major component of wisdom, and the faith-infused and faith-driven attitude of the Christian is one of joy, even when suffering.

Works Cited

Achtemeier, P.
1996   *1 Peter.* Hermeneia. Philadelphia: Fortress.

Adamson, J.
1976   *The Epistle of James.* New International Commentary on the New Testament. Grand Rapids: Eerdmans.
1989   *James: The Man and His Message.* Grand Rapids: Eerdmans.

Allison, D.
2001   "The Fiction of James and Its *Sitz im Leben.*" *Revue Biblique* 108:529–70.

Amphoux, C.
1970   "À propos de Jacques 1:17." *Revue d'histoire et de philosophie religieuses* 50:127–36.
1981   "Systèmes anciens de division de l'Épître de Jacques et compositions littéraire." *Biblica* 62:390–400.

Aune, D.
1987   *The New Testament in Its Literary Environment.* Philadelphia: Westminster.

Austin, S.-J.
2009   "The Poetry of Wisdom: A Note on James 3.6." *Ecclesia Reformanda* 1.1 (forthcoming).

Baasland, E.
1982   "Der Jakobusbrief als neutestamentliche Weisheitsschrift." *Studia theologica* 36:119–39.
1988   "Literarische Form, Thematik und geschichtliche Einordnung des Jakobusbriefes." Pp. 3646–84 in *Aufstieg und Niedergang der römischen Welt* II.25.5. Edited by H. Temporini and W. Haase. Berlin: de Gruyter.

Baker, W.
1995   *Personal Speech-Ethics in the Epistle of James.* Wissenschaftliche Untersuchungen zum Neuen Testament 2/68. Tübingen: Mohr Siebeck.
2002   "Christology in the Epistle of James." *Evangelical Quarterly* 74:47–57.

Barrett, C. K.
1999   "The Historicity of Acts." *Journal of Theological Studies* 50:515–34.

Bauckham, R.
1993   Review of *James and the Q Sayings of Jesus,* by P. Hartin. *Journal of Theological Studies,* n.s., 44.1:298–301.
1996   "James and the Gentiles (Acts 15.13–21)." Pp. 154–83 in *History, Literature, and Society in the Book of Acts.* Edited by B. Witherington III. Cambridge: Cambridge University Press.
1998a   *The Fate of the Dead: Studies on the Jewish and Christian Apocalypses.* Novum Testamentum Supplements 93. Leiden: Brill.
1998b   *God Crucified: Monotheism and Christology in the New Testament.* Grand Rapids: Eerdmans.
1999   *James: The Wisdom of James, Disciple of Jesus the Sage.* London: Routledge.
2001   "James and Jesus." Pp. 100–137 in *The Brother of Jesus: James the Just and His Mission.* Edited by B. Chilton and J. Neusner. Louisville: Westminster John Knox.
2004   "The Spirit of God in Us Loathes Envy: James 4:5." Pp. 270–81 in *The Holy Spirit and Christian Origins: Essays in Honor of James D. G. Dunn.* Edited by G. N. Stanton, B. W. Longenecker, and S. C. Barton. Grand Rapids: Eerdmans.

BDAG
        A Greek-English Lexicon of the New Testament and Other Early Christian Literature. By W. Bauer, F. W. Danker, W. F. Arndt, and F. W. Gingrich. 3rd

edition. Chicago: University of Chicago Press, 2000.

BDF   *A Greek Grammar of the New Testament and Other Early Christian Literature.* By F. Blass, A. Debrunner, and R. W. Funk. Chicago: University of Chicago Press, 1961.

Beck, D.
1973   "The Composition of the Epistle of James." PhD diss., Princeton Theological Seminary.

Betz, H.
1985   *Essays on the Sermon on the Mount.* Translated by L. Welborn. Philadelphia: Fortress.

Beyschlag, W.
1897   *Kritisch-exegetisches Handbuch über den Brief des Jacobus.* Kritisch-exegetischer Kommentar über das Neue Testament 15. Göttingen: Vandenhoeck & Ruprecht.

Bindemann, W.
1995   "Weisheit versus Weisheit: Der Jakobusbrief als innerkirchlicher Diskurs." *Zeitschrift für die neutestamentliche Wissenschaft* 86:189–217.

Blomberg, C.
1999   *Neither Poverty nor Riches: A Biblical Theology of Material Possessions.* Grand Rapids: Eerdmans.

Blondel, J.-L.
1979   "Le fondement théologique dans le parénèse dans l'Épître de Jacques." *Revue de théologie et de philosophie* 29:141–52.

Bockmuehl, M.
2006   *Seeing the Word: Refocusing New Testament Study.* Grand Rapids: Baker Academic.

Bornkamm, G.
1948   "Die Sturmstillung im Matthäusevangelium." *Wort und Dienst*, n.s., 1:49–54.

Brosend, W.
2004   *James and Jude.* New Cambridge Bible Commentary. Cambridge: Cambridge University Press.

Brown, R. E.
1997   *An Introduction to the New Testament.* Anchor Bible Reference Library. New York: Doubleday.

Bruce, F. F.
1974   "The Speeches in Acts—Thirty Years After." Pp. 53–68 in *Reconciliation and Hope: New Testament Essays on Atonement and Eschatology Presented to L. L. Morris on His 60th Birthday.* Edited by R. Banks. Carlisle, UK: Paternoster.

Burchard, C.
1980a   "Gemeinde in der strohern Epistel: Mutmaßungen über Jakobus." Pp. 315–28 in *Kirche: Festschrift für Günther Bornkamm zum 75. Geburtstag.* Edited by D. Lührmann and G. Strecker. Tübingen: Mohr Siebeck.
1980b   "Zu Jakobus 2,14–26." *Zeitschrift für die neutestamentliche Wissenschaft* 71:27–45.

Burge, G.
1977   "'And Threw Them Thus on Paper': Recovering the Poetic Form of James 2:14–26." *Studia biblica et theologica* 7:31–45.

Burkes, S.
2002   "Wisdom and Apocalyptic in the Wisdom of Solomon." *Harvard Theological Review* 95:21–44.

Burton, E. D.
1892   *Syntax of the Moods and Tenses in New Testament Greek.* 2nd edition, revised and enlarged. Chicago: University of Chicago Press.

Byrskog, S.
2000   *Story as History—History as Story: The Gospel Tradition in the Context of Ancient Oral History.* Wissenschaftliche Untersuchungen zum Neuen Testament 123. Tübingen: Mohr Siebeck.

Calvin, J.
1948   *Commentaries on the Catholic Epistles.* Translated and edited by J. Owen. Grand Rapids: Eerdmans. Reprinted Grand Rapids: Baker Academic, 1979.
1960   *Calvin's New Testament Commentaries*, vol. 3: *Matthew, Mark & Luke and James & Jude.* Edited by D. Torrance and T. Torrance. Translated by A. W. Morrison. Grand Rapids: Eerdmans.

Cantinat, J.
1973   *Les épîtres de saint Jacques et de saint Jude.* Sources bibliques. Paris: Gabalda.

Carpenter, C.
2001   "James 4.5 Reconsidered." *New Testament Studies* 46:189–205.

Chaine, J.
1927   *L'Épître de Saint Jacques.* Paris: Gabalda.

Charles, R. H. (trans.)
1917   *The Book of Enoch*. London: SPCK, 1917.

Chester, A.
1994   "The Theology of James." Pp. 6–62 in *The Theology of the Letters of James, Peter, and Jude*. Edited by A. Chester and R. P. Martin. New Testament Theology. Cambridge: Cambridge University Press.

Cheung, L. L.
2003   *The Genre, Composition and Hermeneutics of the Epistle of James*. Paternoster Biblical and Theological Monographs. Carlisle, UK: Paternoster.

Childs, B. S.
1984   *The New Testament as Canon: An Introduction*. London: SCM Press.

Chilton, B.
2001   "James in Relation to Peter, Paul, and the Remembrance of Jesus." Pp. 138–60 in *The Brother of Jesus: James the Just and His Mission*. Edited by B. Chilton and J. Neusner. Louisville: Westminster John Knox.

Chilton, B., and J. Neusner (eds.)
2001   *The Brother of Jesus: James the Just and His Mission*. Louisville: Westminster John Knox.

Cladder, H. J.
1904   "Der formale Aufbau des Jakobusbriefes." *Zeitschrift für katholische Theologie* 28:295–330.

Coggins, R. J.
1998   *Sirach*. Guides to Apocrypha and Pseudepigrapha. Sheffield: Sheffield Academic Press.

Collins, C. J.
1997   "James 5:14–16a: What Is the Anointing For?" *Presbyterion* 23:79–91.

Colson, F. H., and G. H. Whitaker (trans.)
1929   *Philo*, vol. 1: *On the Creation; Allegorical Interpretation of Genesis 2 and 3*. Loeb Classical Library. Cambridge, MA: Harvard University Press.

Cranfield, C. E. B.
1965   "The Message of James." *Scottish Journal of Theology* 18:182–93, 338–45.

Crenshaw, J.
1998   *Old Testament Wisdom: An Introduction*. Revised edition. Louisville: Westminster John Knox.

Davids, P. H.
1978   "The Meaning of Ἀπείραστος in James 1:13." *New Testament Studies* 24:386–92.
1980   "Theological Perspectives on the Epistle of James." *Journal of the Evangelical Theological Society* 23:97–103.
1982   *The Epistle of James: A Commentary on the Greek Text*. New International Greek Testament Commentary. Grand Rapids: Eerdmans.
1988   "The Epistle of James in Modern Discussion." Pp. 3621–45 in *Aufstieg und Niedergang der römischen Welt* II.25.5. Edited by H. Temporini and W. Haase. Berlin: de Gruyter.
2001   "James's Message: The Literary Record." Pp. 66–87 in *The Brother of Jesus: James the Just and His Mission*. Edited by B. Chilton and J. Neusner. Louisville: Westminster John Knox.

Davies, W. D.
1955   *Paul and Rabbinic Judaism*. 2nd edition. London: SPCK.
1964   *The Setting of the Sermon on the Mount*. Cambridge: Cambridge University Press.

Davis, J. A.
1984   *Wisdom and Spirit: An Investigation of 1 Corinthians 1.18–3.20 against the Background of Jewish Sapiential Traditions in the Greco-Roman Period*. Lanham, MD: University Press of America.

DeGraaf, D.
2005   "Some Doubts about Doubt: The New Testament Use of Διακρίνω." *Journal of the Evangelical Theological Society* 48:733–55.

Deissmann, A.
1901   *Bible Studies: Contributions, Chiefly from Papyri and Inscriptions, to the History of the Language, the Literature, and the Religion of Hellenistic Judaism and Primitive Christianity*. Translated by A. Grieve. Edinburgh: T&T Clark.
1927   *Light from the Ancient East: The New Testament Illustrated by Recently Discovered Texts of the Greco-Roman World*. Translated by L. Strachan. Revised edition. London: Hodder & Stoughton.

Denyer, N.
1999   "Mirrors in James 1:22–25 and Plato, Alcibiades 132c–133c." *Tyndale Bulletin* 50:237–40.

Deppe, D. B.
1989   *The Sayings of Jesus in the Epistle of James*. Chelsea, MI: Bookcrafters.

Dibelius, M.
1936   *A Fresh Approach to the New Testament and Early Christian Literature*. London: Nicholson & Watson.
1975   *James: A Commentary on the Epistle of James*. Edited and revised by H. Greeven. Translated by Michael A. Williams. Hermeneia. Philadelphia: Fortress.

Diehl, E. (ed.)
1903–6 *Procli Diadochi in Platonis Timaeum commentaria*. 3 vols. Bibliotheca scriptorum Graecorum et Romanorum Teubneriana. Leipzig: Teubner.

DNTB   *Dictionary of New Testament Background*. Edited by C. A. Evans and S. E. Porter. Downers Grove, IL: InterVarsity, 2000.

Donker, C.
1981   "Der Verfasser des Jakobus und sein Gegner." *Zeitschrift für die neutestamentliche Wissenschaft* 72:227–40.

Dunn, J. D. G.
1977   *Unity and Diversity in the New Testament: An Inquiry into the Character of Earliest Christianity*. Philadelphia: Westminster.
1998   *The Theology of Paul the Apostle*. Grand Rapids: Eerdmans.

Dyrness, W.
1981   "Mercy Triumphs over Justice: James 2:13 and the Theology of Faith and Works." *Themelios* 6/3:11–16.

Edgar, D.
2001   *Has God Not Chosen the Poor? The Social Setting of the Epistle of James*. Journal for the Study of the New Testament: Supplement Series 206. Sheffield: Sheffield Academic Press.

Eisenman, R.
1990   "Eschatological 'Rain' Imagery in the War Scroll from Qumrân and the Letter of James." *Journal of Near Eastern Studies* 49:173–84.
1997   *James the Brother of Jesus: The Key to Unlocking the Secrets of Early Christianity and the Dead Sea Scrolls*. New York: Viking.

Elliott, J. H.
1993   "The Epistle of James in Rhetorical and Social Scientific Perspective: Holiness-Wholeness and Patterns of Replication." *Biblical Theology Bulletin* 23:71–81.
2000   *1 Peter*. Anchor Bible 37B. New York: Doubleday.

Elliott, J. K.
1999   "Five New Papyri of the New Testament." *Novum Testamentum* 41:209–13.

Elliott-Binns, L.
1955   "The Meaning of ὑλή in James III.5." *New Testament Studies* 2:48–50.
1956   "James I.18: Creation or Redemption?" *New Testament Studies* 3:148–61.

Ellis, E. E.
1992   *The Old Testament in Early Christianity: Canon and Interpretation in the Light of Modern Research*. Grand Rapids: Baker Academic.

EncJud   *Encyclopaedia Judaica*. Edited by F. Skolnik. 2nd edition. 22 vols. Detroit: Thomson Gale, 2007.

Epstein, I. (ed.)
1948   *Babylonian Talmud: Seder Zeraim*. London: Soncino.

Ewald, H.
1870   *Das Sendschreiben an die Hebräer und Jakobos' Rundschreiben übersezt und erklärt*. Göttingen: Dieterichschen Buchhandlung.

Fensham, F. C.
1976   "Widow, Orphan, and the Poor in Ancient Near Eastern Legal and Wisdom Literature." Pp. 161–73 in *Studies in Ancient Israelite Wisdom*. Edited by J. Crenshaw. Library of Biblical Studies. New York: Ktav.

Feuillet, A.
1964   "Le sens du mot Parousie dans l'Évangile Matthieu—Comparison entre Matth xxiv et Jac v,1–11." Pp. 261–88 in *The Background of the New Testament and Its Eschatology*. Edited by W. D. Davies and D. Daube. Cambridge: Cambridge University Press.

Fitzgerald, J., and L. M. White
1983   *The Tabula of Cebes*. Texts and Translations 24. Chico, CA: Scholars Press.

Francis, F. O.
1970   "Form and Function of the Opening and Closing Paragraphs of James and 1 John." *Zeitschrift für die neutestamentliche Wissenschaft* 61:110–26.

Frankemölle, H.
1994   *Der Brief des Jakobus*. Ökumenischer Taschenbuch Kommentar zum Neuen Testament 17. Gütersloh: Mohn.

Gammie, J.
1990   "Paraenetic Literature: Toward the Morphology of a Secondary Genre." *Semeia* 50:41–77.

García Martínez, F., and E. J. C. Tigchelaar (eds.)
1997–98   *The Dead Sea Scrolls Study Edition*. 2 vols. Leiden: Brill/Grand Rapids: Eerdmans.

Gempf, C.
1993   "Public Speaking and Published Accounts." Pp. 259–303 in *The Book of Acts in Its Ancient Literary Setting*. Edited by B. Winter and A. Clarke. The Book of Acts in Its First Century Setting 1. Grand Rapids: Eerdmans.

Gertner, M.
1962   "Midrashim in the New Testament." *Journal of Semitic Studies* 7:267–92.

Goodwin, W.
1881   *Syntax of the Moods and Tenses of the Greek Verb*. Revised edition. Boston: Ginn & Heath.
1906   *Plutarch's Morals*. 5 vols. Boston: Little, Brown.

Gordon, R. P.
1975   "*kai to telos kyriou eidete* (Js 5,11)." *Journal of Theological Studies* 26:91–95.

Gowan, D.
1993   "Wisdom and Endurance in James." *Horizons in Biblical Theology* 15:145–53.

Grummere, R. M. (ed. and trans.)
1920   *Seneca*, vol. 2: *Moral Epistles*. Loeb Classical Library 76. Cambridge, MA: Harvard University Press.

Guelich, R.
1982   *The Sermon on the Mount: A Foundation for Understanding*. Waco: Word.

Haenchen, E.
1971   *The Acts of the Apostles*. Translated by B. Noble and G. Shinn. Philadelphia: Westminster.

Hagner, D.
1973   *The Use of the Old and New Testaments in Clement of Rome*. Novum Testamentum Supplements 34. Leiden: Brill.

Halson, B.
1968   "The Epistle of James: 'Christian Wisdom'?" *Studia evangelica* 4:308–14.

Harnack, A.
1897   *Geschichte der altchristlichen Litteratur bis Eusebius*, part 2: *Die Chronologie*. 2 vols. Leipzig: Hinrichs.

Hartin, P. J.
1991   *James and the "Q" Sayings of Jesus*. Journal for the Study of the New Testament: Supplement Series 47. Sheffield: JSOT Press.
1999   *A Spirituality of Perfection: Faith in Action in the Letter of James*. Collegeville, MN: Liturgical Press.
2003   *James*. Sacra Pagina 14. Collegeville, MN: Liturgical Press.

Hauck, F.
1926   *Der Brief des Jakobus*. Kommentar zum Neuen Testament 16. Leipzig: Deichert.

Hayden, D.
1981   "Calling the Elders to Pray." *Bibliotheca sacra* 138:258–65.

Heinrici, C. F. G.
1908   *Der litterarische Charakter der neutestamentlichen Schriften*. Leipzig: Dürr.

Hemer, C. J.
1990   *The Book of Acts in the Setting of Hellenistic History*. Winona Lake, IN: Eisenbrauns.

Hengel, M.
1987   "Der Jakobusbrief als antipaulinische Polemik." Pp. 248–78 in *Tradition and Interpretation in the New Testament: Essays in Honor of E. Earle Ellis for His 60th Birthday*. Edited by G. F. Hawthorne and O. Betz. Grand Rapids: Eerdmans.

Hodges, Z.
1963   "Light on James Two from Textual Criticism." *Bibliotheca sacra* 120:341–50.

Hort, F. J. A.
1909   *The Epistle of James: The Greek Text with Introduction, Commentary as Far as Chapter IV Verse 7, and Additional Notes*. London: Macmillan.

IDBSup   *Interpreter's Dictionary of the Bible: Supplementary Volume*. Edited by K. Crim. Nashville: Abingdon, 1976.

Jackson-McCabe, M.
1996   "A Letter to the Twelve Tribes of the Diaspora: Wisdom and 'Apocalyptic' Eschatology in the Letter of James." Pp. 504–17 in *Society of Biblical Literature 1996 Seminar Papers*. Society of Biblical

Literature Seminar Papers 35. Atlanta: Scholars Press.

2003   "The Messiah Jesus in the Mythic World of James." *Journal of Biblical Literature* 122:701–30.

Jacob, I.

1975   "The Midrashic Background for James II,21–23." *New Testament Studies* 22:457–64.

JE   *Jewish Encyclopedia.* Edited by I. Singer. 12 vols. London: Funk & Wagnalls, 1909.

Jefford, C.

2006   *The Apostolic Fathers and the New Testament.* Peabody, MA: Hendrickson.

Jeremias, J.

1954–55   "Paul and James." *Expository Times* 66:368–71.

1967   *The Prayers of Jesus.* Studies in Biblical Theology 2/6. Naperville, IL: Allenson.

Jobes, K.

2005   *1 Peter.* Baker Exegetical Commentary on the New Testament. Grand Rapids: Baker Academic.

Johanson, B. C.

1973   "The Definition of Pure Religion in James 1:27 Reconsidered." *Expository Times* 84:118–19.

Johnson, L. T.

1982   "The Use of Leviticus 19 in the Letter of James." *Journal of Biblical Literature* 101:341–401.

1983   "James 3:13–4:10 and the *Topos* ΠΕΡΙ ΦΘΟΝΟΥ." *Novum Testamentum* 25:327–47.

1985   "Friendship with the World–Friendship with God: A Study of Discipleship in James." Pp. 166–83 in *Discipleship in the New Testament.* Edited by F. Segovia. Philadelphia: Fortress.

1988   "The Mirror of Remembrance (Jas 1:22–25)." *Catholic Biblical Quarterly* 50:632–45.

1995   *The Letter of James.* Anchor Bible 37A. New York: Doubleday.

Judge, E. A.

1960   *The Social Pattern of Christian Groups in the First Century: Some Prolegomena to the Study of New Testament Ideas of Social Obligation.* London: Tyndale.

Kasser, R.

1961   *Papyrus Bodmer XVII: Actes des Apôtres, épîtres de Jacques, Pierre, Jean et Jude.* Cologny-Genève: Bibliotheca Bodmeriana.

Kennedy, G.

1984   *New Testament Interpretation through Rhetorical Criticism.* Chapel Hill: University of North Carolina Press.

Kilpatrick, G.

1967   "Übertreter des Gesetzes, Jak. 2,11." *Theologische Zeitschrift* 23:433.

Kirk, J.

1969   "The Meaning of Wisdom in James: Examination of a Hypothesis." *New Testament Studies* 16:24–38.

Kittel, G.

1942   "Der geschichtliche Ort des Jakobusbriefes." *Zeitschrift für die neutestamentliche Wissenschaft* 41:71–105.

Kloppenborg Verbin, J.

1999   "Patronage Avoidance in James." *Hervormde teologiese Studies* 55:755–94.

Knox, W. L.

1945   "The Epistle of St. James." *Journal of Theological Studies* 46:10–17.

Kollmann, B.

1996   "Das Schwurverbot Mt 5,33–37/Jak 5,12 im Spiegel antiker Eidkritik." *Biblische Zeitschrift* 40:179–93.

Kümmel, W.

1975   *Introduction to the New Testament.* Translated by H. C. Kee. Nashville: Abingdon.

Laato, T.

1997   "Justification According to James: A Comparison with Paul." Translated by M. Seifrid. *Trinity Journal*, n.s., 18:43–84.

Laws, S.

1973   "Does Scripture Speak in Vain? A Reconsideration of James IV.5." *New Testament Studies* 20:210–15.

1974   "The Doctrinal Basis for the Ethics of James." *Studia evangelica* 7:299–305.

1980   *A Commentary on the Epistle of James.* San Francisco: Harper & Row.

Lenski, R. C. H.

1938   *The Interpretation of the Epistle to the Hebrews and the Epistle of James.* Columbus, OH: Lutheran Book Concern.

Lightfoot, J. B.

1879   *Saint Paul's Epistles to the Colossians and to Philemon: A Revised Text with Introductions, Notes and Dissertations.* London: Macmillan, 1879. Reprinted Grand Rapids: Zondervan, 1959.

L&N   *Greek-English Lexicon of the New Testament: Based on Semantic Domains.* Edited by J. P. Louw and E. A. Nida. 2nd edition. New York: United Bible Societies, 1989.

Lohse, E.
1957 "Glaube und Werke." *Zeitschrift für die neutestamentliche Wissenschaft* 48:9–11.

Longenecker, R.
1975 *Biblical Exegesis in the Apostolic Period*. Grand Rapids: Eerdmans.

LSJ *A Greek-English Lexicon*. By H. G. Liddell, R. Scott, and H. S. Jones. 9th edition with revised supplement. Oxford: Clarendon, 1996.

Luck, U.
1967 "Weisheit und Leiden: Zum Problem Paulus und Jakobus." *Theologische Literaturzeitung* 92:253–58.
1984 "Die Theologie des Jakobusbriefes." *Zeitschrift für Theologie und Kirche* 81:1–30.

Lüdemann, G.
1989 *Early Christianity according to the Traditions in Acts: A Commentary*. Translated by J. Bowden. Minneapolis: Fortress.

Luther, M.
1914 *Tischreden*. Vol. 3 in *D. Martin Luthers Werke*. Weimar: H. Böhlau.

LW *Luther's Works*. Edited by H. T. Lehmann et al. 55 vols. Saint Louis: Concordia; Philadelphia: Fortress, 1955–76.

Machen, J. G.
1976 *The New Testament: An Introduction to Its Literature and History*. Carlisle, UK: Banner of Truth.

Marcus, J.
1982 "The Evil Inclination in the Epistle of James." *Catholic Biblical Quarterly* 44:606–21.

Marshall, S.
1973 "*Dipsychos*: A Local Term? (Jas 1:4)." *Studia evangelica* 6:348–51.

Martin, R.
1988 *James*. Word Biblical Commentary 48. Waco: Word.

Massebieau, L.
1895 "L'épître de Jacques, est-elle l'œuvre d'un chrétien?" *Revue de l'histoire des religions* 32:249–83.

Mayor, J. B.
1897 *The Epistle of St. James: The Greek Text with Introduction, Notes and Comments*. 2nd edition. New York:

Macmillan, 1897. Reprinted Grand Rapids: Baker Academic, 1978.

Mayordomo-Marin, M.
1992 "Jak 5,2.3a: Zukünftiges Gericht oder gegenwärtiger Zustand?" *Zeitschrift für die neutestamentliche Wissenschaft* 83:132–37.

McCartney, D.
1994 "Ecce Homo: The Coming of the Kingdom as the Restoration of Human Viceregency." *Westminster Theological Journal* 56:1–24.
2000 "The Wisdom of James the Just." *Southern Baptist Journal of Theology* 4:52–64.
2002 "Suffering in James." Pp. 477–86 in *The Practical Calvinist: An Introduction to the Presbyterian & Reformed Heritage; in Honor of Dr. D. Clair Davis on the Occasion of His Seventieth Birthday and to Acknowledge His More Than Thirty Years of Teaching at Westminster Theological Seminary in Philadelphia*. Edited by P. A. Lillback. Fearn, Ross-shire, UK: Christian Focus.

McKnight, S.
1990 "James 2:18a: The Unidentifiable Interlocutor." *Westminster Theological Journal* 52:355–64.

Metzger, B. M.
1971 *A Textual Commentary on the Greek New Testament*. Stuttgart: United Bible Societies.
1994 *A Textual Commentary on the Greek New Testament*. 2nd edition. Stuttgart: Deutsche Bibelgesellschaft.

Meyer, A.
1930 *Das Rätsel des Jacobusbriefes*. Beihefte zur Zeitschrift für die neutestamentliche Wissenschaft und die Kunde der älteren Kirche 10. Giessen: Töpelmann.

MHT *A Grammar of New Testament Greek*. By J. H. Moulton, W. F. Howard, and N. Turner. 4 vols. Edinburgh: T&T Clark, 1908–76.

Michaels, R.
1988 *1 Peter*. Word Biblical Commentary 49. Waco: Word.

Minear, P.
1971 "Yes or No: The Demand for Honesty in the Early Church." *Novum Testamentum* 13:1–13.

Mitton, C. L.
1966 *The Epistle of James*. Grand Rapids: Eerdmans.

307

MM   *The Vocabulary of the Greek Testament: Illustrated from the Papyri and Other Non-literary Sources.* By J. H. Moulton and G. Milligan. London: Hodder & Stoughton, 1930. Reprinted Grand Rapids: Eerdmans, 1980.

Moo, D.
1980   *The Letter of James.* Pillar New Testament Commentary. Grand Rapids: Eerdmans.

Moore, G. F.
1927   *Judaism in the First Centuries of the Christian Era: The Age of the Tannaim.* 2 vols. Cambridge, MA: Harvard University Press.

Mussner, F.
1975   *Der Jakobusbrief.* 3rd edition. Herders theologischer Kommentar zum Neuen Testament 13/1. Freiburg: Herder.
1998   "Rückbesinnung der Kirchen auf das Jüdische: Impulse aus dem Jakobusbrief." *Catholica* 52:67–78.

NA²⁷   *Novum Testamentum Graece.* Edited by [E. and E. Nestle], B. Aland, K. Aland, J. Karavidopoulos, C. M. Martini, and B. M. Metzger. 27th revised edition. Stuttgart: Deutsche Bibelgesellschaft, 1993.

Ng, E.
2003   "Father-God Language and Old Testament Allusions in James." *Tyndale Bulletin* 54:41–54.

Niebuhr, K.-W.
1998   "Der Jakobusbrief im Licht frühjüdischer Diasporabriefe." *New Testament Studies* 44:420–43.

O'Rourke Boyle, M.
1985   "The Stoic Paradox of James 2:10." *New Testament Studies* 31:611–17.

OTP   *The Old Testament Pseudepigrapha.* Edited by J. H. Charlesworth. 2 vols. Garden City, NY: Doubleday, 1983–85.

Painter, J.
1999   *Just James: The Brother of Jesus in History and Tradition.* Minneapolis: Fortress.
2001   "Who Was James? Footprints as a Means of Identification." Pp. 10–65 in *The Brother of Jesus: James the Just and His Mission.* Edited by B. Chilton and J. Neusner. Louisville: Westminster John Knox.

Palmer, F.
1957   "James 1:18 and the Offering of First-Fruits." *Tyndale Bulletin* 3:1–2.

Penner, T.
1996   *The Epistle of James and Eschatology: Re-reading an Ancient Christian Letter.* Journal for the Study of the New Testament: Supplement Series 121. Sheffield: Sheffield Academic Press.

Pfleiderer, O.
1911   *Primitive Christianity: Its Writings and Teachings in Their Historical Connections.* Edited by W. D. Morrison. Translated by W. Montgomery. 4 vols. New York: Putnam.

PG   *Patrologia graeca* [= *Patrologiae cursus completus: Series graeca*]. Edited by J.-P. Migne. 161 vols. Paris: Migne, 1857–86.

Pilch, J.
1998   "Mirrors and Glass." *Bible Today* 36:382–86.

PL   *Patrologia latina* [= *Patrologiae cursus completus: Series latina*]. Edited by J.-P. Migne. 221 vols. Paris: Migne, 1844–79.

Popkes, W.
1986   *Adressaten, Situation und Form des Jakobusbriefes.* Stuttgarter Bibelstudien 125. Stuttgart: Katholisches Bibelwerk.
2001a   *Der Brief des Jakobus.* Theologischer Handkommentar zum Neuen Testament 14. Leipzig: Evangelische Verlagsanstalt.
2001b   "The Mission of James in His Time." Pp. 88–99 in *The Brother of Jesus: James the Just and His Mission.* Edited by B. Chilton and J. Neusner. Louisville: Westminster John Knox.

Porter, S.
1990   "Is *dipsychos* (James 1,8; 4,8) a 'Christian' Word?" *Biblica* 71:469–98.

PW   *Paulys Realencyclopädie der classischen Altertumswissenschaft.* Edited by A. F. Pauly and G. Wissowa. Stuttgart: Metzlerscher Verlag, 1921.

Rainbow, P.
1991   "Jewish Monotheism as the Matrix for New Testament Christology: A Review Article." *Novum Testamentum* 33:81–83.

Reicke, B.
1964   *The Epistles of James, Peter, and Jude.* Anchor Bible 37. Garden City, NY: Doubleday.

Richards, E.
1991   *The Secretary in the Letters of Paul.* Wissenschaftliche Untersuchungen

zum Neuen Testament 2/42. Tübingen: Mohr Siebeck.

Richardson, K.
2006   "Job as Exemplar in the Epistle of James." Pp. 213–29 in *Hearing the Old Testament in the New Testament*. Edited by S. Porter. McMaster New Testament Studies. Grand Rapids: Eerdmans.

Ridderbos, H.
1962   *The Coming of the Kingdom*. Edited by R. O. Zorn. Translated by H. de Jongste. Philadelphia: Presbyterian & Reformed.

Riesenfeld, H.
1944   "HAPLOS: Zu Jak. 1,5." *Coniectanea neotestamentica* 9:33–41.

Roberts, D. J., III
1972   "The Definition of 'Pure Religion' in James 1:27." *Expository Times* 83:215–16.

Ropes, J. H.
1908   "'Thou Hast Faith and I Have Works' (James ii.18)." *Expositor* 7:547–56.
1916   *A Critical and Exegetical Commentary on the Epistle of St. James*. International Critical Commentary. Edited by S. R. Driver, C. A. Briggs, and A. Plummer. Edinburgh: T&T Clark.

Scaer, D.
1983   *James, the Apostle of Faith: A Primary Christological Document for the Persecuted Church*. St. Louis: Concordia.

Schlatter, A.
1927   *Der Glaube im neuen Testament*. 4th edition. Stuttgart: Calwer.
1956   *Der Brief des Jakobus*. 2nd edition. Stuttgart: Calwer.

Schmitt, J.
1986   "You Adulteresses! The Image in James 4:4." *Novum Testamentum* 28:327–37.

Schnabel, E.
1985   *Law and Wisdom from Ben Sira to Paul: A Tradition Historical Enquiry into the Relation of Law, Wisdom, and Ethics*. Wissenschaftliche Untersuchungen zum Neuen Testament 2/16. Tübingen: Mohr Siebeck.

Schnackenburg, R.
2002   *The Gospel of Matthew*. Translated by R. Barr. Grand Rapids: Eerdmans.

Schneemelcher, W. (ed.)
1992   *New Testament Apocrypha*, vol. 2: *Writings Relating to the Apostles; Apocalypses and Related Subjects*. English translation edited by R. McL.

Wilson. Revised edition. Louisville: Westminster John Knox.

Seitz, O.
1944   "Relationship of the Shepherd of Hermas to the Epistle of James." *Journal of Biblical Literature* 63:131–40.
1958   "Afterthoughts on the Term *Dipsychos*." *New Testament Studies* 4:327–34.

Sevenster, J. N.
1968   *Do You Know Greek? How Much Greek Could the First Jewish Christians Have Known?* Novum Testamentum Supplements 19. Leiden: Brill.

Shogren, G.
1989   "Will God Heal Us? A Re-examination of James 5:14–16a." *Evangelical Quarterly* 61:99–108.

Silva, M.
2004   "Faith versus Works of Law in Galatians." Pp. 227–34 in *Justification and Variegated Nomism*, vol. 2: *The Paradoxes of Paul*. Edited by D. A. Carson, P. T. O'Brien, and M. A. Seifrid. Grand Rapids: Baker Academic.

Smyth, H. W.
1920   *Greek Grammar for Schools and Colleges*. New York: American Book Company.

Souter, A.
1913   *The Text and Canon of the New Testament*. Studies in Theology. New York: Scribner.

Spitta, F.
1896   *Der Brief des Jakobus*. Göttingen: Vandenhoeck & Ruprecht.

Stagg, F.
1972   "The Abused Aorist." *Journal of Biblical Literature* 91:222–31.

Stein, R.
1978   *The Method and Message of Jesus' Teachings*. Philadelphia: Westminster.

Str-B   *Kommentar zum Neuen Testament aus Talmud und Midrasch*. By H. L. Strack and P. Billerbeck. 6 vols. Munich: Beck, 1922–61.

SVF   *Stoicorum veterum fragmenta*. By H. von Arnim. 4 vols. Leipzig: Teubner, 1903–24.

Tamez, E.
1990   *The Scandalous Message of James: Faith without Works Is Dead*. New York: Crossroad.

Tasker, R. V. G.
1957   *The General Epistle of James*. Tyndale New Testament Commentaries. Grand Rapids: Eerdmans.

TDNT   *Theological Dictionary of the New Testament*. Edited by G. Kittel and G. Friedrich. Translated and edited by G. W. Bromiley. 10 vols. Grand Rapids: Eerdmans, 1964–76.

TDOT   *Theological Dictionary of the Old Testament*. Edited by G. J. Botterweck, H. Ringgren, and H.-J. Fabry. Translated by J. T. Willis, G. W. Bromiley, D. E. Green, and D. W. Stott. 14 vols. Grand Rapids: Eerdmans, 1974–.

Thompson, M. J.
1976   "James 4:1–4: A Warning against Zealotry?" *Expository Times* 87:211–13.

Tov, E., R. A. Kraft, and P. J. Parsons
1990   *The Greek Minor Prophets Scroll from Nahal Hever (8HevXIIGr) (The Seiyal Collection I)*. Discoveries in the Judaean Desert 8. Oxford: Clarendon.

Trudinger, P.
2004   "The Epistle of James: Down-to-Earth and Otherworldly?" *Downside Review* 122:61–63.

UBS⁴   *The Greek New Testament*. Edited by B. Aland, K. Aland, J. Karavidopoulos, C. M. Martini, and B. M. Metzger. 4th revised edition. Stuttgart: Deutsche Bibelgesellschaft, 1994.

Verseput, D.
1997a   "James 1:17 and the Jewish Morning Prayers." *Novum Testamentum* 39:177–91.
1997b   "Reworking the Puzzle of Faith and Deeds in James 2:24–26." *New Testament Studies* 43:97–115.
1998   "Wisdom, 4Q185, and the Epistle of James." *Journal of Biblical Literature* 117:691–707.

Vouga, F.
1984   *L'épître de saint Jacques*. Commentaire de Nouveau Testament 13A. Geneva: Labor et Fides.

Wachob, W. H.
2000   *The Voice of Jesus in the Rhetoric of James*. Society for New Testament Studies Monograph Series 106. Cambridge: Cambridge University Press.

Wall, R.
1990   "James as Apocalyptic Paraenesis." *Restoration Quarterly* 32:11–22.

Wallace, D.
1996   *Greek Grammar beyond the Basics*. Grand Rapids: Zondervan.

Wandel, G.
1893   "Zur Auslegung der Stelle Jak. 3,1–8." *Theologische Studien und Kritiken* 66:683–88.

Ward, R. B.
1966   "The Communal Concern of the Epistle of James." PhD diss., Harvard University.
1968   "The Works of Abraham: James 2:14–26." *Harvard Theological Review* 61:283–90.
1969   "Partiality in the Assembly: James 2:2–4." *Harvard Theological Review* 62:87–97.

Warrington, K.
1994   "The Significance of Elijah in James 5:13–18." *Evangelical Quarterly* 66:217–27.

Watson, D.
1993a   "James 2 in the Light of Greco-Roman Schemes of Argumentation." *New Testament Studies* 39:94–121.
1993b   "The Rhetoric of James 3:1–12 and a Classical Pattern of Argumentation." *Novum Testamentum* 35:48–64.

Westcott, B. F.
1881   *A General Survey of the History of the Canon of the New Testament*. London: Macmillan.

White, J. L.
1988   "Ancient Greek Letters." Pp. 85–105 in *Greco-Roman Literature and the New Testament: Selected Forms and Genres*. Edited by D. Aune. Society of Biblical Literature Sources for Biblical Study 21. Atlanta: Scholars Press.

Wilkinson, J.
1971   "Healing in the Epistle of James." *Scottish Journal of Theology* 24:326–45.

Williams, H. H. D.
2002   "Of Rags and Riches: The Benefits of Hearing Jeremiah 9:23–24 within James 1:9–11." *Tyndale Bulletin* 53:273–82.

Witherington, B., III
1994   *Jesus the Sage: The Pilgrimage of Wisdom*. Minneapolis: Fortress.
1998   *Acts of the Apostles: A Socio-Rhetorical Commentary*. Grand Rapids: Eerdmans.

Wolverton, W.
1956   "The Double-Minded Man in the Light of Essene Psychology." *Anglican Theological Review* 38:166–75.

Wright, N. T.
1992   *Christian Origins and the Question of God*, vol. 1: *The New Testament and the People of God*. Minneapolis: Fortress.

Young, F. W.
1948   "Relation of 1 Clement to the Epistle of James." *Journal of Biblical Literature* 67:339–45.

Zahn, T.
1909   *Introduction to the New Testament*. Edited by M. W. Jacobus. Translated by J. M. Trout et al. 3rd edition. 3 vols. Edinburgh: T&T Clark. Reprinted Minneapolis: Klock & Klock, 1977.

Zerwick, M., and M. Grosvenor
1979   *A Grammatical Analysis of the Greek New Testament*. Unabridged revised edition. Rome: Biblical Institute Press.

Zimmerli, W.
1976   "Concerning the Structure of Old Testament Wisdom." Pp. 175–207 in *Studies in Ancient Israelite Wisdom*. Edited by J. Crenshaw. Library of Biblical Studies. New York: Ktav.

Index of Subjects

Index of Authors

Index of Greek Words

Index of Scripture and Other Ancient Writings

Old Testament

Genesis

1   110, 191n24, 289n22
1:1–2   290
1:14–18   108
1:26   191, 191n23, 191n24, 192, 192n25
1:26–27   121
1:28   191
2:17   261
3:12   104
5:3   192
9   27
9:4   27
12   167, 167n28
15   163, 164, 166, 167, 167n28, 175
15:6   3, 16, 163, 165, 165n24, 166, 167, 168, 169, 170, 170n35, 174, 216
17   167n28

17:5   161
18   165n24
18:25   171
19:28   226
22   3, 16, 111, 163, 167, 167n28, 174
22:1   104
22:1–18   216
22:12   165, 165n24, 166, 168, 174
22:16–18   167, 168
28:18   254, 255
38:26   162
41:38–39   290
48:16   143
49:3   110

Exodus

1:13   142
4:22   111
11:9–10
    LXX   244n10
12   171n39

12:22   171n39
14:31   197
19:17   139n19
20:5   215
20:6   101n19
23:19   110
28:3   290
29:21   254
31:3–4   290
32:6   123n22
34:6   244
34:6–7   151n4
35:5 LXX   110
35:31   214, 289n21
40:15   253

Leviticus

4:26   260
13:36   129n5
17:10   27
19   44, 45, 63, 147, 205, 234, 247, 248n8, 299

19:10   44, 45n68
19:10–18   44, 63
19:12   44, 45, 245
19:12–18   45, 248n8
19:13   44, 234
19:14   44, 45n67
19:15   36, 44, 140, 144, 146, 152, 299
19:16   44
19:17–18   44
19:18   36, 45, 123, 146, 147, 148, 221, 242, 273, 277, 287n17
25:46   85

Numbers

1–4   129n5
3:3   253
3:12   110
11:24–29   218
18:15   111
20   147n2

New Testament

Old Testament Apocrypha

Old Testament Pseudepigrapha

Rabbinic Writings

Babylonian Talmud

Berakot
15b 160n13
Yoma
69b 106n8

Genesis Rabbah
9.7 106n8
24.7–8 192n27
85 290

Mekilta on Exodus
20.26 192n27

Mishnah
'Abot
2.1 290
4.19 101n16
5.4 168
6.2 123n22
6.7 287n14

Pirqe de Rabbi Eliezer
26–31 164

Sipra
on Lev. 19:15 139
on Lev. 19:18 192n27

Sipre Deuteronomy
96.3.2 290

Tanḥuma
23b 91n17
24a 91n17

Targums

Palestinian Targum
on Josh. 2:1 175

Qumran/Dead Sea Scrolls

CD-A
3.12–16 214
9.9–10 245

1QH^a
6.12–13 214
11.26 111
13.8 111
13.22 294

1QM
in toto 108
2.1–3 79

1QpHab
12.3 294
12.6 294
12.10 294

1QS
8.16 149
9.14–15 214
11.5–6 214

4QMMT
in toto 17n27, 275n11

4QpPs^a
2.10 294
3.10 294

4Q185
in toto 283

4Q372
1.16 109n11

Papyri

Oxyrhynchus
4449 20n32

Rylands
77.34 112

Josephus

Against Apion
1.9 §50 32

Jewish Antiquities
5.1.7 §30 175
17.9.3 §214 127n1
19.8.2 §§343–59 9n15
20.9.1 §§197–203 10

Jewish War
7.5.6 §155 260

Philo

Against Flaccus

3 §15 92

Allegorical Interpretation

3.70 §§196–97 111
3.79 §§223–24 194–95

On Sobriety

11 §55

On the Change of Names

22 §127 109n10

On the Confusion of Tongues

28 §144 109n24

On the Creation of the World

2 §10 109n10
18 §56 109n10
24 §72 109n10
24 §74 109n10
25 §77 109n10
28 §86 195n30

On the Decalogue

17 §84 247n6
28 §143 207n1

On the Life of Abraham

46 §273 164n21

On the Migration of Abraham

21 §123 48n71
46 §273 164n21

On the Posterity of Cain

30 §§101–2 147n2

On the Special Laws

4.26 §140 92

On the Virtues

39 §§215–19 214

That Every Good Person Is Free

in toto 123n22
12 §84 245

Classical Writers

Aëtius

De placitis philosophorum
1.2 199n4
2.30.3 112

Apollonius of Rhodes

Argonautica
3.10 111

Aristotle

Metaphysica
4.16 92
De Mundo
392a [13] 109
Rhetoric
1.3.3 41

Arius Didymus

frag. 29 199n4

Arrian

Epicteti dissertationes
4.1.148 91n15

Herodotus

Historiae
1.68 199n4
2.18 127n1
2.37 127n1
2.64 127n1
3.85 199n4

Oppian

Halieutica
3.316 106n9
4.359 106n9

Plato

Alcibiades
132c–133c 121n19
Leges
821b 109
12.942 87

Plutarch

Consolatio ad Apollonium
117 87
Pericles
6.4 112
Quomodo Adolescens poetas audire debeat
33F 194
Tranquillitate animi
13 193n28

Proclus Diadochus

In Platonis Timaeum commentaria
5.330a–b 189n15

Ptolemaeus

Tetrabiblos
37 112
38 112

Seneca

De beneficiis
in toto 149
Epistulae morales
87.25 193n28

Theophilus

Ad Autolycum
1.2 158n9

Thucydides

Historia
1.138.6 173

(unknown author)

Rhetorica ad Herennium
2.18 60–61
2.28 60–61

Xenophon

Anabasis
3.1.39 188n12

Church Fathers

Other Writings

Tabula of Cebes

in toto 210n12

24 121